AMERICAN VEDA

"*American Veda* shows us how we got to where we are. It chronicles a revolution in consciousness and describes India's lasting influence on our culture, from gurus, meditation, and Yoga to sitar music and aromatic curries. Savor it."
  —MICHAEL BERNARD BECKWITH, author of *Spiritual Liberation: Fulfilling Your Soul's Potential*

"This book demonstrates the far reach of Indian thought into the American psyche and sense of spiritual self. A well-written, superbly researched book, it should be read by all the 15 million Americans practicing meditation and Yoga!"
  —CHRISTOPHER CHAPPLE, Doshi Professor of Indic and Comparative Theology, Loyola Marymount University

"In this important and engaging book, Philip Goldberg chronicles the long-neglected history of Hinduism's encounter with the United States. He astutely examines how Hinduism has been constructed and consumed within the larger American spiritual landscape. A must-read for those interested in Hinduism and its transmission."
  —VARUN SONI, Dean of Religious Life, University of Southern California

"Immensely smart, wise, and brilliantly written. This book should be required reading for everyone interested in ecumenical spirituality, which is the one hope for the survival of the human race, and India's great gift to us in our crisis."
  —ANDREW HARVEY, author of *The Hope: A Guide to Sacred Activism* and *The Sun at Midnight*

"*American Veda* documents an important cultural change and is an impressive book: informed and informative, well researched and readable."
  —ROGER WALSH M.D., Ph.D., University of California Medical School, author of *Essential Spirituality: The Seven Central Practices to Awaken Heart and Mind*

"In a delightful, compelling way, *American Veda* shows how India's ancient wisdom has permeated our lives, including many of the self-improvement teachings that have benefited millions."

— MARCI SHIMOFF, *New York Times* bestselling author of *Happy for No Reason* and *Chicken Soup for the Woman's Soul*

"A thrilling examination of how deeply the ancient, vibrant philosophies of India have penetrated Western culture. No American can read this book without being amazed at the degree to which these factors affect our daily life. This book contains wisdom on every page, in Phil Goldberg's splendid style."

— LARRY DOSSEY, M.D., author of *The Power of Premonitions, Reinventing Medicine,* and *Healing Words*

"This book fills a void: Scholars have mined the subject of Indian spiritual philosophy, but mostly for the academy, despite the broad impact of Vedantism on popular culture. Goldberg gets it."

— PUBLISHERS WEEKLY (STARRED REVIEW)

"As Phil Goldberg's masterful *American Veda* shows, we have been under the sway of Hindu spiritual thought for centuries. If you want to understand American spirituality today, and get a glimpse into its future, read this book."

— RABBI RAMI SHAPIRO, author of *Recovery—The Sacred Art*

"Compelling and insightful, Goldberg's fine book is more evidence that we all share the same planet and that we have been influencing one another for millennia."

— NATHAN KATZ, professor of religious studies and director of the Program in the Study of Spirituality, Florida International University

"*American Veda* delights readers as it analyzes developments that enrich the ground from which Yoga in the United States now blossoms."

— YOGA JOURNAL

"Goldberg's chapters are campfire classics, dinner conversation, trivia facts that ignite and excite. He is telling a tale that is part epic melodrama, part detective novel, and, of course, part love story."

— *LA YOGA* MAGAZINE

"An authoritative, engaging survey of why . . . the flowers of Eastern practices have thrived in Western soil."
—Los Angeles Times

"Intriguing reading, fascinating profiles, and great storytelling of Yoga luminaries adapting the teachings to fit their modern American life."
—Lilias Folan, PBS host and author of *Lilias! Yoga Gets Better with Age*

"We are living at a time of a profound awakening of consciousness that is changing the world. Much of that awakening is due to the influence of Indian spirituality and its practical applications. . . . How that came about needed to be documented, and Philip Goldberg has done just that . . . with a novelist's gift for storytelling."
—Common Ground magazine

"*American Veda* is a jewel! A masterful, superbly written, and lucid account of the transformative impact of Vedic thought and practice on American spirituality."
—M. Darrol Bryant, author of *Religion in a New Key* and director of the Centre for Dialogue and Spirituality in the World Religions, Renison University College, University of Waterloo, Canada

"Philip Goldberg surveys the subtle but surprisingly pervasive influence of Vedantic teachings in America with careful scholarship, deft writing, and wit. . . . A superbly researched and written description of Vedanta's migration to the United States."
—John J. Prendergast, Ph.D., editor in chief of *Undivided: The Online Journal of Nonduality and Psychology*, senior editor of *The Sacred Mirror* and *Listening from the Heart of Silence*, and adjunct associate professor of psychology, California Institute of Integral Studies

"Those who read *American Veda* will be amazed by the tremendous influence India has had on America. Readers will appreciate Goldberg's attention to details and sense of humor as he deftly takes them on a delightful journey through time."
—Lola Williamson, Ph.D., assistant professor of religious studies, director of peace studies, Millsaps College

"Based on solid research, but also written in a highly accessible fashion, *American Veda* is a very good starting point for anyone who is interested in

learning more about the influence of Hinduism in America. This chronicle of what may yet emerge as a distinctively American form of Hinduism will continue to be a valuable reference work for many decades to come."
—DR. JEFFERY D. LONG, associate professor and chair, religious studies, and codirector, Asian studies minor, Elizabethtown College

"An excellent overview of the Yoga movement in the West and its Vedic connections . . . a presentation of Yoga that embraces and ennobles the entire human spirit and liberates our deeper Self and consciousness, not simply afford us greater flexibility at a physical level!"
—DAVID FRAWLEY (PANDIT VAMADEVA SHASTRI), founder and director of the American Institute of Vedic Studies

"Nothing short of remarkable. Goldberg manages to cover every major figure, movement, and idea that originated in India's spiritual terrain and arrived on our shores to forever alter the landscape of our thought and culture. An insightful guide to the fascinating history of a phenomenon that will be seen in the future as one of the watershed moments of American history."
—RITA D. SHERMA, Ph.D., executive director, School of Philosophy and Religious Studies, Taksha University

"There have been several books for a mainstream audience that trace Buddhism's history in America . . . but we've been without the equivalent for Hinduism until now. *American Veda,* as entertaining as it is informative, ably fills the void."
—*TRICYCLE* MAGAZINE

"Written with a practitioner's heart and a journalist's eye, this book is indispensable for anyone who wants to understand the deeper philosophy and culture behind today's Yoga boom."
—SALLY KEMPTON, author of *Meditation for the Love of It* and *Awakening Shakti*

AMERICAN VEDA

From Emerson and the Beatles

to Yoga and Meditation—

How Indian Spirituality

Changed the West

PHILIP GOLDBERG

THREE RIVERS PRESS

NEW YORK

THREE RIVERS PRESS and the Tugboat design are registered trademarks of
Random House, Inc.

Originally published in hardcover in the United States by Harmony Books,
an imprint of the Crown Publishing Group, a division of Random House, Inc.,
New York, in 2010.

Library of Congress Cataloging-in-Publication Data
Goldberg, Philip, 1944–
American Veda: from Emerson and the Beatles to Yoga and meditation:
how Indian spirituality changed the West / Philip Goldberg.—1st ed.
p. cm.
Includes bibliographical references and index.
1. Hinduism—United States—History. 2. United States—Religion.
3. Vedanta—History. 4. Yoga—History. I. Title.
BL1168.U532G66 2010
294.50973—dc22   2010011040

ISBN 978-0-385-52135-2
eISBN 978-0-307-71961-4

Printed in the United States of America

1 3 5 7 9 10 8 6 4 2

First Paperback Edition

To the venerable *rishis*, *sadgurus*, and *acharyas*,
a thousand pranams

Passage to India
Lo, soul, seest thou not God's purpose from the first?
The earth to be spann'd, connected by network,
The races, neighbors, to marry and be given in marriage,
The oceans to be cross'd, the distant brought near,
The lands to be welded together.

A worship new I sing,
You captains, voyagers, explorers, yours,
You engineers, you architects, machinists, yours,
You, not for trade or transportation only,
But in God's name, and for thy sake O soul.

—Walt Whitman, "Passage to India"

ACKNOWLEDGMENTS

My gratitude begins with Trace Murphy, who saw the need for a book such as this one and made sure it got written. Profound thanks to my agent, Lynn Franklin, who brought Trace and me together, and whose support, guidance, and friendship have long sustained me. Thanks as well to Gary Jansen, whose astute hands-on editing was invaluable in shaping the book.

A deep bow of gratitude to Huston Smith, whose foreword graces these pages. That he took the time to write it at age ninety-one, with other priorities on his plate, is a testament to the importance he attributes to the subject matter. My added gratitude to Jon and Anna Monday for serving as liaisons to Huston, and for their feedback on sections of the manuscript.

Since I conducted more than three hundred interviews and engaged in countless informal conversations, I can't thank by name all those who generously shared their insights and expertise. I am grateful to every one of them, and especially to certain well-known individuals who are in demand by the media and nevertheless took the time to speak with me.

A number of people offered valuable assistance in a variety of ways, from transcribing interviews to supplying information to vetting passages of the book to extending profound moral support. For those contributions and others, I am thankful to the following: Jeffrey Ainis, Prem Anjali, Bill Barnard, John Roger Barrie, Raveen Battee, Swami Brahmavidyananda,

Robert Brown, Sara Chadwick, Christine Chagnon, Christopher Chapple, Srinivas Chari, Ken Chawkin, Mawiyah Clayborne, Rameshwar Das, Dave DeLuca, my in-laws Betty and Richard Deutsch, Navin Doshi, Bill and Leslie Elkus, Tom Feldman, James Finley, Jack and Roberta Forem, Robert Forman, Elliot Friedland, Robert Gordon, Carlos Grasso, Robert Green, Michael Gressett, Linda Groff, Heidi Hall, Craig Hamilton, Andrew Harvey, Alan Hodder, Kristin Imboden, Jerry Jarvis, Kurt Johnson, Doug Kruschke, Ramdas Lamb, Lauren Landress, Jeffery Long, Jean MacPhail, Sanjay Manchanda, Franz Metcalf, Venkatesan Natarajan, Duncan Newton-Gaines, Jyotish and Devi Novack, Kikanza Nuri, Carter Phipps, John Raatz, Anita Rehker, Gus Reininger, Dana Sawyer, Sara Schrefflers, Michael Schwartz, Rita Sherma, Bahman Shirazi, Dean Sluyter, Stuart Sovatsky, David St. John, Tony Stern, Jim Strohecker, Murthy Subramaniya, Jeremy Tarcher, Mary Ellen Trahan, Jeff Utter, Sirah Vettese, Pravrajika Vrajaprana, Lisa Walford, Andrew Wenger, Melissa West, Sharon Whittle, Lola Williamson, and Connie Zweig.

While this might seem odd, I want to thank the creators of Google and everyone responsible for the miracle of the Internet. In an earlier era, writing this book would have taken at least twice as long, certain details might never have been uncovered, and I might have developed asthma from wallowing in the dusty stacks of a university library, searching for information that is now obtainable in a matter of seconds.

Finally, a deep bow to the dear ones whose encouragement and support over the years has meant more to me than they can possibly imagine: my brother Bob and everyone in my extended family and my wife's family, with special thanks to Aliya Rafei and Ryan Rafei for letting me play with them. Above all, deepest gratitude to my wife, Lori Deutsch, my own private *devi* (look it up), who never wavered in her support, even when it was obvious that this book would consume far more time and resources than anticipated. Without her healing presence, I can't imagine getting through this massive project with mind and body intact.

CONTENTS

FOREWORD

In the Indo-European language—so named because Sanskrit in India and Greek in Europe both derive from it—*v* and *w* were interchangeable. Hence in India the word *Vedanta* and in Europe *wit* (and by extension *wisdom*) are branches of a single linguistic tree.

This common origin, however, is only the framework; the important question is what those two vessels (Vedanta, on the one hand, and the wisdom literature of Socrates, Plato, and their lesser lights, on the other) contained.

Here I will wax personal. As a professor of philosophy and religion, I had been well acquainted with the West's wisdom literature, but I was totally unprepared for the shock of discovering that Vedanta proposes different paths of life tailored to human temperaments—*jnana* for intellectuals, *bhakti* for those who are emotional, *karma* for industrious individuals who like to work, and *raja* for contemplative people who profit from meditating. A verse in the Bible admonishes us to "love the Lord thy God with all thy heart [*bhakti*], with all thy soul [*raja*], with all thy strength [*karma*], and with all thy mind [*jnana*]." But in the Bible the four paths are compressed into a single verse; Vedantins wrote books on how to walk each of those four paths. Swami Nikhilananda's four volumes are beside me in my bookcase.

In *American Veda* Philip Goldberg discusses how the British Empire occupied India for two hundred years and how India in return gave the West its *Sanatana Dharma* (Eternal Religion). It has come to be known as Hinduism, and its scriptures, the Vedas, culminate in the Vedanta, the covering term for the Bhagavad Gita and the Upanishads. Vedanta's philosophical treatises do not concern themselves with Hindu religious practices, such as chanting and ritual bathing.

Early translations of Vedic texts found their way to America in the opening decades of the country's existence and influenced Jefferson, Adams, Emerson, and Thoreau. Goldberg chronicles how these beginnings mushroomed to the point where there are now Vedantic organizations in every major city in the world. He argues that the Vedas hold that religion is rooted in Ultimate Truth, that all authentic religions recognize this, and that that explains Vedanta's appeal to Americans. This is the perspective of perennialism. As Goldberg writes, "Perennialism arose from the frequent observation that the esoteric or mystical components of religious traditions—as opposed to *exoteric* ritual, doctrine, ethics, and the like— call forth strikingly similar descriptions of reality, across cultures and regardless of era."

American Veda also relates how the Vedantic influences found their way back to India through the lens of the American perspective. In a personal story about a visit to India, Goldberg tells of an encounter with an orange-robed monk:

> I watched him methodically plant seeds in the soil as he chanted Sanskrit verses. When he noticed me, he placed his palms together in greeting. After responding to his queries about what had brought me to Rishikesh, I asked about his younger days. Had he been a sannyasi since his youth?
>
> He laughed robustly. As a young man, he had viewed the religion of his ancestors as backward, he said, and went to university to study science.
>
> I asked what prompted his spiritual turnaround.
>
> "I took a class in American literature," he said, "and I read Emerson."

Vedanta quietly surfaces in the daily lives of Americans. *Yoga, karma, meditation, enlightenment* are now household words. How that came about needed to be documented, and Philip Goldberg has done just that.

I hope that I have said enough to whet the reader's appetite to plunge into this significant book.

Huston Smith
Berkeley, California

INTRODUCTION

I n a sense, I started working on this book in 1967, when I first became enchanted by Indian philosophy. As I plunged deeper into my study and began practicing meditation and Yoga, my life changed for the better. Soon I saw the same thing happen to others, then others, and others still. Indian spiritual teachings were clearly affecting a lot of people, not just me and my friends. Then scholars, scientists, psychologists, and others began adapting those ideas and practices to their areas of expertise. By the mid-1980s the imported teachings had seeped into the culture in a profoundly meaningful, although not always obvious, way. Indian imports were changing not only individual lives but also health care, psychology, and religion.

The story seemed intriguing and important, spanning two hundred years and populated by fascinating characters, some of them renowned, others unknown but surprisingly influential. In 1985 I wrote a proposal for a book on the subject but could not interest a publisher. Sometimes "ahead of its time" is an accurate description.

Twenty years later Yoga classes had become as easy to find as a cappuccino, and American spirituality as a whole had acquired a distinctively Eastern flavor; India's influence had spread wider and penetrated deeper into the culture. Trace Murphy at Doubleday saw it too and thought there might be a book in it. He mentioned the idea to my agent, Lynn Franklin, who put the two of us together. When I added formal research to my almost forty years of participant-observation, I saw that the story was even more far-reaching than I'd thought, and far more complex. After three years, hundreds of eye-straining hours of reading, more than three hundred formal interviews, and countless informal conversations, I completed the first draft.

As I was editing the book in August 2009, *Newsweek* published a column by religion editor Lisa Miller titled "We Are All Hindus Now." It was extremely gratifying to have a mainstream publication validate my main thesis: that American society has moved ever closer to a spiritual worldview that resembles the core principles of the Vedic tradition. Many complex forces have given rise to this development, chief among them the two hundred years of access to Indian philosophy chronicled in these pages. Miller's article was like a good advance review.

A second reason her piece intrigued me was its provocative title. Certainly Americans are not becoming Hindus, in the sense of attending rituals in Hindu temples, performing *pujas* (ceremonies) at home altars, celebrating holidays such as Duvali and Shivaratri, and praying to Ganesh or Lakshmi. But that is not what Miller was referring to. Rather, she argued, large numbers of Americans have arrived at a worldview consistent with a principle articulated in the ancient *Rig Veda,* which she translated as "Truth is One, but the sages speak of it by many names."

Miller's title alludes to only one subset of Hinduism, not to the religion as practiced by the majority of Hindus. Which brings us to the name itself.

Why Not *Hinduism*?

This book is about Hinduism—if the word were to be defined narrowly, as a specific set of precepts and practices derived from India's primary religion. But, defined as the everyday religion of India, Hinduism is *not* the subject, and if the title or jacket copy suggested it was, many potential readers would misconstrue the nature of the book. For that reason, I decided to use the terms *Hindu* and *Hinduism* sparingly.

Such linguistic dilemmas have plagued writers, scholars, and practitioners of Hindu-derived teachings for centuries. The origin of the word *Hindu* is more geographic than religious. It initially denoted the land on the other side of the Indus River (originally the Sindhu). Successive invaders—Persians, Muslims, Britons—called the inhabitants of the region Hindus and eventually named its dominant religious strain Hinduism. In fact, what we think of as one religion is a multifarious collection of sects, traditions, beliefs, and practices that evolved from the Vedas, the world's oldest sacred texts, and took shape across the vast Indian subcontinent over the course of many centuries. The other three religions born in India—Buddhism, Jainism, and Sikhism—share the same ancient source.

Varun Soni, dean of religious life at the University of Southern California, calls Hinduism "the oldest and youngest religious tradition"—old because of its ancient origins, and young because "it was codified as an *ism* by colonial Brits more for administrative and political reasons than theological." In many ways Hinduism is more diverse than the sum of Christianity, Judaism, and Islam, which, if history had been reversed, might have been lumped together as Jordanism, after the river valley in which those traditions were born. Hinduism has no central authority, no founding figure, no historical starting point, no single creed or canonical doctrine, and many holy books rather than one—all reasons why it has been called the world's largest disorganized religion. Our understanding of it has been shaped mainly by Western scholars to fit their own system of religious classification. Many adherents prefer the original term, *Sanatana Dharma,* which is commonly translated as "eternal path" or "eternal way."[1]

Due to centuries of distortions—some intentionally perpetrated by colonists and missionaries, some the result of innocent ignorance—Hinduism is widely misunderstood. It is often described as polytheistic, for example, when in fact it recognizes a transcendent oneness, which some call God, that manifests in a multiplicity of forms. Because of such misconceptions, and because the popular mind associates Hinduism with its colorful rituals and iconography, very few Americans of non-Indian descent call themselves Hindus, even if their worldviews and spiritual practices derive from that tradition.

Moreover, the most influential gurus and Yoga masters who came to the West made a big point of saying they were not preaching Hinduism. They were Hindus themselves, of course, but they asserted that all could utilize their teachings without deserting their own religions. Indeed, the ideas and practices they proffered did not have to be viewed religiously at all; they could be seen as a philosophy, a psychology, a science, or even a health-care modality. This was not a marketing gambit; it was an honest, pragmatic adaptation to the West.

As we will see in chapter 1, the components of India's spiritual tradition that most affected Western culture have been the philosophy of Vedanta and the practices of Yoga. Therefore I favor those two terms and use the compound *Vedanta-Yoga* to indicate that combination of imported ideas and practices. (In some instances, I use *Vedic* or *Indian*.) Should Hindu American advocacy groups achieve their laudable goal of correcting the image of their religion, future books will use the term Hinduism freely, without fear of misleading the public.

Where Is Buddhism?

Buddhism and Vedanta-Yoga have interacted and overlapped intimately in the lives of American practitioners, many of whom have drawn liberally from both. Each has helped to legitimize the other, smoothing the way to mutual acceptance in the West. Their compatibility makes sense, given that Buddhism is part of the Vedic legacy. Siddhartha Gautama, the man we call Buddha, was brought up in northern India and became a classic renunciate—a yogi, if you will. He was a reformer, much as Jesus was a reformer of the Hebraic tradition, and the religion that developed in his name stands in relation to Hinduism as Christianity does to Judaism. Also like Christianity, Buddhism became entrenched in foreign lands even as it faded in its place of origin. (Like Hinduism, normative Buddhism in Asia is rather different from its American adaptation.) To keep the book to a reasonable length, however, references to Buddhism were kept to a minimum, despite the tradition's enormous impact. That decision was made easier by the presence of Rick Fields's masterful *How the Swans Came to the Lake* and other informative books on the history of Buddhism in the West.

Difficult Choices

American Veda could easily have been a thousand pages long. Given the space limitations, the amount of coverage devoted to any given subject was primarily based on its impact on American society. Page length should not be taken as a statement about the merit of any teacher, teaching, or institution. Interested readers will find additional details and references to other sources in the notes. And the website www.AmericanVeda.com contains archives, links, photographs, audios, and other supplementary features, including a blog where visitors can contribute information, ideas, and opinions.

I am not an academically trained scholar, hence this is not an academic treatise. I approached the book as a journalist and a participant-observer, and I tried throughout to maintain rigorous standards of objectivity and vigilance about my own possible biases. That said, the book is not without a point of view. It became increasingly evident during my research that America's absorption of Indian spiritual teachings is a positive historical development. As a result, the book is not just a chronicle of the gurus, swamis, and Yoga masters who have come to our shores, but an account of a much larger phenomenon: a religious revolution whose impact is likely to endure. One might compare it to the Great Awakenings of the eighteenth century—vastly different in theology, to be sure, but similar in its egalitarianism and individualism. The story can also be seen in nonreligious terms, as describing a major shift in consciousness; the ideas and practices we've imported from India are changing the way we understand ourselves and our place in the universe. For reasons made clear in the book, I am convinced that this development can help make us a healthier, saner nation and provide a much-needed antidote to religious extremism and intolerance.

I

NAMASTE, AMERICA!

In February 1968 the Beatles went to India for an extended stay with their new guru, Maharishi Mahesh Yogi. It may have been the most momentous spiritual retreat since Jesus spent those forty days in the wilderness. The media frenzy over the Fab Four made known to the sleek, sophisticated West that meek, mysterious India had something of value. Our understanding and practice of spirituality would never be the same.

Today in America limber men and women stride up the street carrying Yoga mats. Doctors and therapists recommend meditation to manage stress. Newscasters toss out words like *mantra* and *guru*. Pop songs and TV shows refer to karma. Christians and Jews delve into their own mystical traditions on silent retreats. People call themselves "spiritual but not religious." All this and a lot more—much of it as subtle as it is profound—can be traced in large part to the Beatles' Himalayan sabbatical. At that watershed moment, Rudyard Kipling's famous prediction that "East is East and West is West/And never the twain shall meet" went the way of the British Empire. The twain had met, and the tectonic plates of Western culture shifted.

The East-to-West flow of ideas actually began with the ancient Greeks. It moved quietly through the age of exploration, when Europeans were too busy extracting resources from the newly discovered lands to learn much from their sages and seers. Then in the early nineteenth century British scholars produced the first English translations of India's sacred texts. Those books reached American shores and fell into the hands of Ralph Waldo Emerson, Henry David Thoreau, and Walt Whitman.

Thereafter, gurus came, lectures were given, books were written, and the message of India proved alluring to more and more people. Predominantly white, urban, and educated, they were seekers of truth, of God, of self-improvement. Some became exponents of Indian teachings themselves. Others absorbed Eastern ideas, incorporated them in their own areas of expertise, and passed along the final products. Through them, Indian philosophy, though not always discernible, has been disseminated deep and wide.

The influence spread slowly and imperceptibly, like a gathering weather system, then surged mightily in the late 1960s, when a constellation of forces came together—mass communication and ease of travel; social unrest; war and nuclear anxiety; psychedelic drugs; and alienated but idealistic youngsters with the time and money to explore new ways of being. The Beatles' journey to the banks of the Ganges blew the gates between East and West wide open. In a flash, more Americans learned about Indian spirituality than in all the previous centuries. Baby boomers read books about Eastern philosophy, took up meditation and Yoga, grooved on the sound of the sitar, chanted Sanskrit in the streets, flocked to gurus, and in some cases trekked to ashrams in India. Hundreds of thousands joined what religious scholar Lola Williamson calls Hindu-inspired meditation movements (HIMMs), which together, she argues, constitute a new religion.[1] But for every committed HIMM member, there were ten or twenty more who never dove into the pool but dipped in enough that their lives were changed and their worldviews were reshaped.

In a few short years Eastern ideas and practices spread from the counterculture to the mainstream, fueling enthusiasm in medicine, psychology, academia, sports, the arts, and entertainment. In time, Indian philosophy seeped into the culture, changing what we know about the mind, body, and spirit, and the way we relate to the sacred.

The story of this powerful, pervasive, and benign current in American life has hitherto been neglected. Understanding it can help us better comprehend who we are, how we got here, and what we might become. If we get to know India as a source of profound and practical wisdom, not just of savory spices and tech support, we will be better able to adapt those treasures to our lasting benefit.

India's Leading Export

The West has always coveted things from India: its minerals, its exquisite fabrics, its cuisine, its cheap labor, and its talent—from the foot soldiers of the colonial period to today's high-tech masterminds. Traders, colonists, soldiers, and business executives have all gone after those prizes. But India's greatest gift has always been the knowledge of its ancient seers, whose insights have never lost their power to astound and instruct. In the 1930s the eminent historian Will Durant wrote, "Perhaps, in return for conquest, arrogance and spoliation, India will teach us the tolerance and gentleness of the mature mind, the quiet content of the unacquisitive soul, the calm of the understanding spirit, and a unifying, pacifying love for all living things."[2]

India's epic tales the *Ramayana* and the *Mahabharata* are so rich in magic, mystery, and metaphor as to make the *Iliad* and the Bible seem like austere short stories. Compared to India's ornate temples, colorful rituals, and pantheon of gods and goddesses, Roman Catholicism seems as plain as vanilla. But India's mythology and the outward forms of its religion have attracted only a small number of Americans. The portions of India's vast spiritual legacy that have most appealed to Westerners are the philosophical system of Vedanta and the mental and physical practices of Yoga. As a unit they can be compared to the theoretical and applied components of a science—biology and medicine, for instance, or psychology and psychotherapy. Like all components of what we now call Hinduism, Vedanta and Yoga derive from the Vedic era (which most scholars trace to the second and first millennia B.C.E.), when seers called *rishis* gave voice to inner revelations about the nature of reality and offered ritual prescriptions for living.[3] These were passed down as oral tradition and eventually codified in the four books of the Vedas (*Veda* means "knowledge").[4] As Indian civilization evolved, Vedic knowledge was obscured and revived, adulterated and readapted many times, most triumphantly by the reformer known as the Buddha and by Shankara, a great medieval philosopher and the primary exponent of Vedanta.

Vedanta literally means "end of the Vedas" and refers to the culmination of that body of knowledge in the Upanishads, the *Brahma Sutras,* and the Bhagavad Gita.[5] *Yoga* typically refers to a collection of methodologies aimed at achieving spiritual transformation and culminating in the union of the individual and the divine. (The word derives from the Sanskrit for "yoking" or "joining.")[6] Taken together, as they usually are in practice, they constitute a science of consciousness.

Vedanta and Yoga are two of the six systems of Indian philosophy (which some call Hindu philosophy). They are so intertwined that all Vedantists advocate Yoga, and virtually all Yoga masters teach Vedanta. Other strains of Vedic spirituality, such as Tantrism, Samkhya, and Vaishnavism have also entered the westward-flowing stream.[7] Gurus and yogis being a pragmatic lot, they draw upon whatever works. But Vedanta and Yoga are India's predominant exports, a conscious choice by exponents who understood that the overtly religious forms of Hinduism would not find as friendly an audience.

These are the core Vedantic principles that we in the West have adapted:

1. Ultimate reality is both transcendent and immanent, both one and many; God can be conceived in both personal and nonpersonal terms, that is, as formless Absolute and in numerous forms and manifestations.

2. The infinite divine, while ineffable, has been given any number of names (Brahman, Allah, Lord, et cetera), descriptions, and attributes. A line from the *Rig Veda* (1.64.46) is frequently cited in this context: *Ekam sat vipraha bahudha vadanti,* typically translated as "Truth is one, the wise call it by many names" and sometimes summarized as "One Truth, many paths."[8]

3. The Ground of Being is also the essential nature of the Self. In the *mahavakyas* (great utterances) of the Upanishads we read: *Ayam Atma Brahma,* or "This Self is Brahman," and *Tat Tvam Asi,* or "Thou art That."[9]

4. Our innate unity with divinity is obscured by ignorance; we identify with our individual egos, when our true identity is the transcendent Self (which is Atman, which is Brahman).

5. Individuals can awaken to their divine nature through any number of pathways and practices; no single one is right for everyone.[10]

6. Spirituality is a developmental process, moving through a progressive series of stages; tangible benefits—joy, compassion, wisdom, peace—accrue in each.

7. Fully realizing one's true nature brings an end to suffering in the state of liberation or enlightenment called *moksha.*

This bare-bones summary does not pretend to do justice to Vedanta, a highly complex tradition with many branches and tributaries.[11] These principles are accompanied by the Vedic concepts of karma (which holds that every action has an equal and opposite reaction; we reap what we sow) and karma's companion, reincarnation. Most applications of Vedanta-Yoga do not require these supplementary ideas, and ordinary practitioners in the West do not necessarily believe in them. As explained in the introduction, the Hinduism practiced by most Indians is outwardly different from (although theologically compatible with) the Vedanta-Yoga that came here. By way of analogy, it would be as if the Christianity exported to Asia and Africa had been a mixture of the intellectual rigor of the Jesuits and the contemplative practices of mystics such as Meister Eckhart and Teresa of Avila, rather than normative Christianity.

Vedanta as described here is similar to perennialism, a perspective championed by the philosophers René Guénon, Frithjof Schuon, and Ananda Coomaraswamy and brought to public attention by Aldous Huxley in his 1944 book *The Perennial Philosophy* (see page 95). Perennialism arose from the frequent observation that the esoteric or mystical components of religious traditions—as opposed to *exoteric* ritual, doctrine, ethics, and the like—call forth strikingly similar descriptions of reality, across cultures and regardless of era. This does *not* mean all religions are the same. That notion has been naïvely promoted by peace lovers because of its harmonious connotations and because every religion has some varia-tion of the Golden Rule. But it has also been attributed, erroneously, to perennialists such as Huxley and Huston Smith, most recently by religious scholar Stephen Prothero, author of *God Is Not One*.[12]

That religions are not the same could not be more obvious. Vedantists and perennialists are not so naïve as to postulate a sameness of theology or of truth claims. The coherence they point to is in the realm of inner ex-perience, the domain associated with mysticism.[13] At the depth of being, they assert, where the individual soul meets the all-encompassing divine, men and women of every spiritual orientation have encountered oneness and have described that revelation in remarkably similar ways.

In other words, while religious customs, rituals, and dogmas vary, all traditions, *if taken deep enough,* can bring practitioners to essentially the same place—our silent origin, or essence, which transcends all notions of place, all words, all concepts, all theologies. Once again, "Truth is one, the wise call it by many names." Vedanta has so seeped into collective aware-ness that the spirit of this premise, if not the literal phrase, is now widely accepted in the United States.

A Perfect Fit

Whether it's a falafel or a philosophy, Americans embrace foreign products when the circumstances are right, and conditions in the United States were right for Vedanta-Yoga from the start. Imagine a savvy entrepreneur running focus groups to see what Americans wanted by way of knowledge and self-improvement. The results would tell him that Indian merchan-dise would go over well with educated people who wanted to better them-selves, whether they were spiritual or secular. He would lick his chops over remarks like this one from the sage Sri Aurobindo: "Indian religion has always felt that since the minds, the temperaments and the intellectual affinities of men are unlimited in their variety, a perfect liberty of thought and of worship must be allowed to the individual in his approach to the Infinite." That emphasis on personalized pathways to the divine—or, for secularists, to personal growth—resonates with the American ethos of individual autonomy and freedom of choice. It also appeals to two seemingly contradictory strains in the national character: romantic idealism and pragmatism. Americans are dreamers, but they're also hard-headed realists; they think big and reach for the sky, but for the most part they invest in what works.

Our promoter might then have dashed off to the Himalayas to cut deals with swamis. For romantics, he could advertise a sublime state of liberated being. For the religious, he could promote union with God. For pragmatists, he could market provable yogic techniques. For the secular, he could promise a healthier, happier life here and now. Step right up!

Absent the crass impresario, the progress of Vedanta-Yoga unfolded more or less that way. My own story is typical. As a college student in the Sixties,[14] I was a political radical, a determined seeker of truth, and a confused mess who couldn't figure out how to live happily in society, much less comprehend any higher meaning or purpose. I had no use for religion, but I was disillusioned with Marx and Freud too. As the era's social tension grew, so did my craving for fulfillment and relief. The descriptions of enlightened yogis and the sublime faces on Buddhist statuary made me think, *I want what those guys had.* I wanted bliss. I wanted wisdom, infinite love, and union with the cosmos. I wanted peace and freedom—not just out there in the world, but inside.

I was also rational and relatively level-headed. One day I was sitting in my funky kitchen in New York, just around the corner from the sex-drugs-and-rock mecca the Fillmore East, reading a book on Eastern mysticism. "Why do they call this mystical?" I said to a friend. It seemed perfectly logical and down to earth. As a modernist who believed that religion was the opium of the people, it was mind-boggling to discover ancient religious teachings that said, essentially, here's what we hold to be true; try it, test it out, see if it works for you—no leap of faith is required, no belief in fanciful tales is necessary, and you need not wait for an afterlife reward. I dashed around Manhattan looking for the Bhagavad Gita (harder to find than a Red Sox fan); I found a Yoga studio (also not easy, believe it or not); I learned Transcendental Meditation as the Beatles had done (but not because of them); I became a teacher of the practice for several years. My discoveries changed my life for the better. Ever since, I have worked diligently to integrate my spiritual priorities with the duties and pleasures of worldly life.

Details aside, my narrative arc is common. With varying degrees of dedication and sophistication, millions of sober, sensible people have taken to one form of Eastern spirituality or another and adapted it to their lives. Their conscious motivations vary, but they all boil down to issues of ultimate concern, and therefore the quest becomes religious.

Form Follows Function

In its most complete form, religion serves five basic functions. I've given each of them a name beginning with the prefix *trans,* meaning "across, through, or beyond":[15]

- *Transmission:* to impart to each generation meaningful customs, rituals, stories, and historical continuity
- *Translation:* to help people interpret life events, acquire meaning and purpose, and affirm their connection to a larger whole
- *Transaction:* to create and sustain healthy communities and provide guidelines for moral behavior and ethical relationships
- *Transformation:* to foster maturation, ongoing growth, and the development of more fulfilled and more complete persons
- *Transcendence:* to satisfy the yearning to enlarge the perceived boundaries of the self, touch the infinite, and unite with the ultimate Ground of Being

By and large, organized religions in the West have emphasized the first three functions and paid far less attention to the last two.[16] For seekers of transformation and transcendence, the vacuum was filled in large part by Eastern spiritual traditions, where they found a vision of possibilities that seemed not only sublime but rational and attainable. When I asked people what initially drew them to Vedanta-Yoga, most referred to the promise of tangible spiritual and psychological benefits; the rewards of the first three functions, such as community and worldview, were usually considered secondary gains. The manner in which Eastern practices have improved the lives of adherents has been described in countless memoirs, research papers, and self-help manuals. The changes lean in the direction of improved well-being: greater peace, self-awareness, happiness, and wholeness, and a connection to something bigger than themselves.

Many people also described an aha! moment upon hearing Vedanta philosophy for the first time.[17] It offered a way of understanding the divine that did not offend their sense of reason or require faith in the miraculous. It was experience-oriented, not belief-oriented; it did not threaten nonbelievers with damnation; and its tent was so wide, it could accommodate people of any faith—or no faith. Above all, to anyone who followed the instruction manual, it held out reasonable hope for transformation and transcendence.

The appeal of Vedanta-Yoga extends to the secular as well as the spiritual. "Religious faith in the case of the Hindus has never been allowed to run counter to scientific laws," wrote the French Nobel laureate Romain Rolland early in the twentieth century. Vedanta-Yoga is a kind of empirical science of the inner life; its postulates can be tested in the laboratory of one's own consciousness, using the test tubes and Bunsen burners of yogic disciplines. And the goal does not have to be union with God, or Self-realization; it can be something instrumental, like reduced stress or a clearer mind. In other words, what some saw as theology, others saw as testable hypotheses. What some viewed as spiritual practices, others viewed as therapies.

Scientists and scholars also found they could study Vedanta-Yoga with the tools of their trades. In so doing they have expanded the databases of psychology, medicine, neurobiology, and even theoretical physics. In turn, science's imprimatur conferred more legitimacy to the Vedic tradition.

Lines of Transmission

Over the decades the influence of Vedanta-Yoga has grown with every person whose life was touched by it. Moved by a yearning for something more, a person seeks out or stumbles upon a source of Vedic wisdom. He or she learns something of value and communicates the discovery to others, some of whom also derive benefit and share their enthusiasm. A zealous practitioner might go to work for a teacher or an organization, as many Americans have. But such committed devotees are just the tip of the lotus petal. The untold story, and perhaps the more significant one, involves ordinary people who assimilate Vedantic-Yogic teachings into their lives and quietly go about their business. They may do nothing more than share ideas with family, friends, and colleagues, but that in itself is a significant act of transmission. And when a disseminator happens to be in a field such as health care, psychotherapy, scientific research, education, journalism, or the arts, the impact can be sizable.

By way of analogy, let's look at the rise of alternative medicine (which, I should note, features meditation and other yogic practices). In the late 1960s and early 1970s, many medical patients, disturbed by the side effects and exorbitant cost of medicine, started searching for natural alternatives. Some physicians, impressed by the results, began investigating the same remedies. Over time methods that proved efficacious were adopted. Eventually integrative medicine achieved legitimacy, amassing millions of dollars in government-funded research. Similarly, people who sought meaning and personal growth and were unsatisfied by existing options, religious and secular, went shopping for alternatives and often found them in the East. Like natural remedies, Eastern teachings were dismissed as a fad and mocked as mystical gobbledygook. In time, however, what proved to be useful seeped into the mainstream. Now physicians recommend Yoga and meditation, scientists study the practices, and ordinary believers hold spiritual attitudes that were once considered foreign and threatening. It's a good old American free-market triumph, led by results-driven consumers.

For decades, advocates have communicated Vedantic ideas, sometimes to persuade, sometimes to explain, and sometimes with no agenda or reference to anything Indian. As a result, millions of Americans have been influenced by Vedanta-Yoga without necessarily being aware of it, just as they devour pasta without knowing its origins in China or watch television without having heard of its inventor, Philo T. Farnsworth. When asked about their religious and spiritual attitudes, a great many people sound vaguely Vedantic, and if you ask where they got those ideas, they don't always know, or they mention a book, a teacher, a friend or family member, a shrink, pastor, or health practitioner, a celebrity, or a self-help author. The influencer might not have used religious language at all but rather that of scholarship, science, or therapy; perhaps they used the generic, religiously neutral argot that has evolved in response to pluralism—a spiritual Esperanto, so to speak. With few exceptions, however, one can trace the line of influence to something Eastern.

Ginny Wright was raised Baptist and married into the Episcopal church. "I became disillusioned with both," she says, "and I started looking for something else." She learned Transcendental Meditation, read Paramahansa Yogananda's *Autobiography of a Yogi*, attended retreats with Ram Dass, and became a devotee of Swami Muktananda's Siddha Yoga. Along the way she earned a doctorate in psychology. Now in private practice in North Carolina, Dr. Wright draws from the Vedic repertoire but rarely refers to it explicitly. "I'll say something like 'God is within you,'" she told me. "I try to show clients that they'll be happier and more fulfilled if they get in touch with the soul, or self, or whatever they wish to call it." Like many therapists, she employs yogic breathing and meditative practices without calling them such.

Jeffery Long was born a year after the Beatles went to India, but as an adolescent in rural Missouri, his heroes were George Harrison, whose life was about as Vedic as a Westerner's can be, and Mahatma Gandhi, whose favorite scripture, the Bhagavad Gita, young Jeffery found "profoundly comforting and compelling." Now a self-defined Hindu convert, Dr. Long is the chair of the religious studies department at Elizabethtown College in Pennsylvania and an advocate of Vedantic pluralism. His students say that he has helped them find their own spiritual paths, some of which led back to Christianity after a period of disillusionment.

Ginny the baby boomer and Jeffery the Gen-Xer represent two ways that seekers become disseminators. Millions of others have done the same, and the people they touch often find their understanding of who they are and how they relate to the cosmos profoundly altered. Each time that happens, the Western zeitgeist shifts a little bit more. As John Friend, the founder of Anusara Yoga, puts it, "The mixing of the cultures is like mixing pigments, giving rise to colors never seen before."

At this point in our history, only the most parochial American is more than a few degrees of separation from an advocate of Vedanta-Yoga, whether they know it or not. Sometimes the connection is only a mouse-click away. In 2008 Oprah Winfrey conducted a series of Internet-based seminars with Eckhart Tolle, the spiritual superstar whose *The Power of Now* had off-the-charts sales. Their cozy salon was downloaded thirty million times. Tolle's spiritual framework has been influenced by both Vedanta and Buddhism, yet he rarely mentions that, and his terminology is mostly generic. His hostess, by the way, has learned well from her guests. Each of us is "a spirit in a human body," Winfrey says, and when she refers to God, she adds that one can just as well call it "source" or "universal energy" because we must not "get hung up on the words"—a rather folksy rendering of Vedantic principles.

Karmic Relief

Cultural trends are reflected in vocabulary, and Indian spiritual terms have infiltrated the language. When the Beatles learned to meditate in 1967, only a handful of people outside India had ever heard the word *mantra*. Suddenly everyone knew that a mantra is a sound used in meditation. Fast-forward to the 2008 presidential campaign, and you could barely go twenty minutes without hearing the word on CNN. Every candidate was said to have a mantra. Barack Obama's was "Yes, we can." John McCain's was "Country first." The political analysts commenting on the mantras were "gurus," a word we now attach to experts of all kinds, or "pundits," from the Sanskrit *pandit,* "learned man." Nor was it just tuned-in media stars who used the word *mantra.* James Baker III, secretary of state under the first President Bush and a pillar of Texas Republicanism, said the title of his memoir, *"Work Hard, Study . . . and Keep Out of Politics!"* had been his grandfather's "mantra." And Zbigniew Brzezinski, Jimmy Carter's national security adviser, scolded George W. Bush for turning *war on terror* into "a national mantra."

As for the ubiquitous *guru,* consider the hugely successful *Guru Guide* books, or Guru Nation, an online learning network for business professionals. *The New Yorker*'s Roz Chast captured the promiscuous usage in a cartoon captioned "In the Guru District," which depicts a dozen bearded seers: Diet Guru, Fashion Guru, Sex Guru, and so on.[18]

Everyone knows the word *yoga,* of course, even if they think it's a new kind of workout, and with Yoga studios on almost every city block, words like *asana* (posture) and *pranayama* (breathing exercise) will soon be as commonplace as *aerobic* and *push-up. Namaste,* the salutation commonly translated as "I recognize the divine in you," is heard—or at least seen, in the palms-together-at-the-chest gesture—more and more frequently and not just in Yoga classes. Celebrities use it when accepting applause (Conan O'Brien is fond of it). A quick Google search reveals Namaste Foods, Namaste Bags, Namaste Solar, Namaste Vineyards, and more. *Samadhi,* defined by one dictionary as "the highest stage in meditation, in which a person experiences oneness with the universe," has also found commercial usage, as in Scent of Samadhi, the "all natural and herbal fragrance of the yogis." *Ananda,* Sanskrit for "bliss," and *dharma,* loosely translated as "duty or righteous action," adorn the names of enterprises from consulting firms to vintage clothing shops. In downtown Sacramento I spotted the Tantric Urban Bistro. When I asked a young man behind the counter about the name, he said that *tantra* was about "channeling divine energy into the world in creative ways." Given the association of Tantra with far-out sex, I was relieved that he meant the sandwich and salad recipes.

Peace activists, civil rights veterans, and fans of Philip Glass's operatic works are familiar with Sanskrit terms made famous by Mohandas K. Gandhi: *ahimsa,* or "nonviolence," and *satyagraha,* "truth force." Most Americans would correctly associate the word *ashram* with a Hindu hermitage, but it's also the name of a $4,000-per-week spa outside Los Angeles. That may not be surprising, but the Louisiana-based United Christian Ashrams, where "Jesus Christ is the center," certainly is. As for *avatar,* well, James Cameron knew that Hindus use the term for divine incarnations such as Krishna and Rama, but he used it to mean "the fleshly incarnation of a living human." If you make the highest-grossing movie of all time, who's going to argue?

The word *karma* crops up everywhere from scholarly journals to cell phone commercials to entertainment reports to conversations of ordinary people who wouldn't know the Vedas from *Vogue.* In back-to-back issues of *Newsweek,* for instance, cultural icons of different eras used it: Norman Mailer and the rapper 50 Cent (who invoked it to explain why he'd been shot nine times).[19] Pay attention, and you'll see the Karma Foundation listed as a PBS sponsor, and any day now you'll see Karma the electric car on the freeway. Now that it's common shorthand for "cosmic justice," *karma* also shows up on the sports pages and in pop culture, where there's always a lot of reaping and sowing. A search of the iTunes Music Store, for instance, yields 150 references to karmic titles, ranging from John Lennon to Willie Nelson to Alicia Keys. TV viewers know that *My Name Is Earl* begins each week with a brief treatise on karma, and fans of *Desperate Housewives* heard Carlos tell Gabi that bad stuff is happening to them because "it's karma. We've been selfish and greedy, and the universe is telling us to be better people."

To a couple of English words, dictionaries have added new meanings. *Meditation* always meant "rumination or the contemplation of ideas"; now it's also a spiritual discipline or a method "to train, calm, or empty the mind." *Enlightenment,* which once referred only to the eighteenth-century philosophical movement, is now also "a blessed state in which the individual transcends desire and suffering and attains nirvana"—*nirvana,* of course, being a Sanskrit word for "spiritual liberation," now joined in Webster's by *moksha.* And while the word *reincarnation* is not particularly novel, this startling piece of data is: a 2004 Gallup Poll found that 24 percent of American adults believe in it, including 10 percent of born-again Christians.

Never mind that these terms are commonly adulterated, trivialized, and misused. Cultures adopt foreign words only when they serve a useful purpose and the native tongue has no equivalent. Some are merely menu items, articles of clothing, or art forms, like *chai,* or *sari,* or *raga.* But the terms I've mentioned have become part of the linguistic furniture because the concepts to which they point have philosophical currency.

The Vedization of America

The way Americans understand and practice religion has become de-cidedly Vedantic—less in form, although there is plenty of that, than in spirit. Survey results from organizations such as Gallup, Harris, and Pew; academic institutions like Princeton's Center for the Study of Religion; university-based social scientists; and media outlets from *Newsweek* to Beliefnet.com all support this conclusion. The body of research over recent decades points to the following trends:

- *Spiritual independence.* One Gallup survey asked, "Do you think of spirituality more in a personal and individual sense or more in terms of organized religion and church doctrine?" Almost three-quarters opted for "personal and individual."[20]
- *Direct experience.* A 2005 Newsweek/Beliefnet survey asked respondents, "Why do you practice religion?" The most frequent answer (39 percent) was "To forge a personal relationship with God."[21]
- *Tolerance.* Exclusivism is in decline; pluralism is in the ascendancy. A 2008 Pew Research Center survey found that 70 percent of Americans agreed that "many religions can lead to eternal life." (Fifty-seven percent of Evangelical Christians also agreed.)[22]
- *Fluidity.* Princeton sociologist Robert Wuthnow has identified a shift from a "dwelling spirituality," in which "a spiritual habitat defines

one's relationship to God," to a "seeking spirituality," where "we seek God in many different venues."[23]

- *Nonliteralism.* Wuthnow says that the number of people who believe the Bible is the literal word of God has "dropped remarkably since the 1960s."[24]

- *A different kind of God.* Over 90 percent of Americans check "yes" when asked if they believe in God. But increasingly they see God as an abstract, nonpersonal force or intelligence, as opposed to an anthropomorphic deity. In the 2001 Beliefnet survey cited above, 84 percent saw God as "everywhere and in everything" as opposed to "someone somewhere."

These trend lines coincide with the appearance of a new religious category: "spiritual but not religious" (SBNR).[25] Robert C. Fuller, a religious studies scholar and author of a book on SBNRs, describes them this way: "Forsaking formal religious organizations, these people have instead embraced an individualized spirituality that includes picking and choosing from a wide range of alternative religious philosophies. They typically view spirituality as a journey intimately linked with the pursuit of personal growth or development."[26] In other words, they are spiritual pragmatists looking for usable wisdom wherever they can find it. Called by some the fastest-growing segment of the religious spectrum, SBNRs make up 16 to 39 percent of the population.[27] That a distinction has emerged between religion and spirituality is in itself a major change, and the fact that I don't need to explain the difference is further proof.

Why is this shift in the spiritual landscape relevant to American Veda? Because it was spearheaded by the trendsetting baby boomers whom sociologist Paul H. Ray labeled "cultural creatives"[28]—the very cohort most likely to have been involved with Eastern spirituality in the 1960s and 1970s—and it spread from them to the mainstream. One of the values shared by cultural creatives, who are now said to number forty to fifty million, is what Ray calls "a new sense of the sacred." In their search for "universal, practical spiritual principles that have intrinsic value and do not depend on ecclesiastical authority," they tend to draw from a variety of traditions.

The data on cultural creatives jibes with a landmark study of boomer spirituality conducted by Wade Clark Roof, a religious scholar at the University of California at Santa Barbara.[29] What Roof calls "the New Spirituality" is marked by questing and driven by autonomy and direct experience of the sacred. One-third of boomers, he reports, agree that people have God within them, and almost half regard "all religions as equally true and good." He cites the rise of panentheism (not to be confused with pantheism), which he defines in Vedantic language: "The self is the indwelling of God. The world is the abode of God. All is one, and one is all. In the tradition of the ancient Upanishads, we find the oneness of our Atman with the all."[30] Ideas like those, says Roof in a subsequent work, "are now rather widely diffused in American culture as a whole—including within the churches, synagogues and temples."[31]

Like all complex social phenomena, these trends have multiple causes. But every reputable analyst says that access to India's spiritual teachings has been a central factor. Tellingly, Roof found that boomers who became independent seekers had a higher degree of exposure to the 1960s counterculture than those who stayed faithful to their religious heritage. Which means they were more likely to read about Indian philosophy, check out gurus, and take off for a Himalayan ashram. While their absolute numbers may have been small, they were trendsetters whose enthusiasms were trumpeted by a voracious media.

Today large numbers of people who never heard the word *Vedanta* are, in outlook and practice, Vedantists. They view spirituality as a developmental process in which each person's path must be constantly adjusted to suit his or her temperament, circumstances, and ever-evolving needs. What could be more American?[32]

The Cart Before the Source

In the late 1940s the writer-philosopher Gerald Heard declared, "A new religion has come into history—that is Western Vedanta." He would probably be surprised by how diverse, unstructured, and subtle that Western Vedanta has become. Even more prescient was Swami Satprakashananda, who ran the Vedanta Society in St. Louis in the mid-twentieth century. When asked if Vedanta would take root in America, the swami apparently replied, "Yes, but the source will not be recognized."

Inevitably the source of any assimilated import grows dim over time. As Americans do their math homework or compute their taxes, how many know that the numerical system they're using was invented in India? In the case of Vedanta-Yoga, however, forgetting the source would not only be sad—because India, having been demeaned through centuries of colonization, deserves the credit—but it could also diminish its potential benefit. The ideas and practices that shape the human soul are not like a spicy dish that can be altered in the kitchen with impunity. If we are careless in our adaptation, the nuanced principles of Vedanta can easily get contaminated, and the practices of Yoga can lose their efficacy. It's happening already. One of the purposes of this book is to make more visible the Vedic footprint on Western spirituality.

In a 1994 essay Ken Woodward, then *Newsweek*'s religion editor, said that America is engaged in a "reconfiguring of the sacred" with a pluralism that "makes any one spiritual path seem inherently parochial." We are now much farther along that path. Data on the generations after the baby boomers indicate that they are even more spiritually exploratory, more likely to fall in the SBNR category, and more curious about religions other than their own.[33] The drift toward personalized, experiential spirituality and freely chosen affiliations—a decidedly Vedantic route—shows no sign of stopping.

This is not a threat to Western religions; Americans are not about to abandon their churches, synagogues, and mosques for Hindu temples. Figures of Shiva and Krishna will not replace crosses in American homes.

No Vedic missionaries have come here saying, "Convert to Hinduism! Give up your heathen God and you will be saved." It has been more like an exchange of goods and services, or of scientific data. The Easterners have said: *Here is what our sages discovered, and here are some practices that can make you a better, deeper, more fulfilled Christian, Jew, Muslim, secular humanist.* In fact, as we'll see, exposure to Eastern spirituality is more likely to strengthen a person's relationship to his or her native religion than to destroy it.

There is, to be sure, a cautionary side to the story. Organizations led by Indian gurus have been rocked by sex scandals and cultish abuses. That dark side must be confronted squarely as we absorb the best of Vedanta-Yoga without compromising either its integrity or bedrock Western values. (We'll examine that issue in chapter 11.)

But overall the impact of India's science of consciousness on American life, like the reverse flow of industry and technology, has been a boon, and it promises to become an even greater one. In 1952 the eminent historian Arnold Toynbee predicted as much. The importance of religion would one day catch up with that of technology, he said, at which point "India, the conquered, will conquer its conquerors." The "catholic-minded Indian religious spirit," he said, "is the way of salvation for all religions in an age in which we have to learn to live as a single family if we are not to destroy ourselves."

THE VOICE OF AN OLD
INTELLIGENCE

I f Ralph Waldo Emerson had been the only American ever to read the sacred texts of India, the Vedic impact on the nation would still have been huge. Far and away the country's leading homegrown philosopher, Emerson has been called "the mind of America" by Yale scholar Harold Bloom. But that mind was shaped in large part by Asia. He was the first public thinker to openly embrace Eastern religious and philosophical precepts, which he blended with a range of other sources and his own fecund musings to produce an unrivaled body of work whose influence pervades the culture to this day. Because of Emerson and his direct heirs, Henry David Thoreau and Walt Whitman, millions of educated Americans have been touched by India since the mid-nineteenth century.

Emerson was born in 1803, at a time when America had no Sanskrit scholars, nor any classes or textbooks in comparative religion. While competing denominations of Christianity existed, by contemporary standards the country was religiously homogeneous. It was also very small: fewer people lived in all the seventeen states than now populate New York City. New information was conveyed through newspapers, books, and handwritten letters that were transported by horses, wagons, and riverboats. But in Emerson's Boston, a bustling seaport, travelogues about India and commentaries on its ancient scriptures and stories trickled in from abroad. Members of the progressive intelligentsia read *Asiatik Researches,* a journal published in Calcutta, and the works of British scholars such as Sir William Jones and Henry Thomas Colebrooke. Many devoured Charles Wilkins's translation of the Bhagavad Gita, the immortal dialogue between the warrior prince Arjuna and the divine incarnation Krishna.[1] It was the first English-language version of India's most revered scripture. (Now there are said to be more than 650.) Much of the New England elite greeted these treasures with the same enthusiasm that the mercantile classes welcomed Asian spices and fabrics. Innovative, exuberant America was on the brink of technological breakthroughs that would eventually bring India's Vedic legacy to all corners of the nation.

The Lure and Lore of the Mysterious East

"Pythagoras, Parmenides and Plato seem to have been influenced by Indian metaphysics," wrote historian Will Durant in *Our Oriental Heritage*. Those philosophers who set the tone for Western civilization must have come upon ideas from India by way of the first adventurers who journeyed east from the Mediterranean—possibly even Pythagoras himself. By 326 B.C.E., Alexander the Great had conquered the Punjab, in what is now Pakistan. According to Durant, the great general was so intrigued by the yogis he came across there that he invited one to accompany him back to Greece. The presumed honor was rebuffed, and the yogis "laughed at the Macedonian's boyish desire to conquer the earth when, as they told him, only a few feet of it sufficed for any man, alive or dead." One ascetic did travel with Alexander, but he became ill and "calmly mounting a funeral pyre . . . allowed himself to be burned to death without uttering a sound." Extraordinary tales of yogic equanimity have enchanted the West ever since. So have accounts of India's exotic people and customs, beginning with the *Indica*, four volumes written by the Greek explorer and diplomat Megasthenes, around 302 B.C.E.[2]

Elaine Pagels, the esteemed Princeton scholar, wrote in *The Gnostic Gospels* that the early Christian mystics known as the Gnostics may have had contact with Hindus and Buddhists in the first and second centuries.

Although it is far from certain, says Pagels, those contacts may have influenced the Gnostics. Certainly their writings, with their emphasis on inner experience of the divine, suggests intriguing parallels.

As the centuries progressed, East-West traffic grew, motivated mainly by trade. India's silk and spices attracted funding for Christopher Columbus's voyage, whose misdirection changed the world. As Europeans increasingly made their way to India, the race for bounty heated up, and another motive for going there arose: saving souls. The sordid history of colonization and conversion produced the residual benefit of making the West aware of the Vedic tradition. As early as the thirteenth century, says Durant, Marco Polo, the archetypal traveling merchant, "gave a vivid description" of Yoga.

The Europeans knew that understanding India's religions would serve their commercial, imperial, and missionary interests. Learned men were commissioned to study its beliefs, practices, and sacred texts. That their earliest accounts were heavy on what they considered pagan rituals and primitive superstitions is not surprising coming at a time when the White Man's Burden was to civilize the savages and convert them to Christianity, which was assumed to be the culmination of religious progress. Some of the first Indologists and Sanskritists were employed by the East India Company, Britain's prototype of the multinational corporation. Even scholars in ivory towers openly served the imperial and missionary agendas. Monier Monier-Williams, an esteemed professor of Sanskrit at Oxford University, wrote that the purpose of translation was to aid in "the conversion of the natives of India to the Christian religion."

In a countervailing trend, some individuals came to see that the Hindu scriptures were far more sophisticated than was commonly imagined. Some conjectured that the religion might even hold some value for Occidentals. That open-mindedness was on display as early as the seventeenth century in some Jesuit missionaries, notably the Italian priest Roberto de Nobili. As religious scholar Harry Oldmeadow notes in *Journeys East*, Nobili and a handful of others were instrumental in "opening European eyes to the spiritual riches of the East."[3] Gradually, more Europeans came to that realization and respectful descriptions of Indian spirituality were added to the mix. As scholarship improved, the translation of Sanskrit texts became more accurate.

Against this backdrop, the information filtering back to Europe about Indian religion was marked by fascination and esteem but also by revulsion, condescension, and belligerence. Often the ambivalence was reflected in the minds of individual scholars, like the renowned Indologist and Sanskritist, Max Müller. The German-born Müller, who never set foot in India, moved to Oxford in the mid-nineteenth century and went on to produce a prodigious number of books, including a fifty-volume series called *The Sacred Books of the East.* "I spend my happiest hours in reading Vedantic books," he wrote. "They are to me like the light of the morning, like the pure air of the mountains" and "I maintain that to everybody who cares for himself, for his ancestors, for his intellectual development, a study of the Vedic literature is indeed indispensable." Clerics denounced Müller for subverting Christianity with his praise of Hinduism; he was so revered in India that after the country achieved independence, it issued a stamp with his likeness. But he was also a paid agent of the colonial regime and wrote, "I do not claim for the ancient Indian literature any more than I should willingly concede to the fables and traditions and songs of savage nations" and predicted that "the ancient religion of India is doomed, and if Christianity does not step in, whose fault will it be?"

In fairness, some of the ambivalence reflected the perception that Hinduism, as practiced at the time, had fallen from the Himalayan heights of the Vedic texts, which Europeans like Müller held in high esteem. A good number of educated Indians shared that assessment, just as many Christians lament the distance their religion has traveled from the original spirit of Christ. What came to be called the Hindu Renaissance was under way even as the early English translators were hard at work, and some of those foreigners aided the reform movement.

To many educated Europeans, knowledge of India and its dominant religion came as a revelation. Most powerfully affected were the philosophers and poets associated with Romanticism and Idealism (the two terms have been applied to key players almost interchangeably), who saw in Eastern philosophy a possible antidote to materialism and the cult of reason. In Germany they were Friedrich Schelling, Johann Gottfried von Herder, Friedrich von Schiller, Georg Wilhelm, Friedrich Hegel, J. G. Fichte, and Arthur Schopenhauer, who said that access to the Upanishads was "the greatest privilege which this still young century may claim before all previous centuries" and who predicted that "Sanskrit literature will be no less influential for our time than Greek literature was . . . for the Renaissance."[4] In England the Romantics included Samuel Taylor Coleridge, Thomas Carlyle, William Wordsworth, William Blake, and others. Their stature lent credibility to the saying *ex oriente lux,* Latin for "from the East, the light."

In America, admirers of the Romantics paid attention, devouring not only the European philosophers' works but the Vedic literature arriving at their harbors from Great Britain. Among the avid readers was former president John Adams. In 1813, twelve years removed from office, Adams wrote to Thomas Jefferson, "I have been looking into Oriental History and Hindoo religion. I have read voyages and travels and everything I could collect."[5] Another aficionado was William Emerson, a Unitarian minister and father of Ralph Waldo. The senior Emerson was the editor of *The Monthly Anthology,* which often published articles about India, and the founder of a society called the Anthology Club, which hosted discussions about Eastern philosophy. Reverend Emerson died in 1811, shortly before his son's eighth birthday, but his passion for India no doubt planted seeds of interest that Ralph Waldo would harvest brilliantly.

Coming of Sage

The young man who would one day be called the Sage of Concord entered Harvard in 1817. He was not a distinguished student, ranking in the middle of his graduating class, but he had an insatiable thirst for knowledge that he satisfied through voracious outside reading. Scholars who have pored over his journals, letters, and school assignments report that he read both ancient Greek and modern European philosophy (he was especially fond of George Berkeley) and works about India provided by his theologically adventurous aunt, Mary Moody Emerson. Robert Gordon, in *Emerson and the Light of India*, says, "By the time he graduated from Harvard, Emerson had read numerous sources on the history, beliefs, and religious practices of India."[6] The eager student derived four key takeaways from those sources, says Gordon: (1) an appreciation of India "as a country of deep spiritual wellsprings," (2) the idea that the material universe is an emanation of divine power and that the purpose of human life is for the soul to realize its inherent unity with its source, (3) the concept of *maya*, which sees the multiplicity of material forms as a kind of illusion that obscures the knowledge of oneness, and (4) "the transmigration of souls from body to body through successive lifetimes."[7]

In 1821, when Emerson began teaching school, the country had grown to twenty-four states with 9.6 million citizens, 83 percent of whom earned their living from agriculture. The nation was in the throes of expansion, the speed of communication and transportation was quickening, and new technologies and gadgets were appearing on the market at a pace that alarmed some of the intelligentsia. Inspired by the European Romantics' love of nature, advocacy of intuitive knowing, and vision of a universe pervaded and guided by an infinite intelligence, some Americans reacted to materialism by creating a counterculture of sorts. Centered in Boston, "the Athens of America," the freethinkers embraced reason and scientific inquiry, deplored machine-driven commerce, and challenged religious dogma.

Emerson, caught up in the ferment, looked for wisdom wherever he could find it, seeking universal principles and discarding beliefs that did not hold up to scrutiny. After teaching for four years in a school for young women he enrolled at Harvard Divinity School. The institution had close links to the Unitarian Church, and Emerson, like his father, was ordained in that denomination. He served briefly as a minister, but "self-defrocked" because of his growing discomfort with doctrines like salvation through faith and the unique divinity of Jesus. Years later, in an 1859 journal entry, he linked his departure from Christian orthodoxy to his discovery of

Eastern texts, which "dispelled once and for all the dream about Christianity being the sole revelation—for here in India, there in China, were the same principles, the same grandeurs, the like depths, moral and intellectual."

A *Rishi* in Concord

In 1834, following the tragic loss of his first wife and a sojourn in Europe, where he met leading philosophers, Emerson moved to Concord, about thirteen miles west of Harvard Square. More than half a century after revolutionary sparks had been lit in that town (and in neighboring Lexington), the spirit of independence still burned bright. Along with kindred spirits who were, like him, aflame with both ideas and social causes, chiefly abolition and women's suffrage, in 1836 the newly remarried Emerson founded the Transcendental Club. One member, the journalist and prototype feminist Margaret Fuller, described her comrades this way: "Disgusted with the vulgarity of a commercial aristocracy, they become radicals; disgusted with the materialistic working of rational religion, they become mystics." A year later, when he was thirty-four, Emerson delivered a lecture to Harvard seniors, one of whom was Henry David Thoreau. Emerson befriended the young man, at one point giving him advice that would prove bountiful to later generations: keep a journal.

Indian philosophy was central to the ongoing education of Emerson and the Transcendentalists. Of the Bhagavad Gita he wrote in his 1831 journal, "It was the first of books; it was as if an empire spake to us, nothing small or unworthy, but large, serene, consistent, the voice of an old intelligence which in another age and climate had pondered and thus disposed of the same questions which exercise us." He also read Sir William Jones's poem "A Hymn to Narayana," the essays and translations of contemporary Hindu reformer Ram Mohan Roy, and other works from and about India. "In all nations there are minds which incline to dwell in the conception of the fundamental Unity," he wrote. "The raptures of prayer and the ecstasy of devotion lose all being in the one Being. This tendency finds its highest expression in the religious writings of the east, chiefly in the Indian scriptures." The central message Emerson drew from his Asian studies, says Robert Gordon, was that "the purpose of life was spiritual transformation and direct experience of divine power, here and now on earth." That insight would shine from his writings and illuminate the lives of millions.

Some scholars have downplayed the impact of the East on Emerson or ignored it entirely. Others, familiar with Vedantic texts and therefore able to recognize their flavor, conclude that Indian philosophy did not just spice up Emerson's philosophical soup, it was a prime ingredient, if not the stock that held it all together.[8] Alan Hodder, a religion scholar and author of *Emerson's Rhetoric of Revelation,*[9] says, "If we are to judge from the plethora of entries Emerson made in his journals from the mid-forties on, in which he transcribed passages from his Hindu readings or reflected on their implications, he read this particular branch of literature more zealously than perhaps any other during the last few decades of his life." What he learned, adds Hodder, "embellished, deepened and extended his own thoughts." *The Dictionary of the History of Ideas* puts it this way: "In his later writings it is practically impossible to separate the Eastern and Western components; Indian monism and Western idealism, the Hindu atman and the Western self, Oriental mysticism and Neo-Platonism transmuted into Emersonian transcendentalism."

Emerson himself said, in an 1842 lecture, that the ideas then catching fire in New England (thanks greatly to him) were "the very oldest of thoughts cast into the mould of these new times." His theory of compensation, for example, was similar to the laws of karma, described in lofty and convincing Americanese. "You cannot do wrong without suffering wrong," he wrote in 1841. ". . . Treat men as pawns and ninepins, and you shall suffer as well as they. If you leave out their heart, you shall lose your own." Later, he added reincarnation to his vision of cosmic justice, writing in his journal that he "discovered the secret of the world that all things subsist, and do not die, but only retire a little from sight and afterwards return again." His essay "The Over-Soul" recapitulates the Vedantic precept that everything in manifest creation is an expression of formless Brahman: "We live in succession, in division, in parts and particles. Meantime, within man, is the soul of the whole; the wise silence; the universal beauty to which every part and particle is equally related; the eternal One." *Maya,* the force that is said to delude us into thinking that the material realm is the sole reality, also figured into Emerson's worldview. In the essay "Illusions" he reproduced a passage from the *Vishnu Purana:* "Thy illusion beguiles all who are ignorant of thy true nature, the fools who imagine soul to be in that which is not spirit. The notions that 'I am,—this is mine,' which influence mankind, are but delusions of the mother of the world, originating in thy active agency."

Homages to Indian literature crop up frequently. His 1846 poem "Hamatreya" is based on a passage from the *Vishnu Purana,* and the essay "Immortality" concludes with a faithful retelling of the story of Yama, the Lord of Death, lifted from the *Katha Upanishad.* Most famously, the opening stanza of his poem "Brahma" ("If the red slayer think he slays/Or if the slain think he is slain/They know not well the subtle ways/I keep, and pass, and turn again") derives from almost identical passages in the *Katha Upanishad* and the Bhagavad Gita.[10] The borrowings were not aesthetic embellishments; they were central to Emerson's worldview.

A Certain Wandering Light

Emerson was not just an exceptional thinker who reasoned his way to logical conclusions. His prodigious intellect was augmented by a deep intuition that yielded insights similar to those of the Vedic *rishis.* He was, in short, a mystic. "The soul *is,*" he wrote. "Under all this running sea of circumstance, whose waters ebb and flow with perfect balance, lies the aboriginal abyss of Being. Essence, or God, is not a relation or a part, but the whole." Such a statement could be taken as speculative philosophy, but it's a description of a felt experience, resembling this 1837 journal entry:

I behold with awe & delight many illustrations of the One universal Mind. I see my being imbedded in it. As a plant in the earth so I grow

in God. I am only a form of him. He is the soul of me . . . A certain
wandering light comes to me which I instantly perceive to be the
Cause of Causes. It transcends all proving. It is itself the ground of
being; and I see that it is not one & I another, but this is the life of
my life. That is one fact then; that in certain moments I have known
that I existed directly from God, and am, as it were, his organ. And
in my ultimate consciousness Am He.

This description of the mystical union with the divine is as close to the
Upanishads' *Aham brahmasmi* (I am Brahman) as can be imagined in the
American idiom.

As a yearning, ceaselessly God-seeking mystic, Emerson was a prototype of the individual who has intimations of the infinite and finds in
Vedanta a way to understand his or her inchoate spiritual experiences
and inspiration and direction for further exploration. Absent Yoga studios and meditation classes his primary *sadhana* (spiritual practice) was
solitary communion with nature. Emerson the mystic resonated with the
numinous perceptions of the Vedic seers; Emerson the learned philosopher packaged his insights in the soaring language of nineteenth-century
America. His genius, says Robert Gordon, was to adapt central Vedantic
teachings "to the modern humanistic culture of the West, thereby creating the most cosmically optimistic faith the world has ever known." That
cosmic optimism was a major reason for Emerson's appeal during his lifetime, when youthful America was feeling its oats, and it remains a key to
his appeal today.

Emerson may have been the first leading American to articulate a vi-
able spirituality apart from traditional Christianity, and also among the
first to recognize that religion is compatible with science. The publication
of Darwin's *Origin of the Species* in 1859 drew the battle lines between science and religious dogma in stark terms. Emerson managed to transcend
both; he saw evolution as an expression of spirit, and the evolution of consciousness as part of the narrative: "In Man the perpetual progress is from
the Individual to the Universal, from that which is human, to that which
is divine." That vision, which some have called spiritual humanism, is

consistent with—and to some extent derived from—the Vedantic view that the divine manifests through ever-evolving expressions of itself. Compatibility with science would prove to be a major reason why Vedanta found favor with educated Americans.

Transcendental Superstar

At midcentury the nation was hurtling into modernity with the muscular speed of the locomotives chugging along the countryside. Between 1830 and the start of the Civil War, more than thirty thousand miles of railroad track were laid; better roads allowed horse-drawn carriages to ride more swiftly; a network of canals brought boats with people and goods to new ports. With information zipping around faster than ever before, a unique and powerful voice could shake things up through ink and speech the way bloggers and talk-show hosts do today.

In 1836 Emerson published a seminal essay, "Nature," that came to be called the Transcendentalist manifesto. It "was heavily debated, condemned by some, praised by others," says Richard Geldard, author of *The Essential Transcendentalists*, and "it launched Emerson's lecture career and America's first homegrown intellectual movement."[11] The essay proclaims that the individual soul and the universal spirit (which he later named the Over-Soul) were one—a direct echo of Vedanta's "Atman is Brahman." He backed the claim with his own transcendent experience: "Standing on the bare ground,—my head bathed by the blithe air, and uplifted into infinite space,—all mean egotism vanishes. I become a transparent eye-ball; I am nothing; I see all; the currents of the Universal Being circulate through me; I am part or particle of God."

He called for individuals to form an "original relation to the universe," thereby making a radical public break with mainstream religion. In place of a fallen, sinful humanity, separate and apart from God, he upheld an ecstatic vision of a divine essence—the "cause behind every stump and clod," as he wrote elsewhere—in which we swim and which swims through us.

Two years later, on July 15, 1838, Emerson elaborated on those themes in a bold address to the graduating class of Harvard Divinity School. "Let me admonish you, first of all," he said, "to go alone; to refuse the good models, even those which are sacred in the imagination of men, and dare to love God without mediator or veil." Accusing Christianity of "noxious exaggeration about the *person* of Jesus," he implored the future ministers to "cast behind you all conformity and acquaint men firsthand with Deity." In place of salvation through faith in Christ, he proposed what Gordon calls "a new metaphysics of consciousness," in which the central obstacle to fulfillment is not inherent depravity but ignorance of our divine nature—a core precept in Vedanta, where that ignorance is known as *avidya* (literally, "nonknowledge") and the agent of ignorance is *maya*. As Diana Eck wrote in her landmark study, *A New Religious America,* "In Emerson himself the perspectives of the ancient Indian Upanishads and the nineteenth-century Transcendentalists came together, directing our human vision toward the oneness of spirit underlying the whole universe."[12]

Emerson made the speech available in print—a bold gesture in the Victorian era and a worthy predecessor to the in-your-face hippies of the 1960s, many of whom revered Emerson and Thoreau as their progenitors. Oliver Wendell Holmes Sr., one of the wildly popular Fireside Poets whose public readings were like nineteenth-century rock concerts,[13] called the Divinity School Address "our intellectual Declaration of Independence." The religious establishment hit back. In a letter to a friend, Emerson said he was "raised into the importance of a heretic." Having prominent enemies is excellent publicity, whether one wants it or not. Banned from speaking at his alma mater, the rebel would return twenty-eight years later as a celebrated public figure to receive an honorary doctorate—not unlike Bob Dylan being honored at the Kennedy Center.

The West was still wild; the Eastern elite could read almost daily about forced migrations of Native American tribes and the army's battles with Sitting Bull, Crazy Horse, Geronimo, and Cochise—then uplift their vision by reading Emerson. His prolific essays and poems appeared in numerous periodicals, including the Transcendentalists' own journal *The Dial,* and many were collected in book form. And while P. T. Barnum was entertaining the suckers he said were born every minute, Emerson

lectured to highbrows on the lyceum circuit, a network of venues for ora-
tors and entertainers and the closest thing to Oprah at the time. Wherever
he went, he packed the house and drew prominent coverage in newspapers, which often printed his speeches verbatim. "Our founding thinker,"
as Richard Geldard called him, became so famous that the terms *Emersonian* and *Emersonism* were already in use during his lifetime. He gave his
audiences and readers more than abstract philosophy; his was a leading
voice for the rights of women, Native Americans, and the enslaved Af-
ricans in the South. But his views on those hot-button issues were not
ordinary; they were built on a Vedic foundation that flipped the prevailing
religious assumption about human nature on its head—from original sin
to original bliss, one might say. "Emerson took the revolutionary notion
that men are essentially good, not fallen, one step further," Robert Gordon
told me. "All human beings are essentially divine."

Emerson died on April 27, 1882. Shortly thereafter the first commercial
power station would light up lower Manhattan, electric cable cars would
run along Chicago's State Street, and telephone lines would link Boston
to Rhode Island, continuing the march of technology that would eventually bring Emerson, and through him Vedanta, to America's classrooms
and bedsides. His impact was magnified by the radiance of his colleagues
and acolytes, like Bronson Alcott (the father of Louisa May Alcott), a
progressive educator who assigned sections of the Upanishads to students; Margaret Fuller, the protofeminist and founding editor of *The Dial*;
and George Ripley, a Unitarian pastor who edited *Harper's* magazine and
started a utopian community called Brook Farm. But two towering figures
who were indebted to Emerson would leave massive footprints on American culture. If, as has been said, Emerson was the mind of America, then
perhaps Walt Whitman was its heart and Henry David Thoreau its soul.

The Karma Yogi

On July 4, 1845, Thoreau moved into the ten-by-fifteen-foot cabin he'd
built next to Walden Pond, on property owned by Emerson, for an early

version of "turn on, tune in, drop out." He had been turned on to Asian philosophy in 1841, while living for a period in Emerson's home, and he brought to the cabin books from his mentor's library. Among them was the Bhagavad Gita, which became a constant companion in his days of silence. In a much-quoted passage in *Walden,* he wrote: "In the morning I bathe my intellect in the stupendous and cosmogonal philosophy of the Bhagavad Gita, since whose composition years of the gods have elapsed, and in comparison with which our modern world and its literature seems puny and trivial." Elsewhere, praising the Gita's "sanity and sublimity," he writes that "the reader is nowhere raised into and sustained in a bigger, purer, or rarer region of thought."

In time Thoreau would read every volume of Indian philosophy available in those days, especially after 1855, when a British friend shipped him a collection of forty-four books. (Appropriately, after Thoreau's death, the finest private Oriental library in America passed to Emerson.) In his notebooks and essays, the Buddha of Walden commended those books and praised their universal vision. Some excerpts:

What extracts from the Vedas I have read fall on me like the light of a higher and purer luminary, which describes a loftier course through a purer stratum.

Whenever I have read any part of the Vedas, I have felt that some unearthly and unknown light illuminated me. In the great teaching of the Vedas, there is no touch of the sectarianism. It is of all ages, climes, and nationalities, and is the royal road for the attainment of the Great Knowledge.

When my imagination travels eastward and backward to those remote years of the gods, I seem to draw near to the habitation of the morning, and the dawn at length has a place.

Like Emerson, Thoreau had mystical experiences that Vedanta helped him to understand. "The texts were a kind of touchstone for his own notions of personal asceticism and introspection," the scholar Alan Hodder told me. "He had moments of euphoria and rapture in nature, but he couldn't really explain them until he started reading the Indian material. Then he actually saw references to what he was experiencing, and he thought, 'Aha! I'm not the only one having this. There's a long tradition to it.'" The sacred books also taught Thoreau the important distinction between philosophical inquiry and spiritual practice. "One may discover the root of an Indian religion in his own private history," Thoreau wrote in his journal, "when, in the silent intervals of the day and night, he does sometimes inflict on himself like austerities with stern satisfaction." He may have been the first American to call himself a yogi. "Depend upon it that, rude and careless as I am, I would fain practice the yoga faithfully," he wrote to a friend in 1849. "To some extent, and at rare intervals, even I am a yogi." Too bad no gurus had yet arrived, or his yoga would not have been limited to those rare intervals.[14]

Of the three classic approaches to enlightenment outlined in the Bhagavad Gita, *jnana, karma,* and *bhakti* (respectively, the paths of the intellect, of action, and of devotion), Emerson's primary inclination was to *jnana,* the yoga that emphasizes knowledge and discernment. Thoreau was a karma yogi, one who follows the path of selfless action rooted in transcendent awareness. His time on Walden Pond is seared so deeply into the nation's psyche that some have called him our first sannyasi, one who renounces worldly affairs for a life of contemplation. His hermetic phase lasted slightly more than two years, however, during which he would walk into town to dine with friends and bring his laundry home to his mother. And while in many ways he did live the *spirit* of renunciation, living alone, eschewing meat, alcohol, and tobacco, he was by nature a warrior who felt duty bound to confront injustice.[15] As most high school and college students learn, he was incarcerated for refusing to pay a one-dollar poll tax, as a protest against slavery and the Mexican War. The most influential jail term in American history lasted only one night, although the prisoner tried his best to extend the sentence, the better to publicize his cause.

Thoreau died of tuberculosis at age forty-four, in 1862, one month after the battle of Shiloh, one of the bloodiest of the Civil War; reports of it must have pained him. Had he lived another four months, he would have rejoiced at the Emancipation Proclamation.

The Bhakti Bard

Walt Whitman, the progenitor of modern American poetry, was not a member of the Transcendentalist cadre, but had he been born a little sooner and lived in Massachusetts, he no doubt would have been. In 1854, when he was thirty-five and working as a carpenter in Brooklyn, he came upon Emerson's essays. They helped him find his poetic voice. "My ideas were simmering and simmering, and Emerson brought them to a boil," he told *The Atlantic Monthly.* Twelve of the poems that bubbled up were collected and self-published as *Leaves of Grass.* Almost every critic who bothered to read the volume ridiculed it, and some denounced it. Undaunted, the poet, in a wily act of self-promotion, sent a copy to Emerson, who was already a virtual God of American letters. In his reply, the sage called it "the most extraordinary piece of wit and wisdom that America has yet contributed," adding prophetically, "I greet you at the beginning of a great career." Thoreau asserted that "Whitman has spoken more truth than any American or modern that I know." In time he and Emerson would meet the wild and woolly voice of freedom in person.

Although Emerson called *Leaves of Grass* "a mixture of the *Bhagavad Gita* and the *New York Herald,*" Whitman probably had not actually read the Gita at the time. But Asia entered the poet's consciousness at some point, at least through Emerson. As the eminent twentieth-century author and literary critic Malcolm Cowley observed, "Most of Whitman's doctrines, though by no means all of them, belong to the mainstream of Indian philosophy." Whitman referred to having read "ancient Hindu poems," and in 1857 he wrote that India "represents meditation, oriental rhapsody, passiveness, a curious schoolmaster-teaching of wise precepts." In his poem "Passage to India" he exalts the ancient land's "myths and fables," "far-darting beams of the spirit," "unloos'd dreams," and "deep diving bibles and legends."

If Emerson's path was *jnana* and Thoreau's *karma*, Whitman's was pure, unadulterated *bhakti*. Poems were his *bhajans* (devotional songs), and earth was his temple. He sang the praises of creator and creation in an exuberant, muscular idiom that captured the emerging American personality. The title, *Song of Myself*, might suggest the ultimate in narcissism, but the poem is a hymn to the Self of all selves, the eternal spirit the Vedas call Brahman:

> *I see something of God each hour of the twenty-four, and each moment then,*
> *In the faces of men and women I see God, and in my own face in the glass,*
> *I find letters from God dropt in the street, and every one is sign'd by God's*
>   *name,*
> *and I leave them where they are, for I know that wheresoe'er I go,*
> *others will punctually come for ever and ever.*

By sacralizing both nature and human flesh, Whitman set the poetic template for what some consider a homegrown Tantra, the stream of Vedic spirituality that sees the divine in the mundane and directs sensory experience toward spiritual realization. "He taught people a way of beholding nature which is itself a form of prayer," said the author and poet Diane Ackerman. She called *Leaves of Grass* "a sacred American text about the essential goodness and perfectibility of people, the sanctity of the common man, the holiness of the human body viewed naked and up close, the privilege of democracy, the need to forge one's own destiny, and the duty of all to discover the world anew, by living in a state of rampant amazement at the endless pocket-size miracles one encounters every day."[16] That is as good a description of an American Tantra as can be imagined.

Transcendental Footprints

In the century after his passing, Emerson acquired nicknames of the highest order: the American Plato, the American Socrates, the philosopher of democracy, even the American Isaiah, suggesting he was not only a sage but a prophet. He has been credited with founding two schools of American philosophy, pragmatism and process philosophy. Princeton professor and cultural provocateur Cornel West, who himself has been labeled "a modern Emersonian," calls the sage "the towering man of letters in the American democratic experiment." Yale's Harold Bloom, one of the preeminent intellectuals of our time, says that "if God appeared in nineteenth century America it was as Ralph Waldo Emerson."[17]

In a 2003 radio interview with journalist Christopher Lydon, celebrating Emerson's two hundredth birthday, Bloom proclaimed that "the whole phenomenon of American culture, on every level down to popular culture . . . is a profoundly Emersonian affair. He has prophesied everything . . . He is the mind of America." That mind produced so many memorable phrases that *Bartlett's Familiar Quotations* devotes more pages to Emerson than to Lincoln, Jefferson, or Franklin, and the *Encyclopaedia Britannica* says he was quoted more than any other American in the twentieth century. The list of prominent figures he influenced is astonishing, beginning with Thoreau and Whitman (who called Emerson "the explorer who went before us and discovered the shores of America") and onward to Emily Dickinson and Robert Frost, Frederick Douglass and Booker T. Washington, Friedrich Nietzsche and Alfred North Whitehead, William James, who was bounced on Emerson's knee as a child, and the New Thought progenitors (see chapter 3).

The Transcendentalist Club that Emerson and his comrades founded lasted less than twenty years, but its footprint has never been erased. Its core perspective, shaped by Vedic precepts, has permeated the culture. No doubt many readers of Emerson, Thoreau, and Whitman have been inspired to take a Yoga class, or buy a Bhagavad Gita (Jack Kerouac did, after reading Thoreau), or book passage to India. But countless more, yearning for an authentic taste of the natural and the sacred, have been nudged by the Transcendentalist song of freedom toward a Vedantic spirituality of individual choice and unmediated connection to the holy, even if nothing explicitly Indian registered in their conscious minds.

It has been said that Whitman lives in virtually every line of poetry and song lyric penned in America since the publication of *Leaves of Grass*. That might be hyperbolic, but it is hard to imagine Woody Guthrie or Allen Ginsberg or Bob Dylan without "the poet of democracy." And the Thoreau of *Walden* lives in the heart of every environmentalist as well as every writer who probes the wonders of nature, from Rachel Carson and Gary Snyder to Mary Oliver and Annie Dillard. Thoreau's much-loved memoir has been blowing minds for a century and a half; it is required reading for thousands of students each semester and is jammed into many a rambler's backpack. Contemporary references to the book show up everywhere—in the *Doonesbury* comic strip, in the film *Dead Poets Society*, in a rock song by the group Wilhelm Scream, in the hippie classic by Robert Pirsig *Zen and the Art of Motorcycle Maintenance*, and in prime-time TV: *Frazier*, *CSI*, *The Simpsons*, and even *South Park*. In addition, the Thoreau of *Civil Disobedience* has inspired generations of peace activists to adopt the tactics of nonviolent protest. In a neat cross-cultural volley, India inspired Thoreau; Thoreau inspired Mohandas K. Gandhi; and Gandhi tossed the ball back to Martin Luther King Jr.

Every American who checks the spiritual-but-not-religious box or shuffles off to a meditation retreat is squarely in the Transcendentalist lineage. A surprising number of the people I interviewed, when recalling the origins of their interest in Eastern philosophy, named Emerson or Thoreau as a catalyst. This was especially true of those who came of age during that unruly period between John F. Kennedy's assassination and Richard Nixon's resignation. While the mid-nineteenth century could not have been more different from the 1960s in some respects—ten times as many people were at the 1967 "human be-in" in San Francisco than lived in Emerson's Concord—the two periods were remarkably similar in others. Both were marked by turmoil and change; by a baby boom following an armed conflict (in the earlier instance, the War of 1812); by political dissent focused largely on domestic injustice and military adventures; by technological advances and commercial booms that triggered both euphoria and revulsion; and by a progressive minority that challenged prevailing values and beliefs. Sixties hipsters fed their intellects with Emerson's essays and poems, nurtured their escapist fantasies with *Walden* and their political ideals with *Civil Disobedience,* and energized their beating hearts with Whitman's throbbing verse. When I moved to Boston in 1967, one of the first things I did was to make a pilgrimage to Walden Pond. The following year, when the Transcendental Meditation center opened in Cambridge, many of those who gathered there were warmed by the thought that they stood on the road Emerson probably traveled to address the Harvard Divinity School 130 years earlier. No wonder the mysterious East figured prominently in both eras.

In a neat bit of karmic reciprocity, Emerson's work bounced back to India even during his lifetime. While the colonial British were still very much in control of the jewel in its crown, literate Indians rejoiced to discover that America's sage cherished their sacred texts. Hindu reformers quoted him. The Nobel Prize–winning writer Rabindranath Tagore told an American journalist, "I love your Emerson. In his work one finds much that is of India. In truth he made the teachings of our spiritual leaders and philosophers a part of his life." Later, in a letter from prison, Gandhi advised a follower to read Emerson: "The essays to my mind contain the teaching of Indian wisdom in a Western garb." And Paramahansa Yogananda, clearly aware of Emerson's position in the American pantheon, quoted him ten times in the footnotes of his seminal *Autobiography of a Yogi.*

So it was that Emerson used India to formulate his philosophy, and India used Emerson to legitimize its ancient wisdom to the modern mind. The effects of that East-West oscillation are more penetrating than we can readily appreciate. In 2001 I was strolling on a path that followed the River Ganges outside the holy city of Rishikesh. It was a sunny day, as the Himalayan foothills warmed up after a chilly spell. The only sounds were my footsteps and the chirping of birds. Then I heard a melodic human voice. I peered over a stone retaining wall and saw a man digging in a garden. He appeared to be in his fifties, and his loose-fitting orange garments indicated that he was a sannyasi, or renunciate. I watched him methodically plant seeds in the soil as he chanted Sanskrit verses. When he noticed me, he placed his palms together in greeting. After responding to his queries about what had brought me to Rishikesh, I asked about his younger days. Had he been a sannyasi since his youth?

He laughed robustly. As a young man, he had viewed the religion of his ancestors as backward, he said, and went to university to study science.

I asked what prompted his spiritual turnaround.

"I took a class in American literature," he said, "and I read Emerson."

NEW THOUGHT IN OLD WINESKINS

B right and early on any Sunday morning, about a thousand people squeeze into tightly packed rows of metal-framed chairs at the Agape International Spiritual Center. They come to this Los Angeles hot spot to meditate, worship, commune, rock to the coolest music ever heard at a service (a kind of R&B-jazz-gospel mix), hear a rousing sermon, and praise God, by which they mean something rather different from the standard-church version of the Almighty. Two hours later another thousand souls arrive, and then another thousand, all three services being necessary ever since Agape's founder, Michael Bernard Beckwith, became a spiritual superstar.

Agape, which boasts about ten thousand members, is perhaps the best-known congregation in America associated with New Thought. There are close to two thousand such venues, most of them in either the Religious Science or Unity Church fold, and they vary in size from living rooms to arenas. Together they draw hundreds of thousands of people each week to services and reach perhaps ten times as many through their publications and websites. Whether they realize it or not, those congregants and readers are receiving messages from ancient India.

Ever since its origins in the late nineteenth century, New Thought's various constituencies have held in common certain premises that could not be more Vedantic. The Association for Global New Thought (AGNT) website summarizes those precepts under the heading "The Principles of Universal Spirituality":

- There is one infinite, all-inclusive, creative, living Intelligence beyond and within the universe. *Whether we call it God, Brahman, Allah, Spirit, or some other name, It is the Great All in which all things exist and of which all things have been made.*
- Our essential nature is spiritual. *We are spiritual beings having a human experience, and as spiritual beings, we share in God's essential nature.*
- We have a creative relationship with our experience of life. *The spiritual universe operates according to spiritual laws, which allows us to co-create our life experience consciously. Through right alignment with spiritual law and conscious contact with the Creative Intelligence within, we can achieve happiness and fulfillment.*
- Life is a spiritual journey toward an awareness of the true source of our being. *The ultimate destiny of every individual soul is to awaken to the true source of its being—God Itself.*

That third point posits that the individual mind is an expression of cosmic mind—a variation on Vedanta's Atman and Brahman. Because this principle was at first applied to physical healing, early New Thought was also called Mind Cure. In 1902, when the movement had an estimated one million followers, William James labeled it the "religion of healthy-mindedness." Before long mind power was applied to all aspects of the good life. It continues today with New Thought's "law of attraction" packaged in the megaseller *The Secret* as the key to unlimited wealth, conjugal happiness, and anything else one might desire.

New Thought began humbly in New England around the time of the Civil War, when its founders, dissatisfied with official Christianity, turned to alternative wisdom sources. Their single biggest influence was Emerson, but they also drew from the German Romantics and British Idealists; metaphysical interpretations of the Gospels; the Swedish mystic Emanuel Swedenborg; spiritualism, which was huge at the time; the Viennese physician Franz Anton Mesmer, whose work gave rise to hypnotism; New

Hampshire clockmaker-turned-healer Phineas P. Quimby; and a Methodist minister named Warren Felt Evans, for whom it was imperative to unveil the true Self, which he explicitly identified with the Vedic Atman and Emerson's Over-Soul.

Significantly, the New Thoughters also drank directly from Vedic wellsprings. By the beginning of the twentieth century, Harvard and Yale had established professorships in Sanskrit, and Indologists were producing textbooks and translations, adding fresh Indian spices to the simmering New Thought stew. In time the seekers who found their way to New Thought became the prime constituency for the first genuine gurus to come here from India. The movement, as it grew in size, became an important disseminator of Vedic ideas, even if some of its own representatives were barely aware of India's impact on the founding mothers and fathers.

The Scientist Christian

Born in 1821 to Calvinist parents on a New Hampshire farm, Mary Baker was a studious, sickly child. As an adult, widowed by her first husband and deserted by her unfaithful second, she coped with loss and illness by reading the Bible and sampling natural remedies, in particular those of Phineas Quimby. In 1866, she slipped on an icy sidewalk and suffered critical injuries, which were miraculously healed, she claimed, by her absorption in the biblical tales of Jesus's healings. She attributed the origins of her Church of Christ, Scientist, better known as Christian Science, to that experience.[1]

Philosophically, Christian Science is marked by a Vedanta-like metaphysic in which human consciousness is contiguous with the infinite spirit that some call God and Eddy (her third husband's name) called Divine Mind. For her, the primary application of that unlimited energy source was healing. In 1875, four years before she created her church (which now has more than two thousand branches worldwide), Eddy published *Science and Health with Key to the Scriptures*.[2] The landmark book, which remains the primary Christian Science text to this day, was revised a number of times before the author's death in 1910. In his 1930 book *Hinduism Invades America*,[3] Wendell Thomas writes that in the first thirty-three editions Eddy quoted the Bhagavad Gita. The references were later expunged, says Thomas.

One of Eddy's acolytes, Emma Curtis Hopkins (1849–1925), was perhaps the best-informed New Thought about Indian philosophy. Hopkins broke with Eddy and struck out on her own. She quoted frequently from the Gita and the Upanishads in her public talks and in articles in the *Christian Science Journal*. A premier teacher of teachers, Hopkins trained many New Thought ministers in her seminaries in Chicago and New York.

The Madame and the Mahatmas

One of the most intriguing characters in the spiritual history of both East and West, Helena Petrovna Blavatsky left Russia in 1848, at age seventeen, escaping marriage to a forty-year-old husband. According to her own account, she took off on a stolen horse and spent ten years abroad before returning to Russia. When her second husband died, she left her homeland for good. Settling in New York in 1873, she impressed people with her alleged psychic powers and her claim to having been initiated by Buddhist masters in Asia. While in Vermont for a séance, she met an American lawyer and journalist named Henry Steel Olcott. They joined forces to create the Theosophical Society, whose aims were "to form the nucleus of a Universal brotherhood of Humanity, without distinction of race, creed, sex, caste or color; to promote the study of . . . the world's religions and sciences, and to vindicate the importance of old Asiatic literature . . . ; and to investigate the hidden mysteries of Nature . . . and the physical and spiritual powers latent in man especially."[4]

Blavatsky, who claimed to receive knowledge telepathically from Himalayan adepts whom she called the Mahatmas (Sanskrit for "great souls"), produced her first book in 1877. The voluminous *Isis Unveiled* draws both from Western metaphysics (Hermeticism, Kabbalah, Rosicrucianism,

Freemasonry, Swedenborgianism, etc.) and from the East: "Isis is the fruit of a somewhat intimate acquaintance with Eastern adepts and study of their science . . . They showed us that by combining science with religion, the existence of God and immortality of man's spirit may be demonstrated." Blavatsky's debt to Asia is also apparent in an 1879 essay, "What Is Theosophy?" in which she ascribes her philosophy to, among other sources, "the Indian Buddh," the Vedas, and "the Rishis of Aryavart." Blavatsky and Olcott moved to India in 1879, where they attracted more members than they had in the West. In addition to translating Sanskrit texts, the organization worked on behalf of the Hindu reform movement.

Over time Blavatsky's use of Buddhist and Vedantic sources grew, culminating in her magnum opus, *The Secret Doctrine* (1888). She died in 1891, a controversial figure considered by some to be a spiritual genius and even a saint, and by others to be a charlatan or a self-deluded poseur. The hundreds of books written about her have not settled the argument, but there is no doubting her impact. "Blavatsky played a significant role in wedding Western esotericism and Eastern religious traditions and in popularizing concepts such as *maya, karma,* and meditation," says scholar of religion Harry Oldmeadow.[5]

After Blavatsky's death, Olcott took over the Theosophical Society and was succeeded, in 1907, by Annie Besant. A British journalist known in London as a birth control advocate and freethinker, Besant became a Theosophist in 1891. (Her former consort, George Bernard Shaw, called her conversion a calamity.) The tireless Besant spent the rest of her days promoting Theosophy, crusading for Indian independence, translating sacred texts, establishing schools, and even serving as president of the Indian National Congress.

By the 1920s, Theosophy had about 45,000 members worldwide, 7,000 in the United States. But the numbers don't begin to reflect the organization's reach, through books, periodicals, lecture tours, and the celebrated figures who were drawn to its teachings: the esoteric philosopher Rudolf Steiner, whose Anthroposophical Society and Waldorf schools remain influential to this day; the mystic and author Paul Brunton (see chapter 7); artists such as Wassily Kandinsky and Piet Mondrian; the poets

W. B. Yeats, T. S. Eliot, and Wallace Stevens; the composer Alexander Scriabin; and storytellers as disparate as Franz Kafka and L. Frank Baum, the author of *The Wizard of Oz*. Baum joined the Theosophical Society in 1892, having written about the philosophy in the *Aberdeen* (South Dakota) *Saturday Pioneer.* (I leave it to others to find mystical themes in the journey of Dorothy and her companions, although it is hard to resist noting the pure Vedanta of waking up to find that you've come home—and that you never left.)

Over the decades Theosophy receded from the public eye; some would say it was co-opted by the New Age movement. But its presence is still felt in the ongoing activities of the Theosophical Society in America; ancillary groups such as the Krotona School of Theosophy; local "lodges" and study centers; and its publishing ventures, Quest Books and the bimonthly *Quest* magazine.[6] If nothing else, its place in history is secured by its formative impact on the New Thought movement, which is still going strong, and by its influence on two Indian superstars whose influence on the West has been immeasurable.

One was a young barrister from the Indian state of Gujarat. While living in London in 1889, he met two Theosophists who asked if he, as an Indian, could guide them in reading the Sanskrit of the Bhagavad Gita. Nonreligious and British-educated, the barrister was embarrassed to say he had never read the classic in any language. He suggested that they read it together. Thus was Mohandas K. Gandhi, the future Mahatma, introduced to the book that he would call "an infallible guide of conduct" and "my dictionary of daily reference."[7] The second was Jiddu Krishnamurti, whose presence in America spanned six decades.

Pathfinder in a Pathless Land

The impossible-to-categorize Krishnamurti (1895–1986) was a slim, handsome thirteen-year-old with haunting eyes when Theosophists discovered him on a South Indian beach and declared him an avatar. "The

Divine Spirit has descended once more on a man," said Annie Besant. The organization schooled him in England and prepped him to lead their Order of the Star of the East. After the First World War, when he was in his early twenties, he was sent forth as the World Teacher. In 1922, seeking a hot, dry climate for his tubercular younger brother, he took up residence in Ojai, California. His brother died three years later, but the hilly village near Santa Barbara remained Krishnamurti's American home until his death at age ninety.

During his first stay in Ojai he had a spontaneous spiritual awakening. "I have seen the Light," he wrote. "I have drunk at the fountain of Joy and eternal Beauty. I am God-intoxicated." Rather than secure his saviorlike status, however, the experience did the opposite. In 1929, at the annual Order of the Star conclave, he disbanded the society, telling several thousand members, "I maintain that truth is a pathless land and you cannot approach it by any path whatsoever, by any religion, by any sect." That included Theosophy. He did not want followers, he said. His one purpose was "to set man free . . . from all cages, from all fears, and not to found religions, new sects, nor to establish new theories and new philosophies." The declaration marked the death of a messiah and the birth of a philosopher who became, ironically, a world teacher. "Imagine you're a rock star, and then say 'I don't want to be one,' and then you become one anyway," said Evelyn Blau, a longtime student and friend of Krishnamurti, who chronicled his life in a documentary and a book.[8]

Doggedly antiguru, he was nonetheless given gurulike treatment as he circled the globe speaking. But for sustained periods of each year he remained at his headquarters in India and Ojai, churning out highly popular books such as *The First and Last Freedom* (1954) and *Think on These Things* (1964). His mind was restless, rigorous, and consistent in its denunciation of dogma, authority, rituals, and techniques. Only through painstaking self-observation, he claimed, could individuals set themselves free. Though he refused to be linked to any tradition, his writings and talks are permeated by the Vedanta that he absorbed early in his life. These excerpts would not be out of place in the Upanishads:

When man becomes aware of the movement of his own thoughts, he will see the division between the thinker and thought, the observer and the observed, the experiencer and the experience. He will discover that this division is an illusion.

That which is eternal cannot be sought after; the mind cannot acquire it. It comes into being when the mind is quiet, and the mind can be quiet only when it is simple.

The emptying of the mind brings unity.

Krishnamurti's antagonism to standard spiritual pedagogy (summed up in the title of a 1986 album by one of his admirers, Van Morrison: *No Guru, No Method, No Teacher*) was a perfect fit for the "question authority" ethos of the baby boomers; his fame peaked when Indian spirituality became all the rage in the 1960s. In the last twenty years of his life, he drew thousands to Ojai for his annual talks in the verdant setting called Oak Grove.[9] "He was asking people to examine their presuppositions and take responsibility for the social constructs they agree to participate in," says Christopher Chapple of Loyola Marymount University. "Once the culturally given constructs are stripped away, there is the inner realization." Or so it was hoped. Ironically, many of his fans, unable to access the inner silence he described, sought help from the gurus and methods that Krishnamurti deplored.

Krishnamurti's singular voice influenced hundreds of thousands, if not millions, among them some of the twentieth century's most prominent thinkers and artists. In the early days of Ojai, Charlie Chaplin, Greta Garbo, and Charles Laughton would motor up from Hollywood in their roadsters. George Bernard Shaw called him "a religious figure of the greatest distinction." Robinson Jeffers composed a poem about him; the opening line reads "My friend from Asia has powers and magic."[10] Later Aldous Huxley, Alan Watts, and Joseph Campbell were friends and admirers. More recently Ken Wilber and Deepak Chopra have acknowledged their debts to him.

So have cutting-edge scientists like biologist Rupert Sheldrake and the eminent quantum physicist David Bohm. Krishnamurti's dialogues with those two are a marvel of East-West synthesis.[11] And, in a shining example of how Eastern philosophical principles can snake into Western culture in unseen ways, Bohm's conversations with Krishnamurti contributed to his "implicate order" hypothesis and the process known as Bohmian Dialogue. That, in turn, led to the Dialogue Project at the Massachusetts Institute of Technology, which was adapted for use by organizational development experts, notably MIT's Peter Senge.[12] Thus Western Theosophists influenced by Indian philosophy groomed an Indian lad, who became an independent thinker whose Vedantic principles, converted into philosophical English, passed through quantum theory, entered organizational theory, and landed, unrecognizable, in corporate team-building sessions.[13]

Unity in the Heartland

Myrtle Page (1845–1931) grew up in pre–Civil War Ohio, an inquisitive child who felt alienated from her family's Methodist church. "There was something in me that protested against the declaration that I was by nature evil and sinful," she said. Teaching school in a small town near Kansas City, Missouri, she suffered from tuberculosis that was said to be untreatable. She sought a cure in the warmer climate of Denison, Texas, where she met Charles Fillmore, a railway clerk nine years her junior. As a ten-year-old in northern Minnesota, Charles had broken his hip ice skating and, after a series of dubious treatments, ended up with one leg three and a half inches shorter than the other. The two seekers married and eventually landed in Kansas City, where Charles made it big in real estate speculation.

In 1886 the Fillmores attended a series of lectures on Christian Science by a former student of Mary Baker Eddy. "I awakened to the Truth that God is my Father and that I inherit from him only that which is Good," Myrtle later wrote. She plunged headlong into the study of spiritual healing. Impressed by the apparent healing of his wife's tuberculosis, Charles followed suit. He had grown up with no formal religious training but had read the Idealist and Romantic philosophers, various metaphysicians, and the Sage of Concord. "The Fillmores looked to Emerson as their primary source," Neal Vahle, a historian of New Thought, told me. "There are more references to Emerson in their writing than anyone else."[14] Charles absorbed Vedic ideas from those sources and from Madame Blavatsky (he called himself "a very earnest student of Theosophy"). His reading of Indian texts increased over time. When I asked Vahle to assess the influence of Eastern philosophy on the Fillmores, he replied, "I would say it was equal to that of Jesus."

The couple began their healing ministry in 1889, under the rubric Society of Silent Help. The name changed several times, but it is now best known as the Unity Church.[15] "We have borrowed the best from all religions," Charles Fillmore once said, "that is the reason we are called Unity." It grew more churchlike with the years, adding Sunday services, sermons, and other features its constituents were accustomed to. The Fillmores held that traditional Christianity had tragically misinterpreted its founders' teachings, distinguishing between Jesus, the human being and master teacher, and "The Christ" or "Christ consciousness," an all-pervasive spiritual energy, sometimes defined as "divinity within," that more closely resembles Brahman than the embodied savior of tradition.

On its official website, Unity Church defines its beliefs about God this way: "God is Spirit, the loving source of all that is. God is the one power, all good, everywhere present, all wisdom. God is divine energy, continually creating, expressing and sustaining all creation. In God, we live and move and have our being." It adds that "each person is a unique expression of God created with sacred worth. Living from that awareness transforms our lives and the world." Because of such beliefs the church has been excoriated as a "New Age cult" by conservative Christians; one Catholic leader said "the Hindu might feel more at home with Unity books than the Christian," because of Unity's belief in reincarnation.

The Vedic influence on Unity's origins is evident in the second issue of *Modern Thought,* the periodical the Fillmores created in 1889. (It later

became *Unity Magazine*.) The issue—which was discovered in Unity's archives by Dave DeLuca, who lectures on Vedanta and New Thought[16]—
contains an essay by Charles Fillmore that opens with all four stanzas of
Emerson's poem "Brahma." Calling the East "the storehouse of a spiritual life" that we cannot "adequately comprehend in our present material
thought environment," Fillmore offered a critique of religion that would
surely have made him a pariah if he hadn't been one already: "The Christian religion has answered our needs up to the present age, but the evolution of the spirit has created a demand for a religion of broader scope, and
we turn to the lore of India, for lack of a better system nearer home." He
extolled the Orient as "the nursery of spiritual philosophies," even specu-
lating that "our Bible is partially of Oriental origin."

Fillmore's essay contains a remarkable early expression of Vedantic pluralism: "But we are all of one God, and it matters not from what source
we get our religion if it has that spirit of love and charity which pervades
the souls of all who find that place of peace which passeth understanding."
References to Indian philosophy virtually disappeared from Unity publications, DeLuca says, presumably to make the church's message more
palatable in the heartland. That would make the Fillmores forerunners of
the many teachers who borrowed Vedic ideas only to downplay their role.
"Their message was very Upanishadic, but their language was not," ob-
serves Marj Britt, the senior minister at Unity of Tustin in Orange County,
California. "Instead of 'Thou art That,' it was something like 'I am an expression of the divine Presence.'" Despite the whitewashing, the Fillmores
must have grown more familiar with Vedic teachings as they became more
accessible. They seem to have attended Swami Vivekananda's celebrated
appearance at the Parliament of the World's Religions in Chicago in 1893
(see chapter 4), and it is hard to imagine two more receptive minds.

Insisting that metaphysical propositions ought to be verifiable empiri-
cally, Charles at one point began sitting in silent meditation every night.
"After exploring differing styles of meditation," writes Neal Vahle, "he
concluded that the meditative techniques of Eastern practitioners, particularly Hindu meditators, were more effective than practices taught

in the West." In 1929 Charles wrote about Indian adepts who intoned
sacred sounds, now commonly known as mantras. Silent meditation became central to the teachings of Unity, which grew into the largest of
New Thought's branches, with 895 ministries and study groups currently
operating worldwide. As for healing, something must have worked: the
tireless Myrtle died at eighty-six, apparently disease free; Charles lived to
ninety-three, and it is said that when he died, both his legs were about the
same length.

A Scientist of Mind

"I studied Emerson, and this was like drinking water to me." So said Ernest Holmes (1887–1960), the founder of Science of Mind (aka Religious
Science), who read Emerson's essays as a teenager. They convinced him,
he wrote, that "there was something in me already that could enlarge and
expand. This was, I sensed, my soul, and I felt it swelling until I almost
burst." Later, his reading of Indian literature illuminated the deeper spiritual implications of Emerson's ideas. "Only in after years, when he had become acquainted with some of Emerson's original sources in the mystical
literature of India, did he come to a full recognition of the significance,"
writes his brother and biographer, Fenwicke Holmes.

Raised on a small farm in Maine, Ernest was by all accounts fond of
confronting preachers with his doubts about church doctrine. After moving to Boston and discovering Emerson, he explored Christian Science
and New Thought metaphysics. In his mid-twenties he moved to southern
California, where Fenwicke had established a small church in Venice. "I
began to read and study everything I could get hold of," Ernest wrote.
Requests to speak led to his first paid gig, in 1916, at L.A.'s Metaphysical
Library. His topic was Thomas Troward's *Edinburgh Lectures on Mental
Science*.

While serving the British Raj as a judge, Troward (1847–1916) had become an ardent student of India's religious corpus. In 1904, two years after
retiring and returning to Great Britain, he delivered a series of lectures

in Edinburgh that were strongly influenced by Vedantic ideas. The book compiled from the talks was widely read on both sides of the Atlantic. It helped shape the ideas of New Thought leaders, most notably Emmet Fox, who addressed more than five thousand New Yorkers a week in the 1930s and 1940s and reached many more through books and pamphlets. (His interpretation of the Sermon on the Mount has sold over half a million copies.)

Fox, it should be noted, was well acquainted with Alcoholics Anonymous founder Bill Wilson, and his sermons were quite the rage in early AA circles. Thus, it is conceivable that Indian philosophy, through Fox and Troward, had some effect on the big bang phase of the twelve-step universe. Perhaps more to the point, Bill Wilson's formative years were in New England, where Emersonian ideals lingered like leaves in a warm November. "What was happening in the 1850s and 60s . . . in New England contributed in a very direct way to what Bill breathed in and out with the Vermont air at the turn of the century," says Wilson biographer Susan Cheever.[17] People who had doubts about received doctrine were receptive to the Emersonian view that, as Cheever puts it, "the divine could exist in the song of a woodthrush or the reflections in a pond and especially . . . in other human beings." Vedic precepts therefore may have seeped into the world's most successful program for conquering addiction. After all, what could be more Vedantic than the phrase "God as we understood him" in the famous third step?

Returning to Ernest Holmes: after delivering that 1916 talk about Troward, he became an increasingly popular speaker. As American boys marched off to the First World War and L.A.'s population marched toward the million mark, so many attended his Sunday-morning talks that the venue was moved to one twice as large. It too proved too small. Eventually Holmes settled in the Wiltern Theater, an art deco landmark that accommodated nearly three thousand. In 1926 he published his first book, *The Science of Mind,* which became the textbook for Religious Science; it is still in print today, having sold well over half a million copies.[18]

Holmes, who was ordained by Emma Curtis Hopkins in the Divine Science Church, started the Institute for Religious Science and School of

Philosophy in 1927, when he was forty. Fenwicke described his brother's philosophy as "a synthesis into one harmonious whole of the teachings of Emerson and Troward, the religions of East and West, the spiritual tenets of Christian Science and New Thought together with whatever he knew or could learn of the 'Mother Doctrine' that had survived in the various depositories of ancient wisdom like the Hermetic teachings, the *Bhagavad-Gita* and the *Zendavesta*." Central to the teaching was a form of prayer whose purpose, said Fenwicke, "was not to change God's mind but to change your own consciousness"—a Vedantic take on prayer that can be found throughout New Thought.

It was the peak of the Jazz Age; Lindbergh flew the Atlantic, Babe Ruth clouted sixty home runs, and Warner Bros. produced the first talking picture in a studio not far from Holmes's headquarters on Wilshire Boulevard. By this time L.A. had a reputation as a welcoming port for unconventional ideas and lifestyles. Not only were books about Indian philosophy increasingly available, but Yoga teachers and swamis passed through, and some put down roots. The enormously influential Paramahansa Yogananda was headquartered in L.A. (see chapter 6) and dined with Holmes on occasion; for a while their respective services were the hottest Sunday morning tickets in town. Fenwicke says his brother was also impressed by the writings of one Yogi Ramacharaka, a shining example of India's influence: he was actually an American who wrote books about New Thought under his real name, William Walker Atkinson.[19]

As his life progressed, Holmes drank more deeply of Vedanta, and he openly acknowledged his debt. In a 1958 lecture to students, he said that New Thought "had its roots in a very deep antiquity." India's sages, he explained,

> believed in one God and only One. They didn't call it God; they
> called it the Absolute, or Brahma [*sic*]; but it doesn't matter what
> you call it. They believed in one Presence and one Power, and only
> One in the Universe. They believed . . . in the mind that sleeps in
> the mineral, waves in the grass, wakes to simple consciousness in the

animal, to self-consciousness in the human and to cosmic consciousness in what they call the upper hierarchies, or an ascending scale of
evolution, ad infinitum.[20]

By then Holmes had become a huge fan of the twentieth-century philosopher and yogi Sri Aurobindo (see chapter 7). When Holmes died in
1960, Aurobindo's magnum opus, *The Life Divine,* was on his chest.

Perhaps the best testimonial to Holmes's debt to India is his last book,
The Voice Celestial, written with Fenwicke and published the year he died.
Composed as an epic poem, its chapter titles include "The Vedic Hymns,"
"Prophets of India," and "Rama, Founder of Faiths," plus two devoted to
the Buddha. Dave DeLuca points out that the book might well be an homage to the Bhagavad Gita. Like that sacred text, *The Voice Celestial* consists
of eighteen chapters; the title is so close to *The Song Celestial,* a traditional
appellation for the Gita, as to invite comparisons. But perhaps the most
obvious mark of Holmes's esteem for Vedanta is the subtitle, *Thou Art
That,* the most famous *mahavakya* (great utterance) in the Upanishads.
His legacy continues through the network of churches (some prefer *centers*
or *institutes*) under the interchangeable rubrics of Science of Mind and
Religious Science.

The New New Thought

Contemporary New Thought adherents may or may not be aware of the
threads that run from the Himalayas to Emerson, to the Fillmores and
Holmes, to the sermons they hear and the publications they read. The primary teachings grew out of the ingenuity of the founders, but they undeniably contain Vedantic nutrients, such as the essential unity of the individual
and the divine, the notion of "one Truth, many paths," the widespread use
of silent meditation, and a strong embrace of karma ("The Law of Cause
and Effect" in Holmes's formulation) and reincarnation. There are, to be

sure, plentiful references to Jesus. But in the New Thought universe, Jesus is a supreme spiritual teacher, a master healer, and an exemplar to emulate. Listen to Hindus speak about the holy man from Nazareth, and you'll hear a similar perspective. Also different from mainstream Christianity is New Thought's view of God—more an energetic force than a person, and more an all-loving creator of an abundant universe than a disciplinarian. As one New Thought minister put it, "We like resurrection symbolism more than the crucifixion."

According to the Association for Global New Thought, there are 800 to 900 Unity churches, 600 to 700 Religious Science venues, and 300 to 400 independent ministries in the United States. A recent survey found that approximately 250,000 people attend at least one New Thought service a month, and various publishing and educational activities reach an estimated 2.5 million a year.[21] Books by Ernest Holmes and other Religious Science authors sell twenty to thirty thousand copies a year.

But New Thought's reach has been far greater than the measurable data would suggest. Its echoes—and by extension, those of Emerson and Vedanta—have been reverberating through American culture for more than a century. Between 1937 and 1955, Dale Carnegie's *How to Win Friends and Influence People* sold more than five million copies. The *Power of Positive Thinking* by Norman Vincent Peale (a 1950s combination of Dr. Phil and Billy Graham) has sold more than seven million copies since starting a 186-week run on the *New York Times* bestseller list in 1952. New Thought echoes today in proponents of mind-body medicine; New Age celebrities and self-help authors like Wayne Dyer and Marianne Williamson (she ran a major Unity Church for a while); purveyors of how-to-succeed advice like Napoleon Hill's perennial *Think and Grow Rich* and the 2006 craze, *The Secret,* by Rhonda Byrne, whose take on New Thought's "law of attraction" (basically, you reap what you think) was championed by Oprah and other trendsetters; and preachers with God-wants-you-to-prosper messages, such as Robert H. Schuller (a protégé of Peale) and Joel Osteen, whose weekly broadcasts from his Houston megachurch reach more than seven million a week. In fact, anytime you hear a self-help maven extol the power of mind, or advocate shifting thought from negative to positive, or recommend affirmations for achieving one's goals, you are encountering the influence of New Thought and therefore of Emerson and Vedanta.

The Yoga of New Thought

In recent decades the direct link to Vedantic philosophy, so instrumental in New Thought's founding phase, has been reestablished. My interviews with leaders and visits to several centers have shown me considerable overlap between modern adherents of New Thought and practitioners of Vedanta-Yoga. The interaction is mutually enriching. New Thought gains from the East a broader understanding of spiritual development, plus time-tested meditative methods; many Vedic practitioners find New Thought techniques such as visualization and affirmation useful for directing their gains in consciousness to worldly concerns. And for many, New Thought institutions provide a spiritual home with familiar trappings.

The board of the International New Thought Alliance (INTA) includes two spiritual teachers from the lineage of Paramahansa Yogananda. Back in the 1920s Yogananda initiated a number of New Thought leaders in his Kriya Yoga practices, among them Joel Goldsmith, whose books remain highly popular on New Thought reading lists. Now Roy Eugene Davis, one of the few direct disciples of Yogananda still alive, and Ellen O'Brian, who was ordained by Davis in the ministry he founded, both sit on INTA's board.

In the late 1960s, when the Beatles put meditation on the front pages, Davis started receiving invitations from Religious Science and Unity churches. "They didn't know actual meditation techniques," he told me. "And when they saw I could explain these matters in plain English, I was invited to their conferences." Reverend O'Brian, who runs the Center for Spiritual Enlightenment in San Jose, California, became involved in New Thought through Davis. Like her mentor, she's taught meditation to New Thoughters and has introduced them to Yogananda's books. O'Brian, whose reading of Emerson as an undergraduate was a spiritual turning point, is also on the advisory council of the Association for Global New Thought, which gives the former political activist a way to apply spiritual principles to social justice issues.

Another example of the modern meeting of New Thought and the Veda is Unity minister Marj Britt. When she was ordained in her forties, Britt had little knowledge of Eastern philosophy. Then she took over a congregation in the Bay Area and was exposed to philosopher Ken Wilber, Buddhist teacher Jack Kornfield, and scholar Andrew Harvey. "The East-West integration brought a vertical deepening of my path," she told me. It also expanded her knowledge base. People drawn to her "campus of consciousness," Unity of Tustin, an hour or so south of Los Angeles, are the beneficiaries. In fact, more and more New Thought ministers are, like Reverend Britt, building all-purpose spiritual centers. In 2008 the United Churches of Religious Science—one of two national Science of Mind organizations—changed its name to United Centers for Spiritual Living because its core constituency favors the language of pluralism over that of doctrinaire religion. This trend has been fueled by New Thoughters who were impacted by the stream of Vedanta-Yoga that poured into the culture starting in the 1960s.

One of those leaders is Reverend Michael Bernard Beckwith. A significant portion of his congregation consists of seekers who are also involved in some form of Vedic spirituality, whether they visit gurus, take Yoga classes, practice Hindu-derived meditation forms, or just read a lot of Eastern-oriented books. Beckwith's own life was transformed by Indian teachings before he found his New Thought calling. I discussed his history with him in his spacious and tasteful office at the Agape International Spiritual Center.

Small in stature and huge in presence, Beckwith is as engaging one on one as he is when speaking to a thousand people, only slightly less exuberant. "When I opened up to the spiritual dimension and began to develop a spiritual practice, I was very influenced by the Eastern traditions," he said. It started in the 1970s, when Beckwith was a psychobiology major at the University of Southern California. "I had a spontaneous spiritual awakening, and my life as I knew it changed dramatically," he said. "Any sense of worry and anxiety dissipated. I just had this awareness that all was well and a divine intelligence governed everything." That opening, and a series of visionary experiences, led to a phase of intense exploration. "I began to do research to discover what had happened to me, and to learn how I could amplify and stay consistent with the awareness I had tasted."

His search brought him to L.A.'s legendary Bodhi Tree bookstore, which had opened in 1970 as a one-room shop. He discovered Sri Aurobindo's *The Life Divine*, Yogananda's *Autobiography of a Yogi*, and other classics. "Most of my insights came internally, and the books would validate it," he told me. "I'd read about the Atman presence, and I knew that it was true—not based on any intellectual exercise, but in my bones. It resonated as reality." He sent away for Yogananda's Self-Realization Fellowship Lessons, learned Transcendental Meditation and other practices, and drove to Ojai each summer for Krishnamurti's lecture series. He spent time with Swami Muktananda, studied the works of Bhagwan Shree Rajneesh (aka Osho), and went to see most of the gurus who came through L.A.

His studies put Christianity in a new perspective. As a teenager, he had turned away from the tradition because he didn't like the dogmatism and "didn't meet anybody who was like Jesus." Now, thanks to his explorations, he said, "I began to appreciate Jesus as a wayshower, an exemplar of the highest possibility of human awareness, a teacher of consciousness with a message for everyone." One day his mother took him to a Science of Mind church. He arrived during the sermon, and when he heard the preacher say "Heaven and hell are not places, they are states of consciousness," he blurted out, "He's right!" He studied Ernest Holmes, who "had blended the best of the East and the West, and was teaching it for the Western mind." Eventually, he was ordained. He started Agape in a living room in the mid-1980s. Now, following his visits to Oprah and Larry King; the publication of his book, *Spiritual Liberation: Fulfilling Your Soul's Potential;* and his PBS series *The Answer Is You*, it's hard to find a seat in Agape's cavernous auditorium.[22]

As the singer-songwriter Leonard Cohen once wrote, "There's a crack in everything, that's how the light gets in." New Thought has been one of the cracks through which Vedic light has entered the American psyche. Behind its pulpits and podiums are hundreds if not thousands of leaders like Beckwith and Britt, who bring East and West together in ways that taste right to modern Americans, many of whom are unaware that they are imbibing Indian spices.

4

THE HANDSOME MONK IN THE
ORANGE ROBE

Chicago was already a broad-shouldered toddlin' town in 1893, and for half that year 27 million people from all over the world poured in for the Columbian Exposition. The six-hundred-acre fair commemorated Christopher Columbus's voyage to what he thought would be India. That was fitting, in light of what transpired at the World's Parliament of Religions, which was held in conjunction with the event. Despite the presence of foreigners, the Chicagoans hustling through the railway station one day that summer must have found the bronze-skinned man in an orange robe and a yellow turban a rather remarkable sight. He needed assistance, as he had little money and had lost the address he'd been given to obtain lodging as a delegate to the Parliament. No doubt some rebuffed him because he was a stranger with a dark complexion, even if his manners and his English were impeccable. Others stepped aside, perhaps because he looked like an oddly dressed hobo after spending the night in a boxcar.[1] And some with good intentions simply did not know how to advise him. As he wandered the neighborhood outside the station, he likely remained unperturbed. He was, after all, a monk on a sacred mission, and he had encountered far greater inconvenience while traveling around India as a mendicant. He sat down on a curb on Dearborn Street to rest.

Young Naren and the Great Swan

He was born Narendranath Datta in 1863 in Calcutta (now Kolkata), his father was a prominent attorney, and his mother was a progressive woman who had steeped her children in the epic tales of the *Ramayana* and the *Mahabarata*. Naren, as he was called, was by all accounts an athletic, cultivated youth, a natural leader with a sharp, inquisitive mind. At a college founded by Scottish missionaries, he studied Western philosophy, logic, and history. The education would prove to be invaluable, but it did not satisfy his hunger to know God and the purpose of existence. While he respected his religious tradition, he was unwilling to accept every premise on faith or to approve of customs that seemed debilitating to the nation. All of which made him a perfect candidate for the Brahmo Samaj.

A socio-religious reform movement founded in 1828 by Ram Mohan Roy (whose writings appealed to the Transcendentalists), the Brahmo Samaj started in Bengal and spread throughout the subcontinent, spearheading what came to be called the Hindu Renaissance (aka the Bengal Renaissance).[2] Its leaders rejected the caste system, scriptural literalism, and various forms of idol worship; but they revered the Vedantic teachings embodied in the Upanishads. They firmly opposed British rule and aggressive missionaries, but admired Western science and the Christian emphasis on social reform. The movement, whose goal was to revive the nation by replanting its spiritual roots in the modern era, could not have been better suited to young Naren's idealism.[3] But as a religious institution, it failed to satisfy his yearning to know the Ultimate. He would ask spiritual leaders, "Have you seen God?" and no one answered to his satisfaction.

In 1881 an English professor told Naren about a raw, unschooled saint in an ashram outside Calcutta, named Sri Ramakrishna. Admired for his effortless ability to transcend doctrines and sects, Ramakrishna was probably the first well-known exemplar of religious pluralism. He was, for starters, equally at home with the austere nondualism of Advaita Vedanta, the ecstatic emotionality of Bhakti Yoga (he was a devotee of the goddess

Kali), and the earthy energy of Tantra, paths that are not always seen as compatible.[4] Even more startling for the Victorian era, he plunged into Christian and Islamic practices as well, famously declaring that all traditions can lead to the infinite. He used various metaphors to illustrate that the one divine assumes a multitude of names and forms. For example: "There are three or four *ghats* [bathing places] on a lake. The Hindus, who drink the water at one place, call it *jal*. The Mussalmans [Muslims] at another place call it *pani*. And the English at a third place call it *water*. All three denote one and the same thing, the difference being in the name only. In the same way, some address the Reality as *Allah*, some as *God*, some as *Brahman*, some as *Kali*, and others by such names as *Rama, Jesus, Durga, Hari*."[5]

Young Naren went to meet the reputed saint and asked, "Have you seen God?" Ramakrishna passed the test by replying matter-of-factly, "Yes, I have seen Him just as I see you here, only more clearly."[6] Naren was initially ambivalent: drawn to Ramakrishna's guileless serenity, he was also wary of his paroxysms of divine intoxication, which had given rise to rumors that he was insane. Eventually Naren's ambivalence yielded to heartfelt surrender and a master-disciple relationship that some have compared to Socrates-Plato and Jesus-Paul. When, in 1886, Ramakrishna died— or as they say in India, achieved his *mahasamadhi* (great liberation)— Naren became the leader of a group of disciples who took formal vows of renunciation, or *sannyasa*. They were the founders of the Ramakrishna Mission, which would have an enormous impact on both India and the West. Naren's monastic name, Swami Vivekananda, would soon become synonymous with Vedanta in America.

In 1890 Vivekananda set out to experience close up and personal the vast homeland he hoped to reform. "This was the great departure," wrote Romain Rolland, the French Nobel laureate who penned biographies of Ramakrishna and Vivekananda. "Like a diver he plunged into the Ocean of India and the Ocean of India covered his tracks." One of thousands of possession-free sannyasis who depend upon the kindness of strangers for food and shelter, he wandered for three years from the Himalayas to the southernmost shoreline, witnessing firsthand India's glories and its sad

degradation from the proud precolonial era. From the depths of meditation arose a sense of calling: to raise up the impoverished and demoralized
nation by awakening its dormant spiritual power.

Go West, Young Man

When Vivekananda learned that religious leaders from around the world
were to convene in Chicago, he thought it might be an opportunity to
educate the West about his nation and its dominant religion, and to raise
funds for his mission. It is hard to imagine a more qualified envoy: Vivekananda's blend of influences included the rational spirituality and social
activism of the Brahmo Samaj; the passion, devotion, and respect for tradition of Sri Ramakrishna; and the language skills and modern knowledge derived from his British education. With the blessing of Sarada Devi,
Ramakrishna's spiritual wife and Holy Mother to his devotees, and with
funds provided by a maharaja and followers in Madras, he set sail from
Bombay on May 31, 1893.

About two months later, after stops in China and Japan and a series of
trains from Vancouver, he arrived in Chicago, only to learn that the parliament would not begin for another six weeks. Moreover, delegates required
credentials, and it was too late to apply for them. To top it off, the Columbian Exposition had inflated the prices of food and lodging. Hearing that
things were cheaper in Boston, he hopped a train. As luck or providence
would have it, on board was a former Smith College professor of literature
named Katherine Sanborn. No doubt charmed by the erudite swami, she
invited him to stay at her home outside Boston. Through her efforts, Vivekananda's first public appearances in America took place on turf made
hospitable by Transcendentalists and New Thoughters. "Despite more
than fifty years of interest in Indian thought, few New Englanders had
met a Hindu," writes Diana Eck, and that summer Vivekananda "attracted
a great deal of attention." He gave about a dozen talks at churches, lecture
halls, and private salons, ranging as far afield as Saratoga Springs, New York.

The exotic visitor was treated with respect by his audiences and the press. This account, from the *Daily Gazette* of Salem, misspellings and all, was typical of the coverage, capturing the purpose of Vivekananda's initial talks:

> Rajah Swani Vivi Rananda of India spoke at the East church Sunday evening, on the religion of India and the poor of his native land . . . The monk was dressed in his native costume, and spoke about forty minutes. The great need of India today, which is not the India of fifty years ago, is, he said, missionaries to educate the people industrially and socially and not religiously. The Hindoos have all the religion they want, and the Hindoo religion is the most ancient in the world. The monk is a very pleasant speaker and held the close attention of his audience.[7]

But there were troubling incidents too, such as the time a hostile mob threw things at him. "A hundred times I had a mind to . . . go back to India," Vivekananda wrote to a friend back home. "But I am determined, and I have a call from Above; I see no way, but His eyes see. And I must stick to my guns, life or death."[8]

The matter of obtaining credentials for the Parliament of Religions was solved by Harvard philologist and historian John Henry Wright, one of many prominent New Englanders who were impressed by the visiting swami. In a letter to the parliament's chairman, Wright called Vivekananda "a man who is more learned than all our learned professors put together." Assured of being credentialed, Vivekananda returned to Chicago, only to lose the address of the parliament en route and end up on the curb on Dearborn Street.

His Kind of Town

"For the faithful, the patient, the hermetically pure, all the important things in this world—not life and death perhaps, which are merely words; but the

things—work out rather beautifully." J. D. Salinger wrote that
once, and it's probably not a coincidence that he, as a budding writer
in the 1950s, spent a good deal of time at the Ramakrishna-Vivekananda
Center of New York. The observation certainly applied to Vivekananda,
for whom things had worked out rather beautifully in Boston and were
about to once again. He had not been sitting long on the curb when a
woman named Belle Hale emerged from her home. When she learned that
the stranger was a delegate to the parliament, Mrs. Hale[9] extended him
every courtesy that a traveler could wish for and accompanied him to the
parliament's offices. In a short while, he would be as big a celebrity as a
foreign religious figure could be.

That June the inflated stock markets of the Gilded Age had collapsed,
but Chicago's economy was robust. The city had recovered from the devastating fire of 1871; buildings were going up, and local companies were
rolling out profitable innovations, like the Sears, Roebuck mail order catalog and Wrigley's Juicy Fruit and Spearmint chewing gums. Visitors to the
Columbian Exposition rode the world's first Ferris wheel and previewed
futuristic machines, all illuminated by lightbulbs powered by alternating
current, a new invention of Nikola Tesla, who would become Vivekananda's friend and student.

Amid the six-month celebration of industrial progress, the World's Parliament of Religions was a seventeen-day island of high-minded tranquility. The invitation to religious leaders had been well received for the most
part, although the Archbishop of Canterbury snubbed the proceedings
because "the Christian religion is the one religion," and he did not wish to
affirm "the equality of the other intended members and the parity of their
position and claims." Some ministers accused colleagues who attended of
"treason against Christ," and the sultan of Turkey offered similar denun-
ciations on behalf of Islam, leaving the parliament with only one Muslim,
a convert from New England. Aside from those discordant notes, enthusiasm for the convocation was overwhelming.[10]

Of the 194 papers delivered, 152 were by Christians. But Buddhism, Taoism, Confucianism, Jainism, Shintoism, Zoroastrianism, and
Hinduism—in the form of Vivekananda and a Brahmo Samaj leader

named P. C. Mazumdar—also had a presence, and William Q. Judge, the vice president of the Theosophical Society, gave two talks on reincarnation. Vivekananda soon emerged as a scene-stealing star; had he not made such a spectacular impression, the parliament would not likely have been remembered, much less revived on its centennial in 1993.

Universal Religion

For the opening ceremonies, four thousand spectators crammed into a hall in a massive new building on Michigan Avenue that would soon house the Art Institute of Chicago. Along with the dark-suited Western clergy, the dais featured, in the words of one reporter, "strange robes, turbans and tunics, crosses and crescents, flowing hair and tonsured heads." Welcoming the audience, Charles Bonney, a prominent Chicago attorney who had spearheaded the effort to convene the parliament, said the occasion heralded "a new era of religious peace and progress . . . dispelling the dark clouds of sectarian strife." (In a sad irony, the date of the event was September 11, precisely 108 years before the world was shaken by deadly evidence of the difficulty of fulfilling those ideals. A further irony: 108 is a sacred number in Hinduism.)

In his opening statement, the parliament's chairman, Dr. John Henry Barrows, set an ecumenical tone: "Religion, like the white light of Heaven, has been broken into many colored fragments by the prisms of men. One of the objects of the Parliament of Religions has been to change the many-colored radiance back into the white light of heavenly truth." It was a remarkably pluralistic message for that era, but Barrows, a Presbyterian minister, would later make clear what he really meant by "heavenly truth."

One of twenty-four delegates to speak on opening day, Vivekananda began his speech with "Sisters and Brothers of America." According to newspaper accounts, he was interrupted by an ovation that lasted two to four minutes. Some have attributed the now-mythic reception to the unusual intimacy of the speaker's greeting; others cite his noble bearing. He went on to say, in part, "I am proud to belong to a religion that has taught the world both tolerance and universal acceptance. We believe not only in universal tolerance but we accept all religions to be true." He recited a traditional hymn: "As the different streams, having their sources in different places, all mingle their water in the sea; so, O Lord, the different paths which men take through different tendencies, various though they appear, crooked or straight, all lead to Thee." Deploring sectarianism, bigotry, and fanaticism, he said, "I fervently believe that the bell that tolled this morning in honor of this convention may be the death-knell to all fanaticism, that it is the death-knell to all persecution with the sword or the pen, and to all uncharitable feelings between persons winding their way to the same goal."

Harriet Monroe, the editor of a well-known poetry journal, reported that "the handsome monk in the orange robe gave us in perfect English a masterpiece. His personality, dominant, magnetic; his voice, rich as a bronze bell; the controlled fervor of his feeling; the beauty of his message to the Western world he was facing for the first time—these combined to give us a rare and perfect moment of supreme emotion. It was human eloquence at its highest pitch." Her impressions were echoed by other reporters, albeit in more sober prose.

For the next sixteen days, sessions were held morning, afternoon, and evening, often to crowds so big that speakers had to repeat their lectures in an adjoining hall. Vivekananda spoke several times, each scheduled appearance drawing a larger crowd than the one before. His primary themes were carried into his postparliament work, and to a large extent, they set the standard for the Vedic teachers who followed in his footsteps. Countering misconceptions about his religious heritage, he presented a modernized Vedanta as the essential core of the tradition. Hindus are concerned with realization, not dogma, he asserted: "Thus the whole object of their system is by constant struggle to become perfect, to become divine, to reach God, and see God; and this reaching God, seeing God, becoming perfect even as the Father in Heaven is perfect, constitutes the religion of the Hindus."

He confronted the image of Hinduism as idolatry: "I may tell you that there is no polytheism in India. In every temple, if one stands by and listens, one will find the worshipers applying all the attributes of God, including omnipresence, to the images." Pointing out that Christians too employed images and symbols, he said that "some people devote their whole lives to their idol of a church and never rise higher, because with them religion means an intellectual assent to certain doctrines and doing good to their fellows." For Hindus, he said, "Idols or temples or churches or books are only the supports, the helps, of his spiritual childhood; but on and on he must progress" in his quest for divine realization.

In making his case he evoked both the Bible ("Father in Heaven") and the modernist spirit of evolutionary progress: "The Hindu is only glad that what he has been cherishing in his bosom for ages is going to be taught in more forcible language and with further light from the latest conclusions of science." This foreshadowed the methods used by most Eastern teachers who came to the West.

Vivekananda's reception has grown to legendary proportions, thanks to the hagiography of his spiritual descendants.[11] Clearly, the dignified swami was a crowd-pleaser. Calling him "a great favorite at the Parliament," a reporter for the *Boston Evening Transcript* said, "If he merely crosses the platform he is applauded, and this marked approval of thousands he accepts in a childlike spirit of gratification, without a trace of conceit." His robust physical appearance didn't hurt. His "barrel chest and broad shoulders," writes historian Carl T. Jackson, gave him "a physique better suited to an athlete than an Indian holy man."[12] Principally as a result of Vivekananda's persuasive presence, minds were changed; the heathens were not as primitive as Westerners had imagined. Lucy Monroe, Harriet's sister, wrote what many must have thought: "The impertinence of sending half-educated theological students to instruct the wise and erudite Orientals was never brought home to an English-speaking audience more forcibly."

The Blowback

The confident assertions of Vivekananda and other delegates from the East irritated those who viewed the parliament as a platform for the Christian gospel. One cleric hoped the gathering would "usher in the triumph of his [Christ's] truth, when at the name of Jesus every knee shall bow." Another said the occasion was "preparing the way for the reunion of all the world's religions in their true center—Jesus Christ." And Reverend Barrows, whose opening remarks seemed to model interreligious understanding, later said: "We believe that Christianity is to supplant all other religions, because it contains all the truth there is in them and much besides . . . and those who have the full light of the Cross should bear brotherly hearts toward all who grope in a dimmer illumination."

Such condescension provoked a proud and defiant response from Vivekananda. He deplored the missionaries who help the hungry "only on condition that the Hindus become Christians, abandoning the faith of their fathers and forefathers." The people of India, he asserted, "have more than religion enough; what they want is bread, but they are given a stone." That remark reportedly drew a round of applause from the liberals in attendance, and the next line prompted an even bigger one: "Send missionaries to teach them how to better earn a better piece of bread and not to teach them metaphysical nonsense." On another occasion he improvised: "We who have come from the East have sat here day after day and have been told in a patronizing way that we ought to accept Christianity because Christian nations are the most prosperous." And yet, he went on, "We look about us and see England the most prosperous Christian nation in the world, with her foot on the neck of two hundred and fifty million Asiatics . . . Christianity wins its prosperity by cutting the throats of its fellow men." After also deploring the Muslim invasion of his homeland, he concluded, "Blood and the sword are not for the Hindu, whose religion is based on the law of love."

In his final address, at the closing ceremonies, he said that the dream of religious unity could not be accomplished by the triumph of any one faith. "Do I wish that the Christian would become Hindu? God forbid. Do I wish that the Hindu or Buddhist would become Christian? God forbid." The parliament, he said, "has proved to the world that holiness, purity and charity are not the exclusive possessions of any church in the world," adding that he pitied anyone who "dreams of the exclusive survival of his own religion and the destruction of the others."

Reverend Barrows, in his own concluding remarks, sounded like a baron who was proud to have invited the help to an estate picnic. The courtesy extended to Asians, he said, was not to be confused with being respected as equals. Philosopher Joseph Campbell would later describe that kind of arrogance cloaked in tolerance as "You worship God in your way, and I'll worship Him in His." But statements like Barrows's were balanced by more ecumenical voices. Merwin-Marie Snell, the president of the scientific section of the parliament, wrote of Vivekananda in *Life* magazine: "Never before has so authoritative a representative of genuine Hinduism, as opposed to the emasculated and Anglicized versions of it so common in these days, been accessible to American inquirers: and it is certain that the American people at large, will, when he is gone, look forward with eagerness to his return." They did not have to wait long.

On the Road

While thousands attended the parliament, and it was covered on the inside pages of many newspapers, most visitors to the world's fair, much less the general public, probably didn't even know it was taking place. Carl T. Jackson, whose research on Vedanta in the West is indispensable, writes that "we can now see that the Parliament of Religions itself was not the watershed event that contemporary enthusiasts proclaimed, nor did it launch a new era in world religious history."[13] Nevertheless it is generally regarded as a landmark event for several reasons: it gave birth to the modern interfaith movement; it was a catalyst for the academic study of comparative religion; it stimulated a reconsideration of missionary practices; and thanks mainly to Vivekananda, it transformed the perception of Eastern religions.

Capitalizing on publicity from the parliament, and with help from a Chicago lecture bureau, Vivekananda toured from Minneapolis to Memphis, speaking as often as fifteen times a week. Jean MacPhail, aka Sister Gayatriprana, a former Vedanta Society nun and author of the memoir *A Spiral Life,* describes his primary audience as "too scientific for most religious people and too religious for most scientific people."[14] He attracted a well-educated, affluent urban cohort, and his principal hosts and organizers were women with the time, resources, and connections to gather a crowd—the same demographics responsible for the success of subsequent gurus.

While many welcomed Vivekananda as an emissary of tolerance and progressive spirituality, conservative Christians denounced him as a threat to all that was good and true and moral. Sometimes he patiently corrected misconceptions about India and its religion; at other times he gave his detractors an earful, accusing them of turning Christ's message into a "shop-keeper religion" whose followers ask God to fill their orders and of filling the world with "bloodshed and tyranny." At the same time, he carefully distinguished between Jesus (whom he held up as an equal to Krishna, Buddha, and other divine personages) and the institutions that claimed to represent him—a perspective common to every Indian teacher who succeeded in the West. The controversy peaked in Detroit with a published volley between Vivekananda and Bishop W. X. Ninde, whose defense of missionaries prompted some to praise him as a prophet and others to label him a hypocrite. Following that tumult, the swami left the Midwest for the sophisticated enclaves of the Northeast.

New York even then was a city of tall buildings and polluted air, only the tallest structures were about twenty stories high, and the air was fouled by dung from the thousands of horses hauling wagons and carts. The city's educated elite welcomed the exotic holy man who had created a stir in the Midwest. In two frenetic weeks Vivekananda spoke in living rooms, churches, and even the Waldorf Astoria Hotel, highlighting core Vedantic principles and sometimes introducing concepts such as karma and reincarnation. From there he returned to Massachusetts, where the reception was more enthusiastic than it had been the first time around. His

lectures at Emerson's alma mater were reportedly attended by such leading intellectuals as the philosopher Josiah Royce and the Sanskrit scholar
Charles Rockwell Lanman. George Santayana ("Those who cannot remember the past are condemned to repeat it") was probably present as
well, along with Nobel Peace Prize winner Jane Addams and the young
Gertrude Stein. In its review the *Harvard Crimson* noted that "whatever
sect the Hindoo belongs to he does not say that his is the only right belief,
and that all others must be wrong. He believes that there are many ways of
coming to God." At least one student, William Ernest Hocking, said that
the message caused him to "rethink my philosophical foundations." He
went on to become a renowned philosopher of religion.

The most celebrated member of the Harvard audiences was William
James. Often called the father of American psychology, James formed an
admiring friendship with Vivekananda and may have coaxed the university to offer him a professorship in Eastern philosophy. (The offer was
declined.) Readers of James's seminal book, *The Varieties of Religious Experience,* learned that he held Vedanta as "the paragon of all monastic systems" and Vivekananda as "the paragon of Vedantist missionaries."

A New Mission

Sometime during his first American sojourn, Vivekananda realized that
his goal of raising funds for reform efforts in India was not going to succeed. Reasoning that East and West could benefit from an exchange of
knowledge and resources, the former to upgrade its material conditions
and the latter to cultivate the inner life, he now focused on establishing an
American Vedanta. Speaking more like a guru and less like an emissary,
he used the term *Hinduism* less and emphasized practical Vedanta and
Yoga over theology and social-historical commentary. The shift was exemplified by a series of lectures that formed the basis of four classic books—
Karma Yoga, Raja Yoga, Jnana Yoga, and *Bhakti Yoga*—that are still widely
read today. (The physical practices of Hatha Yoga were not part of his
repertoire, although he apparently taught some traditional breathing

exercises.) This turning point in the East-to-West transmission set the template for the pragmatic approach that later gurus would take in adapting their tradition to Western audiences. Vivekananda established the ground rules in his introduction to *Raja Yoga:* "It is wrong to believe blindly. You must exercise your own reason and judgment; you must practice, and see whether these things happen or not. Just as you would take up any other science, exactly in the same manner you should take up this science for study."

The book was published in 1896, the year the *Plessy v. Ferguson* Supreme Court decision affirmed the segregationist principle of "separate but equal." Elizabeth De Michelis of Cambridge University calls it "the first fully fledged formulation of modern yoga," marking a seminal moment in the meeting of ancient India and the modern West.[15]

In January 1895, with the help of some earnest students, Vivekananda opened his first facility in America, leasing two small rooms about a block from where the Empire State Building would be built.[16] He taught tirelessly, digging deeply into Vedantic teachings with a handful of sincere devotees and initiating them with traditional mantras for use in meditation. That summer he gathered a group of twelve disciples upstate, in Thousand Island Park, for further training, evidently concerned about the continuation of his teachings once he returned to India. During that time, he ordained the first American sannyasis: New Yorker Leon Landsberg became Swami Kripananda, and a woman named Marie Louise became Swami Abhayananda.[17] To the inner circle, he spoke about Sri Ramakrishna and Sarada Devi for the first time, holding them up as exemplars of Self-realization. In public, he was virtually silent about those venerated figures and about their devotion to Kali—a conscious decision to emphasize a universal, adaptable Vedanta-Yoga, and to keep aspects of Hinduism that might be construed as cultist or idolatrous in the background, as a family might put exotic decor in a closet when conservative guests come over. That too anticipated subsequent gurus.

In 1896, Vivekananda returned to his homeland by way of Europe, summoning from Calcutta two fellow disciples to carry on his work in America. He had left India as a nameless sannyasi, but upon his return he was greeted as a triumphant hero. "Reports of his success in the West had poured into India during his absence, creating in his countrymen a new sense of pride in their great spiritual heritage," wrote the Indian scholar and statesman Karan Singh. He credited Vivekananda with bringing out India's "real spiritual essence" instead of "the mumbo-jumbo that the West had so often mistaken for Hinduism." Newspapers hailed him for elevating the image of the country within India herself. Seizing on his newfound prestige, Vivekananda urged his countrymen to lay claim to their spiritual heritage and revivify the nation. To this end, he established the organizational structure of the Ramakrishna Mission and Math (*math* is pronounced *mutt* and means "monastery"). With the twin goals of teaching Vedanta and engaging in humanitarian works, its centers have been a vital force in India ever since.

In his remaining years, Vivekananda worked tirelessly despite advancing diabetes and a strong desire for seclusion, which he expressed in a letter to a friend in 1896: "The touch of the world is degenerating me . . . I am so tired of talking too; I want to close my lips and sit in silence for years." In the summer of 1899 he returned to the West, spending time in London and New York before heading to California, where his lineage would thrive. He started a Vedanta Society in San Francisco, which in 1906 set up shop in a large Victorian house with turrets representing each of the world's religions. Today tour buses describe it as "the oldest Hindu temple in America." He also attracted followers of diverse backgrounds in Los Angeles with lofty rhetoric such as this passage from a speech in Pasadena:

I accept all religions that were in the past and worship with them all. I worship God with every one of them, in whatever form. I'll go to the mosque of the Muslim, I'll enter the Christian's church and kneel before the crucifix. I'll enter the Buddhist temple, where I take refuge in Buddha and in his Law. I'll go into the forest and sit in meditation with the Hindu who's trying to see the Light which enlightens the heart of everyone. Not only shall I do this, but I'll keep my heart open for all that may come in the future.

Vivekananda returned to his motherland in August 1900. He never got to enjoy the sustained silence he wished for, but he did end his life in the quiet ashram he established in Ramakrishna's name. He passed away on July 4, 1902, a fitting date for someone who stood for spiritual freedom and had come to love America so much that he composed a poem called "To the Fourth of July." Since 1995 the stretch of Michigan Avenue that passes the Chicago Art Institute has been called Swami Vivekananda Way.

A Vedantic Prototype

The trailblazing work of Vivekananda and his handpicked successors established a template for transplanting the core message of Vedantic philosophy into American soil. While maintaining some traditional elements for ardent devotees, such as *pujas* (devotional rituals), guru-disciple initiation, and top-down authority structures, they framed their teaching as a rational science and placed before the public English speakers who were familiar with Western history and values. There is a great irony in this, as the English colonizers had introduced their language and their educational system to wean Hindus from their "idolatrous" religion. The swamis reversed this process, like martial artists who turn their opponents' energy against them. Vivekananda himself said his purpose was "to put the Hindu ideas into English and then make out of dry philosophy and intricate mythology and queer startling psychology, a religion which shall be easy, simple, popular and at the same time meet the requirements of the highest minds." In a country as pragmatic as America, the Vedic presence would hardly have amounted to anything worth writing about if it had come in any other form.

The Vedanta Society never asked anyone to convert to Hinduism or to forsake the religion of their upbringing. Instead, everyone was encouraged to apply Vedantic ideas and yogic practices to his or her own religion. Despite Vivekananda's outspoken critiques of missionaries and what he called "Churchianity," his movement treated Jesus with deep respect. To this day, virtually every Vedanta temple in the West displays images of Christ (and of Buddha) and holds special services on Easter and Christmas.

The Vedanta Society was pretty much the only game in town for Americans drawn to Indian philosophy in the early twentieth century. It enjoyed substantial growth, led by enthusiastic followers such as Josephine Mac-Leod, a socialite who saw to it that Vivekananda's message was heard by prominent citizens. The 1920s were expansionary years, as new centers opened in Chicago, Seattle, and other cities. While the movement has never employed aggressive marketing techniques, its early leaders, notably Swami Abhedananda in New York and Swami Trigunatita in San Francisco, used lectures and publications to get the message out, sometimes speaking to thousands at a time.

One early swami with a knack for public outreach was Swami Paramananda (1884–1940), a charismatic young monk who came to New York as Abhedananda's assistant in 1906 and left a few years later to chart his own course. He crisscrossed the country on speaking tours and established idyllic centers (now called Ananda Ashramas) outside Boston and Los Angeles. A thoroughly modern yogi, he took advantage of commercial air travel and radio to move about and get his message across. Before his death, he made the unprecedented gesture of training a woman, his niece Gayatri Devi, to be his successor. This precipitated an amicable break with the parent organization. Since Gayatri Devi's passing in 1995, an American psychologist named Sudha Puri (née Susan Schrager) has run the two facilities.

Back to the Garden

In the late 1960s, when interest in Eastern philosophy exploded, thousands of seekers found their way to the Vedanta Society or fed their curiosity through books published by the organization's press. Some of the youngsters drawn to the movement then are now its leaders, serving either as lay devotees or as monastics. A prime example is Pravrajika Vrajaprana, a nun at the society's Sarada Convent.[18] In the summer of 1967, while flocks of flower children were cavorting in San Francisco, she was a fifteen-year-old with a thoroughly Western name trying to end the Vietnam War. One hot Sunday she and a comrade were leafleting cars in church parking lots. When they ran out of churches, they took their remaining leaflets to the Vedanta Temple in the scenic hills south of Santa Barbara. (Its convent would later become her home.)

After completing their task, the two curious teenagers tiptoed into the temple. "I thought it was a really nice place with a lovely atmosphere, but I had a problem with the speaker," Vrajaprana told me. "He was a tall swami visiting from India, and he was very skinny. I thought, 'These are religious people who fast, and I'm not into fasting.'" On the way out, she was greeted at the door by the swami in charge. He was not skinny. "When he shook my hand and smiled at me, I burst into tears," she recalls. "I was hell on wheels with 'Stop the war machine,' so my reaction came totally out of the blue. He had a holiness that was transmittable." He was Swami Prabhavananda, the founder of the Vedanta Society of Southern California.[19] The young firebrand was no doubt happy to learn that the famous writer Christopher Isherwood had had a similar reaction to the swami's smile. "It is somehow so touching, so open, so brilliant with joy that it makes me want to cry," he wrote in a memoir.[20]

Raised by Protestants who sent her to Sunday school but had rejected certain doctrines, Vrajaprana had never heard the word *Vedanta* until that day. She returned for a Sunday lecture and kept coming back because the messages made sense to her. One day she discovered the convent. "I want to join," she said. After ten years of indecision, following what she calls "the blessing of a terrible car accident" that she thought had paralyzed her, she finally did. "The round peg was in the round hole for the first time," she says. She is as passionate as ever about peacemaking, only now her means is disseminating Vedantic teachings through writing and public speaking.[21]

Changing with the Times

There are now about twenty Vedanta Society centers and retreat houses in the United States, along with study circles in places without a resident swami. But since the 1970s, the organization's following and its public profile have been dwarfed by famous gurus and hipper, more aggressive organizations. Some centers are doing so well they've had to acquire bigger spaces. One example is the Boston center, which is run by Swami Tyagananda, a well-educated monk from Mumbai who writes scholarly articles and serves as a chaplain at both Harvard and MIT. Others are graying institutions, barely staying afloat. In some cases, the decline in followers has been ameliorated by new Indian immigrants, for whom the Vedanta Society is a taste of the homeland. Some of the swamis in charge—mostly Indian monks sent from headquarters in Calcutta—have accommodated this demographic shift by speaking more about Indian history, invoking sacred Hindu literature, and making traditional observances more available.

Some American followers enjoy the spice (so to speak) of Indian cultural elements, but others—including some of Indian descent—fear that Indianization will drive Westerners away. "If it looks too ethnic, people will think it's an Indian culture club," said one devotee, himself a transplant from Bangalore. Some longtime devotees are concerned that the current leaders are out of step with Vivekananda's vision of a modern Western Vedanta. "They don't know how to reach Americans," said an American nun of the swamis in charge, "and ironically, Americans are more receptive to Indian philosophy than ever before."

In the early 1990s concerned followers started a publication called *Vedanta Free Press* as a forum for openly discussing such issues. "People had gripes, and we gave them a voice," John Schlenck, one of the journal's founders and a former editor, told me. Later renamed *American Vedantist,* the journal takes on controversial issues in addition to printing philosophical articles and personal reflections. To their credit, the powers that be have made no attempt to silence the debate. Schlenck, a composer of sacred oratorios and a devotee for half a century, says that "the concern is for the future. Are we going to turn into just another Hindu sect? Or did Vivekananda have a special message for the West?"

Such dilemmas are common in institutions struggling to adapt their teachings to contemporary America. As the oldest of the lot, and one whose administration is centered in India, the Vedanta Society has challenges that most of the others do not. It will no doubt carry on in its low-key way, serving its constituents and educating interested individuals and groups. At the same time, because some Americans are eager to reach a broader audience, alternative organizations may well spin off in the future.

The Ramakrishna-Vivekananda legacy extends far beyond the walls of its centers and temples. As historian Carl T. Jackson has put it, "Few other religious bodies of such Lilliputian size have equaled the movement's impact or historical significance."[22] That is largely because Vedanta Society swamis mentored some of the twentieth century's most decisive thinkers, and through them Indian philosophy penetrated the intellectual heart of America.

5

THE PUBLIC INTELLECTUALS

On my bookshelf are three thin paperbacks, their covers cracked and torn and their pages yellowed, dog-eared, and heavily underlined. Purchased for $1.25 apiece in the late 1960s, they are: *The Song of God,* a translation of the Bhagavad Gita; *The Crest-Jewel of Discrimination,* a translation of a classic discourse by Shankara, the genius of Advaita Vedanta; and *How to Know God,* a translation and commentary on Patanjali's *Yoga Sutras.*[1] All three books, which were often the only versions of those sacred texts that Americans could find at the time, were coauthored (with Swami Prabhavananda) by the novelist Christopher Isherwood. On that same shelf are four other books, aged and cherished like sturdy pieces of furniture: the anthology *Vedanta for Modern Man,* bookmarked for the essay "Vedanta and Western History" by Gerald Heard; Huston Smith's classic textbook *The Religions of Man;* Joseph Campbell's *The Hero with a Thousand Faces;* and Aldous Huxley's *The Perennial Philosophy.* The eye-opening impact of those books on me was so powerful that I will never part with them, no matter how Kindle-ized my reading habits may become. I am not the only one, not by a long shot.

What these five authors had in common, apart from talent and renown, was that they had as important mentors some of the finest swamis in the Ramakrishna-Vivekananda lineage. In the early twentieth century, Vivekananda's crystalline expositions on Vedanta, and the enthralling tales of

Ramakrishna's mystical pluralism, captured the attention of Western intellectual giants such as Romain Rolland and William James, the historians
Arnold Toynbee and Will Durant, and in Russia novelist Leo Tolstoy and
sociologist Pitirim Sorokin.[2] In midcentury America, the Vedanta Society
furthered the education of those five extraordinary minds—Isherwood,
Smith, Heard, Campbell, and Huxley—and their firepower, like the arsenal of a revolutionary vanguard, would radically transform the way large
numbers of people understand and practice religion.

The British Invasion

Gerald Heard and Aldous Huxley met in London in 1929, two lean, sensitive young men from distinguished families with prodigious intellects
who were deeply troubled by the mounting tension in Europe. Insatiable in their thirst for truth and for ways to change the world, they were
polymaths, interested in everything and comfortable with various modes
of expressing ideas. They became inseparable friends and, through their
early publications, public figures. Heard, five years Huxley's senior, was
destined to be the lesser known of the pair, causing admirers to call him
"the best-kept secret of the twentieth century."

As a catalyst for the propagation of Vedanta, Heard (1889–1971) was
unrivaled, largely because he sparked the interest of people who in turn
reached millions of others. Earlier in his life a crisis of faith had led Heard
to abandon his goal of becoming an Anglican minister. The dark night
of the soul triggered a nervous breakdown, and following a long recovery
period, he embraced secular humanism and scientific materialism. A voracious reader and magnetic speaker, he lectured at Oxford and published
his first book, the enigmatically titled *Narcissus: An Anatomy of Clothes*,
in 1924. In the next few years he rose to fame as a science journalist.
His 1929 book *The Ascent of Humanity* introduced an important theme
in his work, "the evolving consciousness of man." He also edited a short-
lived journal called *The Realist*, whose editorial board included luminaries

such as H. G. Wells, Rebecca West, and the Huxley brothers: Julian, the eminent biologist, and Aldous (1894–1963), by then the author of four novels and five books of essays. By 1934 both men had added to their renown, Huxley with his most celebrated work, the dystopian novel *Brave New World,* and Heard as the author of four more books and the host of a BBC radio program.

Along the way, Heard's spiritual yearning had reawakened, sparked in large part by his study of Buddhism and Hinduism. At one point he suggested that his friend Huxley, who had mystical leanings of his own, try yogic breathing and meditation for his crippling insomnia. So began a shared quest that would transform their lives and countless others.

In April 1937, with the world mired in economic depression, the Spanish Civil War blazing, Stalinist purges in Moscow, Japan invading China, and Hitler aligning with Mussolini, the two pacifists left England for America. It was supposed to be a short visit, centered on a lecture tour for peace. They ended up settling in southern California for the rest of their lives. The Vedanta Society in Hollywood became both a campus for their ongoing education and a platform for their advocacy of Eastern philosophy.

Both men had come to believe that material objects were, like the shadows in Plato's cave, the visible expression of an underlying nonmaterial essence. They had also come to believe, in the words of Huxley biographer Dana Sawyer, "that the unit of world peace is individual peace, that a forest is only as green as the individual trees in the forest are green."[3] The streams of their ruminations came together in Vedanta, whose depiction of ultimate reality as both transcendent of and immanent in everything that exists appealed to them more than the standard Judeo-Christian notion of personified God who stands apart from the world. Of perhaps greater appeal was the practical teaching that awakening to one's divine nature brings what the Bible calls "the peace that passeth understanding." Contrary to conventional wisdom, they concluded, Eastern mysticism did not have to lead to escapism. It could, in fact, make us better citizens. "It is because we don't know who we are," Huxley wrote, "because we are unaware that the Kingdom of Heaven is within us, that we behave in the generally silly, the often insane, the sometimes criminal ways that are so characteristically human."[4]

In 1939, having settled in Los Angeles, Heard sought out the Vedanta Society in Hollywood. The center, built around a small temple with three onion-shaped domes, was located just up the hill from the famous intersection of Hollywood and Vine and a mile from the Hollywood Bowl. It was run by Swami Prabhavananda, who had founded it in 1929.

Prabhavananda (1893–1976) had become a monk in 1914 after graduating from Calcutta University. Upon taking his final vows, he shipped out to the United States, serving in San Francisco and Portland before establishing the Hollywood center. Usually pictured in neat Western clothing, typically a sport shirt and pullover, he is remembered by older devotees as being sometimes cantankerous but a gifted exponent of Vedanta philosophy, a tireless worker, and blessed with the kind of presence that attracts seekers and makes them want to stick around. He left a lasting impression on the American writer Henry Miller, who wrote in *The Air-Conditioned Nightmare* (1945) that "the most masterful individual, the only person I met whom I could truly call 'a great soul,' was a quiet Hindu swami in Hollywood."[5] An erudite, scholarly man, "Swami P," as disciples often referred to him, published at least ten books of his own, including a widely read interpretation of the Sermon on the Mount that is still in print.[6] No doubt realizing that prominent authors would help him get his message out, he took full advantage of the talented scribes.

Heard and Huxley were eager to learn from a genuine representative of the Vedantic tradition and to receive personal guidance in meditation. That summer another celebrated British expatriate, Christopher Isherwood (1904–1986), joined them at the hilltop enclave. Isherwood had just published the collection of stories, set in Berlin, that would be adapted by John Van Druten as a stage play called *I Am a Camera*, which in turn would become the Broadway production and Oscar-winning film *Cabaret*. By 1947, largely through the persuasive Heard, so many artists and intellectuals had been drawn to Vedanta—among them Van Druten, who also wrote the play *I Remember Mama*—that the mystery writer Ellery Queen referred to it as a "western movement" with Heard as its "spiritual godfather."

As eager students and professional writers of the highest caliber, Heard, Huxley, and Isherwood brought intellectual rigor, a modern perspective, and stylistic grace to the literature of what was, at the time, a small, strange cult. From 1939 to 1941 Heard was coeditor with Prabhavananda of the society's journal, *Vedanta and the West*. He served as its editorial adviser from 1951 to 1962, contributing thirty-nine articles over the years. Huxley and Isherwood also wrote for the journal (the latter was editor for a time), and all three were featured, along with other distinguished contributors, in two highly popular mid-1940s anthologies, *Vedanta for Modern Man* and *Vedanta for the Western World*. Isherwood edited both books and supplied elegant introductions. (As mentioned, he also coauthored three classics with Prabhavananda.) The trio also gave well-attended talks at the center, which soon turned into a compound; devotees leased apartments in nearby buildings, and the property expanded to accommodate a convent and a monastery.

Prabhavananda outlived Heard and Huxley, passing away on July 4, 1976, the bicentennial of U.S. independence and seventy-four years to the day after Swami Vivekananda died. The enclave he created still exists, although its original serenity is somewhat compromised by the roaring 101 Freeway a stone's toss away.

An Evolving Consciousness

Of the three expatriates, Heard was the least celebrated, but he might have been the most prescient about Vedanta's importance for America's religious future. In a 1951 essay, he wrote that the system's "blend of empiricism with metaphysic, the width of its cosmology, the vastness of the picture which it gives of human destiny, and the immediate practicalness of its advices and practices—this amalgam seems most suitable to anyone who wants a method which is psychological and a world view that can match modern knowledge of the cosmos."[7] What form would Western Vedanta assume? Heard did not speculate, apparently content to let history determine "what are the actual essentials and what are merely matters of time and place, topical and local," issues still being worked out.

Heard was also by far the most dedicated practitioner of the trio. Although his speaking voice was broadcast quality and his style spellbinding—he lectured at major universities and appeared frequently on television—he was austere by nature and would probably have become a monk if he hadn't been so intent on chasing his curiosity wherever it led him. He took a personal vow of celibacy in 1934; John Roger Barrie, his official literary executor and son of Jay Michael Barrie, Heard's longtime assistant, says that the evidence suggests he kept it. More to the point, Heard pursued enlightenment with the rigor of the scientists he admired, meditating every day, often for as long as six hours.

In 1941 he had a brief falling-out with Swami Prabhavananda; the reasons are vague, but Heard seems to have felt that the swami's lifestyle, though certainly austere, was too comfortable to inspire followers who held monks to a higher standard. Heard may have succumbed to what would become a common error in the 1970s: expecting gurus to be perfect embodiments of purity and grace. Nonetheless, that same year Heard purchased about three hundred acres of dry, hilly land between L.A. and San Diego to establish a utopian community, called Trabuco College, that would combine the rigorous inquiry of a university with the spiritual discipline of a monastery. When the experiment petered out, Heard, having healed his rift with Prabhavananda, turned the facility over to the Vedanta Society in 1949. It remains the Ramakrishna Monastery to this day.

A devoted *sadhak* (yogic practitioner) to the end, Heard had his assistant, Barrie, read passages of *The Gospel of Sri Ramakrishna* to him every night after suffering a series of strokes beginning in 1966. He died in 1971, at eighty-one. One suspects that he would be surprised by the multifaceted, messy way his vision of a world-changing Western Vedanta has unfolded, but he would be pleased to know that his basic prescription, as summarized by Hal Bridges in *American Mysticism,* has proceeded apace:

that "man should now . . . further his psychical evolution by expanding his consciousness through yogic methods."[8]

From Berlin to Brahman

Why a boyish, openly gay chronicler of risqué Berlin between the wars was chosen to collaborate with Swami Prabhavananda on arguably the three most important books produced by the Vedanta Society is unclear, but a better choice could hardly be imagined. To the translations of the sacred works, Christopher Isherwood brought the artistic grace of a first-class novelist. In his introduction to the Gita, Huxley praises the book as "a version which can be read, not merely without that dull aesthetic pain inflicted by all too many English translations from the Sanskrit, but positively with enjoyment." That added bonus of aesthetic pleasure was supplied, no doubt, by Isherwood. He also made the commentaries accessible with the deft use of metaphor and a finely tuned awareness of postwar Western sensibilities.

Isherwood's motive for collaborating is easy to understand. As an "often backsliding disciple but always devoted friend" of Swami P's, working on the books enabled him to spend long periods of time with his guru, discussing the highest knowledge of the Vedas. To optimize the opportunity, Isherwood lived for a while in the monastery, working by day on screenwriting assignments at a Hollywood studio, which he described as "a spectacular example of the world of *maya*." The first of his collaborations with Swami P, *The Song of God: Bhagavad-Gita,* was called by *Time* magazine "a distinguished literary work." The absence of verse numbers and the exquisite mix of poetry and prose make it distinctive among Gita translations. The book has sold well over a million copies since its publication in 1944.

After moving to Santa Monica, Isherwood met with Prabhavananda at least once a week until the swami's death and remained a beloved presence at the Vedanta Society long afterward. All told, he contributed about forty articles to the society's journal, and his commitment to the teachings was mentioned frequently in reviews, profiles, and interviews. Right to the end (he died in 1986 at eighty-one), his literary output was replete with Vedantic themes. *Ramakrishna and His Disciples* (1965) is the most polished account of the legendary saint's life; the stylish memoir of his relationship with Prabhavananda, *My Guru and His Disciple* (1980), is a vivid portrait of a free-thinking, independent Westerner struggling with the traditional demands of discipleship. His epistolary novel, *A Meeting by the River* (1967), tells the story of two brothers, one a renunciate in an Indian ashram and the other a sensualist who tries to talk the swami-to-be out of taking his final vows. And *The World in the Evening* (1954) follows the aptly named Stephen Monk from a life of selfish indulgence to spiritual awakening. Its characters describe vivid inner experiences (a "consciousness that had no name, no face, no identity of any kind" and "knew no feelings, except the feeling of being itself"; "there's a source of life within me—and [I am] much more essentially in It than in I") that rank among the most felicitous descriptions of meditative states ever rendered in fiction.

The Perennial Philosopher

A Renaissance Man if there ever was one, Aldous Huxley had intellectual passions that ranged far and wide, from philosophy, politics, and religion, to the social sciences, the physical sciences, history, and the arts. Since his death in 1963, Huxley tributes have been offered on a regular basis, and Huxley conferences have been convened around the world. Through his work and his friendships, he affected vast numbers of people, some of whom were highly influential themselves. In this regard, he did as much as any other individual to introduce Vedanta to Western culture.

Like Heard and Isherwood, Huxley took formal initiation from Swami Prabhavananda, but he seems to have kept more emotional distance. Independent and free-thinking to the core, he was dismayed by his friends' devotionalism (although by the usual religious standards, neither was especially devotional); he understood that devotion to a personification of the infinite can be a legitimate path to oneness, but bhakti was not his path. As Dana Sawyer notes in his Huxley biography, he was "un-comfortable kowtowing to gurus and gods" and "felt it best to focus one's will directly on trying to connect with the oneness itself." Part of his great contribution, however, was to explain in his writings and public speeches why such issues can be regarded as matters of personality or choice.

The Huxley book most relevant to our topic is *The Perennial Philosophy*, which the *New York Times* called "the masterpiece of all anthologies." Published in 1944, the same year as the Isherwood-Prabhavananda Gita, it presented to a mass audience the idea, still debated by scholars, that the core truths in all mystical traditions are essentially the same, although the language and imagery with which they are expressed varies widely. Huxley describes the perennial philosophy as "the metaphysic that recognizes a divine Reality substantial to the world of things and lives and minds; the psychology that finds in the soul something similar to, or even identical with, divine Reality; the ethic that places man's final end in the knowledge of the immanent and transcendent Ground of all being."[9] He marshals as evidence a mountain of selections from the esoteric teachings of the great traditions. Huston Smith once wrote that Gerald Heard "converted Aldous Huxley from the cynical nihilism of his *Brave New World* to the mysticism of *The Perennial Philosophy*."[10] Indeed, anyone reading the two books back to back would find in the first a statement of humanity's affliction and in the second Huxley's prescribed remedy.

Scholars of religion have not always treated the book kindly. Some accuse Huxley of lacking rigor and of making unverifiable claims while ignoring the many differences among religious traditions. Supporters counter that Huxley was addressing only the mystical branches of the religions, and that he was not expounding a philosophy as such but rather highlighting the common features of a worldview rooted in transcendent experience. Be that as it may, the book was an instant hit, leaving thousands of readers exhilarated by the discovery of universal spiritual principles and introducing a large proportion of them to Eastern philosophy. It remains a must-read for students and seekers.

Huxley's Vedantic-perennialist outlook also came through in his later novels. In *Time Must Have a Stop* (1944), he describes a shift in a character's consciousness: "the little flame in his heart seemed to expand, as it were, and aspire, until it touched that other light beyond it and within; and for a moment it was still in the timeless intensity of a yearning that was also consummation." He also places in a character's notebook ideas that were previously published in the Vedanta Society's journal and would later appear in *The Perennial Philosophy*. His final novel, *Island* (1962), is a utopian counterweight to *Brave New World* set on a fictitious isle off the coast of India, where the citizens live in harmony with nature and use self-development practices drawn from psychology, Yoga, and psychopharmacology. "Everything went into the hopper," Huxley admitted. Published a year before the author's death, the book was lacerated by critics but sold well when it was discovered by the developing counterculture. Ram Dass reproduced a scene from *Island* in the last passage of his manifesto *Be Here Now*. One character whispers to another, who is dying, using a metaphor straight out of the Bhagavad Gita: "Let go of this poor old body. You don't need it anymore. Let it fall away from you. Leave it lying there like a pile of worn-out clothes . . . Go on, go on into the Light, into the peace, into the living peace of the Clear Light."[11]

Though he always maintained an association with the Vedanta Society, Huxley's insatiable curiosity and spiritual experimentation took him far afield. He shared a long, close friendship with the iconoclastic philosopher and erstwhile "World Teacher" Jiddu Krishnamurti, a connection that no doubt reinforced his aversion to organizations and doctrines. His interest in higher consciousness also led him to experiment with psychoactive drugs, as he recounted in *The Doors of Perception*. (The title, borrowed from a William Blake poem, was later appropriated by the rock band The Doors.) The book was published in 1954, that innocent time just before rock 'n' roll, when LSD was a little-known drug being administered legally by a small cadre of researchers. For Huxley, the drugs were in the same category as yogic practices: tools for spiritual growth, to be employed with discernment and restraint. He would no doubt have deplored the disregard for safety and sanity with which the "medicine" was used in the late 1960s, when his book was often cited in defense of the drug culture.

In *The Human Situation,* which was published posthumously, Huxley wrote, "There is no conflict between the mystical approach to religion and the scientific approach . . . You can practice mysticism entirely in psychological terms, and on the basis of a complete agnosticism in regard to the conceptual ideas of orthodox religion and yet come to knowledge—and the fruits of knowledge." No one was better positioned to make that argument to a wide audience. One measure of his reach, as Sawyer notes, is that news reports were interrupted by announcements of his death—on the day John F. Kennedy was assassinated! Perhaps an even better indication is this: Huxley was one of the cultural icons pictured on the cover of the Beatles' *Sgt. Pepper's Lonely Hearts Club Band.*

A Culture Hero's Journey

The East Coast equivalent of Swami Prabhavananda was Swami Nikhilananda (1895–1973). Well-educated, literate, and keen on transmitting Indian philosophy in accessible English, he had come to the United States in 1931 to assist the head of New York's Vedanta Society. After two years of institutional tension, Nikhilananda moved across Central Park and set up his own shop, the Ramakrishna-Vivekananda Center of New York, which he guided until his death. He also built a publishing enterprise centered on his own literary output.

In 1940 he found his equivalent of Christopher Isherwood, when a professor at Sarah Lawrence College came by to meet him. Joseph Campbell (1904–1987) was a popular teacher but not yet the world-famous interpreter of mythology and beloved media personality that he was destined to become. Over the winter of 1939–40, when the news was dominated by Hitler's advances in Europe, Campbell had read an Indian scripture translated by Nikhilananda. He wrote in his journal, "The important thing for me this year was not the war, but the discovery of the *Mandukya Upanishad.*"[12] It was not Campbell's first exposure to Vedic philosophy. He'd received a small dose of it as a youngster through the nineteenth-century German philosopher Arthur Schopenhauer. In his magnum opus,

The World as Will and Idea (1818), which Campbell compared to the *Man-dukya Upanishad,* Schopenhauer had predicted that "one day, India's wisdom will flow again on Europe and will totally transform our knowledge and thought." India certainly transformed the knowledge and thought of Joseph Campbell.

His first major exposure came in 1924, on a steamship voyage to Europe with his parents. He was an undergraduate at Columbia University, an eager student of medieval literature, a multi-instrumental jazz player, and a record-holding track star eager to witness the Olympic Games in Paris. (He had narrowly missed making the American team.) Also on board was the charismatic, brilliant twenty-nine-year-old Jiddu Krishnamurti, whose messiahlike destiny had not yet been announced (see chapter 3). The pair became close and enduring friends. Adding to the Eastern input, one of Krishnamurti's travel companions gave Campbell a book, *The Light of Asia,* Sir Edwin Arnold's portrayal of the life of Buddha.[13] When he read it, Campbell later said, "the fish was hooked."

Between Buddha and Krishnamurti, the voyage precipitated a reappraisal of religion and, in particular, the Roman Catholicism in which Campbell had been raised. It was "like a light going off in my head," Campbell said, confirming his belief in "the unity of the race of man, not only in its biology but also in its spiritual history." That theme of unity—what he called correspondences—would become the overarching leitmotif of his work, separating him from scholars who emphasized the obvious differences among religions.

Over the next five years, as he searched for meaning and vocation, Campbell attended some of Krishnamurti's lectures, exchanged letters with him, and spent time with him privately. "Campbell would never really be a disciple of Krishnamurti, or any other teacher," wrote his biographers Stephen and Robin Larsen, "but he would attest, in his journals and correspondence, to the importance of Krishnamurti's influence upon him as he was shaping his own course."[14] Although uncomfortable with the aura of perfection and infallibility surrounding his friend, Campbell wrote in a letter, "Every time I talk with Krishna something new amazes me."[15] Moreover, during this formative period, he received an indirect taste of

Indian philosophy when he met Fenwicke Holmes, who introduced him to his brother Ernest's book, *The Science of Mind*. It was, say the Larsens, Campbell's "first introduction to a version of what Aldous Huxley called the Perennial Philosophy."[16]

By the time he met Swami Nikhilananda, Campbell had absorbed a broad base of Eastern and Western philosophy, both on his own and in graduate schools in Paris and Munich, where he studied Sanskrit and Oriental studies. The swami was a whirlwind of teaching, translating, and writing, and what Campbell learned at his side informed much of his subsequent work. Among his early insights was that union with the transcendent source was beyond thoughts and words, but was nevertheless attainable. The Larsens called this "a credo by which Joseph Campbell found that he could live."[17]

Nikhilananda recruited Campbell to work with him on his translation of Sri Ramakrishna's conversations with disciples, written in Bengali by a devotee known simply as M.[18] Published in 1942 with a foreword by Aldous Huxley, *The Gospel of Sri Ramakrishna* was called "one of the world's most extraordinary religious documents" by *Time* magazine. The massive volume introduced thousands of Westerners to the unconventional holy man whom Campbell called "the folk-sage who refutes the philistines" and who "cut the hinges of the heavens and released the fountains of divine bliss." One of its readers was the celebrated composer Philip Glass, whose reading of it inspired a piece for orchestra and voices called "The Passion of Sri Ramakrishna."[19] For the rest of his celebrated career, Campbell would pepper his lectures and books with anecdotes from the saint's life.

Campbell became a mainstay of the Ramakrishna-Vivekananda Center, giving occasional talks, serving as president for a time, and working with Nikhilananda on other translations, notably a four-volume Upanishads. The swami and the scholar remained friends until the former's death in 1973, although their closeness—and Campbell's involvement with the center—diminished after their six-month trip to India in 1954. Like any number of Indophiles who have read first and visited second, Campbell was shocked to discover the disparity between the soaring idealism of the country's literature and the conditions of life in its heat and dust. The title of his published journal, *Baksheesh and Brahman,* says it all: the word *baksheesh* is equivalent to the English "tip" but more commonly means "bribe." Nor did he like Nikhilananda's indulgence of what he called the cult of the guru. But he also wrote glowingly of his encounters with two other spiritual teachers, Krishna Menon and the legendary female saint Ananda Mayi-Ma, and he did not let the reality on the ground shade his judgment of Vedic wisdom: "When you look at India from the outside it is a squalid mess and a haven of fakers; but when you look at it from the inside . . . it is an epiphany of the spirit."

Campbell was nearly fifty when he made that trip. In the years leading up to it, he deepened his understanding of East-West connections through two prominent Indologists: Ananda K. Coomaraswamy, the art historian, author, and curator of the Boston Museum of Fine Arts; and Heinrich Zimmer, who became an important mentor. A renowned art historian and mythologist who taught philosophy at Columbia, Zimmer helped the younger man crystallize what would become Campbell's life's work. "To bridge the abyss between science and religion, mind and body, East and West, with the timeless linkage of myths became his task of tasks," said Phil Cousineau, who worked with Campbell on a film and a book of interviews.[20] Cousineau compares that task to Einstein's pursuit of a unified field theory.

When Zimmer died suddenly in 1943, Campbell was asked to complete his mentor's four-volume series on Indian art and philosophy. The books helped to seal Campbell's reputation and enhanced his knowledge of Indian philosophy. Even more significant was his own first and most famous book, *The Hero with a Thousand Faces.* Published in 1949 and greeted with acclaim, *Hero* has been revered by generations of students and used resourcefully by biblical scholars, classicists, novelists, psychoanalysts, and artists like George Lucas, who structured the *Star Wars* plots based on Campbell's outline of the archetypal hero's journey. In the book, which covers the globe and ranges as far back in time as human records allow, Vedanta is evident in the many examples Campbell draws from Hindu and Buddhist literature—he devotes five full pages to Arjuna, the hero of the

Bhagavad Gita, for instance—as well as in its overarching unity-within-diversity viewpoint and its depiction of the hero as one who is transformed by direct communion with the sacred. Campbell concluded his preface with this: "As we are told in the *Vedas:* 'Truth is one, the sages speak of it by many names.'"[21]

Other books, like the four-volume *The Masks of God* (1959–68), followed, and as his fame grew, so did his reputation as a speaker. A witty raconteur with a gift for making esoteric ideas accessible, Campbell spoke everywhere from universities to the State Department to the Esalen Institute, and references to Indian scriptures, symbols, and tales were never far from his lips. One popular lecture series, delivered between 1958 and 1971 at Cooper Union in New York City, was turned into the book *Myths to Live By* (1972). "In the Orient," he explains in one chapter, "the ultimate divine mystery is sought beyond all human categories of thought and feeling, beyond names and forms, and absolutely beyond any such concept as of a merciful or wrathful personality, chooser of one people over another, comforter of folks who pray, and destroyer of those who do not."[22] In the same chapter, he outlines the four yogic pathways, tells the story of the god Shiva and his consort Parvati, and invokes the Upanishadic dictum *Tat Tvam Asi* (Thou art That), which he often used as a guiding motif.

When Campbell died in 1987, *Newsweek* wrote that he "has become one of the rarest of intellectuals in American life: a serious thinker who has been embraced by the popular culture." The reach of that embrace expanded immeasurably a year later when PBS broadcast six hours of his conversations with Bill Moyers. Called *The Power of Myth with Joseph Campbell,* the series and the book derived from it exposed millions of viewers to a new way of looking at religions and the stories they tell. Who knows how many people brought a different attitude to their next Easter Sunday because of passages like this: "The Christ in you doesn't die. The Christ in you survives death and resurrects. . . . Heaven and hell are within us, and all the gods are within us. This is the great realization of the Upanishads of India in the ninth century B.C. All the gods, all the heavens, all the worlds, are within us."

In the Moyers series, Campbell leaped over all boundaries of culture and time, but the Vedantic-Yogic perspective is present in his discussion of the chakra system of subtle energy centers and the kundalini force that rises through them; his explication of the sacred syllable *om;* his description of the symbols in the *Shiva Nataraja,* "the dancer whose dance is the universe"; his references to Indian deities and teaching stories; his quotes from Vedic texts; and his use of Sanskrit terms. It is also present in his depiction of myths as road maps of spiritual development, his portrayal of divinity as both with form and without form, and his insistence on the primacy of inner experience over belief. When Moyers calls him a man of faith, Campbell responds, "I don't have to have faith. I have experience."

Campbell would not have been pleased that one of his phrases, "Follow your bliss," was taken to mean "Do your thing" and bliss was confused with simply feeling good. He tells Moyers, "I came to this idea of bliss because in Sanskrit, which is the great spiritual language of the world, there are three terms that represent the brink, the jumping-off place to the ocean of transcendence: *sat-chit-ananda.* The word *sat* means 'being.' *Chit* means 'consciousness.' *Ananda* means 'bliss' or 'rapture.'" In other words, "follow your bliss" points to self-transcendence, not self-indulgence.

Toward the end of his life, the Larsens report, Campbell read the Bhagavad Gita every day. Others say that he kept a copy of the Upanishads in his hospital room.

The legion of people Campbell influenced includes: Jean Houston, a prolific author, founder of the Mystery School, and an adviser to UNICEF and, famously, to Hillary Clinton; the anthropologist, consultant, and popular seminar leader Angeles Arrien; the poet Robert Bly; transpersonal psychology pioneers Stanislav and Christina Grof; anthropologist-turned-Zen-teacher Joan Halifax; and countless others whose names are not well known but who have quietly affected many lives. "In the twenty years since Joe died," Cousineau told me, "I've received thousands of letters from artists, soldiers, policemen, Buddhists, Catholic nuns, rabbis, people of every imaginable persuasion, who say that Campbell enabled them to see their spiritual life in a new way." Directly and indirectly, he may have exposed more people to Vedic precepts than any other Western scholar, with the possible exception of his good friend Huston Smith.

The Man of Religions

In his foreword to Gerald Heard's *Pain, Sex and Time,* Huston Smith said that "the book in hand converted me from the scientific worldview (which takes the visible world to be the only world there is) to the vaster world of the mystics." It was 1943, and the scholar who would write the all-time bestselling book on comparative religion was a graduate student at Berkeley. Needing to do research on the subject of pain, he brought home some library books and turned first to the one with the provocative title. He read through the night and in the morning found that he was "living in a new world that has housed me ever since." Heard's premise was that humanity is on the brink of an evolutionary leap forward that will be guided by the insights of the mystics, whom Smith would later call "the advance scouts of mankind who have transcended their egos, and in exceptional cases, merged with God completely." Their spiritual technologies, he added, were practical means to achieve the "breakout" in human evolution that Heard predicted.[23]

I had the privilege of interviewing Smith in a stately sitting room at the Vedanta Society's Santa Barbara compound. He was eighty-eight and rather frail, and he had to be helped into a chair. Yet he seemed as bright-eyed and curious as a graduate student. My first query was, "How important was Vedanta in shaping your life's work?" His back straightened, and his voice rose to a robust exclamation point. "Immense!" he proclaimed.

He went on to say that, after reading *Pain, Sex and Time,* he made two promises to himself. One was to not read anything else by Heard until he had completed his Ph.D. The second was to then read *everything* Heard had written. After keeping both vows he hitchhiked to Southern California from Denver, where he'd begun his teaching career, and met with

Heard at Trabuco College. Heard introduced him to Aldous Huxley, with whom Smith enjoyed a long and fruitful friendship. *The Perennial Philosophy* became "my bible for the next ten years," he said.

At the time Smith was about to move to St. Louis to teach at Washington University. Either Huxley or Heard told him about Swami Satprakashananda, a learned scholar in that city whom other swamis consulted on translations and interpretations. As soon as he was settled, Smith sought out the St. Louis Vedanta Society, where he met the ochre-robed swami, who looks in photos like a well-tanned sibling of Harry S. Truman. That day Smith bought a copy of the *Katha Upanishad*. "I was overwhelmed in just two pages," he told me, "astonished by how much truth could be compressed into so few words. I was hooked."

He took up a meditation practice and probed deeply into Vedanta, meeting with Satprakashananda for tutorials virtually every week for ten straight years. When the center grew and was able to purchase a building of its own, Smith served as front man for the transaction, placing the deed in his name because someone—the owner, the realtors, or the city—refused to sell to a dark-skinned heathen like Satprakashananda. Vedanta provided a framework for understanding all religions, he said, and its delineation of different approaches to spiritual development for different personality types "came as a welcome revelation." So did the Vedantic elaborations on the dictum "Truth is one, sages call it variously," which, along with Huxley's book and various scholarly works made Smith what he called a "perennialist with a capital P." He maintained that stance through his decades as a revered educator, always distinguishing the exoteric aspects of religion (rituals, forms, behavioral codes, stories, etc.) from the esoteric (the innermost experiences resulting from spiritual practices). "Exoterically, they're very different," he summarizes, "but esoterically they are one."

Smith's first foray beyond the academy was a televised course called *The Religions of Man*, broadcast in 1955 by a St. Louis educational channel. About one hundred thousand viewers tuned in—a lot of eyes for a local public station at a time when *I Love Lucy* ruled the airwaves and comparative religion for most midwesterners meant Methodist versus Baptist. They were treated to the sight of a tall, lanky professor in a neat suit and tie, cheerfully clambering onto a desk, removing his shoes, and demonstrating the lotus position. The response was so strong that the series aired in twenty other cities and prompted Smith to write his now-classic book, *The Religions of Man* (later retitled *The World's Religions: Our Great Wisdom Traditions*).[24] Published by Harper in 1958, it still sells four thousand copies a month. It was, as Smith wrote, "a different kind of book on world religions," centering on "the *meaning* these religions carry for the lives of their adherents."

The book was a landmark. "To treat the religions as equals was unusual, since there tended to be a Christian or Western bias at the time," says Dana Sawyer, Smith's authorized biographer. "When they *were* treated as equals by academics it was as antiquated curiosities, all equally useless, not as relevant sources of wisdom." In the 1950s religion was treated as an anthropological curiosity in academia, Sawyer told me. "At the same time, Christian theologians were launching polemics about why other religions were theologically inferior. So, to take religion seriously, rather than deconstruct it out of existence, and to see them as equals was very unusual."

The book's description of Hinduism might have been heard in any Vedanta Society. Smith wrote it with the active guidance of Swami Satprakashananda, and his decision to place that chapter before those of other religions was probably not arbitrary; the Vedantic point of view sets the tone for the rest of the book. He highlights the notion that "the various major religions are alternate and relatively equal paths to the same God" with a classic Vedantic image: "It is possible to climb life's mountain from any side, but when the top is reached the pathways merge. As long as religions remain in the foothills of theology, ritual or church organization they may be far apart." The mountaintop, in this famous metaphor, represents the heights of union with the divine. The book's final two pages consist of a long excerpt from Sri Ramakrishna's teachings on the unity of religions, which Smith calls "Hinduism's finest voice on this matter."

In Smith's hands, as in Campbell's, the ancient and foreign become

fresh and relevant. The book was not only far ahead of the curve on pluralism and interfaith respect (values Smith demonstrated in his own long life,
as a Methodist and a Vedantin who also adopted Zen and Sufi practices)
but also in its use of terms like "states of consciousness" and in its reference to Yoga as "one of the most realistic, matter-of-fact, practical-minded
systems of thought and training ever set up by the human mind." This was
radical stuff in midcentury America, and its impact on how students and
ordinary people viewed India, Hinduism, and religion in general cannot
be exaggerated.

When I asked Smith how he would assess his own influence, he looked
as though he wished I hadn't asked. "I like the Vedantic statement that
the impact any human being has on history is like putting a finger in a
glass of water and taking it out," he said. But some fingers make a bigger
splash than others, and Huston Smith's have been tsunamic. His best-
known book has sold more than three million copies.[25] Other books of
his have had a substantial impact, notably *Forgotten Truth: The Primordial
Tradition* (1976), which states the case for the perennial philosophy, and
Why Religion Matters (2001), a passionate response to both fundamentalism and postmodern secularism.[26] Add to that the dozens of prefaces and
forewords to other books (including this one); the numerous chapters in
anthologies; the thousands of times he's been quoted by other authors; the
countless classes at Washington University, MIT, Syracuse, and Berkeley;
the guest lectures at dozens of other universities; the professional conferences and public events; the documentary films; and his guest appearances in the media, and it's no wonder the *Christian Science Monitor* called
him "religion's rock star."

One indication of Smith's fame, and his ability to unite worlds, is that
the New Age movement in the 1970s trotted him out as a reputable advocate of mysticism and unconventional religion—as did New Age *critics* because he warned against the promiscuous eclecticism of dilettantes,
comparing them to hungry people at a buffet who get too much of what
they want and not enough of what they need. That same balance was on
display in the hothouse of Cambridge in the early 1960s, when Smith par-
ticipated in the Leary-Alpert psychedelic experiment. "Entheogens" can

be of value in "a solid religious context of belief and responsibility," he proclaimed, but he deplored their careless and indiscriminate use. The point of spiritual experience, he pointed out repeatedly, is not altered states but altered *traits*.

The culmination of Smith's celebrity was the same forum that made his friend Joseph Campbell a household word: a five-part Bill Moyers series on PBS. In *The Wisdom of Faith with Huston Smith*, which aired in 1996, he discourses in endearingly personal terms on the world's religions. Of special note is a segment in which he speaks warmly of the decisive impact of Vedanta on his life and work. He recalls how, every year on Christmas Eve, he and his family would attend the four p.m. services at the Methodist church where he was an associate minister, then go home, have supper, and put the kids to bed, at which point he would head to the Vedanta Society for Swami Satprakashananda's annual talk, "Jesus Christ, the Light of the World." Smith loved the togetherness of his church community and the magic of Christmas. But, he tells Moyers, "when it came to spiritual depth, what the swami said about the incarnation fed my soul more than any Christmas sermon." He goes on to say, "I have drawn spiritual succor from an alien tradition, which however was true to the metaphysical teachings of original Christianity more than my church, which had been diluted by modernism."

Smith tells Moyers that the origin of *yoga* is the same as the English *yoke,* and its purpose is to yoke human spirit to ultimate spirit. He describes the eight limbs of Classical Yoga; he rises early every morning to practice, he says, because "it makes the days go better." He even demonstrates some masterful standing poses and a headstand. Extolling the spiritual emissaries from the East, who "are bringing an emphasis on experience and a method for attaining that," he concludes by noting that spirituality is ultimately beyond words, citing a Hindu prayer: "O Thou before whom all words recoil."

According to Dana Sawyer, Smith and Campbell agreed to a division of labor in which the latter would emphasize the power of myth and Smith would focus on the importance of transcendent experience. That he did. He stood up for the efficacy of deep religion in a secular age, illuminating lofty ideas and ancient texts for the masses. In his life and his work, he was, in the best sense, a Vedantist. When I asked him if that was an accurate statement, he said with a twinkle, "Yes, but not exclusively." And that too is rather Vedantic when you think about it.

The process by which the five men profiled in this chapter digested Vedic ideas, combined them with other sources and their own fresh insights, and passed them along to others would be repeated by many of the millions who read their works or heard them speak. Those who say they're indebted to one or all of them include some of the leading voices of progressive spirituality, among them Deepak Chopra, Ken Wilber, and Ram Dass. Like many popular intellectuals, they were never taken as seriously as they might have been in academia. But they were educators in a bigger way, and they understood that. Perhaps that is why all five were instrumental in establishing the Esalen Institute, whose seminars served as a prototype for the learning formats that helped to promote alternative spirituality in the West.

A more rational, unsentimental, worldly-wise quintet could scarcely be imagined. They issued no exhortations to convert or to take on faith what they said. They offered no sugarcoated pablum, made no inflated promises. They persuaded with reason, logic, evidence, and graceful prose. If American spirituality is better off because of the infusion of Indian philosophy, it is largely because those five chose to be spokespersons, each in his own way.

6

THE YOGI OF THE AUTOBIOGRAPHY

The passenger in the window seat spent most of the boarding process staring at the tarmac and gnawing her cuticles. When the plane started to taxi, she tightened her seat belt, clenched her jaw, and opened a paperback, clutching it so tightly that her fingertips drained of blood. On takeoff, she thrust her head forward and closed her eyes for a minute, as if in prayer. Then she continued reading. Her grip on the book obscured the title and the author's name, but I knew what it was from the light orange cover. Once we achieved flying altitude, she relaxed and closed the book. It was, as I had thought, *Autobiography of a Yogi* by Paramahansa Yogananda. She told me she had a pathological fear of flying, and the book got her through the takeoff.

Among the people I interviewed about their key spiritual influences, a high percentage named a book, and by far the book most often mentioned was Yogananda's unique memoir. A distant second was *Be Here Now* by Ram Dass, and he mentioned the *Autobiography*. My seatmate's use of it might have been unusual, but so many people have derived benefit from it that the Self-Realization Fellowship, which represents Yogananda's legacy, is justified in using the slogan "The Book That Changed the Lives of Millions." It has sold more than four million copies and counting, plus it has long been one of the most-borrowed books in spiritual circles.[1]

Aside from the presence of a genuine guru, nothing has made the allure of India and the promise of spiritual enlightenment as vivid as the five hundred pages of the *AY*, as devotees call it. Filled with miracle-making yogis and magical moments, the life story of the most influential Indian guru to settle in America is, for some readers, just a good yarn and an exotic travelogue. But for those with the heart of a seeker, it's an introduction to Vedic philosophy, yogic practices, and concepts such as karma, kundalini, and *siddhi* (extraordinary power). As the distinguished scholar W. Y. Evans-Wentz wrote in the preface, it is uniquely "a book about yogis, by a yogi."

The yogi of the autobiography was born Mukunda Lal Ghosh in the northern city of Gorakhpur in 1893, the year of Vivekananda's triumph in Chicago. His father, a railway company executive, provided handsomely and lived rather ascetically. His mother, who raised eight children, died at age thirty-six, when Mukunda, her fourth, was only eleven years old. Both parents were initiated disciples of a guru named Lahiri Mahasaya, who is said to have been empowered by Mahavatar Babaji, a legendary yogi alleged to be hundreds of years old and able to materialize at will for the good of humanity. Lahiri Mahasaya numbered among his followers Swami Sri Yukteswar, who would become Mukunda's guru. He met him shortly after finishing high school, and declared his wish to enter the monastic life. Sri Yukteswar told him to go to college, saying it would serve him well when he went to the West, as he was destined to do.

Mukunda spent more time at the ashram than he did at school but managed to graduate from Calcutta University in 1915. He was then initiated into a monastic lineage and given the name Swami Yogananda. (The honorific *Paramahansa*, literally "great swan," came later.) In 1917, when he was twenty-four, Yogananda founded a school for boys that combined modern education and traditional spiritual teachings. Three years later it was time to fulfill his predicted destiny, which, he tells us in the *AY*, was confirmed by a dramatic appearance by Babaji. With a generous check from his father and blessings from his guru, he sailed to America on a steamer and checked into a small, spartan room in a Boston YMCA.

The Coming of the Heathens

Between Vivekananda's departure and Yogananda's ascendancy, other proponents of Indian spirituality added contributions of their own, like the builders of minor structures surrounding the work of illustrious architects. Swami Rama Tirtha, a math-professor-turned-monk who called his message "practical Vedanta" and "a religion without a name," spent only two years in America, 1902–4, but attracted a number of followers, mainly in the Bay Area; his writings would inspire later gurus, notably Swami Sivananda (see chapter 10) and Yogananda, who translated some of Tirtha's poems from Bengali to English. Another 1902 arrival, a former journalist named Premananda Bharati, was the first guru to offer Americans a devotional form of Hinduism. Linked to the same lineage that would give us the Hare Krishna movement in the 1960s, Bharati stayed for nine years, teaching in New York and Los Angeles, and left behind a book, *Sri Krishna: The Lord of Love,* which was recently reissued. Perhaps the first teacher from India to promulgate Hatha Yoga for physical health, Shri Yogendra worked with New York medical researchers to establish the scientific credibility of the system; he stayed in the United States from 1919 to 1924, then carried on his Yoga research in Bombay.[2] But the best-known voice of India at the time was Rabindranath Tagore, the first Asian to win the Nobel Prize for literature. The great novelist, poet, and philosopher visited three times, attracting standing-room-only crowds on his 1916–17 lecture tour. With his erudite passion and his ability to blend Vedantic messages and poetic images, he did much to legitimize Indian philosophy in the minds of educated Americans.

Whereas Tagore was treated like an honored guest, the swamis and yogis drew a more ambiguous response. The success of the Vedanta Society, home to the most visible Indian teachers in the early twentieth century, triggered a predictable and often ludicrous backlash, mainly from Christian groups. A proper Bostonian named Sara Bull bequeathed money to the Vedanta Society, only to have a court nullify her will because the poor girl must have been duped by the inscrutable Orientals.[3] Panicky articles with titles like "American Women Going after Heathen Gods" and "A Hindu Apple for Modern Eve: The Cult of the Yogis Lures Women to Destruction" stoked fears of innocent women being seduced by dark-skinned pagans. In 1911 a widely circulated screed by one Mabel Potter Daggett, "The Heathen Invasion," argued that Yoga "leads to domestic infelicity, and insanity and death."[4]

In those days, the lurid fear of Asians—both bronze-skinned and yellow-skinned—was intertwined with jingoism toward all exotic foreigners, especially the tidal wave of immigrants from Italy and the Jewish ghettos of Eastern Europe. The nativist hysteria gave rise to immigration laws that prohibited Indians from becoming citizens and made it difficult for them even to visit. The legislation slowed the progress of American Veda until the mid-1960s, when reforms opened the gates to a fresh wave of gurus, not to mention millions of productive immigrants.

These early teachers, along with some American propagators (see chapter 10), added to the westward flow of Vedanta-Yoga, but they were minor tributaries compared to the long-running torrent that was Yogananda. He arrived three years after the First World War and taught through the Roaring Twenties, the Great Depression, the New Deal, World War II, the dawn of the Cold War, McCarthyism, and the Korean conflict. When his boat docked in Boston, America was a nation of trains, farmers, and newspapers; by the time he passed away, during Dwight D. Eisenhower's 1952 presidential campaign, it had become a nation of cars, consumers, and TV viewers. It had also become, in large part due to him, a culture ripe for a Vedic tidal wave.

Maiden Voyage

The impetus for Yogananda's journey was an invitation to speak in Boston on October 6, 1920, at the International Congress of Religious Liberals, a conference organized by the American Unitarian Association. His speech was called "The Science of Religion." It set the tone for his next three decades of work, and in many ways it summarized the message of most

Vedic emissaries. "In fluent English and with a forceful delivery he gave an address of a philosophical character," read the conference's official account. "Religion, he maintained, is universal and it is one. We cannot possibly universalize particular customs and conventions; but the common element in religion can be universalized, and we can ask all alike to follow and obey it."[5]

The following excerpt from Yogananda's published version of the speech captures the central points:

> If by religion we understand only practices, particular tenets, dogmas, customs, and conventions, then there may be grounds for the existence of so many religions. But if religion means primarily God-consciousness, or the realization of God both within and without, and secondarily a body of beliefs, tenets, and dogmas, then, strictly speaking, there is but one religion in the world, for there is but one God. In reality, God and man are one, and the separation is only apparent . . . As the sun's true image cannot be perceived in the surface of moving water, so the true blissful nature of the spiritual Self—the reflection of the Universal Spirit—cannot be understood, owing to the waves of disquietude that arise from identification of the self with the changing states of the body and mind.[6]

He used a minimum of Sanskrit and Hindu terms, referring to "centers," for instance, rather than chakras. The scientific Kriya Yoga of his lineage, he said, "consists of magnetizing the spinal column and the brain, which contain the seven main centers, with the result that the distributed life electricity is drawn back to the original centers of discharge and is experienced in the form of light," thus freeing up the "spiritual Self" from physical and mental distractions.[7] He also invoked the Bible, quoting Saint Paul and claiming that the "seven stars" in the Book of Revelation were actually the seven energy centers. This combination of scientific rationality and respect for the Judeo-Christian tradition would become hallmarks of his approach and were no doubt key to his success in winning minds and hearts.

Sea to Shining Sea

There could have been no more hospitable location for Yogananda's debut than the New England that birthed Transcendentalism, and he liked
it well enough to stick around. "Four happy years were spent in humble
circumstances in Boston," he wrote. It was the beginning of a love affair with America that lasted throughout his life. Walking around Beacon
Hill, shopping for his vegetarian meals at Haymarket Square, rolling over
the countryside in the Model Ts of well-heeled students, he came to love
the country's optimism and freedom of thought so much that in the *AY*
he quotes George Washington's Farewell Address and Walt Whitman's
"Hymn to America."

Following his debut at the religious congress, he gave his first public
lecture at Boston's Jordan Hall, followed by speeches at such prestigious
locations as Harvard University and the iconic Park Street Church, where
passionate abolitionists had preached. During that initial phase of his
ministry, he founded the Self-Realization Fellowship (SRF) to disseminate his teachings,[8] and he wrote the poems that were collected in the
book *Songs of the Soul*. This was the beginning of a prolific outpouring of
largely old-fashioned verse filled with nature imagery, praise to God, and
lots of *Thous* and *Thees*.

In November 1923 he ventured to a New York City booming with Pro-
hibition jazz and stock market fervor. Enthusiastic followers organized
events at Town Hall, the Waldorf Astoria, and other major venues and
introduced him to prominent people, including Margaret Woodrow Wilson, the daughter of the former president, who became his student.[9] In
1924 Yogananda set off on a transcontinental tour of virtually every sizable city, sometimes drawing thousands to talks such as "How the Teachings of India's Great Masters Can Help America." Ads described him as
"India's Great Saint and Savant, Poet, Psychologist, Educator who has
taken America by Storm." Among the dignitaries who became devotees
were George Eastman, founder of the Eastman Kodak Company; the
poet Edwin Markham; Leopold Stokowski, the renowned conductor of

the Philadelphia Orchestra; and Luther Burbank, the so-called Wizard of Horticulture, who transformed botany and grew so close to Yogananda that the *AY* was dedicated to him.[10]

On the Los Angeles tour stop, Yogananda dubbed the rapidly developing city "the Benares of America." Since nothing resembling the Ganges flows through the hot, dry town, he was presumably comparing its spiritual energy to that of India's holiest city. On January 13, 1925, eight days after his thirty-second birthday, he spoke at L.A.'s Philharmonic Auditorium on "Mastering the Subconscious by Superconsciousness." According to the *Los Angeles Times,* the three-thousand-seat hall was filled, and thousands were turned away. The article described the speaker as "a Hindu invading the United States to bring God in the midst of a Christian community, preaching the essence of Christian doctrine."

L.A. became his home, and a hilltop five miles from downtown became his movement's international headquarters. Purchased in 1925 with money from wealthy disciples, the twelve-acre property atop Mount Washington, formerly a resort, now houses a temple, administrative offices, a convent, and a monastery. The verdant grounds are landscaped with nooks and gazebos for contemplation, mango and pepper trees, and stately gardens. It was the first dividend for what must be the best real estate karma of any guru who came to America. In addition to that prime site, SRF owns a spacious temple on Sunset Boulevard in Hollywood; a clifftop hermitage with a magnificent view of the Pacific in Encinitas; the Hidden Valley ashram in the rolling hills north of San Diego; smaller temples in Pasadena, Fullerton, and other communities; and the crown jewel, the ten-acre Lake Shrine in Pacific Palisades, where some of Mahatma Gandhi's ashes are interred and tourists stroll around lush grounds with a waterfall, flower beds, tributes to the major religions, and swans gliding on a picturesque lake. Maybe Yogananda's personal mantra was "location, location, location."[11]

With the establishment of the Mother Center, the swami had property, offices, and a staff to deal with. He was now not just a teacher, but an executive; not just a spiritual leader but a manager. These Peter Principle add-ons have been the bane of many a guru and sometimes a fatal trap.

Yogananda seems to have handled them well, although he did write in his autobiography, "Sometimes (usually on the first of the month, when bills rolled in for the upkeep of Mount Washington Center . . .) I thought longingly of the simple peace of India. But daily I saw a widening understanding between West and East; my soul rejoiced." The East-West harmony he set out to further was not just about the material West meeting the spiritual East, although it was certainly that. He also defined it in provocative religious terms, claiming a dispensation to "reveal the complete harmony and basic oneness of original Christianity as taught by Jesus Christ and original Yoga as taught by Bhagavan Krishna; and to show that these principles of truth are the common scientific foundation of all true religions."

He spent much of the 1920s on the road, lecturing and teaching the techniques of Kriya Yoga to tens of thousands. The venues ranged from colleges and professional conferences to churches and synagogues to grand auditoriums like Boston's Symphony Hall and New York's Carnegie Hall, where he packed the house for a series of programs complete with chamber music. Some of his lecture titles suggest that he or someone around him was wise to the American psyche: "Everlasting Youth," "Science of Healing," and "The Science of Success and the Art of Getting What You Want." He was photographed with mayors and governors, and President Calvin Coolidge invited him to the White House for a chat. Under the headline SAGE SEES COOLIDGE, the *Washington Herald* reported that the president agreed with his guest that "it is only spiritual understanding between all nations that can bring lasting peace." By the end of the 1920s, he was by far the best-known representative of Indian spirituality in America.

Consolidation and Expansion

The decade that roared was a boundary-breaking burst of knowledge and innovation. The booming economy made everyone giddily optimistic. Automobiles and airplanes, radio and phones lines obliterated the barriers of time and distance; abstract painting, free verse, movies, and jazz shattered the conventional structures of art; quantum mechanics and relativity revealed a vision of the universe unfettered by time and space; Freud and his colleagues unveiled the shadowy realms beneath the conscious mind; standards of sexuality and gender roles were flaunted. The world was not what it appeared to be, and the old constraints no longer applied. But the surge of romantic idealism came to an abrupt halt with the stock market crash of 1929. It was a time that affected everyone, even monks.

In the 1930s Yogananda traveled less, leaving L.A. only for occasional public appearances. One was the World Fellowship of Faiths at the Chicago World's Fair; he spoke on September 10, 1933, one day shy of forty years from Vivekananda's debut in the same city. He also spent a year in India, where, again like Vivekananda, he was greeted as a conquering hero for his work in the West. For the most part, he focused on writing, solidifying and expanding his organization, and furthering the training of dedicated followers. "I am not interested in crowds," he said, "but in souls who are in earnest to know God."[12]

Toward that end SRF began publishing collections of Yogananda's talks, poems, and prayers in books like *Metaphysical Meditations* and *Whispers from Eternity*. Ministers were trained to perform pastoral services such as weddings, funerals, and counseling. The monastic order was established in 1931, becoming the focal point of leadership training. Perhaps most important, Yogananda found a way to bring his practical teachings to more people, using a new innovation: mail order. In an unprecedented departure from tradition, he converted the instructions he had been offering on a one-to-one basis, as gurus had always done, into a home-study course. A sequence of lessons promising "to recharge the body with energy, to awaken the mind's unlimited power, and to experience a deepening awareness of the Divine in one's life" would arrive in the mail at regular intervals (as they do to this day) with guidance on "the art of spiritual living," plus instructions for meditation, concentration, and "energization" practices. The Self-Realization Fellowship Lessons were the spiritual equivalent of the groundbreaking Sears Roebuck catalog, the Amazon.com of the era; both offered high-quality goods at affordable cost, with convenient, reliable delivery. The innovation was a prime factor in SRF's success.[13] The number of students, temples, and centers expanded steadily.

Yogananda was the face of Indian spirituality in America, but other teachers also made ripples in that era. In Chicago, Sri Deva Ram Sukul started the Applied Yoga Institute, and he too offered a correspondence course. Swami Omkar, a follower of Rama Tirtha, established centers in Philadelphia and L.A. Also based in L.A., Yogi Hari Rama taught classes and published a book titled *Yoga System of Study*. In New York, Kedarnath Das Gupta set up Dharma Mandala, emphasizing that "no one is required to renounce his particular form of religion to become a member." In the 1930s, the silent mystic and purported avatar Meher Baba made his initial tour; the British author Paul Brunton published an immensely popular account of his spiritual quest, *A Search in Secret India,* which introduced the legendary Ramana Maharshi; and gossip columnists linked celebrities like Cole Porter, Mae West, and Greta Garbo (who visited Yogananda with Leopold Stokowski) to the practice of Hatha Yoga. But as historian Carl T. Jackson put it, most Indian teachers "disappeared from view as suddenly as they appeared," whereas "as early as 1937 . . . Yogananda had initiated over 150,000 persons."

In 1946, as America was finding its footing as a superpower and the first wave of baby boomers took their first breaths, *Autobiography of a Yogi* was released. *Newsweek* said it was "rather an autobiography of the soul than that of the body," calling it "a fascinating and clearly annotated study of a religious way of life, ingeniously described in the lush style of the Orient." In 1950, SRF convened its first annual convocation, and that same week more than fifteen hundred people turned out for the opening of the Lake Shrine and Gandhi World Peace Memorial. In his dedication speech, Yogananda said, "This shrine is dedicated to all religions, that all may feel the unity of a common faith in the Fatherhood of God." It stands today as an urban oasis and a living advertisement for the Vedantic promise of serenity in the midst of everyday life.

Yogananda passed away on March 7, 1952, immediately after a banquet to honor the Indian ambassador. The official cause of death was "acute coronary occlusion." In his speech he said, "Somewhere between the two great civilizations of efficient America and spiritual India lies the answer for a model world civilization." He worked tirelessly to achieve that dream, leaving behind anointed successors, organizational structures, and instructions for the future of his teachings and publications.

Twenty days after the Paramahansa's death, Harry T. Rowe, the mortuary director at Forest Lawn, the famous resting place of Hollywood luminaries, sent a notarized letter to SRF. Quoted in newspapers at the time, the letter stated, "The absence of any visual signs of decay in the dead body of Yogananda offers the most extraordinary case in our experience." The complete letter is excerpted on a black-bordered page in the *AY*.[14] For Yogananda's devotees, of course, it stands as proof positive of his saintly status and the transformative power of yogic discipline.

The Secrets of Success

SRF continued to flourish after the passing of its charismatic founder, an accomplishment not always achieved by spiritual movements. It grew slowly through the 1950s and 1960s, then enjoyed a boom when the Beatles ignited interest in India and depicted Yogananda and his line of gurus with the other icons on the *Sgt. Pepper* cover. According to spokespersons, SRF now has more than 500 temples and centers in more than fifty countries. That's not counting the Yogoda Satsanga Society of India, which operates another 152 centers. To this day, Yogananda's name and autobiography are mentioned by celebrities in the media: Judy Collins on *60 Minutes;* Russell Simmons in his bestseller, *Do You!;* Andrew Weil, the natural medicine guru, who said, in an ad, that the book "inspired me to change my diet, meditate and pay attention to my spiritual well-being"; Mariel Hemingway on *Larry King Live;* and Madonna, when the material girl turned into a spiritual girl. Elvis Presley visited the Lake Shrine on occasion and popped up at SRF's Mother Center at least once in the late 1960s. Sister Daya Mata, the longtime SRF president, said about the occasion, "Here was someone who had everything the world could offer, [but] it didn't satisfy him . . . He was nourished in every other way, but where was the nourishment for his soul?"

Celebrities have helped put many spiritual movements on the map, but in SRF's case they were incidental. The real celeb was Yogananda himself, and his primary medium of exposure was his celebrated memoir. In the 1960s and 1970s that coral cover, with the then-unfamiliar word YOGI in big print and the author's long-haired visage with the knowing eyes and serene smile, was a fixture on brick-and-plank bookshelves and milk-carton end tables in counterculture living rooms. Copies circulated from one pad to another like flyers for an antiwar rally. Quite a number of the readers sent away for the Lessons, and some who became devotees are now the respectable elders in Yogananda-inspired communities. Their children and grandchildren have grown up in the tradition, reading the books, learning the practices, and maybe attending youth programs.

The book never stopped circulating, despite its anachronistic prose and the plethora of choices that grew like kudzu on the spirituality shelves of bookstores. According to SRF, sales have actually increased in each of the last ten years, averaging about 55,000 a year. Subscriptions to the Lessons have increased at a similar rate, they say—a notable achievement in an era when yogic practices are as easy to come by as running shoes. Yoga's trendiness, rather than cutting into the market for Yogananda's teachings, has probably helped. In Yoga studio gift shops, alongside the organic cotton shirts and sticky mats, you'll usually find some books, and one of them is likely to be the *AY*.

There are other reasons for SRF's enduring success, and they are worth exploring because they shed light on successful East-to-West transmission.

The Personal Touch

Anyone who's been in the presence of a genuine holy man or woman knows it can be a powerful experience. Such people exude a unique blend of serenity, compassion, knowingness, and magnetism that makes others want to be near them. That attraction can be fatal when the magnet is unscrupulous or exploitative. Yogananda seems to have had little of that dark side, and he served his followers for three full decades as a wisdom

source, vision holder, organizational architect, object of devotion, and—
perhaps most important—living exemplar of life in higher consciousness.
That he was active in America for over thirty years was a major reason for
the durability of his legacy.

The fine people who succeeded him would be the first to say that the
fall-off in stature was drastic. This is typical of a spiritual movement after
the departure of an illumined founder; like the clarity of radio signals as
the distance from the transmitter grows, the wisdom of the source di-
minishes with time. SRF's president following Yogananda's passing was
Rajarsi Janakananda (formerly James J. Lynn of Kansas City), who led the
organization for only four years before his death. His successor, Sri Daya
Mata, had been Faye Wright when she met Yogananda in Salt Lake City
in 1931 and joined his monastic order. Now in her nineties, she has led the
worldwide organization since cars had tailfins. She and a cadre of longtime disciples have been fierce guardians of Yogananda's legacy, always
keeping "Master," as they call him, in the forefront. Officially, Yogananda
is the last in his line of gurus.

Like the Ramakrishna-Vivekananda lineage, SRF has invested its primary leadership in monastics. This arrangement has advantages: ideally,
monastics are driven more by selfless service than by careerism; they are,
by definition, single-mindedly devoted to spirituality; and they are, by virtue of their vows, inclined to obedience. It also has its downside, as monks
and nuns can be hopelessly out of touch with the real-life concerns of
constituents. Be that as it may, SRF's monastic leaders differ from the Vedanta Society's in three key respects: first, they are Americans; second, the
organization is governed from Los Angeles, not Calcutta; and third, many
high-ranking positions, including the top one, are occupied by women. In
a radical departure from Hindu tradition, Yogananda placed women in
key administrative posts, and the SRF board of directors has always had
more women than men. Those factors have no doubt contributed to SRF's
skillful community building. Its annual convocation draws as many as six
thousand people to downtown L.A. for a week every August.

The sailing has not been entirely smooth by any means, and how well
the organization can adapt to future social conditions remains to be seen.

So far, by virtually any measure, it has made a successful transition after the ministry of its founder.

Natural Selection

Like all successful gurus who came west, Yogananda knew how to speak to the minds and hearts of the natives. Listening to his recordings, now available in digital form, one gets the impression of a gifted speaker who could be warm, intimate, and endearingly personal, and then, as if changing channels, let loose the soaring oratory of a nineteenth-century actor reading Milton. Also like other successful gurus, he maintained the integrity of traditional teachings but also adapted to the times: he invoked science at every opportunity, he broadcast radio talks when that medium was as new as the iPad is today, and he used up-to-date metaphors, comparing his "scientific" route to realization to an airplane ride, while presumably lesser approaches moved with the speed of a bullock cart.

Perhaps his most important adaptation to the West was his enthusiastic embrace of Jesus. While respect for the person of Jesus was common among gurus, Yogananda took it further. He reached out to clergy and believers of all faiths, but he gave Jesus an unparalleled place of honor. Christmas and Easter were not just occasions for a lecture; they were serious celebrations, highlighted by an eight-hour group meditation. He also used Western-style God language more than most yogis; most of his prayers would not seem out of place in a Protestant church.

More important, on every altar at a Yogananda facility you will see six portraits, in this order from left to right: Lahiri Mahasaya, Mahavatar Babaji, Jesus Christ, Lord Krishna, Yogananda, and Sri Yukteswar. In other words, Jesus is treated as part of a *sampradaya*, or teaching lineage. Cynics have argued that Yogananda was pandering to his market. But anyone who reads the *AY* or even glances at his massive, two-volume *The* *Second Coming of Christ*,[15] is bound to conclude that he believed it was his mission to revive "original Christianity."

The subtitle of *The Second Coming*, which was pulled together by SRF editors from everything Yogananda said or wrote about Jesus, is *The Resurrection of the Christ Within You*. What does that mean? "A thousand Christs sent to earth would not redeem its people unless they themselves became Christlike by purifying and expanding their individual consciousness to receive therein the second coming of the Christ Consciousness, as was manifested in Jesus." In true Vedantic fashion, he has Jesus calling for a transformation of consciousness, not belief in him. While much of what he says about Jesus would be considered poppycock, if not blasphemy, by mainstream pastors and theologians, they came as revelations to Christian seekers who had become disillusioned by, contemptuous of, or furious with their own churches. They found through Yogananda a way to forgiveness and reconnection. And an awful lot of Jewish Yogananda fans have made a similar passage from misconception, stereotype, or resentment to respect for the rebbe of Nazareth.

Ironically, some Jews and embittered Christians have found the featured role of Jesus to be an obstacle, although many eventually adjust. "When I turned to SRF, I was trying to get as far away from the Presbyterian Church as I could," one devotee told me. He's now happy to call himself a "Hinduterian," although he wishes SRF were more Hindu and less "terian." A former SRF nun who had attended strict Catholic schools confessed that she was never able to put the picture of Jesus on her private altar along with the other gurus. Another devotee, Lauren Landress, had a similar problem, having grown up in a secular Jewish home. "I had no problem with Krishna," she told me, "but Jesus was a struggle." After taking Yogananda as her guru, she prayed for two full years before she could finally place Jesus on her altar. She is now the head of publicity for SRF.

However one assesses Yogananda's interpretation of the Christ gospel, one thing is certain: his reverence for Jesus—along with the format of SRF's Sunday services, which are quite Protestant-like, right down to the collective prayer and the collection basket—was clearly a major reason for his acceptance in America.

Practice, Practice, Practice

As every Eastern tradition emphasizes, the menu is not the meal. Seekers want the tangible benefits that gurus and Yoga masters promise, and their personal transformations have made for great word-of-mouth marketing. For Greg Mooers, for instance, the transformation that initially impressed him was his mother's. "Basically, she had always been frenetic, and now she wasn't worried all the time," he recalled when we met in a shady nook at SRF's Lake Shrine. Still, he had been a skeptical engineering student, so he asked his mother for a book, intending to tear it apart with logic. She sent a collection of Yogananda's sayings. To his surprise, he says, "I didn't find anything to argue with."

Yogananda's recommendation to give his techniques a one-year trial period appealed to Mooer's scientific bent. He sent away for the SRF Lessons, applied them as instructed, and liked the results so much that he applied for the next step available to students who complete the 180 Lessons: initiation into the Kriya Yoga tradition, pledging their loyalty to the lineage and accepting Yogananda as their guru. (If you meet people who call themselves "kriyabans," it means they've taken that initiatory step.) A few years later, having built a successful artificial intelligence company but feeling trapped by life in the fast lane, Mooers dropped it all and moved into the SRF ashram. He left after eight years. Now married and living in L.A., he runs a company called LifeCamp, which utilizes principles he learned as a monk.[16] Like Mooers, hundreds of thousands of seekers have taken to Yogananda's teachings because they have improved their lives.

Overall, Yogananda's long tenure in this country, his personal charisma, his results-driven package of offerings, and his ability to appeal to both the secular and the religious made him what the *Los Angeles Times* called "the 20th century's first superstar guru." To one degree or another, the most successful gurus of the second half of the century shared those same qualities.

Shadows and Light

Yogananda's movement has not enjoyed uninterrupted peace and progress. During his lifetime he was subject to rumors and legal entanglements as one of the swarthy swamis targeted by guardians of morality. In 1928 he fled Miami, either because suspicious husbands filed suit or because he was threatened by a racist police chief, depending on your source. In 1939 a lawsuit filed in Los Angeles depicted the Mother Center as a virtual harem and the nuns as concubines. The plaintiff, a former disciple named Nerode Chowdhury, sued SRF for half a million dollars, claiming that Yogananda violated an agreement to make him a partner in his work. The case was thrown out of court by a judge who called the charges "slanderous and libelous." Even as late as 1995, a sixty-two-year-old man filed suit claiming that Yogananda was his father; in 2002 DNA evidence determined otherwise.

As for the organization he founded, SRF can boast of a high percentage of satisfied students. But like all spiritual institutions, it also has its share of critics, ranging from the mildly disappointed to virulent faultfinders, whose attacks sound like depositions in a bitter divorce. The latter group includes former monks and nuns, some of whose critiques need to be tempered by the understanding that very few are cut out for the demands of monasticism.[17] Some of the grievances seem relatively trivial, such as yawn-inducing services and a style of chanting that one Sunday regular calls "Lawrence Welk Hinduism." Other critiques have more serious implications, mostly centering on the monastic monopoly on authority. Terms like "groupthink" and "pressure to conform" are tossed about, as they are in most spiritual organizations, and many express the desire for more transparency and rank-and-file involvement. While SRF's monks and nuns are generally admired as knowledgeable and good-hearted, many members consider them out of touch with their worldly concerns. The organization has been called prissy, puritanical, and guilt-inducing because renunciation is considered a spiritually superior way of life. "Yogananda said his parents had sex only for procreation," one member complained, "and that's held up as an ideal."

That split between renunciation and worldly engagement is a common feature of Vedic organizations with monastic roots. Yogananda was a monk from a conservative time and place, so it's no surprise that SRF's lifestyle guidelines seem austere by modern standards. The result, I'm told, is that many students struggle with feelings of shame or spiritual inadequacy. For all these reasons, the monastic bias has troubled many SRF members.

I mention these issues here to introduce an important piece of the story: virtually every guru and institution from India has had to struggle with culture shock, disappointed followers, and organizational dysfunctions. Some of these difficulties are endemic to *all* spiritual organizations and to some extent secular ones as well; others are unique to Asian spiritual imports. Still, compared to many others, SRF appears to be a paragon of virtue and efficiency. Most disgruntled members stress that their grievances have no more bearing on the efficacy of Yogananda's teachings than complaints about a utility company demean the value of electricity.

The Spinoffs

So popular is Yogananda that various therapists, Yoga teachers, and gurus have attempted to establish their credibility by claiming a connection to him. Daniel Hart, for instance, uses Kriya Yoga techniques at his Yogoda Self-Help, an addiction recovery system in Phoenix, and Sri Goswami Kriyananda (né Melvin Higgins), founder of the Temple of Kriya Yoga in Chicago, says his guru, one Sri Shelliji, was Yogananda's disciple.

Two Indian teachers with verifiable connections to Yogananda and his lineage have made a mark in the West. Paramahamsa Hariharananda (1907–2002) was a disciple of Yogananda's guru, Sri Yukteswar, and ran one of Yogananda's Indian ashrams before striking out on his own in 1959. He visited America often beginning in 1975 and established the Kriya Yoga Institute in Homestead, Florida, which is now run by his successor, Paramahamsa Prajnanananda.[18] The second was Swami Premananda

(1903–95), who was summoned to America in 1928 by Yogananda and ran SRF's Washington, D.C., chapter. After Yogananda's death, he split with SRF and established the Self-Revelation Church of Absolute Monism in suburban Maryland. The facility, which also houses the Mahatma Gandhi Memorial Foundation, has been run since 1975 by an American woman, Srimati Kamala (formerly Sally Slack).[19]

The best-known Americans with links to Yogananda are a pair of direct disciples who met him in the late 1940s. Both have been teaching on their own for more than forty years and say they offer the same practices their guru authorized but in a different format from SRF's. The main difference is that one has had cordial relations with SRF, while the other has a history of antagonism and litigation.

Roy Eugene Davis, whom we met in chapter 3, was a teenager on an Ohio farm when he saw an ad for the AY in a fitness magazine. He read the book, ordered the Lessons, and in 1949, at age eighteen, hitchhiked to California. Two days after meeting Yogananda, he moved into the Mother Center, where he lived for four years. Davis, who never took final monastic vows, ran SRF's center in Phoenix for two years, then joined the military to gain some real-life experience. Upon his discharge, he started writing and lecturing on his own. In 1973, married with two children, he established the Center for Spiritual Awareness, an eleven-acre retreat in the wooded hills of Georgia. He's written a number of books, publishes a bimonthly journal, and continues to teach new students and work with initiates.[20]

Better known and more controversial than Davis, Swami Kriyananda (né Donald Walters) is a courtly man with the twinkle of an elder who has lived well and is still on the ball; the late John Gielgud would have played him to perfection. In 1948, at twenty-two, he read the AY and hopped a bus from New York to Los Angeles. Like Davis, he moved into the ashram right after meeting Yogananda. After being given unusual authority for a young monk, his relationship with some of his elders grew tense. He remained a leader after Yogananda's passing, at one point serving as an SRF vice president and board member, but in 1962 he was ordered to leave. SRF won't say exactly what prompted the ousting. Kriyananda says his burning desire to bring Yogananda's teachings to more people—which he understood to be "Master's" mission for him—did not sit well with officials, who accused him of being self-serving.

In his mid-thirties, while living in the Bay Area, he began getting invitations to speak and to perform devotional music.[21] One thing led to another, and in 1968 he built a spiritual community for householder devotees in the foothills of the Sierras, a venture he says was in line with Yogananda's intention to create "World Brotherhood Colonies." Ananda Village, on 840 acres of woods and meadows, is now home to about 250 residents.[22] It includes a tranquil retreat center called The Expanding Light and the Crystal Clarity publishing house, an outlet for Kriyananda and other Ananda authors and the distributor of Ananda's own version of the *AY*. (If you're browsing, theirs is the one with the periwinkle-blue cover and the spelling *Paramhansa* instead of *Paramahansa*.) Ananda promotes its version as Yogananda's original, asserting that SRF has made hundreds of changes to the classic; SRF says that the only changes were factual updates and those ordered by Yogananda before his death. The disagreement, details of which can be found on the Internet, is a minor chapter in a saga that stands as a classic example of the ruptures that can occur after the passing of a beloved guru.

While Ananda has endured (a rarity among intentional communities), life there has not always lived up to its name, which means "bliss," or as they translate it, "joy." From 1990 to 2002 the community was embroiled in an expensive legal battle with SRF as well as a sexual harassment suit filed by a former resident. The Ananda-SRF dispute centered on Ananda's use of terms such as *self-realization,* which SRF greeted as Disney would an animation studio using mouse ears in its logo. Listening to both sides, I felt as though I were watching the Japanese movie *Rashomon,* which depicts the same incident from different points of view. Each claims some degree of victory, and each portrays itself as a victim. (Interested readers will have no trouble finding details on the Internet.) Anyone who respects Yogananda's work can only hope that the organizations representing his legacy remain faithful to the teachings that have served Western seekers well for almost a century.

Ongoing Transmission

Yogananda's presence remains so vital that it is strange to remember that he died when Harry Truman was president and Jackie Robinson patrolled second base in Brooklyn. His impact will no doubt continue to be felt, through official teaching institutions, through the vast numbers of admirers who recommend his books and teachings, and through the many individuals whose lives have been touched by his work and who further his influence in their own ways.

As for the institutions representing Yogananda's legacy, they will no doubt thrive to the extent they can adapt to the coming generations of seekers while remaining faithful to their tradition. Schisms may well develop when Yogananda's direct disciples are gone. No matter what happens to the organizations, however, that iconic memoir will remain, whatever the color of its cover. While researching this book, I went to a gathering for one of the newer gurus visiting America. During a break I sat with four twenty-somethings and asked how they first became interested in Indian spirituality. Each of them had read *The Autobiography of a Yogi*. As a measure of how things have changed since people had to search high and low for the book, one of them had chanced upon a copy in a high school library in Kansas.

7

BLOWIN' IN THE WIND

The twenty or so years between the end of World War II and the volcano we call the Sixties are associated with conformity, materialism, suburbanization, songs of innocence, and gray flannel ennui. But beneath all that, a subterranean current was making the culture a fertile field for a bumper crop of gurus and Yoga masters. A vanguard was forging new directions in art, science, and the frontiers of thought. While the interstate highway system and the infrastructure for mass communication were being built, and jet planes and rockets soared into the sky, and African Americans began their march to equality, the same drive for expansion and freedom stirred the souls who blew bebop into jazz, shattered the structures of poetry and painting, and questioned received wisdom in philosophy, psychology, and religion.

In many ways, these developments represented a resumption of the boundary-breaking trends that had burst forth in the Roaring Twenties, only to be curtailed by depression and war. Now beatniks took over what bobby-soxers began, and they would soon give way to hippies. Ideas from the mystical East contributed quietly to these currents at first, but in 1967 they would surge onto the public stage like Niagara.

For most Americans, the living symbol of India was Mohandas K. Gandhi. The image of the abstemious, frail-looking man could not have been more different from that of mighty George Washington, which made it all the more awe-inspiring that he too led his nation to freedom from the British Empire. Gandhi's image had been appearing in newspapers and newsreels since the 1920s; it graced the cover of *Time* magazine three times, once when he was named *Time*'s Man of the Year.[1] Surely the average American knew the Mahatma was a religious man with Christ-like ideals, but only a few understood the Hindu roots of his nonviolent philosophy. Those who were curious about the source of his strength learned about Vedanta and perhaps even read the Bhagavad Gita, which seldom left Gandhi's side. Appreciation for that spiritual legacy would grow as the civil rights movement marched on and Martin Luther King's application of Gandhian tactics became better understood. (In 1959 King made what he called a pilgrimage to India.)

It is hard to know how many Americans thought of Gandhi strictly as a political figure as opposed to a spiritual one, but at the very least their respect for him made them more favorably disposed to other Indian ascetics. The two best known at the time were towering figures whose impact on America has been remarkably profound given that neither one ever set foot on the continent or lived to see 1951.

Deathless Spirit

For many in postwar America, the first exposure to a Gandhi-like figure came in 1949, when *Life* magazine printed a twelve-page feature titled "Holy Man."[2] The man was Sri Ramana Maharshi (1879–1950), the most revered saint in India at the time. The exquisite black-and-white photos of the seventy-year-old sage, with his clipped white hair and beard and what *Life* reporter Winthrop Sargeant called the look of "a superior human being" with "unshakable peace of mind," may have reminded readers of Gandhi, who had been assassinated sixteen months earlier. But Ramana was different. He was a living exemplar of an ancient archetype: the *jivamukti*, an enlightened being alive in the world. The pictures no doubt made a strong impression on many Americans. One was a twelve-year-old girl in Boston. "I had no clue as to who he was, but some transference of energy happened," said Lilias Folan. She would grow up to become the face of Yoga for millions through a string of books and a syndicated PBS series, *Lilias! Yoga and You,* which ran from 1972 to 1992.

The article's text was remarkably accurate about the variety and depth of Indian spirituality, and for good reason. Winthrop Sargeant was a journalist and music critic who would go on to publish one of the best translations and commentaries on the Bhagavad Gita.[3] "What the West calls theology," Sargeant wrote in *Life,* "has expanded in India to the proportions of a universal science." Of the Gita he said, "Seldom in the history of religion and philosophy has so much profundity been encompassed in a few pages," comparing it to the Sermon on the Mount. He also described the types of Yoga as different approaches to attaining "harmony with the eternal essence known as Brahman." Heady stuff for a mainstream magazine in the Truman era.

Some Westerners had read about Ramana before the *Life* article appeared, either in Yogananda's homage in the *Autobiography* or in British writer Paul Brunton's books, *A Search in Secret India* (1934) and *The Secret Path* (1935). They would have read that Venkataraman, as he was named, was born in 1879 to South Indian brahmin parents. At seventeen he was seized by an existential crisis that makes normal adolescent angst seem like just a bad dream. Overcome by the reality of inescapable death, he plunged into an inquiry that did not stop until he realized that, in his words, "the material body dies, but the spirit transcending it cannot be touched by death. I am therefore deathless spirit." Before long, he traveled to the temple city of Tiruvannamalai, where for many years he sat in silent meditation, in shrines, vermin-infested holes, and finally in caves on the slope of the sacred mountain—more of a large hill, really—called Arunachala. He became a living legend and something of a pilgrimage site himself. Eventually, responding to the equivalent of public demand, he started answering questions and writing poems, hymns, and commentaries on sacred texts. Virtually every word he spoke or wrote was made available in books (and now on the Web).[4] They constitute a crystalline rendering of Advaita Vedanta, returning again and again to the fundamental message, "Thou art That."

In time, an ashram was built at the foot of Arunachala. There the Bhagavan, as his disciples call him, held forth until his passing in 1950, while a constant parade of pilgrims came for his *darshan* (literally, "sight"; in common usage, the presence of a holy person). If they had suddenly stopped coming, one suspects that it would have affected Ramana no more than if a familiar squirrel were to stop appearing in a suburban backyard.

Thanks to Brunton's compelling descriptions, spiritually inquisitive Westerners began trekking to Tiruvannamalai even before the war, and the traffic picked up when peace was declared. One early visitor was the British novelist Somerset Maugham, who used the sage of Arunachala as the model for the fictional guru Shri Ganesha in *The Razor's Edge,* a widely read tale of an American seeker published in 1944. Brunton was probably the best-read Western author on Eastern spirituality at the time, but he stopped writing and lecturing in the 1950s to work on his own inner development. Some of the individuals he met in the course of his travels considered him their spiritual guide. One was Anthony Damiani, a Brooklynite who supported his wife and six children by selling subway tokens and taking tolls on the New York Thruway, jobs that afforded him time to read metaphysical books. Eventually he opened a small bookstore and study center near Cornell University, where up to a hundred students would gather. One of them, Paul Cash, told me that he and two other regulars founded Larson Publications to make available in book form about twenty thousand pages of Brunton's unpublished work as well as books by Damiani. (Brunton died in 1981; Damiani in 1984.)[5]

In such ways may a guru who never left India influence the West through the efforts of articulate followers. Another example involves a cross-cultural volley. In 1941 a twenty-eight-year-old Indian schoolteacher named Bhagawat Prasad Singh read a Hindi translation of Brunton. After studying journalism at the University of Iowa and working at the Indian embassy in Washington, D.C., he made his long-postponed pilgrimage to Ramana's ashram. There he met a British devotee named Arthur Osborne, the author of biographies of Ramana, who urged him to make the sage better known to Americans. Taking the name Arunachala Bhakta Bhagawat, Singh opened a temple in Queens, which still draws Ramana devotees long after its founder's death in 2000.

Ramana and his brand of Advaita Vedanta influenced a number of important disseminators of Indian spirituality, from the great Indologist Heinrich Zimmer and his student Joseph Campbell, to prolific commentators such as Georg Feuerstein, Ken Wilber, and Andrew Harvey. An alert reader will also find echoes of Arunachala in Eckhart Tolle's books, Ramana being one of the few sources the author acknowledges. The interesting cross-fertilization of Vedanta and contemplative Christianity also owes a lot to the Maharshi: the seminal Catholic mystic Thomas Merton wrote about him, as did the famous Christian sannyasis, Bede Griffiths and Dom Henri Le Saux (aka Swami Abhishiktananda), and more recently Francis X. Clooney, a Jesuit priest and Harvard professor, in *Hindu Wisdom for All God's Children.*[6]

Remarkably, Ramana is better known now than ever. Gatherings in his name are held regularly in living rooms throughout America. Some are peer-oriented and leaderless; others are run by teachers known as neo-Advaitans (see chapter 17). Meanwhile Tiruvannamalai, like Rishikesh up north, has become a mecca for seekers. Reservations for Sri Ramanasramam have to be made months in advance, and the nearby hotels are often filled. In 2008, as I waited to check into mine, I glanced at the bulletin board and felt as though I were in a New Age bookstore in California. There were flyers for all manner of workshops and *satsangs,* most of them led by Americans and Europeans.

Spiritual Evolution

It is hard to imagine a sophomore mistake having a bigger impact than the one Michael Murphy made in 1950, when the Stanford pre-med student walked into the wrong lecture hall. The chain of events that followed led, twelve years later, to the creation of the Esalen Institute. For many, the name Esalen conjures images of naked bodies in hot tubs, drug-fueled sexual abandon, and cathartic encounter groups—all to some extent accurate, but far from complete. Esalen became a forum for cutting-edge ideas about human potential, a cauldron for personal growth, and the mother church of America's "religion of no religion."

That last phrase was coined by the professor whose class young Murphy stumbled into, Frederic Spiegelberg. A specialist in Indic studies in Stanford's Department of Religion, Spiegelberg was a world-class scholar and an electrifying speaker. That day he spoke of Atman and Brahman, and his resonant voice reached something deep in Murphy. "I'll never be the same again," he thought on his way back to his frat house. He stayed in the course, and by semester's end, he said in our phone interview, "I was completely on fire." Of all that he heard and read, what stoked his ardor most was the evolutionary vision of Sri Aurobindo.

Born in Bengal in 1872, Aurobindo Ghose was educated in England and graduated from Kings College, Cambridge, where he absorbed Darwin and other modern ideas. He sailed back to his homeland in 1893, the same year Vivekananda went to Chicago, Yogananda was born, and Gandhi set sail for South Africa. After teaching for several years at a college, he got involved in the Indian independence movement, earning a reputation as a firebrand essayist and inspirational leader. He was the first political figure to publicly call for complete independence from foreign rule. Arrested twice for sedition and once for conspiracy, he spent more than a year in a British prison, using the time to meditate and study Vedantic texts. He went to jail as a Che Guevara and emerged as a Swami Vivekananda, who, he claimed, came to his cell and instructed him. The task, as he now saw it, was spiritual revolution.

Acquitted but still a marked man, he sailed down the Bay of Bengal to the French outpost of Pondicherry. As his stature as a teacher and thinker grew, an ashram took shape around him. In 1920 a Frenchwoman of Egyptian and Turkish descent named Mirra Alfassa became his partner and collaborator. Declared by Sri Aurobindo to be an incarnation of the Divine Mother, she was known as the Mother and remains to this day a focus of devotion. She took over the management of the ashram, freeing Sri Aurobindo to produce essays, poems, and books that were

astonishingly ahead of their time in their synthesis of Western science and
Vedantic scholarship.

Breathtaking in scope and vision, his body of work—most notably *The
Life Divine* and the epic poem *Savitri*—have inspired a veritable library
of commentary and analysis.[7] His "integral yoga," combining elements of
Karma, Bhakti, and Jnana Yogas, departed from the dominant mode of
his time by rejecting otherworldly renunciation. Its aim, he wrote, is "to
manifest the Divine here and create a divine life in Matter." Like all yogic
teachings, Sri Aurobindo's begins with the development of individual consciousness. But that was just his starting point. "Sri Aurobindo held that
the human race was by no means the final product of evolution," wrote
Karan Singh, the renowned Indian statesman and philosopher. "Rather
man today is an intermediate creature, halfway between the animal and
the divine consciousness . . . [W]ith the advent of the human race a species has emerged which is self-conscious and can therefore cooperate ac-
tively in the process of evolution." In short, through yogic disciplines, an
individual can advance not only his or her own evolution but that of the
universe itself.

Widely considered India's greatest modern philosopher, Sri Aurobindo
was also revered as a spiritual figure. On August 15, 1947, the day of India's official independence and his seventy-fifth birthday, he was asked to
address the nation. He spoke of his dreams. One was that "the spiritual
gift of India to the world" would be realized. Another was for "a step in
evolution which would raise man to a higher and larger consciousness."
No one devoted more energy to those tasks than he did. He passed away
in 1950, eight months after Ramana Maharshi. But his work in India was
advanced and expanded by the Mother, who lived until 1973. The Sri Aurobindo Ashram flourished, adding schools, athletics, arts, and other modern components. Westerners settled in Pondicherry to be part of it, and
in 1968 an international community took shape on an enormous swath of
undeveloped land separate from the ashram. Called Auroville, its intent
was to create "a universal township where men and women of all countries
are able to live in peace and progressive harmony, above all creeds, all poli-

tics and all nationalities." About two thousand people from forty countries live and work there now.[8]

Sri Aurobindo was transported to the West by Americans and Europeans who were enchanted by his writings and practiced what followers call "the Yoga." One of them was Michael Murphy. For a kid who once thought of becoming an Episcopal priest only to become "a classic teenage atheist," Vedantic philosophy was life-altering. He ditched pre-med and finished his degree largely through independent study with Spiegelberg. What turned him on most, as both a seeker and a social activist, was Sri Aurobindo's vision, which he described as "the divine disclosure through the course of time through evolution." After graduation Murphy devoted long hours to meditating and reading everything he could get his hands on, from the Eastern canon to Emerson to the Christian mystics. After a two-year army stint and a brief flirtation with graduate school, he took off for India, spending sixteen months at the Sri Aurobindo Ashram. Back home, his quest took him to San Francisco, which was fast becoming a hotbed of Eastern philosophy.

Golden Gates

The American Academy of Asian Studies (AAAS) was established in 1951 by a businessman named Louis Gainsborough. It was to be a graduate school for Eastern philosophy, religion, and culture, areas sorely neglected by universities at the time. The first scholar Gainsborough lined up was Frederic Spiegelberg. He in turn recruited two colleagues who would become prime disseminators of Asian wisdom. Dr. Haridas Chaudhuri, an Indian philosopher, had written his thesis on integral yoga and had been recommended by Sri Aurobindo himself. Chaudhuri soon started a separate organization, the Cultural Integration Fellowship (CIF), which was "devoted to the concepts of universal religion, cultural harmony, and creative self-unfoldment," with an emphasis on the teachings of Sri Aurobindo.

The second Spiegelberg recruit was the estimable Alan Watts (1915–1973). As a teenager in his native England, Watts had developed a strong interest in Buddhism, publishing his first book, *The Spirit of Zen,* in 1936 at age twenty-one. Two years later he moved to America, where he was ordained as an Episcopal priest and served as a chaplain at Northwestern University. In 1951, after the first of his three marriages had ended and he had given up the priesthood, he moved to the Bay Area at Spiegelberg's behest. At the time, San Francisco was to the West Coast what Greenwich Village was to the East, a bohemian mecca—just the sort of place where Watts's iconoclastic, eclectic, and decidedly nonascetic spirituality would flourish.

The Friday-night colloquia at AAAS, led by Watts, Spiegelberg, and Chaudhuri, drew huge crowds from the city's coffeehouse intelligentsia. Among the regulars were the young Beat poets—Allen Ginsberg, Gary Snyder, Michael McClure, Philip Whalen—who absorbed ideas that would find their way into their verse and, among other things, turn on the avant-garde to Eastern spirituality. The Beats were called poets of revolt, but as Ginsberg would later remark, theirs was a revolt of consciousness, not just of politics and social mores.

Watts ran AAAS until 1957, when, in his words, "It was becoming clear that I was as much out of place in the groves of academe as in the Church, that I was never, never going to be an organization man, and that I must make up my mind finally to go it alone."[9] He became perhaps the leading figure in the so-called San Francisco Renaissance of the 1960s and surely the best-known interpreter of Eastern philosophy in the West, thanks to his clever prose, captivating speaking style, and roguish personality. A rascal and a renegade who seemed to know and influence everyone, his ability to express esoteric concepts with wit and clarity made him a folk hero in the beat and hippie subcultures. While he was known primarily for his role in popularizing Zen, he did as much as anyone to elucidate Vedanta, after his friend and fellow Brit Aldous Huxley convinced him to study it. *The Book: On the Taboo Against Knowing Who You Are* (1966) was a succinct restatement of basic Vedanta. In the preface, Watts states his thesis: "The prevalent sensation of oneself as a separate ego enclosed in a bag of skin is a hallucination which accords neither with Western science nor with the experimental philosophy-religions of the East—in particular the central and germinal Vedanta philosophy of Hinduism."[10] His more than twenty-five books and hundreds of public radio broadcasts were devoured by both dilettantes and serious seekers long past his death in 1973—and to a surprising extent they still are.[11]

Other habitués of the AAAS and the CIF also went on to become important disseminators. Richard Hittleman, for instance, would pioneer the use of video to teach Hatha Yoga. His daily TV show, *Yoga for Health*, debuted in Los Angeles in 1961 and was later syndicated nationally. He published a book by the same title, followed by a host of others that have reportedly sold eight million copies. Another regular was Rama Jyoti Vernon, who went on to create the International Yoga College and to become not only a leading advocate for Yoga but an international peacemaker. And Michael Toms would create, along with his wife Justine, New Dimensions Radio, which is still an important voice for cutting-edge spirituality. They and a host of others were schooled by the scholars at the AAAS and the CIF, but not in a purely academic manner. "We were concerned with the practical transformation of human consciousness," said Watts, "with the actual living out of the Hindu, Buddhist, and Taoist ways of life at the level of high mysticism."

Also attending those classes was Michael Murphy. In 1951 he took up residence in the CIF's townhouse near Golden Gate Park to immerse himself in study and meditation. There he met a fellow Stanford grad named Richard Price, who responded well to the Aurobindo-inspired idea to create an institution, neither ashram nor university but something like both, for the free and open exploration of the Big Questions. Murphy thought he might have just the place: an undeveloped piece of heaven on the Big Sur coastline that belonged to his family. His grandmother, who controlled the property, turned him down; she feared he'd "give it to the Hindus." It took some time, but she eventually changed her mind in the hope that her grandson would clear the place of the grungy locals who had been sneaking onto the property to party in the natural hot springs. In a lovely historical irony, the Esalen Institute, which became known as a haven for hippie hedonism, started as an antidote to same.[12]

East Winds

While Murphy and Price were hatching their zeitgeist-shaping project, other Johnny Appleseeds were implanting Asian wisdom in American soil. Two important Zen Buddhists established footholds in the 1950s and were embraced by the emerging counterculture. The scholarly D. T. Suzuki taught at Columbia University from 1952 to 1957 and later spent time in the Bay Area. His books *Essays in Zen Buddhism* (1927–34) and *Introduction to Zen Buddhism* (1948, with a foreword by the great Swiss psychiatrist Carl Jung) were required reading for anyone interested in the subject. In 1959 Shunryu Suzuki (no relation) arrived from Japan and founded the San Francisco Zen Center, which became a magnet for seekers and remains (along with its retreat centers, Green Gulch and Tassajara) a fixture on the Bay Area spiritual scene. In 1970 this Suzuki published the classic *Zen Mind, Beginner's Mind.* The popularity of Zen made the culture even more receptive to Vedanta as another form of Asian nondualism.

In the mid-1950s, an Indian physician named Ramamurti S. Mishra began working at a Manhattan hospital and, in his spare time, founded the Yoga Society of New York. He later gave up medicine, changed his name to Shri Brahmananda Sarasvati, and opened the Ananda Ashram retreat center north of the city. The ashram, which still exists, attracted seekers from all over the Northeast.[13] Also arriving on the scene in those years were two important gurus who are discussed in forthcoming chapters: Swami Vishnudevananda, founder of the Sivananda Yoga Vedanta Centers, and Maharishi Mahesh Yogi, whose Transcendental Meditation would soon become a global phenomenon.

Also adding kindling to the Vedic bonfire that would erupt in the 1960s was the growing awareness of Hatha Yoga. During the Eisenhower era, Hollywood stars like Gary Cooper, Marlon Brando, and Marilyn Monroe were mentioned as practitioners in the press. (Gossip columnist Walter Winchell reported that Marilyn did it "to improve her legs.") One of the leading teachers was Bishnu Charan Ghosh, Yogananda's youngest brother, one of whose students, Bikram Choudhury, went on to create an empire of Yoga studios. (He is now busy turning Yoga asanas into a competitive sport.) Another prominent teacher, European-born Indra Devi, drew the likes of Gloria Swanson and Olivia de Havilland to her Los Angeles studio, and two of her students, Walt and Magaña Baptiste, opened San Francisco's first Yoga studio. The Baptistes went on to train future Yoga leaders, including their children, Sherry and Baron, and the aforementioned Rama Jyoti Vernon.

Books on Eastern teachings started to reach an ever-widening readership. In addition to authors published earlier, seekers now found illumination in Watts's early works *(The Way of Zen; Nature, Man, and Woman; Beat Zen, Square Zen, and Zen)*. The scholarly inclined may have found their way to *Yoga: Immortality and Freedom*, a 1954 book by the eminent Mircea Eliade. Also hitting the bookshelves were philosophical treatises and instruction manuals on Yoga, by the likes of Sir Paul Dukes, a British journalist and, by the bye, a secret agent *(Yoga for the Western World*, 1954); Theos Bernard *(Hindu Philosophy*, 1947; *Hatha Yoga*, 1950); and Indra Devi *(Yoga for You*, 1948; *Forever Young, Forever Healthy*, 1953).

These developments had created a groundswell for Eastern-oriented self-exploration by the time Michael Murphy and Richard Price were ready to launch their experiment in Big Sur. In 1962 the two innovators—the inner life's equivalent of, say, Apple's Steve Jobs and Steve Wozniak—took Sri Aurobindo's integralism one American bootstep further, bringing together East and West, mind and body, science and spirit, scholarship and art, individual and social, ancient past and unseen future. "Esalen began out of the founders' mutual involvement in Asian studies, coupled with Western social and psychological thought," stated an institute catalog. "If out of a chaos of events and programs Esalen strives for anything, it is the development of a sadhana appropriate for the West."

Seekers of personal growth, drawn in part by a landscape so breathtaking that if the workshops didn't get them closer to God, the scenery would, chose from among offerings whose variety belied an underlying coherence. The focal point was what Aldous Huxley termed "the human potential," and Esalen became the primary laboratory for its exploration. The brainpower listed in its early catalogs constitutes a who's who of cutting-edge thought, and virtually every one of them was influenced by Eastern philosophy: Huxley, Spiegelberg, Watts, Timothy Leary, Richard Alpert, Joseph Campbell, Huston Smith, Gerald Heard (with whom Murphy consulted in the planning stage). The faculty also included Abraham Maslow, Stanislov Grof, Anthony Sutich, and other revolutionary psychologists (see chapter 16).[14] Esalen's sublime setting was as conducive to diving into the mind and spirit as it was to sinking into the famous hot tubs.

Over the years, periodically surviving its predicted demise, Esalen has welcomed about ten thousand visitors a year to over twenty thousand workshops all told. Jeffrey Kripal, the author of a massive history of the institute, says that Esalen "holds a legitimate place in America's religious history and spiritual landscape, offering a kind of secular mysticism that is deeply conversant with democracy, religious pluralism, and modern science." He suggests that Esalen has been a sort of petri dish for a uniquely American Tantra, using Tantra in the sense of an embodied, in-the-world spirituality.[15]

Aurobindo's Legacy

Had Sri Aurobindo given nothing more to America than the inspiration for Esalen, his influence would have been profound. But his impact runs deeper. His books alone have been the primary spiritual references for thousands of seekers. Among the first was Judith Tyberg. A Californian who was raised in Theosophy and became a Sanskrit scholar, she learned about Aurobindo while studying in Benares and became a direct disciple with the guru-given name of Jyotipraya. She taught at the AAAS with Watts, Choudhuri, et al., and in 1953 founded the East-West Cultural Center in Los Angeles (now the Sri Aurobindo Center). Other centers, mostly in devotee living rooms, have since cropped up all over the country, some with interesting stories attached to them.

In postwar New York, for instance, Aurobindo salons were hosted by two society women, Eleanor Montgomery and Marjorie Spalding. Montgomery first heard of the sage when she read about a woman who got so

Engraving of Ralph
Waldo Emerson, 1846.
*Used with permission of the Joel
Myerson Collection of Nineteenth-
Century American Literature, Rare
Books and Special Collections,
University of South Carolina
Libraries*

Poster of Swami
Vivekananda at the 1893
World's Parliament of
Religions. *Used with permission
of the Vedanta Society of Southern
California*

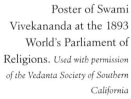

Swami Prabhavananda, Aldous Huxley, and Christopher Isherwood (portrait of Sri Ramakrishna on the wall) at the Hollywood Vedanta Society, circa 1940s. *Used with permission of the Vedanta Society of Southern California*

Ramana Maharshi, 1948. *Used with permission of the Sri Ramana Ashram Archives, Tiruvannamalai, India*

Paramahansa Yogananda, with *Autobiography of a Yogi*, 1949. *Courtesy of Self-Realization Fellowship, Los Angeles, California*

Sri Aurobindo and the
Mother, 1950.
*Photograph by Henri Cartier-
Bresson, copyright © Sri
Aurobindo Ashram Trust,
Pondicherry, India*

Louis Gainsborough,
Frederic Spiegelberg,
Judith Tyberg,
Haridas Chaudhuri,
and Alan Watts, at
the American
Academy of Asian
Studies, circa 1951.
*Courtesy of the California
Institute of Integral
Studies Archives*

Maharishi Mahesh Yogi with the Beatles and other meditators, Rishikesh, India, 1968. *Photograph by Deborah Jarvis*

Poster for Mantra Rock Dance at San Francisco's Avalon Ballroom, 1967. *Poster designed by Harvey Cohen, used with permission of Bhaktivedanta Book Trust International, Inc.*

Swami Muktananda hugging Fritjof Capra, with Christina and Stanislav Grof in the background, 1982. *Used with permission of Stanislav Grof*

Guru Maharaj Ji (Prem Rawat) arriving in the United States, 1971. *Copyright © The Prem Rawat Foundation*

Swami Satchidananda at Woodstock, 1969. *Copyright © Satchidananda Ashram-Yogaville/Integral Yoga Archives*

B.K.S. Iyengar in Switzerland, circa mid-1960s. *Used with permission of the Ramamani Iyengar Memorial Yoga Institute, Pune, India*

Neem Karoli Baba with devotees, circa 1971; *kirtan* artist Krishna Das at lower right. *Photograph by Balaram Das*

Ram Dass and Huston Smith at the Esalen Institute, circa late 1980s. *Photograph by Cynthia Johnson Bianchetta*

George Harrison and Ravi Shankar at the Esalen Institute, circa 1968. *Photograph by Paul Herbert, used with permission of the Esalen Institute*

Jiddu Krishnamurti and physicist David Bohm, 1984. *Photograph by Mary Zimbalist, copyright © Krishnamurti Foundation of America*

Shiva Nataraja statue at the European Organization for Nuclear Research (CERN), Geneva, Switzerland. *Photograph by Giovanni Chierico @ CERN 2004*

Mata Amritanandamayi (Amma) hugging a devotee in Los Angeles, 2001. *Photograph by Dave English, copyright © MA Center*

The author interviewing Sri Sri Ravi Shankar, 2007. *Photograph by Larry Nemkov, used with permission of William and Leslie Elkus*

absorbed in one of his books that she was locked in the New York Public Library overnight. That woman, who spent her last days in the Sri Aurobindo Ashram, was President Woodrow Wilson's daughter. Some years later two other New York devotees, Sam Spanier and Eric Hughes, created a retreat center called Matagiri (home of the Mother) upstate. Shortly after it opened, in the town of Woodstock, devotees coming to Sri Aurobindo's birthday celebration on August 15, 1969, fought a monumental traffic jam because hippies were trying to get to the music festival down the road.

Then there's the Boston center. Located in a small apartment a few blocks from Fenway Park, it was started in the late 1950s by an unlikely disciple named Mickey Finn. A thief and a heroin junkie, Finn was arrested fifty-three times, but was such a gifted con man that he served time only once. At one point he stole a book about Yoga from a library. His motivation? To sharpen his mind, so he could con educated rich people. When he was around forty, Mickey stumbled onto Sri Aurobindo. He flew to India, met the Mother, and promptly went straight. Driving a taxi to earn an honest living, he used his gift of gab to promote "the Yoga" to anyone in Boston who would listen. His widow, Angel, has carried on since his death in 1993.

Sri Aurobindo's prodigious intellect has made him a prime source of Eastern philosophy for leading thinkers, such as futurist Barbara Marx Hubbard, who sees his extension of evolutionary theory to consciousness as applicable to global problems. Aurobindo conferences are held annually in the United States and India, and some of the Bay Area's links to Pondicherry continue to thrive. The AAAS folded in 1968, but the CIF picked up the slack by creating an educational division called the California Institute of Asian Studies. In 1980 the name was changed to the California Institute of Integral Studies (CIIS), and its fully accredited undergraduate and graduate programs have become key settings for the integration of Eastern and Western disciplines, psychology in particular.[16] To cite one example, Brant Cortright, chair of the CIIS's counseling psychology program, draws heavily from Sri Aurobindo in examining psychotherapy from the lenses of Karma, Bhakti, and Jnana Yogas.[17] Given the scope of his ahead-of-its time output, Sri Aurobindo will likely be firing up young minds like Murphy's long into the future.

The JFK Years

The early 1960s were, on the surface, still very 1950s. But the torch of leadership had been passed to JFK's generation, and an even younger one, the baby boomers, was wading into its teenage years in uncharted waters. If any one word captures the era that was about to arrive, it would not be *protest* or *revolution* but *freedom*—freedom of expression, and freedom from poverty, bigotry, repression, and everything else that stifles the fullness of being human. This aligned with a basic property of Eastern spirituality: freedom to pursue one's spiritual goals on a path of one's choosing, and the promise of ultimate freedom in liberated awareness.

Oddly enough, the Catholic Church played a role in freeing American minds to explore Eastern ideas. The Ecumenical Council known as Vatican II lasted for three years (October 1962 to November 1965), during which time the church's bishops wrestled with how to align Christian doctrine with the rapidly changing modern world. While the meaning and implications of Rome's pronouncements are debated to this day, provocative statements from the Vatican, such as "religions to be found everywhere strive variously to answer the restless searchings of the human heart" and "many elements of sanctification and of truth are found outside its [the Church's] visible confines," undoubtedly freed open-minded Catholics to roam beyond the borders of received dogma. This crack in the stained glass led many to alternative interpretations of the Gospels and to their own tradition's long-buried esoterica (*literally* buried, in the case of the Gnostic parchments unearthed in Egypt in 1945). For inquisitive Catholics, many of whom were inspired by Trappist monk Thomas Merton's praise of Eastern teachings, Vatican II was like being given a passport stamped with an Asian entry visa.

At the other end of the religious spectrum, a cabal of rogue scientists and scholars in Cambridge, Massachusetts, made history of their own. In 1960 a Harvard psychologist named Timothy Leary ingested psychedelic mushrooms on a trip to Mexico. "I learned more about the mind, the brain, and its structures than I did in the preceding fifteen years as a diligent psychologist," he said of his four-hour trip. Among other things, he realized that "normal consciousness is one drop in an ocean of intelligence." He was not the first Western intellectual to sample mind-altering chemicals; Aldous Huxley had documented his own psychedelic experiences in *The Doors of Perception* in 1954, and serious researchers had been conducting studies on the substances for therapeutic use since the early 1950s. To build on that scientific enterprise, Leary devised experiments on the effects of psylocibin (he later switched to LSD) and enlisted the help of a colleague named Richard Alpert.

The experimenters experimented on themselves and invited others to join them. Allen Ginsberg hopped aboard, as did Huxley, Smith, Watts, and lesser-known adventurers like psychologist Ralph Metzner and a Harvard undergrad named Andrew Weil, now America's best-known proponent of integrative medicine. Two factions emerged: those who advocated caution and restraint with this atom bomb of the psyche, and those who wanted to turn on the world. Leary and Alpert were in the latter group, and when they were dismissed by Harvard in 1963, they became the Butch Cassidy and Sundance Kid of the psychedelic era.

The outlaw pair became counterculture icons and, to authorities, a menace to society. Richard Nixon dubbed Leary "the most dangerous man in America." To the dismay of serious researchers, the furor led the government to ban the experimental use of LSD, but personal use could not be squelched. Psychedelics threw open the gates of consciousness to the transcendent, raising the question, What is going on here? People like Huxley and Smith, who were well versed in spiritual literature, saw resonance in the drugless mysticism of the East.[18]

Acid heads combed libraries for books on Asian mysticism, and some set their sights on getting to Mother India herself. After reading a few books and thinking they were the next Alan Watts, some anointed themselves gurus. Most of them disappeared without approaching Andy Warhol's allotted fifteen minutes of fame. But at least one deserves mention. Stephen Gaskin had already crossed the Maginot Line of trust by turning thirty. Perhaps because of that extra maturity, he recognized early that LSD could scramble minds as well as expand them, and he found alternatives in the mystical East. His English classes at San Francisco State College evolved into far-ranging dialogues, and after his dismissal from the school, they morphed into his legendary Monday Night Class at the Family Dog, a spacious dance hall. At its peak, Gaskin's free (in more ways than one) neo-Tantric-yogic-Buddhist talks drew over a thousand people. Many of them have been quietly propagating Vedic ideas ever since.[19]

The desire to understand the expansion of consciousness, and to find ways to produce it safely and reliably, led in 1967 to Alpert's trip to India and his metamorphosis into the spiritual leader Ram Dass (see chapter 12). The broad strokes of that journey were recapitulated in the lives of hundreds of thousands of coming-of-age baby boomers as the 1960s, the decade, evolved into the Sixties, the phenomenon.

The Times Were a Changin'

In 1965 major announcements from President Lyndon B. Johnson came with the frequency of Sandy Koufax strikeouts: bombing raids on North Vietnam escalated; the draft call-up doubled; antipoverty programs were created; Medicare and the Voting Rights Act were passed into law. With monumental events like those taking place, it is small wonder that LBJ's signing of the Hart-Cellar Act at the foot of the Statue of Liberty is seldom remembered. But by revising a quota system that had effectively kept Asians out since 1924, the immigration bill turned Lady Liberty's beacon toward the East. It not only opened the door to millions of future citizens, it also made it easier for spiritual teachers to come and stay.

Some of the prominent gurus we'll meet in the coming chapters arrived around that time. So did several whose influence was smaller but still noteworthy, such as Eknath Easwaran. A professor of English in India,

Easwaran came to the Bay Area on a Fulbright in 1959 and returned in 1965. His talks on Vedic philosophy began to attract people, including the American woman he married. He went on to establish the Blue Mountain Center of Meditation in Berkeley and publish a number of books.[20]

As the decade progressed, the appetite for Indian spirituality grew stronger among trendsetting boomers, who were catching the spirit of Romanticism that had animated the Transcendentalists a century earlier: the urge to get back to nature; to find one's soul through art and music and unmediated mysticism; to celebrate the body and at the same time transcend it. Now it was amplified by electric guitars and fueled by affluence and cheap gasoline. Like all Romantics, they called into question conventional religious beliefs and cultural assumptions. And as family ties and communal mores lost their grip, the search for answers grew more intense.

In fact, religious doubt was not confined to the young. A large segment of American society was questioning what they had been taught about God. The April 8, 1966, cover of Time magazine—perhaps the most famous cover in the magazine's history—consisted of a three-word question, in bloodred, against an all-black background.[21] The question was: IS GOD DEAD? To true believers, it was blasphemy. To atheists and secularists, it was the death knell for religion, confirming that the relentless march of rationality and science had finally crushed the last vestiges of faith. In fact, the article said no such thing, as the question mark in the headline indicated. The text describes a struggle to redefine God and find new ways to express the timeless urge to know the infinite. "The new approaches to the problem of God," said Time, may, among other possibilities, "lead to a more realistic, and somewhat more abstract, conception of God."

To a growing number of individuals, religious debate was not just a matter for theologians. The modern zeitgeist made the personal spiritual quest an imperative, and the East's approach to what theologian Paul Tillich called "the ground of being" seemed more compatible with science and secularism than with conventional religion. Among other things, it did not require God language, with all its untenable anthropomorphic connotations. What was called mysticism seemed less mysterious than a church sermon: no virgin births, resurrections, or sea-parting miracles were required.

By the summer of 1966, the emerging counterculture had begun to acquire the distinct aroma of sandalwood incense and patchouli oil. One could chant with Hare Krishnas in the street. Places to learn Yoga and meditation were becoming easy to find. And Eastern-themed books to suit anyone's taste were being passed around dorms and crash pads and low-rent districts. Among the gotta-read authors were Watts, Huxley, and Yogananda. Books on nondual Buddhism, like Philip Kapleau's *The Three Pillars of Zen* and Paul Reps's *Zen Flesh, Zen Bones,* made the rounds, along with sacred texts such as the Bhagavad Gita, the *Dhammapada,* and especially the *Tao Te Ching,* with its implied endorsement of go-with-the-flow spontaneity and other hippie ideals. New books on Yoga appeared: the journalist Jess Stearn's *Yoga, Youth, and Reincarnation* (1968), a part-memoir, part-instruction manual, would remain highly popular for years; and B.K.S. Iyengar, whose Hatha Yoga system would become arguably the most influential in the West, introduced himself with *Light on Yoga,* which is still a standard manual.[22] Intellectual types were drawn to the scholars of mysticism Rudolf Otto and Evelyn Underhill, or to Krishnamurti, or Carl Jung, or Abraham Maslow, whose *Toward a Psychology of Being* introduced concepts like "peak experience" and "self-actualization" into the lexicon.[23] Lovers of fiction devoured classics like Hermann Hesse's *Siddhartha* and Somerset Maugham's *The Razor's Edge,* and new works such as J. D. Salinger's post–*Catcher in the Rye* stories, with their explicit references to Vedanta and Buddhism (see chapter 15).

Indian ambiance reverberated from record players too. Having discovered the sitar on the set of *Help!* George Harrison introduced the instrument on "Norwegian Wood," on the Beatles' *Rubber Soul* album. Its hypnotic drone came to define the psychedelic subculture as the tenor sax defined jazz. The rockers who dabbled in the sitar were derided as amateurish by aficionados of classical Indian music, but its popularity called attention to a genuine virtuoso with deep spiritual roots: Ravi Shankar. The maestro's sold-out concerts, and his revelatory set at the 1967 Monterey Pop Festival, which was also the climax of the concert movie *Monterey*

Pop, moved thousands to explore the spiritual tradition that had birthed music that was at once serene, exuberantly free, and transcendent. Even Jimi Hendrix got into the act; the cover of his 1967 album, *Axis: Bold as Love,* depicts him and his bandmates amid a pantheon of Hindu deities.

The generational torch was passed from the Beats to the hippies at the Human Be-In on January 14, 1967, which drew some twenty thousand to San Francisco's Golden Gate Park.[24] Billed as "A Gathering of the Tribes," the event had decidedly Indian overtones, thanks in large part to the ubiquitous Allen Ginsberg. Although he was primarily identified with Buddhism, Ginsberg had spent fifteen months in India earlier in the decade, visiting ashrams, meeting gurus, and hanging out with Bengali poets.[25] His Bhakti (devotional) Yoga found expression in Vedic chanting. Throughout that period, the media frequently displayed images of the counterculture's poet laureate dancing with the Hare Krishnas, intoning *om* to pacify political rallies, and chanting mantras at flower power gatherings.[26] That morning he and Gary Snyder circumambulated the gathering space in a traditional Hindu ritual. As the day progressed, he could be seen chanting Sanskrit mantras in what seemed to be a perpetual state of joyful astonishment, as young people in Indian fabrics, blousy shirts, and billowy skirts danced and sang and played on Indian and Western instruments—that is, when they weren't grooving to the Grateful Dead and the Jefferson Airplane.

Among the featured speakers were the Pied Pipers of acid, Timothy Leary and Richard Alpert. Leary, wearing a string of heavy beads and a yellow flower in the graying hair above each ear, issued his clarion call to "turn on, tune in, drop out," and it was easier to do the first of those than to find a water fountain. The celebration resumed a few months later in the famous and infamous Summer of Love. By now a hundred Americans a week were dying in Vietnam, and riots were erupting in Newark and Detroit, and the need for a new kind of consciousness had never been more obvious. As the Beatles sang on the sitar-drenched "Within You Without You"—released that summer on the seminal *Sgt. Pepper* album—"With our love we could save the world" and it's "all within yourself."

As summer began, the San Francisco air was as thick with hope as it was with marijuana smoke. But as the days grew shorter and the breezes blew cooler through Haight-Ashbury, the dark side of flower power became more and more evident. Streets and clinics were filled with strung-out hippies who looked more like casualties than merry jesters, a turnabout captured by a *Mad* magazine cover depicting a zoned-out, flower-haired Alfred E. Neuman and the phrase "Turn On, Tune In, Drop Dead." In that context, finding a way to expand one's mind without endangering life and limb started to seem pretty attractive.

To the shock of many, authentic exponents of Eastern wisdom re-inforced that notion. The gurus who had appeared on the scene—A. C. Bhaktivedanta Swami of the Hare Krishnas and Swami Satchidananda of the Integral Yoga Institute—were uniformly antidrug. So was Ravi Shan-kar, who was viewed as some combination of Charlie Parker and Buddha. At a concert I attended in 1967, the sitar master told a packed theater that he was dismayed to learn they were coming to his performances stoned. Drugs are pollutants, he said. Better to come with clean, clear senses. In the stunned silence, you could practically hear a thousand brains thinking, *Bummer!*

By the fall of 1967, a lot of young people were hungry for nonchemical, nondropout ways to expand their minds. As word spread that the Beatles had found one, attention turned to London. Spirituality in the West would never be the same.

8

MAHA MASS MEDIA

In August 1967 Maharishi Mahesh Yogi gave a public lecture at the Hilton Hotel in London. It was probably the most consequential public event by an Indian spiritual teacher in the West since Vivekananda in 1893—not so much for what was said but for who was in attendance. In the overflow crowd were three lads named John, Paul, and George. After meeting Maharishi backstage, the Beatles said they were eager to learn the guru's Transcendental Meditation (TM) technique.[1]

They were primed for that moment by the same forces described in chapter 7. When I interviewed Donovan, the Pan-like folk rocker and Sixties megastar, he recalled what had led him and his friends, the Beatles, to Maharishi. Dressed like an elegant gentleman in a dark blazer and a mock turtleneck—although his hair was as long as it was in 1968—he sipped tea in the rooftop café of his L.A. hotel and reeled off his early influences: Kerouac, Zen, the *I Ching,* Huxley, the Celtic mystics and English bards, and Yogananda's autobiography. He and George Harrison had read voraciously, he said, posing cosmic questions to one another and talking about consciousness, especially after George studied sitar with Ravi Shankar and delved into yogic texts. "We were aware of the need for meditation," said Donovan. "The only thing missing was the initiation. Where do we do it and how do we do it? We needed a guide."

Two days after meeting Maharishi, the Beatles, now completed by

Ringo, along with Mick Jagger, Marianne Faithfull, and others, boarded a train for Wales and a ten-day course with Maharishi. On both ends of the trip, the station was crammed with reporters, photographers, police, and fans. The media backed off while the group settled in and received their mantras and meditation instructions. Then the idyll was shattered. Brian Epstein, the group's manager, had died of a drug overdose. Dazed and distraught, the Beatles rushed back to London, facing the press with their usual aplomb. In footage that was seen around the world (and that can now be seen on YouTube), John said Maharishi told them "not to get overwhelmed by grief, and whatever thoughts we have of Brian, to keep them happy, because any thoughts we have of him will travel to him, wherever he is." He added, "Meditation gives you confidence enough to withstand something like this." George, already the metaphysical Beatle, said, "There's no such thing as death anyway. I mean, it's death on a physical level, but life goes on everywhere, and you just keep going really."[2] For youngsters who hung on every word a Beatle uttered, there could have been no more compelling introduction to Eastern spirituality.

Throughout that fall, the face of "the giggling guru," with his long black hair and full beard with a white chin patch that added a touch of Santa, stared out from posters on campuses and telephone poles, and the media reminded everyone that the Beatles had ditched LSD in favor of meditation. David Frost devoted two of his popular TV talk shows to the subject, with guests John and George. Thanks to meditation, said John, "I'm a better person, and I wasn't bad before."[3] George echoed one of Maharishi's key messages: meditators don't have to change their lifestyles or renounce material wealth. "It's just that this gives them some spiritual wealth to go with it." In the tabloid *Daily Sketch* John said, "You can make it with meditation if you're a Christian, a Mohammedan or a Jew. You just add meditation to whatever religion you've got." When told that journalist Malcolm Muggeridge, an outspoken Christian, had raised concerns about TM, he replied bluntly, "The Maharishi is a completely happy man. Malcolm Muggeridge isn't." It's easy to imagine a chorus of youngsters shouting "Right on!"

The steady tip-tap of TM references spread around the world, turning

into a drumroll the following winter, when the Beatles flew off to Maharishi's ashram in Rishikesh, India, accompanied by Mia Farrow, Donovan,
and the Beach Boys' Mike Love. What could be more intriguing than
celebrities who had everything and could go anywhere deciding to sit
with their eyes closed for several hours a day? George explained, telling
the press: "For every human, it is a quest to find the answer as to 'Why
are we here? Who am I? Where did I come from? Where am I going?'
That, to me, became the only important thing in my life. Everything else
is secondary."

For the youth market, this was the gold standard in endorsements.
Gretchen Woelfle, an American who had gone to "Swinging London" a year
earlier, when she graduated from Berkeley, thought, "If meditation is good
enough for John Lennon, it's good enough for me." In outfits purchased
for the occasion at the Apple Studios clothing store—brightly colored bell-
bottoms with a floral design; satin shirts with billowing sleeves—she and
her flatmate, a Swarthmore grad, skipped down to the TM center, an elegant townhouse in a posh neighborhood. To their surprise, they were
greeted not by fellow hippies but by the proper, middle-aged men and
women who were Maharishi's earliest followers. Undeterred, they signed
up for the course. So did thousands of others in North America and Europe, including refugees from the Summer of Love, who plucked the flowers from their hair and offered them up in the five-minute ceremony *(puja)*
that precedes TM instruction. Among the other advantages of finding
bliss through meditation instead of drugs, Kurt Vonnegut Jr. quipped in
Esquire magazine, was that "the fuzz can't bust you."[4]

The Making of a *Rishi*

The man who came to be known as Maharishi Mahesh Yogi was born
Mahesh Prasad Varma in either 1917 or 1918, in a village near the Central
Indian city of Jabalpur.[5] Some say his family was of the *kshatriya* (warrior)
caste, although the lineage was *kayasth,* a sort of subcaste of scribes and
administrators.[6] Not much is known of Mahesh's childhood except that

he was sharp enough to earn admission to Allahabad University, where he majored in, or perhaps only took courses in, physics. His familiarity with modern science became one of his chief assets in the West.

While in college, Mahesh heard that a saint named Swami Brahmananda Saraswati was in the area. He went to the ashram where the swami was staying, "as a thirsty man arrives at a well."[7] When he declared that he wished to become his disciple, the man he would call Guru Dev (the term means "divine teacher" but has been mistaken for a proper name) told him to first finish school. By the time he graduated and was formally accepted as a *chela* (disciple), his guru had been persuaded, at age seventy, to fill the long-vacant seat of Shankaracharya of Jyotir Math, heading a monastic lineage established centuries earlier by the philosopher-saint Shankara.[8]

As Bal Brahmachari Mahesh,[9] the future Maharishi served his master for thirteen years as a clerk and all-around organizer. After Brahmananda Saraswati passed away in 1953, Mahesh lived in Himalayan seclusion for some time before traveling to South India to visit sacred sites. In Trivandrum, a stranger asked him to give a public talk. Before long he was touring the country as a "loudspeaker" for his guru. In 1955, at a religious festival in the state of Kerala, he was first referred to as Maharishi—*rishi* meaning "sage" and *maha*, for "great." The appellation stuck. In late 1957 he announced to a crowd of ten to twenty thousand people in Madras—reportedly without having contemplated it in advance—a program to "regenerate spiritually the whole world with meditation."

In the written record of his early talks, one can see that Maharishi shared with Vivekananda and Yogananda more than a Western-style education, fluency in English, and an astrological sign. (His birthday, January 12, was also Vivekananda's; Yogananda's was January 5.) These were his central points:

- *India needs to revive its spiritual tradition:* "This spirituality tends to be ignored today in the heat of the modern currents and Western ideologies. If India is to become strong and great, let her not sleep over spirituality, the science of the very motive force of existence."
- *Spiritual development is for everyone, not just renunciates:* "Caste, creed

or nationality is no hurdle . . . every body has every right to enjoy permanent peace, Bliss Eternal, which is the nature of his own soul."

- *Vedanta is compatible with science:* "Now if we are able to conceive that the whole material universe is nothing but formless energy, then it is easy to conceive, on similar lines, that all this concrete universe is nothing but the Abstract Formless Brahman."[10]

The same sources also reveal two features that made Maharishi's approach distinctive: a laserlike focus on meditation, which he considered the most important component of the yogic repertoire, and an insistence that meditation is so simple and natural that anyone can derive benefit from it. In modern parlance, he was branding the technique that came to be called TM.[11]

After teaching six months in the South, Maharishi later said, he calculated that it would take two hundred years to enlighten the world at the rate he was going. The solution was to head to the United States, "the most advanced country," where people "would try something new very readily." Once they did, he reasoned, the rest of the world, including his homeland, would take notice. En route to California, he stopped in Honolulu and ended up in the YMCA for a month, teaching his first Western students. The *Honolulu Star-Bulletin* noted that the yogi with "puppy eyes" and "no money" claimed that "meditation leads to blissful peace and happiness," and "the glare of material life is further brightened by the glow of inner self." That was the basic message he carried to the mainland. His meditation was both a means for secular self-improvement and a jet plane to enlightenment—an upgrade of Yogananda's airplane metaphor.

The *Ozzie and Harriet* Years

Maharishi's movement took root in Los Angeles, but it wasn't hipsters who gravitated to him at first. His earliest supporters, drawn by invitations from friends or small ads in local newspapers, were citizens of *Ozzie and Harriet*'s America—clean-shaven dads with neat haircuts and good jobs, and apron-wearing moms who supervised nuclear families in homes equipped with the latest appliances. But underneath the straight-laced exteriors beat the hearts of spiritual adventurers, and the charmer from the East inspired a zeal to promote his work. Among them were one celebrity, Efrem Zimbalist Jr., the star of the popular TV series 77 *Sunset Strip,* and prominent citizens with the time and resources to make things happen. Socialite Nancy Cooke de Herrera, for instance, got Maharishi into the press and introduced him to tobacco heiress Doris Duke, who put up the cash for the ashram that the Beatles would make famous.[12]

Maharishi made steady inroads, teaching meditation to ten here and twenty there as he circled the globe annually, going to new places and returning to old ones where friends of satisfied meditators awaited him. His insistence that meditation was easy came as a surprise to most seekers, since the practice was thought to require exceptional powers of concentration. This was not a marketing ploy; it was a statement about the nature of the mind. Like a bumblebee in search of nectar, Maharishi contended, the mind restlessly seeks satisfaction. But we mistakenly direct that urge outside ourselves, to sources of happiness that are, without exception, fleeting. What the sages counseled, he said, was not to control the mind but to nudge it gently inward, toward the inexhaustible bliss of the supreme Self, and that is what his technique did. TM caught on slowly and steadily. Those who wished to learn it either waited for Maharishi to return or were instructed by the one American he had trained as an "initiator," San Diego resident Beulah Smith.

By 1965 TM centers had opened in many world capitals, and Maharishi had published two books, *The Science of Being and Art of Living* and his commentary on the first six chapters of the Bhagavad Gita.[13] Then the movement stumbled upon a ripe new constituency: college students. Ninety million Americans, almost half the population, were under twenty-five at the time, and whatever captured their fancy reverberated throughout society. By tapping into the youth market, TM would do for Indian spirituality what rock 'n' roll had done for the record industry.

The campus campaign was led by Jerry Jarvis, who was half a generation younger than most of Maharishi's followers and half a generation older than college students. Jarvis and his wife Debby were both former reporters who had learned TM in 1961. An articulate speaker with a calm demeanor and a cherubic smile, he had been delivering lectures, mostly in living rooms, reading from a script written by Maharishi. Now, as the word spread on California campuses, the groups grew larger. By 1966 the Students International Meditation Society (SIMS) had branches at Berkeley, Harvard, Yale, and other schools, and its national offices near UCLA became the administrative engine of the TM movement.

Within You Without Drugs

Like saplings in a dreary forest, disaffected youngsters bent toward the light of the East, with cutting-edge artists leading the way. Following the Beatles' lead, other rockers—members of the Jefferson Airplane, the Beach Boys, and the Grateful Dead (reportedly, Maharishi suggested they switch to Grateful Living)—followed suit, making meditation hipper by the day. (Three of the four Doors had jumped the gun two years earlier.)[14] When classes resumed in the fall of 1967, SIMS was a busy place indeed. Feature articles on the campus craze appeared in outlets large and small. One, in *The Village Voice* (November 9, 1967), stands out as a signpost of the times. The front-page lead, "What's New in America? Maharishi & Meditation," dropped the names of meditating rock artists and opined that "with 2,000 students waiting anxiously in Berkeley for their introductory lectures and initiation, it looks now that Maharishi may become more popular than the Beatles." The reporter worried that meditative bliss might lead people away from political protest, a common concern among activists. Sharing the front page was a profile of filmmaker Conrad Rooks and his guru, Swami Satchidananda. It was written by a respected young reporter named Sally Kempton, who would, in the coming years, become initiated into the Siddha Yoga lineage as Swami Durgananda.

A cover story in the *New York Times* Sunday magazine, titled "Chief Guru of the Western World" (December 17, 1967), prompted the TM movement to hastily arrange a couple of East Coast appearances for

Maharishi. The first drew a capacity crowd of 3,600 to the Felt Forum at New York's Madison Square Garden; the second, with Mia Farrow in the front row, packed Harvard's Sanders Hall on a frigid weekday evening. The events triggered a burst of saturated hoopla that a publicist would kill for. Print coverage of the Garden lecture, which went nationwide if not world-wide, cited highlights from the talk: everyone can live "two hundred per-cent of life" (100 percent spiritual, 100 percent material); if one percent of the population meditated, it would "dispel the clouds of war for thousands of years."[15] At a VIP gathering at the Plaza Hotel, Allen Ginsberg, ever the provocateur, gave the coverage some juice by chastising Maharishi for putting down psychedelics. "There wouldn't be all these people sitting around here listening to you if it wasn't for LSD," the poet railed. He also busted him for not taking a stand against the Vietnam War. According to a newspaper account, the guru demurred: "Many young people ask me, should they go to the army and fight or not. I say meditate, try some yoga. But if I were young I would not participate in mass murder."

"Amen to that," said Ginsberg, concluding the argument with a melodi-ous "Om."[16]

The mother lode was two nationally televised interviews, one with Johnny Carson on *The Tonight Show* and one with Joe Garagiola on *To-day*. Likely no spiritual teacher, except perhaps the pope or Billy Gra-ham, had ever been heard by that many Americans at once. Sitting on his customary deerskin and gesturing with a flower as if it were a pointer, Maharishi showed a national audience that Indian holy men could have a sense of humor and speak in the modern idiom. In his form of medita-tion, he explained in his cheery, high-pitched voice, the mind "travels from the grosser state of thought to the subtle state of thought, to the subtler and subtlest state of thought till it arrives at the source of thought," at which point "the conscious mind gains the state of bliss consciousness, or transcendental consciousness, or pure consciousness." Probably very few viewers understood what he was talking about. But the words, "more ener-getic," "more productive," and "happier" no doubt registered, and citizens concerned about wars and riots were at least intrigued by the statement "If we want to change the world, we must change the individual."

After Harvard, Maharishi flew straight to India, on the same plane as Mia and her sister Prudence (soon to be immortalized by the Beatles' song "Dear Prudence"), and the world's press was on their heels.

Here Comes the Hurdy-Gurdy Man

The rich and famous had helped spread Indian spirituality since the days of Emerson, but this was of another order of magnitude. It was the Beatles, after all, not the Dave Clark Five. Yogananda had had Luther Burbank and Leopold Stokowski, but he would have needed Albert Einstein and Judy Garland to match the wattage of Mia and the Fab Four, and even then he would not have had television to beam their images to the masses. Headlines screamed "Hippies Flock to Maharishi," "Beauty and the Yogi," and "Indian Priest Casts Hypnotic Spell: Mia Lured Away from Frank" (Sinatra, that is, from whom the media's favorite gamine had just separated).

Pre-cable and pre-Internet, a story in a national magazine was *maha* exposure, and Maharishi had several of them. *Life*'s article hyping the "Year of the Guru" hit the stands just as the Beatles arrived in the holy city of Rishikesh.[17] It focused on the celebrity meditators, of course, but it also quoted the Bhagavad Gita and offered a definition of Vedanta. A companion piece by Jane Howard reported that parents of meditating youngsters are "brought around when they see how much their kids have changed." TM, she concluded, "may be the most wholesome mystique to attract a youthful following since . . . the Boy Scout movement." Druggies got clean; slackers got serious about schoolwork; drifters settled down; the sullen got friendly; the estranged got along with their families. Worried adults can overlook a lot of weirdness when they see such changes in their children.

That same week, *Look*'s cover showed a bright-eyed, clean-cut cluster of Yale meditators.[18] The article, accompanied by a photo essay by jazz flutist Paul Horn, about his time in India with Maharishi, was titled "The Non-Drug Turn-On Hits Campus." The reporter, William Hedgepeth, concluded that TM was "compatible with living in the modern world" (a relief, no doubt, to adults who feared that their sons and daughters might drop out) and that its sudden popularity is "part of what some believe is an evolutionary social development: the practice of 'turning on' without drugs in order to expand the conscious mind into new realms of awareness." Maharishi, he said, "couldn't have come at a better time."

The image of a bearded man in white flowing garments, sitting cross-legged, and smiling as though amused by all the fuss, now became the symbol of guruhood. It cropped up everywhere, in films, photos, cartoons, and caricatures, sometimes with respect and sometimes with ridicule.[19] For the most part, the media blitz was surprisingly positive. The predominant message was that poverty-stricken India had something to offer the prosperous West. At the same time, there was also a loud and energetic backlash from across the cultural spectrum. Christian preachers saw the young being diverted from the true path of salvation. Hindu purists accused Maharishi of watering down the tradition and "selling mantras."[20] To political conservatives, meditation was another way for escapists to drop out and leech off society. Lefties thought their ground troops were being lured to some spiritual neverland. Law enforcement suspected that Maharishi was a cult leader ripping off the gullible.

Asked to explain the appeal of the East, social scientists theorized about alienation and the breakdown of tradition, family, and community. Few of the commentators took the Occam's razor approach of accepting the simplest explanation, the one offered by meditators themselves: they wanted to change their lives from the inside. As theorist of religion Harry Oldmeadow wrote, "The interest in Eastern spirituality met some deep yearning for a *vision of reality* deeper, richer, more adequate, more attuned to the fullness of human experience, than the impoverished world view offered by a scientifically-grounded humanism."[21]

Meanwhile a battalion of photographers and reporters invaded Rishikesh, some of them perching in trees like the monkeys that populate the Himalayan foothills. The ashram staff tried to keep the compound undisturbed, but reports filtered out on a regular basis, raising interest in meditation even more and fueling rumors that persist to this day. Ringo and his wife Maureen left after ten days, reportedly because the drummer's tummy couldn't handle the food; Paul and his girlfriend Jane Asher stayed for two months, telling reporters that "the meditation is great"; and two weeks later John and George, wives in tow, left angrily because they'd heard that Maharishi was hitting on women, probably Mia, who had bolted from the scene earlier. The always-candid John recorded his displeasure in "Sexy Sadie," whose original lyrics, "Maharishi, what have you done . . . ," were changed for either ethical or legal reasons. For the rest of Maharishi's days, even in his obituaries, journalists could hardly mention his name without referring to the incident, more often than not assuming that the allegations were true.

For the record, no evidence of hanky-panky has ever surfaced. Mia wrote in her memoir, *What Falls Away,* that her state of mind was so tenuous that she freaked out when Maharishi went to touch her after a private meditation session, and "if Jesus Christ Himself had embraced me, I would have misinterpreted it." Cynthia Lennon wrote that a member of the Beatles' entourage named Magic Alex had plied John and George with lurid stories "without a single thread of evidence or justification." According to reports, George visited Maharishi in 1992 and apologized for his and his mates' behavior. People who were present in Rishikesh told me they wished Maharishi had not relaxed the usual rules to accommodate the celebrities. Then again, because they used their spare time to write songs, we have the *White Album,* most of which was written in the ashram on the Ganges.

Maharishi's Little Helpers

Every mention of the Beatles and meditation seemed to increase demand on campuses, where students flocked to introductory lectures, sometimes by the thousands, drawn by posters with copy like this:

EXPAND YOUR CONSCIOUS MIND
Using a Safe, Spontaneous and Simple Technique of
Self-Exploration

As anxiety over the Vietnam War grew in intensity, Jerry Jarvis and the few other trained teachers—including Paul Horn, who left the jazz scene to teach TM—dashed around the country like presidential candidates, dispensing inner peace. At the end of 1965 only 220 Americans had learned TM. When 1968 began, there were nearly 5,000, and by the election of Richard Nixon that November the number had tripled.[22] To meet the demand, Maharishi decided to train more teachers—"multiply myself," as he put it. He certified a couple of hundred more the following year, and then, with the number of applicants exceeding the capacity of his Rishikesh academy, he leased temporary facilities in the United States. In the summer of 1970, he drew over a thousand to four-week courses in Maine and northern California. Then he turned the Colorado Rockies into the Himalayas for three months. By Christmas, about three hundred new teachers became the first and last to complete their training in America.[23] For the next few years the movement turned off-season European resorts into temporary ashrams, and fresh batches of happy graduates, almost all under thirty, were turned loose to soothe a nerve-wracked society.[24]

Maharishi got his army of teachers to do something their parents could not: clean up their acts. Razors were purchased and scissors borrowed, and shorn hair filled trash cans from Miami to Seattle. Guys raided the closets of their fathers and brothers for hand-me-down suits, or picked up something that didn't quite fit at the Salvation Army. The women did the equivalent, fixing their hair neatly and replacing miniskirts with shin-length, high-necklined outfits that would not have attracted attention at a Junior League tea party. Few would have gone that far for a job, or for dinner at Granny's, but they got spiffy for Maharishi, like those who got "clean for Gene" McCarthy in the 1968 Democratic primary campaign. As spiritual warriors, they were happy to don a uniform to save the world one mantra at a time.

Earlier, the TM action had been in college towns like Cambridge, Berkeley, Ann Arbor, and Boulder. Now the youth brigade ushered the exotic product into the mainstream, telling their elders they could conquer their tension without the pills that the Rolling Stones called "mother's little helper." Like their kids, the grown-ups replaced their drugs of choice with a natural remedy from India. Most of the fresh-faced teachers were callow and naïve; some had never had a job or paid their own rent. But they had youthful zeal, and the testimony of their own transformed lives.

There were two other reasons the young TM teachers were taken seriously, both of which sprang from Maharishi's systematic mind. He trained his representatives to make logical presentations in language suitable for their audiences, and he equipped them with a methodical procedure for imparting meditation instructions. Because meditators were asked to keep their mantras secret, there was a great deal of speculation about how they were chosen, and they were often invested with the mystique of magic words. (In Woody Allen's *Annie Hall,* a then-unknown Jeff Goldblum panics on the telephone, "I forgot my mantra.") Suffice it to say that selecting mantras was as cut-and-dried as determining someone's shoe size.[25] What was truly distinctive was that teachers guided students into the practice with a series of algorithmic steps: if A, then X; if B, then Y; if neither A nor B, then Z; and so on. This enabled wet-behind-the-ears youngsters to lead anyone into a satisfying meditative experience and to ensure that a distinctive aspect of Maharishi's teaching would be practiced, not just preached: TM, he said, was effortless; it did not involve concentration, mind control, contemplation (in the sense of contemplating ideas), or chanting.

The Science of Vedic Science

The systematic procedures also opened the door to what might be Maharishi's most durable contribution: the scientific study of meditation. Science requires repeatable experiments, and TM's uniformity and ease of instruction meant that large numbers of ordinary meditators, not just the rare Himalayan hermit, could be experimental subjects. Having had a scientific education, Maharishi knew this. He also knew that hard data would be as useful in the marketing of meditation as it was for medicines or machines. Decrying the fact that Vedic teachings had been "shrouded in the garb of mysticism," he dressed them instead in the language of science, and he urged experts to conduct research on TM.

While the Beatles were in India, the first study on the physiology of meditation was being prepared by a boyish-looking UCLA graduate student named Robert Keith Wallace. In 1970 a version of his Ph.D. dissertation was published in *Science* magazine, the prestigious journal of the American Association for the Advancement of Science.[26] Here was quantitative evidence that a mental technique could induce dramatic changes in key bodily measures, principally oxygen consumption, heart rate, respiratory rate, and other indices of profound relaxation. Wallace then teamed with Harvard cardiologist Herbert Benson for a pair of studies whose publication represented a landmark in the marriages of East and West, ancient and modern, spirit and science.[27] The relaxation message quickly overshadowed the more profound reasons for meditating, but the data armed TM teachers with charts and graphs that impressed not only the public and the press but physicians and scientists as well. Maharishi launched a virtual Manhattan Project on meditation, establishing research institutions in the United States and Europe. By 1976 his movement was able to publish a seven-hundred-page volume of papers from fifty-one institutions in thirteen countries.

The studies also gave the TM movement the language of stress reduction. The message was simple: as scientists like Hans Selye had revealed, excessive and prolonged stress agitates the nervous system, distorts the mind, and damages the body; TM reverses the physiology of stress; mental, physical, and behavioral benefits follow. So step right up; no belief necessary, no change of lifestyle required. It was presented as a scientific procedure, with results as predictable as those of any medicine, and no bad side effects. This rebranding of meditation was the first step in the secularization and medicalization of yogic disciplines. Maharishi called the profound stillness of meditation "deep rest" rather than *samadhi*. He contended that regular practice would eliminate not just ordinary stress but also the residue of traumas, emotional wounds, and other karmic disturbances embedded in the nervous system. In essence, he used *stress* as a catch-all term for *samskaras* and *vasanas*, the past impressions and subtle inclinations that trigger desires and obscure the apprehension of our divine nature.

He also set out to translate Vedanta philosophy into scientific language. Calling his formulation the Science of Creative Intelligence (SCI), he sponsored symposia in which he dialogued with leading thinkers such as Selye, Buckminster Fuller, Marshall McLuhan, Jonas Salk, and a host of prestigious scientists. Whatever the speaker said, Maharishi praised it, drew parallels to Indian philosophy, and added the dimension of consciousness. Between 1970 and 1973 about ten thousand people were said to have attended the conferences, which can be seen as an expansion of Vivekananda's and Yogananda's outreach to scientists and as a precursor to the conclaves hosted by the Dalai Lama in the 2000s.

SCI also became the cornerstone of Maharishi International University, which the TM movement opened in the summer of 1973, in a rented apartment complex outside Santa Barbara. A year later the operation moved, lock, stock, and videotapes, to the campus of defunct Parsons College in Fairfield, Iowa. Now called Maharishi University of Management, the school has never had more than three or four hundred students at a time, but its few thousand graduates, soaked in Vedanta and meditation, have no doubt served as a quiet advertisement for India's spiritual legacy as they made their way in the world.

Maharishi's appropriation of science was clearly part of his agenda from the beginning. His organization was incorporated as an educational nonprofit, not a religious one; teachers charged a course fee rather than pass around a collection basket; he established a university, not an ashram or a church. "On the surface at least, the movement and method seem more Western than Asian," writes religious historian Carl T. Jackson.[28] That skillful adaptation was no doubt a big reason for its friendly reception. Above all, it was hard data, that most convincing form of argument, that moved meditation from student dorms and hippie pads to suburban living rooms and plush offices.

Physicians and psychotherapists began recommending meditation; hard-nosed business leaders endorsed it as a performance enhancer; and new celebrities joined the parade—not just stars such as Goldie Hawn and Shirley MacLaine but Hall of Fame jocks like Arthur Ashe, Bill Walton, Steve Carlton, and even Broadway Joe Namath, all of whom said that meditation helped their game. As the TM demographic grew steadily older and more respectable, its main constituency was affluent, well educated, and white, but the African-American population also responded, thanks in part to a feature article in the first issue of *Ebony* after Martin Luther King's death (May 1968). Maharishi's solution to race relations? Raise the consciousness of both races.[29]

TM centers bloomed like crocuses to serve the growing demand. As the 1970s dawned, 24,000 Americans had learned TM. Two years later nearly 200,000 had done so, and that number was about to increase fivefold.

Merv Mainstreams Meditation

One night in 1975, in the charming seaside town of Carmel, California, a TM teacher named David Rosenkranz went to a restaurant with someone he had taught to meditate. The meditator spotted a friend of his: Merv Griffin, the TV producer and talk-show host, whose daily program was the *Oprah* of its day. Coincidentally, said Merv, he had just been speaking to a tennis buddy who practiced TM, one Clint Eastwood. Merv thought it might be interesting to devote an entire show to the subject. Rosenkranz taught him and his staff to meditate, and the program was placed on the calendar for that spring.

Griffin opened the nationally syndicated show by welcoming Maharishi to the orchestral strains of "The Fool on the Hill." Then he announced, "I'm a meditator, and I've never felt better in my life." By the first commercial, a few million people were probably opening the Yellow Pages to find a TM center. The show was a virtual infomercial, with personal testimony, name-dropping, and constant references to science. The other guests, all meditators, appealed to different segments of the audience: Ellen Corby, the actress who played the grandmother on the wholesome TV series *The Waltons;* California state senator Arlen Gregorio; and Yale psychiatrist Harold Bloomfield, who added the medical stamp of approval.

The show aired in more than a hundred cities, giving 30 to 40 million viewers a *Cliff's Notes* version of Vedanta 101. When summer came, the program was repeated in most major markets. TM centers could barely keep up with demand, even with thousands of teachers now armed and ready. Bloomfield's newly released book (coauthored with two others), *TM: Discovering Inner Energy and Overcoming Stress,* appeared on the *New York Times* bestseller list almost as soon as Merv held it up for the camera.[30] It remained on the list for six months, rising as high as number two before starting a fresh run in paperback. All together it sold well over a million copies, furthering the spread of meditation and launching Bloomfield as a self-help star whose bestsellers were laced with Vedantic ideas. Also enjoying the fortuitous timing was *The TM Book,* a collection of basic facts and whimsical cartoons that quickly hit the paperback list. Publishers large and small leaped in, and within a year bookstore shelves were glutted with so many tomes on meditation and Maharishi that there was no space left for new ones. Before long books on other forms of stress reduction were also selling big, not least of them Herbert Benson's megaselling *The Relaxation Response* (see chapter 16).[31]

Newspapers and magazines latched onto TM as they had in the Mia-Beatles days, only now the meditators profiled ranged from the snazzy (Broadway magician Doug Henning) to the sublime (jazz great Peggy Lee) to the sober and serious (playwright William Gibson, author of *The Miracle Worker;* and diplomat Alfred Jenkins, who advised Kissinger and Nixon in China). Articles appeared everywhere from *Reader's Digest* and *Saturday Evening Post* to in-flight magazines and *Mechanix Illustrated.* In October 1975 *The Atlantic Monthly*'s cover story was the meditation portion of Adam Smith's soon-to-be-bestseller, *Powers of Mind.*[32] *Time*'s October 13 cover featured a psychedelicized portrait of Maharishi with the headline "Meditation: The Answer to All Your Problems?" Calling TM "the turn-on of the '70s," the piece offered more data, more testimonials, and more big-time names, concluding that TM is "the most visible manifestation of the industrialized nations looking for relief from the pressures of modern life in Eastern spiritual or quasi-spiritual movements."

The coup de grâce came in November, when Merv Griffin did an encore. Fundamentalists picketed the studio with signs reading JESUS IS THE LORD, NOT MAHARISHI. They were no match for Merv's high-voltage guests: America's sweetheart, Mary Tyler Moore, said that she'd been meditating, and "things that used to be problems are now just situations with which I must deal"; and Clint Eastwood, the nation's top box-office star and living symbol of macho power (not diminished one photon by his handing Maharishi a flower), said TM helped him think better. The other guests were window dressing, but they reinforced the message of respectable pragmatism: Richard Nolan, a U.S. congressman from Minnesota, and Bernard Glueck, M.D., who cited his three-year study of TM on psychiatric patients. Once again the phones at TM centers rang off the hook.

Those around Maharishi knew it was a source of both amusement and frustration that he had come west to speak of enlightenment and was forced to speak of stress. But like Vivekananda, Yogananda, and others, he was applying a maxim from the Bhagavad Gita: "Let not the wise man who sees the All disturb the unwise who sees not the All." Most of the people who suddenly crowded the TM centers were interested only in reducing tension or getting a decent night's sleep, but many found a port of entry into something deeper. They heard about, and perhaps tasted, the possibility of higher consciousness and inner peace, and they took their first earnest steps on a spiritual path. So it has been with all Vedantic teachings in the West, and so it remains in millions of Yoga classes, where some just work out and others work within as well.

About three hundred thousand people learned TM in 1975, and by the end of the bicentennial celebrations in 1976 the total exceeded a million.[33] No one knows how many of them continued with the practice. But most would likely express some variation of what Ringo Starr said when asked in 2008 about his time in India forty years earlier: "You can take the car, you can take the house, whatever. But the mantra's mine. It's in my soul." In a sense, the same could be said of America in general. Meditation had entered the national soul, and with it core Vedantic ideas. Countless people were making their way to alternative spiritual outlets. New gurus and Yoga masters rose to prominence, and attendance at established institutions surged. Secular venues for spiritual inquiry and self-improvement flourished. Esoteric bookstores, such as Weiser's in New York, Shambhala in Berkeley, and the Bodhi Tree in L.A., did booming business, as did similarly themed magazines and radio programs, such as Lex Hixon's *In the Spirit* on New York's hippest public station, WBAI, and Michael and Justine Toms's West Coast–based New Dimensions Radio.[34] Following Benson's lead, physicians, therapists, and seminar leaders offered up meditation techniques of their own. The New Age was suddenly upon us; it would further propagate Eastern ideas and practices, albeit in modified and often highly adulterated forms.

It added up to a watershed moment in the meeting of East and West. For the first time in history, the possibility of having a fruitful spiritual life outside conventional religion had become a distinct possibility for everyone. It was, arguably, the birth of "spiritual but not religious."

Living the Vida Veda

For Maharishi's movement, new competition combined with the inevitable decline in media attention led to what businesspeople call diminished market share. Other factors contributed as well, such as intense opposition from Christian fundamentalists and a 1978 New Jersey court ruling that barred TM from being taught in public schools as religious in nature. In addition, the organization stepped on its own toes by succumbing to institutional neuroses that alienated some of its constituents. For all these reasons, once the so-called Merv Wave petered out, the number of new initiates returned to pre-Beatles levels; centers closed or moved to smaller spaces; teachers went back to school or looked for jobs. TM would remain one of the most influential branches of Indian spirituality in the West, but its priorities shifted, and its public profile diminished.

Post-Merv, Maharishi unleashed a series of new ventures. Some of them, like the plan to build Vedic theme parks (headed by the magician Doug Henning) and the Natural Law Party (which ran physicist John Hagelin for president three times), attracted media attention but flamed out in time. Other projects were more durable, and more in keeping with Maharishi's stated purpose of ushering in an "Age of Enlightenment" through the revival of Vedic knowledge.[35] The new phase got off the ground, literally and figuratively, in mid-1977 with the TM-Sidhi Program. It drew from the enigmatic third chapter of Patanjali's *Yoga Sutras,* which describes extraordinary powers called *siddhis* (extrasensory perception, intuitive knowing, invisibility, levitation, and more) and suggests the possibility of developing them by honing the mind with yogic discipline.[36] That Maharishi would systematize such practices was shocking to those who had heard him pooh-pooh supernormal powers as distractions from the goal of self-realization. The purpose, he maintained, was not the powers as such but the holistic development of consciousness.

The program quickly became a must-have for TM enthusiasts, who begged and borrowed to pay for it. Had Maharishi kept it in the family, his movement might have been better off. Instead, he launched a publicity campaign. Newspaper ads promised "the ability to levitate by mere intention." Young representatives, gleeful and guileless, held press conferences, making it sound as though hundreds of people were flying through the air on the wings of the mind and otherwise exhibiting mastery over matter. Since no actual proof was forthcoming, the coverage was often scathing. The TM reps giggled their way back to their meditation rooms—now padded with foam so levitators could make soft landings—certain that their claims would soon be validated. They're still waiting. All that has been demonstrated is what the TM movement calls the first stage of yogic flying—essentially, hopping froglike for a foot or two, looking more like gymnasts than helicopters lifting off.

The practice disappointed many practitioners but also satisfied those content with the deepened inner peace and heightened awareness that they said they experienced. In terms of public perception, however, TM sacrificed much of the respectability it had worked to acquire. Prominent supporters were so embarrassed that they severed their ties. Then came another controversial claim. TM scientists predicted that if the square root of one percent of a population engaged in yogic flying, peace and harmony would reign.[37] Presumably the orderly EEG waves generated by individuals are amplified geometrically, and the coherence radiates outward like broadcast signals.

To prove the assertion, teams of yogic flyers were dispatched to various places to see if their group practice would reduce crime rate and other indices of social disorder. The data were published, and the phenomenon, dubbed both Super Radiance and the Maharishi Effect, became the focal point of the movement's activities. Undeterred by attacks on the validity of the research, Maharishi urged TMers to get their butts onto the foam-lined meditation domes in Fairfield, Iowa, to create world peace. Flocks of the faithful heeded the call.[38] To his diehard supporters, the program was evidence of Maharishi's visionary genius. Critics thought he suffered from delusions of grandeur. He was just getting started.

One new offering followed another, each bearing the Maharishi brand, and meditators were implored to partake of them, for the sake of their own development and the good of the world. There was Maharishi Sthapatya Veda, "the eternal system of architecture and city planning"; Maharishi Jyotish, a Vedic form of astrology; Maharishi Yagyas, Vedic rituals to ward off negative influences; Maharishi Gandharva Veda, music that "replicates the vibrations of Nature"; "consciousness-based education" for students in Maharishi Schools; and Maharishi Ayur-Veda, the TM version of the ancient medical system, with a product line of herbal supplements, oils, teas, and spices.

Each element of "Vedic Science," designed to orient life to "natural law," was introduced at intervals from the mid-1970s onward. The one that attracted attention outside TM circles was Ayurveda. The movement's aggressive promotion put the ancient system on the map. Practitioners already at work in the West, such as Vasant Lad, founder of the Ayurvedic Institute in New Mexico, became much better known; early exponents like Robert Svoboda, the first American certified to practice Ayurveda in India, expanded their reach; and institutes such as the California College of Ayurveda started training practitioners. Eventually, the National Ayurvedic Medical Association was created to advance and protect the profession. Most cities now have Ayurvedic clinics; books on Ayurveda compete for space in the health sections of bookstores; and a number of practitioners are prospering.[39]

The advent of Ayurveda did more than add new nostrums to alternative medicine's bag of tricks; it opened a fresh new spigot from which the

Vedantic worldview flowed into the culture, since the system's philosophical roots are inseparable from its application. Perhaps most important,
TM's Ayurveda push launched into orbit a new international celebrity,
Deepak Chopra. Heavily promoted as the TM spokesperson, he eventually went out on his own and became arguably the leading voice of Vedanta in the West (see chapter 12).

Growing Pains

Within the TM movement, some embraced the new offerings like kids
let loose at Toys "R" Us. But the majority resisted what they saw as Vedic orthodoxy and were dismayed by the apparent reversal of Maharishi's
original message: just meditate regularly, no radical change of lifestyle is
needed. Now, it seemed, if you *really* wanted to get enlightened, your every waking moment had to be dictated by rules derived from the ancient
Vedas. Conformity was by no means required, but the pressure to keep
up with the yogis next door was intense, as it always is when the stakes
are nothing less than the fulfillment of human destiny—*moksha*, nirvana,
salvation, whatever. Over time, because of the high cost and the less-than-
advertised results, fewer and fewer TMers kept up the Vedic lifestyle. At
the same time, followers felt increasingly pressured to donate money for
TM's worldwide outreach and alienated from what they saw as an organizational drift toward authoritarian governance. For many, the last straw
was a series of price increases for the basic TM course.

For all those reasons, from the 1980s onward former loyalists reduced
their involvement with institutional TM and many cut themselves off completely. In Fairfield, Iowa, where about three thousand had moved to get
enlightened and save the world together, the cognitive dissonance grew
thicker than the humidity. By the year 2000, the community, once spiritually homogeneous, had diversified. It is now in many ways a microcosm
of baby boomer spirituality. On one extreme you find the diminishing
cohort of TM diehards. On the other extreme are rejectionists who think

Maharishi was a fraud. In the middle are the great majority, who for the most part kept the babies and tossed the bathwater. They still meditate, they are still dedicated to the pursuit of spiritual realization, but they have declared independence, and their quests have become so eclectic that the tiny, inconvenient town in the cornbelt is now a favorite stop for touring gurus and seminar leaders.

Back to the Future

Despite the attrition after the Merv Wave subsided, the TM movement continued to field aggressive activists, and the tireless Maharishi was featured in the media from time to time. Some of the coverage—a *Life* magazine spread in 1990,[40] for instance, and a Larry King interview via satellite in 2002—was substantive enough to introduce his Vedantic perspective to a new audience. TM also cropped up in the occasional celebrity profile. Promoting *The Bee Movie* in 2007, for instance, Jerry Seinfeld answered a reporter's query about his "Zenlike equilibrium" by revealing that he'd been practicing TM his whole adult life. Even Howard Stern would occasionally interrupt the vulgarity to say he'd been meditating since the 1970s, and when Maharishi died, the shock jock offered a shockingly moving tribute.[41] More significantly, major articles and news reports regularly mentioned TM in stories about stress. In 2003, for instance, actress Heather Graham graced the cover of *Time* in meditative repose, her neckline plunging to her heart chakra, behind the headline "THE SCIENCE OF MEDITATION."[42] The article focused on the extraordinary amount of scientific research that had been conducted since the first TM studies more than thirty years earlier.[43]

That research, and the legitimization of meditation in general, will likely stand as Maharishi's lasting legacy. Always a polarizing figure, he was revered as a modern Buddha by some and ridiculed as a P. T. Barnum by others. But when he passed away in February 2008, the press coverage was consistently respectful, largely because he had kick-started a valuable scientific enterprise. Hollywood glamour may attract attention, but the data gathered by lab geeks is far more enduring.

The TM movement has produced a huge number of meditators who have played a significant role in the propagation of Vedanta-Yoga in other contexts. Some occupy leadership positions in other spiritual institutions, as swamis, Zen *roshis*, rabbis, and ministers; others operate on their own. Ben Collins, for instance, created Puja.net, a podcast of Hindu stories and Sanskrit chants. Others are psychotherapists, health care providers, and artists. Executives might arrange for employees to learn meditation, and educators might bring a Vedantic perspective to the classroom, like Ed Sarath, who heads the University of Michigan's jazz department and teaches courses on consciousness and creativity. Most simply go about their business, occasionally adding a brick to the edifice of American Veda by recommending meditation or tossing a Vedantic perspective into a conversation. Those bricks add up, especially if you're in a high-profile position, like *über*-record producer Rick Rubin or John Raatz, a Los Angeles publicist who learned his trade promoting TM in the 1970s.

Perhaps most notably, the TM movement spawned a remarkable number of nonfiction and self-help authors. The bestsellerdom that started with Harold Bloomfield and peaked with Deepak Chopra and John Gray (of *Mars-Venus* fame) also includes relationship expert Barbara De Angelis (*How to Make Love All the Time*, 1991); Peter Russell (*The Global Brain*, 1983; *From Science to God*, 2002), who weaves Eastern philosophy with scientific themes; and Marci Shimoff, whose premise in *Happy for No Reason* (2009)—"happiness is inherent in the true nature of what we are"—could not be more Vedantic. Maharishi's heirs also include a bevy of lesser-known authors whose additions to the Vedic stream should not be underestimated.[44]

It remains to be seen whether the TM movement, in the absence of its charismatic founder, will continue to be a force. Its international operation, headquartered in Holland, is now headed by the Lebanese-born doctor Tony Nader (aka Maharaja Adhiraj Raja Raam) and, in the United States, by physicist John Hagelin. Press releases announcing new scientific findings are dispatched regularly, ambitious new projects are initiated frequently, and the university in Iowa continues to turn out a few hundred graduates a year. As I write this, the TM world is rocking with the return of the celebrity factor. Film director David Lynch, who began meditating in 1973, started a foundation in 2006 to provide TM instruction to students.[45] To garner support, he rolled out a series of well-publicized lectures on consciousness and creativity and organized conferences for educators, using testimony from scientists, teachers, and celebrities like Russell Simmons, who tells kids it's cool to meditate. On April 4, 2009, Lynch organized a benefit bash at New York's Radio City Music Hall to raise money to teach at-risk students to meditate. Titled "Change Begins Within," it featured current stars like Eddie Vedder and Sheryl Crow, along with cameos by meditators Seinfeld and Stern. Bringing it all back home, the concert reunited artists who had meditated together in India in 1968: Donovan, Paul Horn, Beach Boy Mike Love, Ringo Starr, and the headliner, Sir Paul McCartney.

9

THE BABY BOOMERS' BABAS

In a sense, Maharishi was the Henry Ford of American Veda, and TM was the Model T. In each case, what had been a luxury item—cars for the wealthy; meditation for the mystically inclined elite—was made accessible to everyone, resulting in a radically altered landscape, geographic or spiritual. Maharishi was similar to Ford in another way: his success created a market for competitors. Just as other brands of automobiles, with different colors, accessories, and features, rolled onto American byways next to the black Model T, other Vedic offerings rose to prominence in the wake of the TM media frenzy. Not only did new gurus start arriving—in most cases sponsored by American pilgrims who met them in India—but those who had been laboring in relative obscurity suddenly found eager students at their feet. *Life*'s "Year of the Guru" coverage of TM noted that other stops on New York's "Swami Circuit" would need more space because "none is big enough to handle the swelling crowds who drop by to exercise, chant or meditate."[1]

Well-established institutions, notably the Vedanta Society and Yogananda's SRF, enjoyed a fresh surge of interest that swelled their memberships, their coffers, and their supply of future leaders. Even Krishnamurti, who denounced the suddenly famous gurus as mantra merchants, benefited from their notoriety. His public appearances drew bigger audiences than ever, albeit a younger and scruffier crowd than he was accustomed to.

In 1982 three thousand showed up at each of his two Carnegie Hall appearances, and the following year even more piled into Madison Square Garden.

In a spiritual version of supply responding to demand, the gurus brought out different components of the Vedic repertoire to suit the spiritual inclinations of Americans: devotional practices, both God-centered and guru-centered; new philosophical orientations, such as Tantrism and Kashmir Shaivism; and, of enormous consequence, body-based Hatha Yoga. It was as though artisans and engineers were adding wings, rooms, furnishings, and decor to the edifice of American Veda. Underlying the variety, however, were the same core principles of universality, pluralism, pragmatism, and nonsectarianism emphasized by all successful gurus in the West. They not only influenced many lives for the better, they trained students to become disseminators of Vedanta-Yoga in their own right.

The gurus' sudden popularity triggered a spate of books, articles, and public commentaries analyzing the lure of the East. Mainstream religious leaders feared that charismatic Hindus were luring youngsters away from traditional houses of worship, if not taking them straight to hell. In truth, most students of gurus had already ditched their ancestral religions and were surprised when their new teachers told them to honor those traditions and augment them with yogic practices. In one well-publicized book, *Turning East* (1977), Harvard theologian Harvey Cox said that the young seekers were looking for community, immediacy of experience, trustworthy authority, and involvement in something natural, less patriarchal, and more ecological. While not entirely off the mark, Cox missed the most essential factors driving the latter-day Romantics. "Notably absent from Cox's list," wrote scholar Christopher Chapple, himself once a 1970s seeker, "are the two prime reasons given in Indian texts as to why people pursue a religious quest: desire for knowledge (jijnasa) and desire for liberation (mumukshu)."[2] To which I would add one factor that was especially compelling to activist boomers: a different way to change the world, this time from the inside out.

For the most part, the gurus were able to satisfy those longings, although not always to the extent that devotees hoped for—or were promised. In addition to dashed expectations, many experienced pain, trauma, and the shock of scandal. The dark side of the guru story offers important lessons for seekers and history alike. But first we'll look at the leading teachers of the 1970s: a multifaceted, idiosyncratic, hard-to-categorize bunch, each of whom attracted a different type of student and left a unique mark.

The Divine Minstrel

He arrived by ship in 1965, a sixty-nine-year-old man with a shaved head, dressed in an orange robe, and possessing fewer personal effects than a child could carry in its hands. Formerly Abhay Charan De, a Calcutta business executive and family man, he was, since taking monastic vows in 1959, A. C. Bhaktivedanta Swami. His mission was to promulgate the teachings of Gaudiya Vaishnavism, a bhakti lineage founded in the sixteenth century by Sri Chaitanya Mahaprabhu (1486–1534) and centered on exuberant devotion to Lord Krishna, the avatar whose story (mythology to some, history to others) is recounted in the *Shrimad Bhagavatam* and the epic *Mahabharata*.[3]

The humble monk rented a dilapidated storefront on New York's Lower East Side. Across the street were symbols of the transient existence for which he saw his work as an antidote: a bar and a funeral home. Once the locus of immigrant assimilation, the neighborhood was now becoming known as the East Village, and its center of energy, Tompkins Square Park, would soon be a haven for hippies, folksingers, protesters, and drug dealers. There Bhaktivedanta spoke of God and led the chanting of the soon-to-be-famous Hare Krishna *mahamantra*.[4] Those singing along found in the *kirtan* (participatory chanting) a dose of unfiltered, nonchemical joy.

One frequent reveler was the neighborhood's best-known citizen, Allen Ginsberg, who helped spread the word to the West Coast through the counterculture grapevine. In Ginsberg's distinctive syntax: "And a second center for chanting Krishna's Name was thereafter established in San Francisco's Haight-Ashbury at the height of the spiritual crisis and breakthrough renowned in that city, mid-sixties twentieth century." In January

1967 Bay Area newspapers ran headlines like SWAMI INVITES HIPPIES TO HIPPIELAND TEMPLE. Posters appeared for a "Mantra-Rock Dance" at the Avalon Ballroom, which was second only to the Fillmore as a rock mecca. The event, presided over by Bhaktivedanta and Ginsberg, featured the Grateful Dead, Big Brother and the Holding Company (with lead singer Janis Joplin), and other stars of the promiscuous, drug-driven scene. They were joined onstage by the celibate, drug-rejecting, vegetarian musicians of the newly established International Society for Krishna Consciousness (ISKCON).

The Hare Krishnas became a fixture in the Haight and a camera-ready presence during the Summer of Love. To onlookers, they were just a more exotic version of the freaks and dropouts gravitating to hip enclaves and college towns. But they were, in many ways, the polar opposite, and not just because the men shaved off their hair instead of growing it. In their austere behavioral code, they were closer to Orthodox Jews or the Amish—the antithesis of hippie mottoes like "Do your own thing" and "If it feels good, do it." Initiates took Sanskrit names and lived communally; their *sadhana* included morning and evening classes, group chanting, and private *japa* (mantra recitation).[5] No meat, gambling, nonmarital sex, or intoxicants were allowed, including caffeine and tobacco. Bhaktivedanta saw ISKCON's future in the unkempt, orgiastic hippies because "they are already dissatisfied with material life." Once they get a taste of Krishna consciousness, he predicted, they would abandon their toxic frivolities. Most hippies said no thanks to anything more than the chanting and dancing and—praise Krishna!—the free, belly-filling Sunday feasts. But some did prefer austerity to nihilism, and the movement grew. Soon their public chanting and their hawking of books and *Back to Godhead* magazine earned them a reputation as the Hindu version of Jesus Freaks.

Bhaktivedanta—Srila Prabhupada to his followers—traveled the globe, opening temples, cultivating disciples, and working on *The Bhagavad Gita As It Is,* which became the most visible translation of the sacred text. In 1968 he established a communal compound in West Virginia, called New Vrindaban after the holy city of Krishna's youth. The following year ISKCON got a huge boost when George Harrison, the most diligently spiritual of the Beatles, discovered Krishna bhakti. Harrison funded ISKCON's London temple and the printing of Bhaktivedanta's 1970 book, *Krishna: The Supreme Personality of Godhead,* even penning a foreword.[6] He then produced and performed on an album of chants that brought Krishna consciousness to a global audience.

In August 1969 Apple Records released a single called "Hare Krishna Mantra." An international smash, it was followed by another single, "Govinda," and then by the album *Radha-Krishna Temple.*[7] With Harrison's help, the Krishna musicians toured Europe, opening for name acts like the Moody Blues. "Sometimes in earnest, sometimes in jest, the chanting of 'Hare Krishna' spread around the world," writes Joshua Greene in his account of Harrison's spiritual journey.[8] That would continue for decades: not only did George praise Krishna in some later songs, but references to the avatar and the *mahamantra* showed up on tunes by the Beatles ("I Am the Walrus"), Stevie Wonder ("Pastime Paradise"), and others, on into the punk era, when a subgenre called Krishnacore emerged, and in the 1990s recordings by Boy George and Kula Shaker (named for a Vaishnavite poet named Kulashekhara).[9]

In the mass media, the jesting outweighed the earnestness. Ever since the chanting scene in the landmark musical *Hair* (1967), everyone from Cheech and Chong to Woody Allen to the Simpsons has used the image of orange-clad Krishnas to comic effect, usually to depict a hippie scene or cultists who irritate pedestrians, drive parents up a wall, and sometimes require deprogramming. The outlandish public face of Hare Krishna actually helped other Vedic groups at the time, just as the Black Panthers helped Martin Luther King, by making them seem respectable by comparison.

The devotional aspect of Vedic tradition had not been totally sidelined by previous gurus; it was, for instance, emphasized by Yogananda. But Bhaktivedanta placed it front and center, with virtually all the trappings of its Indian origins. It was too exotic to attract large numbers of followers, but by the time of its founder's death in 1977, the movement had established hundreds of temples and initiated about ten thousand devotees worldwide. The uncompromising swami passed away with his reputation intact, but the Krishna community was ruptured in the 1980s when some of its leaders were accused of racketeering, kidnapping, child molestation, and even murder. Devotees left, temples closed, and property was sold to cover legal costs. But the faith of most adherents was strong; it just took on more private forms of expression. "ISKCON has become a far more family-oriented and household-based, and therefore less temple-centered, congregation," says sociologist Burke Rochford. Prabhupada's dropout followers dropped back in. They married, had kids, shed their dhotis and saris, and started careers as late-blooming adults. "Their miracle has been to find the ashram within the mainstream, within themselves, and still function in the world," the scholar of religion Graham Schweig told *Newsweek* in 2006. The guy with the shaved head who tried to sell you a book in the airport might now be your insurance agent.

The assimilation of minority religions is a slow, steady process, says Michael Gressett, a scholar who specializes on Hare Krishna in America. He said the Krishnas mirror what is called the cult-to-church movement—a cult being a new religious movement that's in tension with its environment, while a church is an established form that accommodates society's values. "They are so distinct that it will be a slow, steady process," he says. "They will always be at least a small minority." Its influence, however, has been far greater than its number of adherents would suggest. For one thing, a number of early Hare Krishnas became scholars whose work constitutes a quiet but important stream of Vedic influence.[10]

In addition, the Hare Krishnas have probably generated more interest in reincarnation and vegetarianism than any other single source. And most Americans over forty got their first taste of Sanskrit chanting from them, whether they liked it or not. Now *kirtan* is a veritable industry. CDs blending Indian and Western motifs sell briskly, and Yoga studios rock like rave clubs on certain evenings, when mostly young crowds test out George Harrison's hypothesis that by chanting the names of the Lord "you'll be free."[11]

Most important, the visibility of the Krishna devotees furthered interest in all Indian spiritual forms, even if most seekers chose other paths. For over forty years, they've been drawing people of all inclinations to their colorful temples, festivals, feasts, restaurants (called Govinda's), and outreach programs at schools. And not just in liberal enclaves: if you drive south on the I-15 from Provo, Utah (home of Brigham Young University), you'll see the ornate, fifty-foot-high Sri Sri Radha Krishna Temple. Set on fifteen acres, the temple is the brainchild of a devotee named Caru Das, who grew up as Christopher Warden outside Pittsburgh. He told me that 15,000 to 20,000 people a year drop by to sightsee and browse the bookstore and displays. This in the home of Mormonism and perhaps the most conservative state in the Union![12]

Shakti Rising

With his dark glasses, funky red ski cap, and scruffy beard, Swami Muktananda looked more like an edgy jazz musician than a standard-issue holy man. Which is fitting, since he introduced new melodies and rhythms into America's Vedic repertoire: Kashmir Shaivism, a nondual system developed in mountainous Kashmir centuries ago; *shaktipat,* a form of initiation by which a *sadguru* (true teacher) awakens in the devotee the primal energy called *shakti;* and an emphasis on the guru as an embodiment of the divine and an object of devotion.

The second and third elements were not exactly unknown when Muktananda arrived on the scene. Students of Indian spirituality knew that kundalini, or *shakti,*[13] is a potent force that sits coiled like a serpent at the base of the spine. Yogic techniques, it was understood, raise that energy through subtle channels to enliven the centers called chakras, culminating at the crown of the head *(sahasrara chakra),* which produces the enlightenment experience.[14] Muktananda introduced kundalini concepts to massive audiences in the context of what has been called Guru Yoga. Whereas most Indian teachers in the West downplayed guru devotion except among their closest disciples, he placed it front and center. "Realization of God is possible only through a Guru," he said, and while he distinguished between the human guru and "the Cosmic or Transcendental aspect," he treated surrendering to the personal guru as a spiritual practice.

Born in South India in 1908 and given the name Krishna, Muktananda was a teenager when he met his future guru, Bhagawan Nityananda. Considered an *avadhuta* (an ascetic so free of worldly concerns as to make what we call eccentrics seem like conformists), Nityananda wore only a loincloth, spoke few words, and behaved cryptically. Inspired by the encounter, young Krishna wandered India on foot in the time-honored tradition of monks, studied with yogic masters, and was initiated into a sannyasi order as Swami Muktananda. He was nearly forty when he was accepted as a disciple by Nityananda. In 1956 his guru gave him a piece of land in Ganeshpuri, not far from Bombay, on which he built an ashram (now called Gurudev Siddha Peeth) that was probably visited by more Westerners in the last quarter of the twentieth century than any other ashram in India.

When Nityananda passed away in 1961, Muktananda assumed the mantle of what he called the Siddha Yoga lineage,[15] *siddha* being a Tantric term for "one who has attained perfect enlightenment."[16] He quickly attracted a following and in 1970 was brought to the West by devotees. His tour drew sizable crowds in New York and California, in part because his opening act was the enormously popular Ram Dass, né Richard Alpert. By all accounts, the atmosphere at those appearances was electric. Muktananda led chanting sessions and gave discourses (translated from Hindi), whose central message was "Honor your Self, worship your Self, meditate on your Self. God dwells within you as you." His dynamic presence blew away the prevailing image of the placid guru. It was like seeing Mick Jagger when you expected Tony Bennett.

Muktananda's next tour, sponsored in part by Werner Erhard, whose est seminars were all the rage, spanned the two-plus years from Richard Nixon's resignation to Jimmy Carter's election. During this period he introduced the practice that branded him: *shaktipat.* He touched students with a wand of peacock feathers, presumably triggering the release of kundalini energy. Reactions ranged from a bath of inner peace to lightning bolts up the spine, paroxysms of noise-making, and spontaneous gestures called *kriyas* that resemble the positions of Hatha Yoga. Theoretically, it is an initiation into an ongoing transformative process. "Once shaktipat is bestowed," writes scholar Paul Muller-Ortega, "the path of yoga unfolds spontaneously and ineluctably within."[17] Muktananda essentially democratized *shaktipat,* dispensing what had been a rare guru-disciple transmission to hundreds, sometimes thousands, at weekend retreats called Intensives.

On this tour, he also established an organizational structure under the rubric Siddha Yoga Dham (*dham* means "abode"), aka the SYDA Foundation. Devotees' homes became centers, and a run-down hotel in Oakland became a residential ashram. Still in operation, the ashram was significant on two counts. First, because it was in a predominantly black neighborhood, it gave SYDA the largest percentage of African-American followers of all the Vedic imports. Second, it set the template for SYDA's disciplined ashram lifestyle: celibacy, vegetarianism, service *(seva),* and a rigorous schedule of meditation, chanting, and other forms of *sadhana.* (Devotees outside of ashrams were given a different routine.)

In the ensuing years, Westerners were trained to lecture, lead courses, and run SYDA centers. Some were initiated as sannyasis.[18] In 1978 Muktananda returned to the West for his final tour, which lasted more than three years. He made media appearances, filled venues as big as Carnegie Hall, developed a prison project and other charitable ventures, hosted conferences, and turned an old hotel in South Fallsburg, New York, into his international headquarters.[19] These activities, aided by celebrity cachet from John Denver, Phylicia Rashad, and others, attracted a good deal of media attention.

After his death in October 1982, Muktananda's legacy was blemished by reports that he'd had clandestine sexual liaisons, some with adolescent girls. The furor intensified in 1983 when the allegations were made public in a widely circulated article in *CoEvolution Quarterly.*[20] That upheaval was followed by another one over the SYDA line of succession. In 1981 Muktananda had announced that his chosen successor was Subhash Shetty, an eighteen-year-old sannyasi whom he had honored with the name of his own guru, Swami Nityananda. Six months later, he declared that his translator, Nityananda's older sister Malti, would share the leadership. Malti was named Swami Chidvilasananda, and became famous as simply

Gurumayi. The siblings ruled uneasily until Nityananda stepped down in 1985, admitting he had broken his vow of celibacy. Later, he claimed his resignation had been coerced under duress by his sister's henchmen. When he declared himself a guru again, he was denounced and reportedly harassed by Gurumayi's supporters.[21] All this and more was reported in harrowing detail by Lis Harris in *The New Yorker* in 1994.[22]

Remarkably, Siddha Yoga not only survived the turmoil, it thrived. Gurumayi blossomed as a guru in her own right, like a child actor who blows out the klieg lights with a sparkling grown-up performance. A cocoa-skinned beauty with a toothpaste-commercial smile, she was young, charming, fluent in vernacular English, and female—an inspiration to American women at a time when gurus were all graybeards. Over the course of two decades, she expanded SYDA's reach, attracted a fresh crew of celebrities (Diana Ross, Meg Ryan, Don Johnson, Melanie Griffith), and founded two philanthropic organizations.[23] In 2001 she closed the South Fallsburg ashram to visitors, and in 2004 stopped appearing live. "Gurumayi wants people to be more self-reliant," an official told me. More use is now made of local facilities and the Web to disseminate teachings. Perhaps as a direct result of Gurumayi's withdrawal, SYDA's membership and public awareness of its programs has declined drastically.[24]

Whatever else may be said, Siddha Yoga affected hundreds of thousands of lives and expanded the range of Vedic teachings in the West. Long after his departure, Muktananda's legacy continues to spread through his and Gurumayi's followers in various walks of life, from business to education to the academic study of religion.[25] The movement attracted an exceptional number of psychologists, thanks in large part to Muktananda's friendship with Stanislav and Christina Grof, two leading figures in transpersonal psychology. The Grofs described their encounters with Baba (as devotees called him) in various publications and arranged for him to speak at professional conferences.[26]

Siddha Yoga also turned out spiritual teachers who made a mark on their own. (Two American gurus with early connections to Muktananda are described in chapter 10.) In the 1970s Sally Kempton was a highly regarded New York journalist. Then she met Muktananda and served

SYDA for more than two decades as Swami Durgananda. The author of *The Heart of Meditation,* she now teaches under her original name and writes a column for *Yoga Journal.*[27] And at least two prominent Yoga teachers, John Friend and Steven Ross, spent chunks of their formative years in Siddha Yoga ashrams.[28] Then there's Eugene Callender, a legendary Harlem preacher and social activist (he delivered the eulogy at Billie Holiday's funeral, among other things), who met Muktananda in 1979 and was SYDA's president for fifteen years during Gurumayi's reign. Now almost ninety, he says of that association, "I'm a better Christian and a better minister because of it. It made me a more powerful person, and showed me the possibilities of what someone can become."[29]

SYDA's future as a force in Western spirituality will probably depend on several factors: whether it can put to rest concerns about its controversial past; how well it transitions from its dependence on a magnetic guru to a more democratic, educational model; and whether it can reach the younger generation of seekers—a task faced by all the lineages that set down roots in earlier times.[30]

The Olympian Guru

Born in 1931 in what is now Bangladesh, Chinmoy Kumar Ghose was orphaned at eleven and spent the next twenty years in the ashram of Sri Aurobindo. He came to New York in 1964 and worked as a clerk at the Indian consulate before becoming known as Sri Chinmoy, the leader of a spiritual community centered in Queens. In the early 1970s, he came to public attention when he attracted some well-known musicians: guitar great Carlos Santana; fusion star John McLaughlin, whose Mahavishnu Orchestra was named by Chinmoy (see chapter 15); and Roberta Flack, one of the biggest pop singers of the era. By the time he passed away in 2008, at seventy-six, Chinmoy had known so many movers and shakers that statements were read at his memorial service from the likes of Nelson Mandela, Bill Clinton, and Mikhail Gorbachev.

As a teacher, Chinmoy was situated squarely in Vedanta but emphasized the personal aspect of the divine. Kusumita Pederson, a historian of religion, says he was "radically theistic" and emphasized "the need to approach God with love, devotion, surrender, and most of all with gratitude."[31] He evidently ran a tight ship; regular meditation, attendance at communal events, vegetarianism, celibacy, and abstention from drugs and alcohol were expected, all in the service of realizing union with "the Supreme."

Compared to other popular gurus of the era, Sri Chinmoy had relatively few disciples. There are now said to be some seven thousand worldwide, and more than three hundred small, loosely affiliated centers sustained by followers through independent enterprises such as vegetarian restaurants and health food stores.[32]

But Sri Chinmoy's influence was larger than those numbers would suggest. Creatively prolific, he is said to have written more than 1,500 books, 115,000 poems, and 20,000 songs—an output that John Updike would have envied, even though most of the books were compiled from his talks, and the poems could be as pithy as aphorisms. He also turned out paintings and drawings by the basketful, and performed at nearly eight hundred self-produced "peace concerts." But he was unique in his gusto for sports; exceeding the apparent limits of the body and mind was, to him, a means of self-transcendence. With teams of devotees, he ran in marathons and ultra-distance races. He gave exhibitions of his weightlifting prowess, shoulder-pressing a reported thirteen hundred pounds (with the help of special apparatus) and lifting celebrities who ranged in weight from Yoko Ono to Muhammad Ali. To critics, the events were self-aggrandizing stunts; to disciples, they were teaching tools. Either way, they brought attention to Indian spirituality. Perhaps most important, from 1971 until his death he led twice-weekly meditation sessions for the staff and delegates at the United Nations. It is hard to think of a better place to highlight the Vedantic message of oneness.

A Child Shall Lead Them

In July 1971, shortly after the *New York Times* published the Pentagon Papers and the voting age was lowered to eighteen, an Indian lad arrived in the United States and was hailed by a welcoming throng as Guru Maharaj Ji, "the 13-year-old Perfect Master." Born Prem Rawat in 1957, he was the youngest son of a spiritual leader named Hans Ji Maharaj, founder of the Divine Light Mission. At age nine, when his father died, Prem was named successor.[33] Four years later Americans who met him in India introduced him to the West with messianic fervor. As one reporter put it, Maharaj Ji's devotees, known as "premies,"[34] saw him as "the guy who will out-Christ Christ." His mother and brothers, with whom he traveled, were called the "Holy Family." When he arrived in a new town, flyers announced, "The Lord Has Come."

At a time when gurus were long-bearded and middle-aged, it was not surprising that the media would have a field day with one who looked to them like a Hindu bar mitzvah boy. Most of the coverage was predictably cynical. But while the sensationalism played out, Maharaj Ji was quietly transforming thousands of lives. By mid-1973 the U.S. branch of the Divine Light Mission (DLM) had given Knowledge—the movement's term for the four meditative techniques to be practiced about an hour a day—to an estimated forty thousand people.[35] Committed premies lived in communal settings where celibacy, service, *sadhana,* and devotion to the guru were expected. As in most groups of that nature, compliance was thought to correlate with rapid self-realization.

The fanaticism and media attention peaked with Millennium '73 at the Houston Astrodome. Called by DLM "the most holy and significant event in the history of mankind," it was to usher in "a thousand years of peace." The buildup attracted copious coverage, much of it generated by Rennie Davis, one of the Chicago Seven who stood trial after the riots at the 1968 Democratic Convention and now Maharaj Ji's loudest disciple. "I feel like shouting in the streets," he shouted. "If we knew who he was, we would crawl across America on our hands and knees to rest our heads at his feet."[36] Organizers expected 100,000 at the Astrodome; they came up 80,000 short. The letdown may have hastened the guru's maturation; he soon asserted more control over his U.S. operation. He was also said to be living so lavishly that the press ridiculed him as a materialistic brat. Then, while still under the age of consent, he married a twenty-four-year-old American follower and moved to a choice four acres in Malibu. His mother disowned him, flew home, and installed her eldest son as head of DLM in India.

The media lost interest after that, but Prem Rawat never stopped teaching. The last of his ashrams closed in 1983, and in time he eliminated virtually all of the Indian accessories, renounced the messianic claims, and renamed his organization Elan Vital. Still married and living in Malibu, the father of four, now in his fifties, has been traveling the world in a business suit, teaching a secularized Vedanta with the central message: "The peace we are looking for is within. It is in the heart, waiting to be felt. When people in the world are at peace within, the world will be at peace."[37]

While some ex-premies are bitter to this day over what they see as false promises and lost years in an oppressive cult, others are grateful for the association and still use the techniques they learned. Michael Nouri, for example, has had a distinguished acting career (playing Glenn Close's husband on the FX series *Damages*). "I seldom miss a day," he said of his practice. "It's been the most consistent commitment in my life." Another 1970s premie who is still at it is Timothy Gallwey, who met Maharaj Ji in 1971, then wrote a bestseller, *The Inner Game of Tennis*.[38] Gallwey, who went on to create an "Inner Game" empire of writing, coaching, and consulting, remains Prem Rawat's friend, student, and adviser. "You don't get tired of love, you don't get tired of joy, you don't get tired of peace," he said when I asked why he continues with the practices he learned nearly forty years ago. That is a consistent theme among the aging population that followed the gurus of the 1970s.

The Radical Iconoclast

Naughty, bawdy Bhagwan Shree Rajneesh was so unconventional and anti-tradition that he would not wish to be included with the gurus in this chapter. No doubt they would prefer it that way as well. Called "the swami of self-indulgence" by one reporter, he was to the spiritual scene what the Yippies were to the 1960s antiwar activists or the Dadaists were to modern art—an up-front, in-your-face provocateur. But his story is much more nuanced than that. Whereas the questionable behavior of other gurus had to be extracted from the shadows of their benign images, Rajneesh's reputation as the poster boy for exploitative cult leaders obscured his many incisive books and his positive impact on thousands of lives.

Rajneesh Chandra Mohan, born a Jain in 1931, was a brilliant, incendiary philosophy teacher at Indian universities before quitting in 1966 to devote his time to spiritual teaching and public speaking. By 1974 he had acquired the honorifics Bhagwan and Shree,[39] along with an ashram in Pune (aka Poona). Americans and Europeans flocked to his wildly eclectic mix of Vedic teachings, Western philosophy (he was fond of Nietzsche), psychological techniques drawn from the human potential movement, and meditation practices that he either adapted or created. Ever the iconoclast, he called his disciples sannyasins, even though sannyasi-like renunciation was not in the plan.

He actually ran a tight, disciplined operation, but the grapevine and the media made it sound like Woodstock East, with throngs of people letting loose in a frenzy of shouts and uninhibited movement, sometimes in the nude, and orgies of unrestrained sex. It was to a large extent true. But according to the people I interviewed, there was method in the madness. Rajneesh was out to awaken the unbounded awareness of the unitary Self that he, presumably, had realized. In preaching the liberation of consciousness, he was a traditional Vedantin. In other ways, he was a blend of George Carlin and Hugh Hefner.

The thrashing about was part of his Dynamic Meditation, in which the practitioner lets out pent-up energies before settling into a period of silence. Transcendental awareness was the aim, but Rajneesh felt that Westerners were too stressed out to meditate in the usual ways, so he had them unload first. Similarly, he agreed with the yogic principle of directing sexual energy upward to the higher centers, but he was aware of the pitfalls of a repressed libido, so he told his hormonally charged disciples to get it out of their systems. Those who did so would usually get more serious about pursuing realization. Those who came for kicks tended to leave after a while, because the ashram ethos was to spiritualize the sensual. Rajneesh encapsulated his vision with the term "Zorba the Buddha," combining the enlightened one with the lusty character portrayed by Anthony Quinn in the 1964 film.[40] Such a person, he said, would be "in the senses, enjoying the body," and also possess "a great consciousness."

Rajneesh contradicted himself; he acted arbitrarily, abrasively, and abusively; he made impossible demands; he said disgusting things and cracked offensive jokes. All of it he justified in the name of blowing minds in order to clear them. The approach, called "crazy wisdom," has a long history in the esoteric traditions. Georg Feuerstein, the founder-director of the Yoga Research and Education Center, defined it as "a unique mode of teaching, which avails itself of seemingly irreligious or unspiritual means in order to awaken the conventional ego-personality from its spiritual slumber."[41] In the hands of a compassionate and skillful master, the offbeat methods apparently work to the aspirant's benefit. In the hands of an incompetent or a con man, the student becomes a victim. Which category Rajneesh was in is a matter of debate. Faithful followers think he was a spiritual genius. His enemies, and they are legion, think he was a madman or a sadist. One thing is certain: his four years in America were marked by more crazy than wisdom.

Upon his arrival in 1981, he declared himself "the messiah America has been waiting for." At its height, the 64,000-acre spread he acquired in Oregon, christened Rajneeshpuram, had about three thousand residents and a constant flow of guests. Along with modern amenities, the virtual city boasted an airstrip, a reservoir, a private security force, an arsenal that the NRA would envy, and business operations that brought in millions. Rajneesh flaunted his infamous herd of Rolls-Royces, a symbol of ostentation that the media loved to exploit.

Paradise was lost when conflict with the surrounding community flared up. Ma Anand Sheela, the highest-ranking staff member, adopted insurgency tactics that prompted a criminal investigation. The media portrayed the ashram as a free love commune and a potential Jonestown, the notorious cult that had ended in mass suicide in 1978, and Rajneesh's appearances on *60 Minutes* and *Nightline* did nothing to assuage concern. The complete tale, including Rajneesh's reputed addiction to Valium and nitrous oxide, has enough bizarre twists to make a great Coen brothers movie. Suffice it to say, Sheela ended up doing time and Rajneesh cut a deal with immigration officials. He left the country in 1985. Changing his name to Osho, he resumed teaching in Pune, but his health went rapidly downhill and he died in 1990.

It is easy to conclude that Rajneesh-Osho took advantage of the naïve self-indulgence of the Me Generation and dealt a body blow to the reputation of Eastern spirituality. But the picture is more complicated than that. For one thing, thousands of his followers, now grandparents and solid citizens, continue to practice his techniques, study his writings, and in some cases live near one another and operate Osho-inspired businesses. His Pune facility, now the Osho International Meditation Resort, is an upscale personal growth center that has been called the Esalen of India. A prodigious archive of written and spoken material is being harvested by Osho International and turned into a steady flow of books.[42]

Hugh B. Urban of Ohio State University points to Rajneesh's contribution, calling him "one of the key figures in the remarkable transformation of 'Tantra' from a highly esoteric and elaborate ritual tradition into an extremely popular and widely marketed spiritual commodity for a Western audience."[43] At the risk of oversimplifying, it could be said that Tantra emerged to counter the strain of Vedanta that emphasized renunciation over worldly engagement. While many Westerners treat it strictly as a vehicle for sacred sex (sometimes only for *better* or *more* sex), its practices are designed to unite within the individual the silent, unmoving aspect of the divine (Shiva) and the dynamic aspect (Shakti).

If Rajneesh tolerated any label, it was that of *neo-Tantra*. Strictly speaking, his would be considered "left-hand Tantra," which attempts to transmute and spiritualize the so-called lower urges by indulging them rather than suppressing them. Even in the context of that unconventional tradition, however, Rajneesh was unconventional, and his legacy will be debated for a long time. However it turns out, his story clearly offers lessons on the pros and cons of spiritual eclecticism; on the uses and misuses of Tantra; and on the profits and pitfalls of brilliant, outrageous teachers. One former disciple summed it up with Dickensian flair: "He was the best of gurus, he was the worst of gurus."

Other Tributaries

The teachers profiled so far were major players in the Vedization of American spirituality in the post-Sixties era, but they were not the only ones. An astonishing number of relatively obscure teachers were active at the time. Their direct contributions may have been small trickles in the Vedic stream, but their influence has spread through the activities of some of their students. The silent yogi, Hari Das Baba (he communicates by writing on a chalkboard) has presided over the Mount Madonna Center outside Santa Cruz, California, since 1971, when Ram Dass brought him here from India.[44] Sant Keshavadas, a bhakti guru who made the United States a regular pit stop from the 1970s into the 1990s, trained perhaps the best-known expert on mantras in America, Thomas Ashley-Farrand (Namadeva Acharya)—who, in turn, trains Vedic priests and teachers.[45] Gurani Anjali, one of the rare female gurus, taught in Amityville, Long Island, from the 1960s until her death in 2001. A householder with a family, her Yoga Anand Ashram had a small group of followers that included Christopher Chapple, who is now a well-published scholar and the creator of the unique Yoga Philosophy Program at Loyola Marymount University.[46]

Swami Amar Jyoti established ashrams in Arizona and Colorado; his followers now run them and also publish books and the quarterly *Light of
Consciousness.*[47] And Paramahamsa Hariharananda, from the same lineage
as Yogananda, passed through America frequently and left behind an ashram in Florida. He died at age ninety-five in 2002, having influenced numerous followers, including Swami Vidyadhishananda Giri, who started
the Self Enquiry Life Fellowship in Santa Barbara, and Andrew Cohen, an
American guru and founder of *EnlightenNext* magazine (see chapter 14).[48]

Countless other gurus had an impact on the West without ever leaving their homeland, thanks to the many pilgrims who returned from their
journeys with stories, knowledge, and sometimes training. Of course, in
India, gurus and swamis are as easy to find as rickshaws, so most of them
are known to only a handful. But some, such as Neem Karoli Baba, Sri
Aurobindo, and Ramana Maharshi, who are discussed elsewhere in the
book, continue to influence Americans long after their deaths. You will,
for example, find the stunning image of Anandamayi Ma on the altars
of Americans who never laid eyes on her in person. One of India's most
beloved spiritual figures, the "Joy-Permeated Mother" was a magnet for
ordinary villagers, Indian dignitaries, and even other gurus. In the 1970s
her *darshan* was coveted by Westerners on the guru trail.[49]

So too was the *darshan* of Sathya Sai Baba, and it still is. If you've been
to a Hard Rock Café, you will probably have seen the phrase "Love All,
Serve All" and a photo of a dark-skinned, smiling man in a big fuzzy Afro.
You may have thought the slogan was aimed at the restaurant staff and
the picture was of an Earth, Wind & Fire musician, but both belong to the
guru whom Hard Rock cofounder Isaac Tigrett credits with changing his
life. Tigrett, who funded Sai Baba's five-hundred-room hospital in South
India, is not the only one. I am told that there are about two hundred
Sathya Sai Centers in the United States, mostly in people's homes, serving
about ten thousand devotees.

What sets Sai Baba apart are the alleged miracles he performs on a
regular basis. Much less practical than turning loaves to fishes, they involve conjuring, seemingly out of nowhere, *vibhuthi,* an ashlike substance
alleged to be a manifestation of divinity, and sometimes watches, rings,

and other trinkets. Needless to say, sleight-of-hand artists and filmmakers have attempted to prove that the manifestations are merely parlor tricks.[50]

Far more disturbing are allegations that Sai Baba has sexually molested young boys. Neither charge has reduced the flow of pilgrims to the guru's spacious ashram near Bangalore. Some visitors are merely curious; others find the atmosphere spiritually rejuvenating; and many are devotees who believe that Sai Baba is an incarnation of God who has come to set things right in the world. According to the Sai gospel, he will live until 2022. Considering the state of the planet, if he is "the avatar of this age," he has his work cut out for him between now and then.

In addition to the thousands whose lives have been affected by his message to realize their divine nature, honor all religious traditions, and serve God by serving others, Sai Baba's devotees include two gurus with American followers of their own. One is Sai Maa Lakshmi Devi, a woman of Indian descent from the African island of Mauritius who is headquartered in Crestone, Colorado. She is a kind of Auntie Mame guru, frank and clever, with a flamboyant flair, and her teachings are typically Vedantic with a strong dose of the occult and some unique creations, such as her Brain Illumination Meditation. Also a disciple of Sai Baba was the late Swamini Turiyasangitananda, aka Alice Coltrane. The musician-composer embarked on an intense spiritual quest after her renowned husband, John, died in 1967. Eventually she took sannyasi vows and in 1975 began teaching. While continuing to compose and perform, she presided over her ashram, Shanti Anantam, in the hills between Malibu and the San Fernando Valley, until her death in January 2007.[51]

Every guru described in this chapter was a yogi and a teacher of Yoga in that they pointed followers to the liberating union of self and Self and instructed them in methods of achieving it. But the physical practices that have come to define Yoga in the West—predominantly the postures known as asanas and, to a lesser extent, the breathing exercises called pranayama—were either left out of their inventories or treated as incidental. Muktananda, for example, trained instructors to teach Hatha practices to those who wanted to learn. Others had similar policies. The gurus in the next chapter placed the familiar postures and movements front and center and made prominent use of the term *yoga* in their presentations, their marketing materials, and in some cases, the names of their organizations. While they were by no means the first to do so (we've already mentioned some of their predecessors), because they taught in an era of unprecedented receptivity and media exposure, they played a seminal role in putting Yoga as we know it on the map.

THE YOGA BEARERS

I f your Yoga teacher references a traditional text as *the* authoritative source on the subject, it is likely to be the *Yoga Sutras,* a pithy series of aphoristic statements (*sutra* means "thread") composed by the sage Patanjali, who lived, most scholars believe, in the second century B.C.E. What surprises most people who read an English translation—and there are dozens—is that Patanjali barely mentions *asana,* the word associated with the stretches and bends that occupy 90 percent or more of their Yoga classes. The *sutras'* main concern is the attainment of union, or yoga, through the cessation of the mind's incessant fluctuations.[1] The now-familiar asanas were developed as a way to foster that purpose through physical means, mainly as prelude to meditation. That they are also terrific for getting in shape, beating stress, and staying healthy was always considered a fringe benefit.

The Yoga masters who became popular in the 1960s and 1970s understood that larger context. They taught what is often called Classical Yoga, addressing all of Patanjali's eight limbs, of which asana is but one (and mainly in reference to sitting posture). Casual students may have seen the Yoga masters as instructors, but to their close followers they occupied the exalted position of guru. At the same time, their classes set the template for today's physically oriented Yoga boom. That is why they are grouped together in this chapter.

The Integral Yogi

He was right out of central casting if you were looking for a leading-man alternative to Maharishi's diminutive cuteness: tall, lean, and muscular, with a thick mane of wavy black hair and a gray pillow of a beard, both of which turned snow white in the nearly four decades he lived in America. For most of that time, Swami Satchidananda was the most visible face of Yoga.

Born C. K. Ramaswamy Gounder in 1914 in South India, he was a husband and a father who had worked in various businesses when his wife died tragically young. Placing his sons in the care of his family, he wandered for eight years from ashram to temple, mountaintop to jungle. His pilgrimage led north, and in 1949 he arrived in Rishikesh. There he met his guru, Swami Sivananda (1887–1963), who had, at age thirty-six, given up a lucrative medical practice to become a monk and eventually would turn a cowshed into an ashram. Among its early visitors was a young Romanian named Mircea Eliade, who studied with Sivananda for six months in the 1920s. Eliade (1907–1986) became one of the most distinguished academic figures of the century, publishing numerous classics in the study of religion, some of which—*Yoga: Immortality and Freedom* and *Patanjali and Yoga*—bear the obvious stamp of India.[2] Eliade taught at the University of Chicago from 1956 until his death; the chair in history of religions is named for him. Sivananda's ashram, the Divine Life Society, grew to dominate the western bank of the Ganges. It remains the cornerstone of the holy city, and Sivananda, a strapping, vigorous monk with a shaved head and face, remains synonymous with Yoga around the world, thanks to his hundreds of books and pamphlets and the teachers he sent forth with his aphorism "Serve, Love, Give, Purify, Meditate, Realize."[3]

By far the most famous of Sivananda's successors, Swami Satchidananda was teaching at his guru's behest in Sri Lanka (then Ceylon) when, in 1966, an American filmmaker named Conrad Rooks sought him out for help with his drug addiction. An heir to the Avon cosmetics fortune, Rooks flew Satchidananda to Paris, where he was working on a movie titled *Chappaqua*. The film was eventually released to resounding derision.

But its making was a turning point in American Veda, not just because Satchidananda appeared in it, but because he met two then-unknown artists who were working on the film with Rooks: painter Peter Max and composer Philip Glass. Max invited the guru to visit New York, putting him up on a foldout bed in his living room and gathering a bunch of hipsters to listen to him speak.[4] Max and friends chipped in to keep the guru around. An apartment on West End Avenue was leased, and Hatha Yoga, meditation, chanting, and Vedantic discourses were offered. Before long, so many were showing up that the Friday-night talks were moved to a Unitarian church.

In its 2002 obituary the New York Times wrote of Satchidananda, "Among the many Indian gurus then appearing in America, he was regarded as more tolerant of the often heavily medicated flower children." His message about drugs—you can't take a pill to become enlightened any more than you can take one to become a doctor—prompted many to replace acid with asanas. One side effect of hippies turning onto Yoga was a change in Peter Max's art. "I found myself creating images that depicted a peaceful, euphoric cosmos," he later said. His whimsical, color-saturated posters became the visual backdrop of the flower-power era.

Satchidananda established his Integral Yoga Institute (IYI) in 1966.[5] The system is defined as "the complete Yoga, which integrates all aspects of life and maintains our natural condition of an easeful body, peaceful mind, and useful life." Musician Stephen Fiske, a longtime devotee, calls its blend of traditional practices "deep yoga, not cosmetic photo-op yoga." IYI grew steadily, and when the Beatles made gurus as hip as long hair, the place took off.

In January 1969 Satchidananda lectured to a packed Carnegie Hall. That August he was invited to open what posters quaintly called the Woodstock Music and Art Fair. Helicoptered in from the city, he sat cross-legged on an elevated platform and greeted the four hundred thousand tightly packed youngsters with a salutation that recalled Vivekananda's at the 1893 parliament: "My beloved sisters and brothers." Excerpts of his talk were viewed by millions in the film Woodstock, which won the Academy Award for best documentary in 1970. "America is helping everybody in the material field," he said, "but the time has come for America to help the whole world with spirituality also." He added, "Let us not fight for peace, but let us find peace within ourselves first." He concluded with a traditional chant, followed by a short period of silence. To this day followers credit his calming influence with averting what might have been a catastrophe when the rains came and food and shelter grew scarce.

Having outgrown its West Side apartment, IYI moved in 1970 to a Greenwich Village townhouse, aided by funding from Alice Coltrane, who studied with Satchidananda before meeting Sai Baba and becoming a swami herself. The Thirteenth Street ashram and teaching center remains a Village fixture, along with Integral Yoga Natural Foods, Integral Yoga Natural Apothecary, and Integral Yoga Bookstore. In the mid-1970s, another music legend assisted IYI's real estate needs when Carole King donated her northern Connecticut estate, Music Mountain.[6] The property was soon sold to purchase land in central Virginia, which was turned into a compound called Yogaville in 1979. Occupying about a thousand acres along the James River, it contains the headquarters of Integral Yoga International as well as the Satchidananda Ashram, which conducts a busy schedule of workshops, retreats, and teacher-training programs. The surrounding area has been settled largely by householder devotees.

While a number of organizations lay claim to jump-starting the Yoga craze, IYI can make a strong case for the title. In the early 1970s, its teachers began fanning out across the continent, and many of the monks and nuns Satchidananda started training in 1975 went on to become leaders. The "Woodstock guru" also left a mark as a tireless emissary for the Vedic principle that became his motto: "Truth is one, paths are many." In the 1970s, interfaith activities were far less commonplace than they are now, and only rarely did they include the Eastern traditions. Satchidananda was instrumental in changing that. He was photographed with popes, priests, ministers, and presidents (Carter, Bush 41, and Clinton), and received numerous awards from humanitarian organizations. He also teamed with Rabbi Joseph Gelberman for a series of popular dialogues, "The Swami and the Rabbi," and helped Gelberman create the New Seminary, the first institution to ordain interfaith ministers.[7] His commitment to the interfaith ideal is symbolized in Yogaville's stunning Light of Truth Universal Shrine (LOTUS). Surrounded by landscaped grounds, ponds, fountains, and plazas, the domed shrine is to interfaith what the Taj Mahal is to earthly love.[8]

Satchidananda's legacy is perhaps most profoundly felt in health care, through the efforts of two early followers, Drs. Sandra (Amrita) McLanahan and bestselling author Dean Ornish, to bring yogic principles to medical practice (see chapter 16). He also produced a host of other emissaries, like folksinger Stephen Fiske. "I see the world through a yogic filter," Fiske told me. He conveys that vision in performances at interfaith, peace, and environmental gatherings. Another longtime devotee, psychotherapist and business consultant Bruce Fern draws on Vedantic principles and yogic practices without making reference to either. He cites by way of example a technique for replacing a negative thought pattern with its polar opposite. He calls it "opposite substitution"; in Patanjali's *Yoga Sutras* it goes by the name *pratipaksha bhavana*.

Since the passing of its leader in 2002, IYI has continued to grow, adapting to changing times while holding true to its origins. "We won't do what others have done—pull out two limbs, asana and pranayama, and call it yoga," says Swami Asokananda, a former IYI president who first laid eyes on Satchidananda at Woodstock when his name was Jeffrey.[9]

The Flying Swami

Satchidananda was Swami Sivananda's best-known emissary to the West, but he was not the only one. Two German-born disciples, Sita Frankel and Sylvia Hellman, made a mark in North America. As Swami Radha, Hellman established an ashram in Vancouver.[10] Sivananda's successor, Swami Chidananda, visited several times and influenced numerous Western teachers, including Lilias Folan. And one direct disciple who preceded Satchidananda to America was vital to the development of Western Yoga.

Swami Vishnudevananda became a sannyasi in 1949 at age twenty-two. He quickly proved to be so adept at Hatha Yoga that Sivananda put him in charge of that aspect of ashram life and, in 1957, sent him to the West with, it is said, less than a dollar's worth of rupees and this farewell: "People are waiting." From the time he arrived in California, Swami Vishnu (as he was often called) traveled incessantly, propounding what Sivananda called the "Yoga of Synthesis" because it combined Karma, Jnana, and Bhakti Yogas for the development of "hand, head and heart." In 1960 he published *The Complete Illustrated Book of Yoga,* which has since sold over a million copies. The next year he established his first center, in Montreal, and followed that with the Sivananda Ashram Yoga Camp in the mountains of Quebec. A brownstone in the Chelsea section of Manhattan became the Sivananda Yoga Vedanta Center in 1964. (It is still there.) In quick succession, ashram/retreat centers were set up in the Bahamas (1967); Grass Valley, California (1971); and upstate New York (1974).[11]

In his early years Vishnudevananda was the guy New Yorkers turned to for Yoga. Later he spent most of his time at his headquarters in Canada and at his winter location in the Bahamas—where, it is said, he taught Yoga to the Beatles when they were filming *Help!* The swami also had a bit of the showman in him. He earned the nickname "Flying Swami" by piloting his own two-seater into the airspace of trouble-spot countries and "bombing" them with flowers and peace leaflets. Carrying only a "Planet Earth Passport," designed by Peter Max with doves and religious symbols, he flew over Northern Ireland, the Suez Canal, the Berlin Wall, and the West Bank. Needless to say, these missions attracted more media attention than his tireless teaching. He was among the first, if not *the* first, to design training programs to certify Yoga teachers. His organization claims to have trained about twenty thousand around the world.

Long after the founder's death in 1993, and despite the ubiquitous presence of hip Yoga studios, Sivananda centers continue to thrive, attracting students who are drawn to a classical Yoga that sticks to its spiritual roots. In addition, teachers trained by the organization have carved out niches of their own. Back in the 1960s, for instance, one of Swami Vishnu's students, Ganga White, opened the Center for Yoga, which played a central role in establishing Hatha Yoga in Los Angeles. The author of *Yoga Beyond Belief,* White now runs the White Lotus Foundation in Santa Barbara.

That tradition continues with Sivananda-trained teachers like Suvani Stepanek, a mainstay of Bay Area Yoga who teaches classes for credit at San Francisco City College, and Durga (née Catherine O'Neill), whose Yoga of Recovery combines yogic practices, Ayurveda, and twelve-step tools. Finally, Vishnudevananda's centers are largely responsible for the ongoing popularity of the Divine Life Society in Rishikesh as a pilgrimage destination for Westerners, many of whom disseminate Vedantic teachings when they get home.[12]

Himalayan Mastery

Six foot one and clean-shaven, the forty-four-year-old Swami Rama arrived in America in 1969 to teach what he called the Himalayan tradition. Born Brij Kishor Kumar, he studied at European universities after taking monastic vows, then headed to the United States. It is said that his first office was a Chicago motel room with a double-entendre sign taped to the door: "Swami Rama: Inquire Within." People did inquire, and before long he came to the attention of Elmer Green, a biopsychologist and founder of the Voluntary Controls Program at the famed Menninger Clinic in Topeka, Kansas. Green and his wife, psychologist Alyce Green, having heard that yogis could mentally control involuntary physiological processes, invited Swami Rama to the clinic.

During an extended residency in 1970 and 1971, he changed the temperature of his skin, raised and lowered his heart rate, altered his brainwave patterns, and stopped his heart from pumping blood.[13] The scientific documentation of these feats was a leap forward in the West's understanding of the mind-body relationship and a major step in the development of biofeedback training. With articles about him appearing in national publications, and students eager to learn from him, Swami Rama established the Himalayan International Institute of Yoga Science and Philosophy in Chicago. Branches and affiliated centers cropped up, and in 1977 the institute moved to its present location on four hundred acres in the Pennsylvania Poconos. The following year Swami Rama's name and teachings were again made widely known through physician Rudolph Ballentine, who made a big splash with *Diet and Nutrition: A Holistic Approach.*[14]

In addition to serving as an ashram, the Himalayan Institute has been a popular destination for retreats, seminars, and Yoga-teacher training. The emphasis, an institute spokesperson told me, is on "systematic personal transformation" based on "the full range of yoga philosophy." When Swami Rama died in 1996 he was succeeded by his chief disciple, Pandit Rajmani Tigunait, a married man with two children and two Ph.D.'s, one in Sanskrit and one in philosophy.[15]

Swami Rama's influence endures through several channels. The Himalayan Institute Press distributes dozens of his books, most famously *Living with the Himalayan Masters,* as well as books by Pandit Tigunait, Ballentine, and others. Its bimonthly magazine, *Yoga + Joyful Living,* goes to about one hundred thousand readers. The thousands of instructors trained by the institute are active everywhere from affiliated centers to independent studios and YMCAs. Swami Rama also initiated several Americans into the monastic life, some of whom now teach on their own.[16] Other disciples spread the word in their own ways. An acupuncturist named Ragani, for example, met Swami Rama at age eight, after her mother read Ballentine's book. She later became the guru's personal assistant and studied Indian vocal music under his guidance. Now living in Milwaukee, her monthly *kirtan* evenings draw three hundred to four hundred enthusiasts from all religious backgrounds—this in a city known mainly for beer, *Laverne and Shirley,* and Green Bay Packer fanatics.[17]

Rebirth in the Berkshires

Unlike most other gurus, Amrit Desai was a married man, not a monk. He and his wife emigrated to Philadelphia in 1960. While working as an artist at design and textile companies, he started teaching Yoga in his home. He had studied in India with Swami Kripalvananda, for whom he named the system he developed, Kripalu Yoga, which adds to the standard toolkit an element of spontaneous flow that Desai called "meditation in motion."

Before long he gave up his day job. In 1972 he moved to an ashramlike setting in the countryside and began to function more like a traditional guru.
In 1983 he and a couple of hundred *chelas* (disciples) settled in a former
Jesuit seminary in Lenox, Massachusetts, on a scenic Berkshires hilltop
down the road from the famed Tanglewood Music Center. Now able to
draw students from New York and New England, Kripalu blossomed.

In an instructive example of East-West adaptation, the institute offered
courses by outside health practitioners, spiritual teachers, and psychologists in addition to its own Yoga programs. Meanwhile, the residents
lived in an austere environment in which the guru was king, individual-
ity was subordinated, single devotees were expected to observe celibacy,
and couples were advised to exercise monkish sexual restraint. The clash
of those two worlds proved decisive in Kripalu's death and resurrection.
"The traditional guru-disciple relationship was keeping a lid on personal
empowerment and on the energy of cocreativity in the community," writes
psychologist Stephen Cope in *Yoga and the Quest for the True Self,* and that
atmosphere "collided directly with the spirit of American pluralism, democracy, realism, and self-reliance." There was, says Cope, "a longing for a
new level of authenticity."[18]

The karma hit the fan in 1994, when it was revealed that the still-
married Desai had had affairs with longtime staff members. We'll return
to the crisis in chapter 11. Suffice it to say that Desai was forced to leave,
and after a tumultuous period of legal battles, internal squabbling, and
personal anguish, what is now the Kripalu Center for Yoga and Health was
reborn as an educational nonprofit. It is the leading residential Yoga center
in the country, and its workshops attract more than fifteen thousand a
year, including many Yoga teachers who come to bolster their skills. The
institute also works with scientists to study the effects of Yoga on various
parameters of well-being.[19]

Like the community he created and let down, Amrit Desai demonstrated a phoenixlike capacity to rise from the ashes. He now runs the
Amrit Yoga Institute in Salt Springs, Florida.[20]

The Postural Yogis

The gurus mentioned so far were instrumental in making *yoga* a household word during the 1970s. Also playing a role was Yogi Bhajan, a Sikh economist who gave up a promising position in the New Delhi government to teach his form of Kundalini Yoga, which combines meditation, prayer, asanas, and breathing exercises. Eventually his 3HO Foundation (for "healthy, happy, holy") turned out hundreds of certified teachers, many of whom are recognizable by the white garments and turbans of traditional Sikhism. Married with three children, Yogi Bhajan also led the effort to get Sikhism recognized as a religion in America and as an entrepreneur started several natural foods lines (e.g., the multiflavored Yogi Tea brand in health food stores).[21]

But the direct antecedent of the bustling Hatha Yoga scene, with its almost exclusive emphasis on asana practice, was the arrival of K. Patthabhi Jois and B.K.S. Iyengar in the mid-1970s. They were *gurubais* (brother devotees of the same guru) of an innovative master who might be called the Thomas Edison of modern Hatha Yoga. Whichever system your favorite Yoga studio emphasizes, the chances are that, as Fernando Pagés Ruiz put it in a *Yoga Journal* article, "your practice stems from one source: a five-foot, two-inch Brahmin born more than one hundred years ago in a small South Indian village." The diminutive innovator was Tirumalai Krishnamacharya, who straddled tradition and modernity as a devout Vaishnavite (worshipper of Vishnu) and a polymath with degrees in both Western and Indian disciplines. Born in 1888, in the midst of the Hindu Renaissance, he researched ancient sources that had been buried under the sludge of colonialism and adapted them to the modern era with relentless experimentation. His formulation of asana and pranayama became the foundation of today's physical Yoga.

In the 1920s and 1930s, under the patronage of the Maharaja of Mysore, Krishnamacharya delivered countless lectures and demonstrations. He also trained three students who would become key propagators of his teachings in the West. In a double break from orthodoxy, one was both European and female. Indra Devi, born Zhenia Labunskaia in Latvia, displayed such dedication and competence that Krishnamacharya made her his emissary. From 1947 until 1985, when she moved to Argentina (where she was a celebrity until her death in 2002), she introduced Yoga to the American masses through her book *Forever Young, Forever Healthy,* public appearances, and press coverage of the stars who attended her Hollywood classes.

Krishnamacharya's other principle *chelas,* Jois and Iyengar, developed systems whose elements suffuse today's Hatha Yoga as African rhythms permeate popular music. From 1937 to 1973 Jois headed the Yoga department at Sanskrit College in Mysore, and in 1948 founded the Ashtanga Yoga Research Institute, which became one of the prime training grounds for Western teachers. He came to America in 1975 at age sixty and returned fifteen times, at one point making news as the teacher of Madonna and Sting. His Ashtanga Yoga is a vigorous system whose trademark feature, *vinyasa,* denotes flowing movement, synchronized with breath, through a sequence of asanas.

Iyengar, Jois's classmate in the 1930s, became the most influential figure in the creation of what British scholar Elizabeth De Michelis terms Modern Postural Yoga.[22] His own life is a testimonial to Yoga's health benefits. "I was suffering from influenza, malaria, tuberculosis, typhoid, and so on and so forth," he says in the excellent documentary *Yoga Unveiled.* At age sixteen, his sister's husband, Krishnamacharya, suggested that Yoga might improve his brother-in-law's condition. Iyengar took to it big time, then took it worldwide, through the institute he created in Pune in 1947. "It's hard to imagine how our yoga would look without Iyengar's contributions," wrote Ruiz, "especially his precisely detailed, systematic articulation of each asana, his research into therapeutic applications, and his multi-tiered, rigorous training system which has produced so many influential teachers." Not to mention the props he invented to help students enter into difficult postures.

Jiddu Krishnamurti was a student of Iyengar's (and vice versa, apparently). So was violinist Yehudi Menuhin, who introduced him to the West in the mid-1950s.[23] In 1973, on Menuhin's recommendation, an American musician named Mary Palmer studied with Iyengar in India, then invited him to teach at the Ann Arbor, Michigan, YMCA. By then Iyen-gar's book, *Light on Yoga* (1966), had "brought the performance and teach-ing of *asana* . . . to new, impressive standards of completeness regarding range of postural variation and performance proficiency," writes De Mi-chelis. During his ensuing visits to the United States, Iyengar began train-ing teachers, who then fanned out across the land. The training became formalized, certification procedures were introduced, and the methods became so popular that Iyengar conventions were held about every three years. By now those who teach under the banner of what came to be called Iyengar Yoga constitute only a portion of those who were influenced by the master's techniques. De Michelis calls Iyengar Yoga "arguably the most influential and widespread school of Modern Postural Yoga worldwide."

If longevity is any measure of Yoga's value, consider that Krishna-macharya lived to 100, Indra Devi to 102, Patthabhi Jois to 94, and the once-sickly Iyengar, born in 1918, still teaches at his institute in Pune. Meanwhile, Krishnamacharya's son, T.K.V. Desikachar, born in 1938, has carried on his father's legacy since 1976 as head of the Krishnamacharya Yoga Mandiram in Chennai.

Unlike the other gurus in this and the previous chapter, Iyengar and Jois did not establish American ashrams or communities of disciples. Like visiting professors, they spent most of their time at their home campuses in India. "They emphasized professionalization, not discipleship," says longtime Iyengar teacher Lisa Walford. As a result, they were untouched by the rumors, scandals, and revelations that attended other gurus in the 1970s (the subject of chapter 11). They do, however, bear the burden of another concern: that Yoga is now widely seen as just a calmer form of fitness training.

This unmistakable trend, a side effect of Yoga's tremendous success, is troublesome to those who esteem the larger meaning of the word and who pursue the tradition's deeper purpose. "It's an American talent to take something deep and make it as superficial as possible," the veteran L.A. Yoga teacher Steve Ross told me. Many place the blame at the feet of Iyengar and, to a lesser extent, Jois, for making one of classical Yoga's eight limbs—asana—so prominent as to virtually redefine the ancient system in its own terms. One longtime practitioner compared it to the popularity of pizza, which is, for many young Americans, the beginning and end of Italian food. The concern is real, but as we'll see, countervailing forces make it highly doubtful that Yoga's spiritual treasures will get buried by the weight of twenty million bodies stretching and bending. In fact, the opposite may be true: the Yoga masters who came here, regardless of their orientations and specialties, created a foundation for the wider dissemination of Vedic teachings as a whole. Students may come for a workout, but their minds stretch and bend too.[24]

In the 1970s and beyond, enthusiastic young women and men were drawn to Yoga classes, ashrams, and institutes. Some of them led the way to today's Yoga phenomenon. They trained hard, learned how to teach others, and adapted what they'd been taught to the language and social ethos of contemporary culture. Some established their own studios, their own hybrid teaching styles, and their own brands. Some, like David Life and Sharon Gannon at New York's Jivamukti Yoga, experimented with musical forms as background atmospherics, practically creating a new genre of music in the bargain. Some started to train teachers themselves. Magazines were launched (not just *Yoga Journal,* the most successful of the lot, but a host of local and institutional publications with loyal readers), conferences were held, products were invented and marketed, teacher certification procedures were established, and organizations were formed to maintain standards. The end result is the biggest and most sustained penetration of the Vedic tradition in America since the post-Beatles heyday of TM.

II

SEX, LIES, AND
IDIOSYNCRASIES

Tibetan Buddhists compare gurus to fire: stay too far away, and you don't get warm; venture too close, and you can be burned. Ever since seekers of the sacred first bowed at the feet of holy men on mountaintops and riverbanks, they have sought the right psychic distance, where they can be both warm and safe. In the rowdy period from Kent State and *M*A*S*H*, through Watergate and *Star Wars,* to Ronald Reagan and *Apocalypse Now,* when gurus were new and especially hot, those who turned to them for spiritual guidance struggled to find their balance point. The gurus who attracted large followings were uncommonly brilliant, charismatic, and skilled. Their timeless call to awaken the divinity within was alluring, and their methods brought peace to millions of tremulous souls. But their all-too-human flaws and, in some instances, misbehavior, also caused pain.

A certain irony brings smiles to the lips of boomers who lived through it: many members of the most antiauthoritarian generation in the history of the most antiauthoritarian nation in the world relinquished their spiritual autonomy to authority figures. Freedom lovers in guru-centered movements willingly gave up freedoms they would have scratched and clawed to protect in the outside world. Youngsters who didn't trust their parents or teachers—or presumably, anyone over thirty—trusted gray-bearded gurus, sometimes to the point of puppylike obedience, on the theory that the master's heart is so pure and his awareness so perfectly attuned to divine intelligence that surrendering to his will is not a sacrifice but an act of supreme self-interest, for it would surely lead to the highest freedom of all. For many, that leap of faith yielded rich rewards, if not exactly *moksha*. But it also led to disillusionment and pain, some of which lingers still. Thousands of young people had difficulty extracting themselves from the grip of authoritarian communities, and even from benign institutions that unwittingly fostered childlike dependence. Many grew cynical and resentful when they discovered chicanery or incompetence on the part of spiritual leaders whom they'd placed on the highest of pedestals. And some were deeply wounded by a guru's betrayal of his own moral standards.

The scandal involving Swami Muktananda was the most sensational of the era, because of his fame, the media exposure, and the fact that the allegations involved adolescent girls. But sex-related upheavals also rocked other communities.[1] Even gurus who were *not* caught with their dhotis down had accusations and rumors attached to them, sometimes long after their deaths. In 2007, more than thirty years after the passing of Swami Prabhavananda, Vivekananda's best-known heir in the United States, the Hollywood Vedanta Society shook as though an L.A. temblor had hit it when a former nun, Vijali Hamilton, published a memoir alleging a two-year affair with the swami in the 1960s.[2] To this day, long after the Mia Farrow rumors were put to rest, stories circulate about Maharishi Mahesh Yogi having had affairs in the early 1970s. You can even find online arguments over whether Paramahansa Yogananda messed around with his nuns in the 1920s!

In most of these cases, it is unlikely the allegations will ever be proved or disproved. But others are widely assumed to be grounded in fact, since witnesses and participants have come forward with consistent stories. The charges against Swami Rama, for instance, were reported in a 1990 *Yoga Journal* article by journalist Katharine Webster, and after the guru's death one of the alleged victims was awarded damages by a Pennsylvania court.[3]

Most instances centered on liaisons between adult female disciples and a revered guru who advocated celibacy for his followers and had taken a vow of celibacy himself.

Denials and Denunciations

The reactions of devotees to the charges against their gurus ranged along a continuum. At one extreme was outright denial: our guru could never do such things; the women making the allegations are either lying or delusional. Next to that was spiritual rationalization: if it happened, there has to be a cosmic reason for it because whatever the guru does is in accord with divine will. Under that rationale the women most people saw as victims were sometimes considered blessed. Some of the faithful adopted a nonjudgmental but loyal position. As one longtime follower of an accused guru told me, "It was always my feeling that it's not for me to question the guru, so I never wavered." In the middle of the spectrum were rational and pragmatic responses, basically: maybe it happened, maybe it didn't; either way, it doesn't detract from the benefits I've gained from the practices. Among those who accepted the charges as true, some shrugged it off on the principle that it's all about the teaching, not the teacher. Those who felt that way were likely never to have seen the guru as perfect to begin with. Others were devastated. Some disciples were so outraged they left their communities, either in search of a more perfect master or to continue their spiritual quests guru-free, while others were so disgusted that they concluded that Eastern spirituality is a fraud and plunged headlong into the material world. The most indignant filed lawsuits and launched truth-telling campaigns, some of which still rage on the Internet.

Many followers who had once dismissed the charges as ludicrous have since come to accept them as valid, or at least plausible, as evidence mounted and their emotional attachment to the guru diminished. But conflict remains over how to interpret what happened. Some, of course, consider it sexual exploitation, plain and simple, and where underage victims were involved, it was criminal. But where consenting adults are concerned, the question of interpretation gets quite complicated. Was the guilty guru just a horndog in holy garb? Was he a spiritual paragon who succumbed to human urges as he aged? Was he exploiting innocent victims? Or was he master of esoteric techniques of genital union for the purpose of driving spiritual energy to the higher centers?

Tantric literature offers precedent for the last view, giving some devotees reason to believe that even Muktananda's alleged juvenile consorts had not been victimized but rather were initiated by a true *siddha*.[4] To which opponents say, poppycock: Tantric sexuality is meant for consenting yogis properly trained in the sacred rites, not for naïve acolytes in the most unequal of relationships. Similar arguments have been proffered in defense of other guru dalliances. In the case of Sathya Sai Baba's alleged fondling of young boys, while some call for his arrest many loyal devotees either vehemently deny the charges or claim that the avatar, in his wisdom, was healing the boys' karmic wounds.

One institution, Kripalu, has earned respect for its mature response to its trauma. The secret of Amrit Desai's dalliances had been festering among close disciples for years, according to a former devotee who compared it to a cancer that had been diagnosed but left untreated. It might never have been exposed at all had the visiting experts who taught at the center not encouraged residents to examine their communal dynamics. When the truth came out, friends such as Jungian scholar Marian Woodman helped them to face it head-on. The stunned followers confronted their guru, demanded his resignation, and forced him to publicly confess and make amends. Kripalu's subsequent success would likely have been inconceivable had they responded with denial or circled the wagons defensively, as other institutions did in similar circumstances.[5]

Bureaucratic Follies

The sex scandals haunt people to this day, and they captured the attention of the media. But they weren't the only issues to disturb the peace of guru-based communities. Others had to do with organizational defects;

some involved the kinds of foibles that drive office workers crazy (as in the comic strip *Dilbert*), while others centered on the misuse of money or abusive leadership.

Every spiritual tradition extols the importance of community. In Sanskrit, it's called *sangha,* and it's one of the three "jewels" (aka gems) in which Buddhists take refuge.[6] Most gurus created structures for communal support and the propagation of their teachings. The institutions are structured like atoms, with a series of orbits around a nucleus. In the center sits the guru, alone like the sun. Around him circle the closest disciples and the highest-ranking officials, often the same people. Because the orbits nearest the nucleus are said to be the most spiritually rewarding, devotees tend to do their best—some might say their worst, since the competition can get pretty rough—to gain entry and stay there. But those inner orbits also demand the most in conformity, obedience, and surrender, so most followers eventually drift to more distant circles, where the organizations feel less like religions or cults than educational institutions where one can partake of the teachings without giving up one's autonomy.

That's what happened in most Vedic organizations as they grew in size and ambition and more and more dysfunctions surfaced. Some of those flaws can be viewed as typical of all organizations, especially those with lofty aims staffed by volunteers. But even minor annoyances and small ethical lapses hit members of guru-centered communities hard because they show that the leaders they looked up to, or even worshipped, do not possess the level of wisdom, kindness, or integrity they assumed they had. The blow is especially devastating when organizational blemishes are more than petty.

During the interviews I conducted for this book, anger surfaced when former devotees recounted tales of financial chicanery: constant pressure to donate money or sign up for pricey programs; funds diverted to the personal enjoyment of officials or the aggrandizement of the guru; and mysteries about where the money went. (In their defense, many organizations describe a Robin Hood–like transfer of funds from the affluent West to projects in the developing world.) Other stories centered on authoritarian control: lack of transparency; members ostracized or punished for unexplained reasons and without a chance to defend themselves; edicts handed down from the top without discussion; intolerance of dissent; doubt treated as a personal shortcoming; and the demand for obedience. The worst stories resembled the chilling tales of defectors from totalitarian regimes, with spies, informants, physical threats, disinformation campaigns, bribery, doctored photos . . . the list goes on, and anyone interested in the details can find them on the Web.[7]

Grist for the Mill

To some extent these follies and tragedies can be attributed to culture clash: a top-down, hierarchical management model, with long roots in tradition and monasticism, was transplanted to the egalitarian, democratic West, where "question authority" is a bumper sticker. But the takeaway transcends organizational dynamics. The larger issues that came to the surface in the 1970s centered on the nature of gurus: who and what they really are, and how Western seekers can best relate to them. Cynical outsiders see any whiff of authoritarianism as proof that all gurus are brainwashing charlatans who exploit the gullible for money, sex, or both, and any sign of scandal as confirmation that Asian spirituality is as unwelcome as Asian flu. The hostility was especially virulent in the late 1970s, after the mass suicide at Jonestown, when even the most benign spiritual communities were suspected of being dangerous cults.

The reality is far more nuanced, since the same gurus who ran dysfunctional organizations, and perhaps engaged in unethical conduct, also consistently displayed love, compassion, humility, and kindness and bestowed upon their followers teachings that led to genuine growth and spiritual breakthroughs. For that reason, the scandals and cultish abuses became an important part of the curriculum. A generation of seekers was forced to learn sobering lessons about the pitfalls of spiritual dependency and the danger of elevating gurus to godlike status, exempt from the normal rules of social engagement. It also led to a collective inquiry into important

issues about the nature of spiritual development and the relationship between higher consciousness and moral behavior. Those explorations, still
ongoing, were crucial in the maturation of baby boomer yogis, and the
lessons learned smoothed the way for subsequent students of charismatic
teachers.

The most egregious problems, those requiring the most difficult adjust-
ments on the part of followers, came from the assumptions of what has
been called Guru Yoga. When the guru is taken to be an embodiment of
the divine, his or her intuitive wisdom is assumed to surpass anything that
ordinary people can aspire to, unless they ascend to the same enlightened
heights. Therefore one's guru should be obeyed, or at least given the benefit of the doubt. A related assumption is that it accrues to the followers'
advantage to give up their egos and attune themselves, through practice
and surrender, to the guru's mind and will. Examples of how that alchemy
of consciousness turned humble disciples into masters abound in the sacred literature, and there is no reason to doubt their veracity. Like all great
teachers, the best gurus guide their students to the point where they are
no longer needed. But not all gurus are equal, and they don't all measure
up to the standards of their own tradition, which is why the Vedic texts
counsel discernment in choosing one.

The 1970s upheavals taught yogic practitioners that when a purportedly enlightened master does something that seems illegal, unethical, or
simply bizarre, they should not take it as a sign of cosmic genius. Aspirants learned to relate to gurus as something other than perfect masters
to whom one must surrender—as respected mentors, savvy guides, caring
friends, expert advisers, revered exemplars, or admired role models. And,
thanks in large part to the efforts of developmental theorists like Ken
Wilber, they learned that there is not necessarily a one-to-one correlation
between elevated states of consciousness and moral or ethical behavior.
"I always claimed that I'm not perfect," Amrit Desai said in a postscandal
interview. "What I always said is, 'Trust the guru within you first *before*
you can trust the outer guru.'" Some of his wounded ex-disciples question the sincerity of that remark, but its spirit has been almost universally
embraced.[8]

The Teaching on Teachers

Those hard-earned lessons were taken to heart. It took a long time, and the cost in mental anguish and emotional pain was high, but eventually naïve devotees matured into stronger, more autonomous spiritual practitioners. And newer seekers learned from the mistakes of their predecessors. There is still plenty of dewy-eyed zeal around gurus, and there always will be, but the evidence suggests that today's spiritual aspirants are less vulnerable to flawed gurus and oppressive institutions. John Raatz, a publicist who's in touch with current spiritual trends, says, "We [boomers] were more innocent. Now they're better informed, and they're starting from a more mature place. They don't give themselves over as easily." Furthermore, the hazards of sex in unequal power relationships are well understood now. All of which adds up to a shift away from the traditional guru-disciple model to a pedagogy more in line with modern teacher-student standards.

The scandals were deeply injurious. The actions that created them must be condemned and remembered, not just dismissed as aberrations from an era when virile, captivating men walked barefoot out of ashrams and caves into a freewheeling society in the throes of sexual revolution, to be greeted by adoring young women in short skirts. Similarly, the institutional corruption that caused so much pain should not be written off as a bump in the road to the full assimilation of Asian traditions. At the same time, the seedy side of the history should not be allowed to diminish the contribution the gurus made to individual lives and to American spirituality. To make too much of their personal flaws would be tantamount to disparaging Picasso's art because he was a boorish womanizer, or to belittle the U.S. Constitution because Thomas Jefferson owned slaves and slept with one.[9]

Somewhere in between the hagiography of ardent disciples and the hatchet jobs of sneering detractors is the reality of exceptional human beings with unexceptional human flaws. In the long run, the efficacy of Vedic teachings will matter more than the shortcomings of their proponents. To the extent that gurus are seen as religious figures, any scent of hypocrisy or chicanery will be deplored. But if they are seen as representatives of a science of consciousness, their behavior becomes less relevant and their teachings can be viewed not as divine truths but as hypotheses to be tested. "If Einstein turned out to be a thief," said a disciple of a disgraced guru, "it would not make the theory of relativity wrong."

Most of the 1970s gurus are gone now, but the institutions they left behind are established features of the spiritual landscape. While the dramas were unfolding within their communities, and to some extent in the press, Vedanta-Yoga in general was spreading from the counterculture to the mainstream, propelled by good old American pragmatism: if it works and the price is right, buy it, and who cares if the salesman is a little sleazy or the ad campaign promises too much? A Gallup poll taken in 1978 found that ten million Americans were "engaged in some aspect of Eastern religion."

As the next decade unfolded, new gurus came along—Sri Sri Ravi Shankar and Mata Amritanandamayi chief among them—to till the soil made hospitable by their predecessors. Of perhaps greater significance, a veritable army of scientists, physicians, psychologists, educators, writers, artists, and other professionals, as well as entrepreneurs ranging from shameless hucksters to gifted teachers, were now positioned to disseminate what they learned from the gurus. We have met some of them already. In the chapters ahead, we'll meet others.

MADE IN THE U.S.A.

In 1905 Dr. Pierre Bernard started teaching what he called Tantrik Yoga in San Francisco. Born thirty years earlier in Iowa, his real name was Perry Arnold Baker and he had apprenticed in Nebraska with a Syrian teacher named Sylvais Hamati. Bernard was arrested on morals charges, following complaints by two young women. When the charges were dropped for insufficient evidence, he headed east and established the Tantrik Order in America and the New York Sanskrit College. In 1910 he served time for abducting young women for the purpose of illicit sex. The tabloids had a field day, branding Bernard with the oddball nickname Oom the Omnipotent (aka the Great Oom).

Flashy and grandiose but by all accounts a serious teacher—he called himself "a curious combination of the business man and the religious scholar"—Bernard continued to teach Hatha Yoga and esoteric Tantric practices with his wife, a dancer with the Tennessee Williams name of Blanche De Vries. In 1920 he acquired a seventy-six-acre estate outside the city and built a combination ashram and resort with the innocuous name of Clarkstown Country Club. Despite recurring tabloid slander, he attracted numerous followers from the upper crust (the Vanderbilts were prime patrons) and created what one scholar called "in its day, the most renowned private library of materials related to the study of Indian philosophy and religion in the United States." He died in 1955.[1]

So went the strange career of America's first Yoga teacher, and the first American to create an organization to promulgate Vedic teachings. Needless to say, a lot of others have emerged from American soil, beginning in Bernard's lifetime and mushrooming after the guru wave of the 1970s, when followers matured into leaders. One of the first, incidentally, was the Great Oom's nephew, Theos Bernard. Presumably inspired by his uncle, Theos studied in India and Tibet and earned a doctorate at Columbia with a dissertation that he turned into the book *Hatha Yoga: The Report of a Personal Experience* (1943). It may have been the first text with photos of Yoga postures. (The author served as model.)[2]

Westerners who, like the Bernards, disseminate Eastern teachings are examples of what Carl Jung called gnostic intermediaries. Psychiatrist Roger Walsh defines the term this way: "someone who imbibes a wisdom so deeply that they are able to transmit it in another language and culture, so the person who is hearing is able to understand." The intermediary's challenge is to find skillful means (what Buddhists call *uppaya*) for translating spiritual ideas and practices from one culture to another. Psychologist Joan Harrigan, the first Western representative of a small, Rishikesh-based lineage, described the task this way: "to maintain the authenticity and integrity of the teachings without distorting or diluting them for Western consumption, while adapting them so people from a different cultural base can understand, integrate, and utilize them." A key component of that challenge has been to rethink the job description itself.

The intermediaries whom I call Vedic transmitters are a disparate lot, and they function in a variety of ways. I separate them into three categories: *pandits, acharyas,* and *gurus. Pandits* are what we would call scholars: learned individuals who are steeped in the sacred literature and theological minutiae of the religions they study—and who, it is hoped, are skilled at conveying their knowledge to others. Dictionary definitions of *acharya* include "a wise religious teacher" and "a learned religious teacher and guide." For our purposes, *acharyas* differ from *pandits* in that their role is not just to convey information but also to address the personal concerns of spiritual aspirants. One could define *guru* in precisely the same way, but gurus are not just educators: their spiritual attainment is presumed to be of a higher order of magnitude than that of ordinary teachers. They are held up as living embodiments of realization—in some cases, divine incarnations—and as such are treated with far greater reverence and are granted far more authority. Gurus have disciples, not just students, and classically, they take responsibility for disciples' spiritual lives, if not their lives as a whole. In return, disciples vow fealty and attempt to surrender to the guru's will. In many cases, their mere presence, or *darshan,* is thought to confer spiritual boons. (Hence the elbow-flailing attempts to get as close to them as possible.)

In the wake of the crises of the 1970s, many intermediaries have made a point of declaring themselves *non*gurus. They do not take on formal disciples, oversee spiritual communities, or allow students to treat them as exalted beings. They teach self-sufficiency, not dependence. Joan Harrigan, for example, was initiated into a monastic lineage by her guru, Swami Chandrasekharanand Saraswati, in 1987 and was later named his eventual successor. In India she might be seen as a guru. But she runs Patanjali Kundalini Yoga Care in Knoxville, Tennessee, more like an educational institute than an ashram. Students come for short retreats and are given personalized yogic repertoires based on systematic evaluations.[3]

There are many variations on this nonguru guru theme. Perhaps the most ungurulike of all is a man who never sees students in person and insists on anonymity. He calls himself Yogani, and all he would say about himself is that he lives in Florida with his wife and has devoted much of his life to studying yogic techniques. His system, Advanced Yoga Practices—"an integration of hatha, kundalini, and tantra techniques"—is taught online, for free.[4]

Some intermediaries are harder to define. Jean Klein, a Czech-born French citizen, taught the nondualism of Advaita Vedanta in Europe and America for nearly forty years until his death (in Santa Barbara, his part-time home) in 1998. He was revered as a spiritual master, and his devotees basked in his presence. But when I asked one of his students, psychologist John Prendergast, if Klein was a guru, the answer was ambiguous: "He functioned as guru in the sense of a 'dispeller of darkness' "—a traditional descriptor—"but he had no formal disciples, no initiatory rituals, and made no demands on his students." No doubt some saw Klein as a guru and others saw him as an *acharya*. He probably couldn't have cared less.

Ambiguity can arise when teachers are treated with disciplelike adoration despite their best intentions. So it was, apparently, with Franklin Merrell-Wolff, a mathematician-philosopher who attracted a small but devoted following to his Advaita-based teachings from the 1930s until his death in 1985, at ninety-eight. "Franklin didn't like people coming to sit at his feet," Doroethy Leonard, the chair of the Franklin Merrell-Wolff Fellowship, told me. But some of those who journeyed to his center in Lone Pine, California, did so anyway.[5] Muddled definitions also arise when teachers disavow guruhood but surround themselves with gurulike trappings. The South African–born (in 1970) Mirabai Devi relates to students informally and tries to empower them with a "guru is within you" message. She does not consider herself a guru. But at the *satsang* I attended, she was surrounded by white-clad assistants, sat cross-legged in flowing silks on an upholstered chair flanked by flower displays, transmitted *shakti* by touching individuals' foreheads, and led chants and healings. Hers might be a hybrid style we will see more of in the future.[6]

In short, the categories can be fuzzy, and there is wide variation within each of them. That should be kept in mind as we turn to America's omgrown Vedic transmitters, beginning in this chapter with *acharyas*, and moving on to *pandits* and gurus. Because of space limitations, I include only the most influential in each category. That meant leaving out a lot of worthy individuals who have contributed to the understanding and practice of Vedanta-Yoga. It also meant summing up figures whose work deserves greater attention, such as the following three *acharyas* who have distinct personalities and histories but share a wealth of knowledge and a passionate regard for India's spiritual heritage.[7]

Passions for India

David Frawley (b. 1950) was too busy reading Vedic scriptures to finish college. But when his youthful reflections on the Upanishads were published by the Sri Aurobindo Ashram, he was off and running. Now he is recognized in India as a *Vedacharya* (teacher of the Veda) as well as a *vaidya* (Ayurvedic doctor), a *jyotishi* (Vedic astrologer), and a *puranic* (Vedic historian). Given the name Vamadeva Shastri in 1991, he teaches at several Indian institutions. In America, his public profile centers mainly on Ayurveda; he has written several books on the subject and helps to train practitioners. A self-identified Hindu and a tireless defender of Vedic authenticity, his stated objective is to help "revive Vedic knowledge in an interdisciplinary approach for the planetary age."[8]

For Georg Feuerstein (b. 1947) interest in India began at age fourteen, when he read Paul Brunton, and persisted through a doctorate in Indology at England's Durham University and a variety of spiritual mentors, including the controversial American Adi Da, whom he met after moving to the United States in the 1970s. Feuerstein is a meticulous chronicler of India's spiritual history and an interpreter of Vedic texts, and his books have won the admiration of both lay readers and scholars. Some of them—*The Yoga Tradition: Its History, Literature, Philosophy and Practice,* for example—are encyclopedic in scope but never lose the connection between philosophy and spiritual practice.[9] In addition to his thirty-plus books and countless articles, Feuerstein reaches his audience through the Web-based Traditional Yoga Studies (TYS). He now lives in Saskatchewan, Canada, "in full retirement."

Vedic tradition has no more passionate advocate—and no more frank a critic of its contemporary foibles—than Andrew Harvey (b. 1952), a true child of the East-West marriage. British, Christian, born and raised in South India, and educated at Oxford, he has written about virtually every mystical tradition, but all of his personal and scholarly pursuits, he says, "have been profoundly shaped by the experience of India and its magnificent and still-vibrant spiritual traditions." With his accent and palpable passion, Harvey combines the erudition of Alan Watts, the prophetic eloquence of Winston Churchill, and the flair of Elton John in his lectures, workshops, films, and books. In 1993 his profile surged with a BBC documentary, *The Making of a Mystic,* and a *New York Times Magazine* piece, "The Merry Mystic." Soon thereafter he made waves in spiritual circles with a scathing antiguru critique, which arose from an unsettling split with Mother Meera, his guru of fifteen years, whom he accused of homophobia. (Her devotees deny the allegations.)[10]

Now living outside Chicago, Harvey has aimed his ardor at uniting "two great fires": the mystic's passion for divine realization and the activist's passion for justice. His mission, spelled out in his latest book, *The Hope: A Guide to Sacred Activism,* tallies with an important pattern in the long East-West exchange: from India, the inward march to liberated awareness; from the West, the outward march to social justice. "Mystics are addicted to being," says Harvey, "and activists are addicted to doing." He's raising the bar of recovery for both.[11]

The impact of Frawley, Feuerstein, and Harvey on the dissemination of Vedanta-Yoga has been substantial. But the next two *acharyas* have left a massive footprint on the nation's spiritual terrain—one that deepens by the day.[12]

There Then, Here Now

Born in 1931, Richard Alpert grew up in an affluent Boston suburb as, in his words, "a Jewish, middle-class, upwardly mobile, anxiety-ridden neurotic." After earning his Ph.D. in psychology at Stanford, he joined Harvard's Center for Research in Personality. Before he was thirty, Alpert had academic prestige and goodies galore—and seething discontent. "I felt that something was wrong in my world, but I couldn't label it in any way so as to get hold of it," he later recalled. "I felt that the theories I was teaching in psychology didn't make it, and that the psychologists didn't really have a grasp of the human condition."

Then Timothy Leary joined the department. Alpert and his mischievous older colleague worked, hung out, and pondered new ideas together. After Leary discovered psychedelics, they also tripped together and did research on lysergic acid diethylamide, or LSD-25.

During his first psychedelic experience, in March 1961, everything the blown-away psychologist identified as "Richard Alpert-ness"—his social identity, his physical form, his thoughts—dissolved. "I realized that although everything by which I knew myself, even my body and this life itself, was gone, still I was fully aware!" he later wrote in *Be Here Now.* "Not only that, but this aware 'I' was watching the entire drama, including the panic, with calm compassion."[13]

In time, Alpert came to know that the drug experience pointed to something beyond what drugs could supply. "I was aware that I didn't know enough to maintain these states of consciousness," he wrote. "And I was aware that nobody else around me seemed to know enough either." In search of an intellectual framework in which to place his experiences, he turned, at the urging of friends, to Eastern texts.[14] Next stop, India.

Servant of God

One day in Katmandu, Alpert, then thirty-five, met a long-haired beanpole from Laguna Beach, California, named Bhagavan Das. As surfer dude Michael Riggs, he had tasted cosmic consciousness in the early 1960s while floating on the ocean. After high school he traveled to Europe and, having figured out that "it was an inside job, and I needed to find that inner connection," he hitchhiked to India. He lived in caves, visited ashrams, and went on pilgrimages. One day, in a small temple on the lower slopes of the Himalayas, he met a sadhu who touched him on the head. "It was like he knocked my brains into my heart," Bhagavan Das would recall. He had found his guru, Neem Karoli Baba.

At the time, Maharaji, as devotees called him, was probably in his mid-sixties. In his photos he looks like a combination of the bald, grizzled Sean Connery and the Ben Kingsley of *Gandhi*—wise, kind, somewhat mischievous, and a little on the crusty side. It is said that sometimes during gatherings he would sit in silence, while at others he would pour forth trenchant teaching stories, exaltations of love, goofball gossip, and foul-mouthed putdowns. A bhakti yogi, the only *sadhana* he gave to disciples was devotional chanting *(kirtan)* and service to others *(seva)*. For those who wanted to learn meditation and other yogic practices, he had a referral service of sorts.

Bhagavan Das took his new friend to meet his guru. The highlights of Alpert's encounter with Neem Karoli Baba are now part of spiritual lore: the aging sadhu who owned nothing blew the mind of the spoiled Ivy Leaguer by knowing things about him he couldn't possibly have known; the scientist fed the guileless guru a huge dose of LSD and watched incredulously as nothing happened; the ice of scientific skepticism melted in the white heat of unconditional love. Instead of leaving India two days later, as scheduled, he stayed five more months, soaking up his guru's *darshan* and learning about Vedanta and Yoga.

He returned to the States in 1968, bearded, beaded, berobed, and redubbed Baba Ram Dass.[15] *Ram Dass* means "servant of God," and he served God and guru as a kind of Pied Piper, turning on the turned-on generation to an ancient path of liberation, spinning tales, cracking jokes, and expounding Vedanta-Yoga (with generous servings of other wisdom traditions) at *satsangs* and retreats. Many of the young seekers treated him as a guru, and like most mortals, he probably enjoyed it. But by all indications, the adulation wore thin after a while. "A teacher points the way, and a guru *is* the way," he once said, "so I guess I'm not a guru. I'm a teacher." It was probably for that reason that he dropped the paternal *Baba* from his name.

A Ram Dass road show materialized, complete with tour manager and *kirtan* band. Part Himalayas, part Harvard Yard, part vaudeville, it was a huge hit, and not just with the hippies. "It was as if the whole culture was waiting to be turned on by the East," Ram Dass said. His academic credentials made him a perfect crossover figure, especially among psychologists. Despite all the hoopla, or maybe because of it, he made regular visits to his guru for "heart-to-heart resuscitation."

In 1971 Ram Dass published the iconic *Be Here Now*. It contained an autobiographical overview, a how-to "cookbook" with a variety of yogic practices, cogent quotes from the wisdom traditions, advice for living more consciously in the world, a fourteen-page list of recommended books, and the famous brown pages. Read by turning the book sideways, it's the print equivalent of an extended jazz solo, with the lyrics, so to speak, juiced up with decorative fonts and lines that circle and curl, and a rhythm section of pen-and-ink drawings. To be sure, a lot of hippies took the injunction to "be here now" as an excuse for self-indulgence: if it feels good, do it—*now*. But many understood what it really was: an invitation to discover eternal, ever-present Being through spiritual practice. The square-shaped book has sold more than two and a half million copies.

In the summer of 1974, with oil prices soaring in the wake of OPEC's embargo and Nixon resigning the presidency, Ram Dass and the Tibetan lama Trungpa Rinpoche presided over the inaugural sessions of the Naropa Institute, a radically new college in Boulder, Colorado, with an East-meets-West curriculum. As many as a thousand people turned out for their evening sessions. By the end of the decade, the Ram Dass audience would expand, to universities, medical institutions, and even service clubs like Rotary, mirroring the mainstreaming of meditation.[16] In the midst of that transition, however, Ram Dass got caught up in "worldly play," he said, and "felt more and more depressed and hypocritical." Hilda Charlton, a mainstay of the New York spiritual scene who had known some of India's most illustrious teachers, introduced him to a young, female guru in Brooklyn called Joya Santana. Originally Joyce Green, she had what Ram Dass called "powerful charisma and chutzpah," and she claimed to be in touch, psychically, with Neem Karoli Baba, who had died the previous year. She told Ram Dass her job on earth was to prepare him for his future as a world spiritual leader. "I easily let myself be convinced," he confessed in a mea culpa in *Yoga Journal* titled "Egg on My Beard," saying he'd conned himself into believing an "incredible tapestry of half truths and lies."[17] The episode taught him that his attempt to live the pure life of renunciation wasn't working. "I finally realized, I had to fully participate and delight in life, rather than rejecting it," he later said.

By sharing that lesson with everyone who looked to him as a role model, Ram Dass helped shift the emphasis of enlightenment seekers away from escapism. And by presenting himself with a new level of candor, he added psychological authenticity to the equation. He made sure everyone knew that he, like them, struggled with how to integrate spirituality and "real life." He wrestled with his ego, his relationships, his sexuality, and all the rest of it—all grist for the mill, he said, and made that the title of his next important book.[18] He was not a *bhagawan* or a *maha* anything or a such-and-such-*ananda*. He was just a guy who knew more than most and could explain it exceptionally well—and get laughs in the bargain, making everyone feel like they were in some cosmic sitcom together. That mix of expertise and self-honesty made him not just respected but beloved among seekers who wanted to identify with someone more like themselves than an exalted guru.

By shifting into responsible service with the Seva Foundation, an international public health organization, and the Hanuman Foundation, which served prisoners and the dying, Ram Dass was once again modeling the course that others would follow as they matured. Quite likely, he did it again when he suffered a stroke in 1997. That too was grist for the mill. "For me to see the stroke as grace required a perceptual shift," he wrote. "I ended up looking at the world from the Soul level in my ordinary, everyday state. And that's grace." Fierce grace, he called it, the title of a moving documentary about him by filmmaker Mickey Lemle.[19]

When I interviewed Ram Dass in 2007, by phone from his home in Maui, his stroke-impaired speech was much improved since the time I had heard him lecture a few years earlier, but he still had to pause at times to wait for the words to crawl into his awareness "from the lobby." I asked him to assess the role he played in conveying Vedic teachings to the Sixties generation. There was a long pause, either because of the stroke or because he wanted to find the right image. "I was an uncle," he finally said. *Uncle* was the right word. He was a trusted elder and a believable guide, like your parents' cool kid brother—older, but not too much older, with Ivy League authority and the cachet of having left the establishment. Before he hung up the phone, he deferred to his guru. "I was just playing with Maharaji's energies," he said. "I was Charlie McCarthy"—the puppet of ventriloquist Edgar Bergen.

The Ram Dass appeal now extends to the children and grandchildren of his original entourage. I've met Yoga buffs in their twenties and thirties who were directed eastward, at least in part, because someone turned them on to *Be Here Now*. I asked Dean Sluyter, who uses the book in a course called "Literature of Enlightenment" at the Pingry School in New Jersey, how today's teenagers respond to it. "The responses cover a broad spectrum," he said. "At one end was the girl who asked whiningly why we were reading a book about hippies taking drugs. At the other end are kids who tell me it's the coolest book they've ever seen. They're completely taken by the explosion of spiritual information, by the persuasive synergism of stories, vocabulary, and insights from various traditions, all pointing to the same ultimate reality, and probably most of all by the idea that there are people who have devoted their lives to realizing and living that reality—and that *they* could too."

Ram Dass would probably find that very far out.[20]

Love, Serve, Remember

Ram Dass had promised his guru not to tell anyone who or where he was, but he couldn't help himself. From the time he returned to India in 1970 until Neem Karoli Baba's death three years later, a few hundred Westerners found him. They went to India for reasons ranging from a passionate search for the divine to hippie narcissism, but a remarkable number have made a mark on American culture, inspired by the old man whose motto was "Love, serve, remember." His emphasis on service produced living counterarguments to the criticism—not entirely erroneous in the 1970s—that Indian teachings led to social detachment.

The all-stars who jogged onto the playing field of life from Neem Karoli's dugout constitute a perfect example of how one *acharya*—in this case Ram Dass, the unanimous MVP—brings others to Vedanta-Yoga, and how they in turn further the teachings in myriad ways.

They include leading American Buddhist teachers like Lama Surya Das, Jack Kornfield, Joseph Goldstein, and Sharon Salzberg,[21] as well as Harvard-trained psychologist Daniel Goleman, who wrote prolifically about Eastern philosophy and practices (e.g., *The Varieties of Meditative Experience*, 1977) and later on cutting-edge science as a *New York Times* correspondent and the author of several books, including the megaselling *Emotional Intelligence* (1998). Another member of the tribe was Mirabai Bush, the former executive director of the Center for Contemplative Mind in Society, whose mission is "to integrate contemplative awareness into contemporary life in order to help create a more just, compassionate, reflective, and sustainable society." Prior to that, Bush served as project director of the Seva Foundation, which was started by a fellow devotee, physician Larry Brilliant, to wipe out curable blindness.

Dr. Brilliant's career of service began in Neem Karoli's ashram, when the guru told Doctor America (as he called him) to work with the World Health Organization to eradicate smallpox in India. As a young, long-haired American, Brilliant got turned away repeatedly, but once he was hired he rose from the lowest rungs to directing a team in charge of South Asia. Smallpox was eradicated. In 2006 the epidemiologist became the director of Google.org, the giant firm's philanthropic arm, and three years after that took charge of the Skoll Urgent Threats Fund, which works to prevent pandemics. Named one of *Time* magazine's one hundred most influential people in the world in 2008, Brilliant does not hesitate to say that when making decisions, he asks himself, "What would Maharaji say?"

Another young professional whose life was turned around by Neem Karoli was Michael Jeffery. Like the others, he sought out the guru because of Ram Dass. During a five-year immersion in the ashram, he says, his connection to Christianity deepened because Neem Karoli urged people to be true to their own faiths and one day said to him: "Christ said to serve the poor and the sick. Will you do it?" He vowed to use his law training to do so. Now a superior court judge in Barrow, Alaska, where Eskimos constitute 60 percent of the population, he keeps a picture of Maharaji in his office, next to a portrait of Jesus.

Finally, two Neem Karoli devotees have affected the spiritual scene through devotional music. Think of Krishna Das and Jai Uttal as the Ray Charles and Chuck Berry of *kirtan*—crossover artists who helped usher an esoteric musical form into the mainstream. Both native New Yorkers with secular Jewish backgrounds, they found their way to India circa 1970 and eventually combined the traditional mantra repetition they first heard at Neem Karoli's ashram with Western rhythms and instrumentation. Uttal, who studied classical Indian music with the legendary Ali Akbar Khan, brings an eclectic East-West blend to his concerts and workshops, which are far more popular now than at any time in his career. Krishna Das, whose baritone is probably the best-known *kirtan* voice in the West, was turned on to India as a basketball-and-blues-playing college student, when he saw the Apu Trilogy by the great filmmaker Satyajit Ray. Starting in 1968, he says, he trailed Ram Dass from one retreat to another before realizing "there was a real guru behind the throne." At that guru's ashram, he learned to chant, but he didn't do so publicly until 1994, when he performed at the Jivamukti Yoga School in New York. Four people showed up. In 2008, when he played the same venue, seven hundred squeezed into the room.

Neem Karoli Baba passed away in 1973, but through Ram Dass he has touched a lot of souls since then. Bo and Sita Lozoff, to cite an interesting example, read *Be Here Now* in 1972, and says Bo, "The picture of Neem Karoli Baba stopped me cold." It was a face he'd seen in dreams. He wrote to Ram Dass, forming a connection that led to the Prison Ashram Project, which the Lozoffs created to "help prisoners use their time for spiritual practice." There is no set teaching, just friendship, advice, some music, and Bo's 1984 book, *We're All Doing Time*, which "the spiritual Johnny Cash" has given away to more than four hundred thousand inmates.

Mysterious though it may be, the connection to departed gurus is not without precedent, and in Neem Karoli Baba's case, it continues. I have visited a biweekly *kirtan* gathering in the Los Angeles living room of Randall Reel, a fortyish real estate developer who has made pilgrimages to Neem Karoli's ashrams in India. Most of those who gather in his home had not yet been born when the guru whose photo graces the altar "left his body," as yogis tend to put it. One of the musicians, Shiva Baum, is Ram Dass's godson. His parents had been with Neem Karoli in India, and the house he grew up in was adorned with the guru's photos. As a kid, he'd tell friends that the old man was his grandfather. There are similar gatherings elsewhere in the country, and a Neem Karoli ashram in New Mexico.

As for the scraggly hippie who started it all, Bhagavan Das returned to the United States in 1971 to discover that *Be Here Now* had made him a legend. "I hadn't worn shoes in years," he told an interviewer, "and suddenly I was living in a New York town house." He did public events for a while, then "left the whole guru trip" to settle down with a wife and three kids. He sold cars, insurance, and solar energy, and then, affluent but unhappy, he once again rejected the straight life. Back to being Bhagavan Das, his long hair and beard now gray, he teaches and performs *kirtan,* happy to be a kind of grandfather to youngsters who are "looking for something more than shopping." His book, published in 1999, is called (what else?) *It's Here Now (Are You?).*

From Doctor Chopra to Just Plain Deepak

At a time when his Western contemporaries were enchanted by India, Deepak Chopra was riding the tide the opposite way. The son of a New Delhi cardiologist, he was immersed in the study of medicine when the Beatles were meditating on the Ganges. As American seekers flocked to ashrams, he went to New Jersey for residency training and adopted the lifestyle the seekers had rejected. He smoked, drank, tried recreational drugs, and sprinted on the career treadmill. By the late 1970s, he had a successful endocrinology practice, was chief of staff at Boston Regional Medical Center, and taught at Tufts and Boston universities. But something was missing.

"Two things were happening," he told me when we met at the Chopra Center, on the lush grounds of the La Costa Resort and Spa near San Diego. "I was a good technician," he said. "I knew everything about the human body. But I was not a healer, because I didn't know anything else." He was also unhappy. Determined to change, he gave up toxic substances and searched for answers to existential questions. One day in 1985, while browsing, he chanced upon a used book that led him to the Cambridge

TM center.[22] Before long he had his life-changing first encounter with Maharishi Mahesh Yogi at a conference in Washington, D.C.

Evidently spotting something he liked, the guru invited the doctor to his suite for a rare face-to-face chat. In time, Chopra accepted an offer he couldn't refuse, to serve as TM's voice of Ayurveda. It's easy to see why he was chosen: attractive, charming, and articulate, with impeccable scientific credentials and (as he put it) the right accent, Chopra was a living bridge between East and West.

The TM movement pulled out all stops, placing him in front of large audiences and promoting break-out books such as *Quantum Healing* (1989) and *Perfect Health* (1991), which presented Ayurveda in an updated, scientific context. He got so busy with public appearances, setting up clinics and spas, and overseeing Maharishi Ayur-Veda Products International (MAPI), that he gave up his medical practice. Within the TM organization, he was assumed to be Maharishi's heir apparent. It was not all glory, however. In 1991, after running a Chopra article on Ayurveda, the prestigious *Journal of the American Medical Association* discovered the author's commercial ties to MAPI and commissioned a follow-up piece that accused him of deception.[23] Chopra sued for defamation. The case was settled in 1993, but only after a good deal of inflammatory press coverage.

At one point Maharishi named Chopra *Dhanvantari,* which translates as "Lord of Immortality." But gurus have been known to inflate egos only to burst them like party balloons. A guru-centered universe has only one pole star, and the atmosphere can be as redolent with jealousy as with incense. Maharishi was told that his famous devotee was, in effect, usurping his premier status. Chopra said he had no desire to be a guru or to lead the organization, but Maharishi gave him a choice: withdraw from public life and remain at his side like a traditional disciple, or leave. Chopra, a family man who was already feeling "hemmed in" by organizational dynamics, opted for departure. The rest is modern spiritual history. Like Diana Ross after leaving the Supremes, Chopra established his own voice and became a superstar.

While the massive fame he accrued after his departure from the TM world is unique, his trajectory was in many ways typical of devotees of a guru or lineage who branch out on their own. He kept on bridging the East-West and science-spirit divides, but now he could choose his own vocabulary and style. His book *Ageless Body, Timeless Mind* (1993) linked quantum mechanics and mind-body wellness. To ordinary readers, it was a visionary leap; to many scientists, it was a simplistic interpretation of physics made worse by grandiose claims. But never mind the critics—Deepak had *Oprah*. According to *Time* magazine, the day after his appearance on that most coveted venue, his book sold 137,000 copies. It remained on bestseller lists for close to a year, launching the now-prolific doctor into the stratosphere of commercial authorship. Soon he was no longer just an advocate of alternative medicine, ranging farther afield, from success and relationship manuals to *How to Know God* to novelized takes on the lives of Merlin and Buddha.

Dr. Chopra became Deepak, the one-name global celeb. He was called a money-guzzling egotist who's dazzled by celebrity admirers like Barbra Streisand and the late Michael Jackson; attacked by Christians for promoting Hinduism in the guise of science; and parodied for dispensing New Age nostrums. But he comes across in person as unaffected by it all. "I happened to be in the right place at the right time," he told me, "with the right education and the right understanding and the right desire to explore Vedanta." For more than two decades he has probably been the best-known proponent of Indian philosophy in the world, selling more than twenty million books, producing dozens of CDs and DVDs, delivering keynote speeches to hundreds of thousands, and appearing on virtually every major talk show many times over. The host of a weekly program on Sirius XM Satellite Radio, he blogs prolifically and maintains a highly active website. Plus, he's tight with everyone from Mike Meyers to Mikhail Gorbachev, and he seems to be the go-to guy whenever Larry King needs a nonconventional spiritual perspective. As he draws on everything from astronomy to psychology, from Rumi to Oscar Wilde, the average listener might not know there's anything Indian about him aside from his accent and his name, but the beating heart of everything he does is a Vedantic sensibility.

In this regard Chopra, an American citizen and the father of two American-born children, is a paradigm for the West's assimilation of Eastern spirituality. His mentor was adept at distilling Vedic teachings into a form that would go down easily on this end of the globe. A generation younger, thoroughly modern and worldly, Chopra stripped away even more of the Indian religious and cultural artifacts. The meditation form that his center teaches utilizes traditional mantras (selected differently from TM) but dispenses with the ritual *puja,* and in some settings he drops the Sanskrit and the individualized instruction altogether. Whether this is a gain or a loss can be debated. Undeniably, it opens doors.

Over time there has been a demographic shift in Chopra's base. "It used to be women, mostly between the ages of thirty and fifty," he said in 2008. "Now it's just as many men, and also young people in their twenties, even teenagers." It's also denizens of corner suites and examining rooms; he leads seminars for physicians at places like Harvard Medical School and for high-level executives at Northwestern University's Kellogg School of Management. "Some guys in ancient times had it figured out, because they had a science of going inward," he said. "My hope is that a consciousness-based science will emerge that will influence everything we do." If it does, he will have been a prime mover in its development.[24]

We turn now to American *pandits*—not pundits, the bloviating political commentators on television, but scholars who have added clarity and nuance to our understanding of Hinduism, Indian philosophy, and all things Vedic.

NOT JUST ACADEMIC

Starting in the late 1960s, meditators, yogis, and guruphiles with an intellectual bent developed a passion to learn more and more about India's spiritual heritage. Some had unsettled career plans, and it dawned on them that one way to combine their interests with the need to earn a living was to become a scholar. They came from Siddha Yoga, from the Hare Krishnas, and from all the other *sanghas* (communities), large and small, and they entered graduate programs in religious studies, theology, philosophy, Asian studies, and other relevant disciplines. Those who stuck it out earned doctorates and launched careers as professors and researchers.

At the time the academic study of religion was coming into its own, but most religion courses were still taught by philosophers, historians, and social scientists, most of whom approached the subject in the spirit of anthropologists observing exotic cultures or entomologists studying insects. Many brought to their research a theoretical framework—Marxist or Freudian, typically—that was antagonistic to religion. This was especially true of Hinduism, which outsiders associated with everything they found deficient in Indian culture, such as the caste system and customs that oppressed or demeaned women. Now came young spiritual types making their way through graduate school with stacks of books, trips to India, and hundreds of hours of Yoga, meditation, chanting, and lectures from gurus under their belts. It was a game-changer: Western scholars who were not only sympathetic to Asian traditions but also intimately engaged in their practices.

Practitioner-*Pandits*

The influx into the academy of Western-born adherents of Hindu and Buddhist traditions brought a new twist to an old debate about the difference in perspective between insiders and outsiders, or practitioners and non-practitioners. Can scholars who practice a particular faith bring sufficient objectivity to the analysis of that faith? Do scholars who are *not* engaged in a religion lack the intimacy and familiarity to properly study it, and are their own biases and assumptions as potentially distorting as those of religious practitioners? In the case of Eastern religions, the insider-outsider dilemma is even more complicated because Western practitioner-*pandits* occupy a murky middle ground: they are insiders because they are personally engaged with the Vedic tradition; but they are also outsiders because they are not Indian and in most cases practice not normative Hinduism, but a Westernized form of Vedanta-Yoga. Further complicating matters is the shortage of scholars from India, or of Hindu descent, with training in Western-style religious studies.

The new insider-practitioners brought to academic life a dimension that had previously been limited to rarities like Mircea Eliade and Huston Smith. Because of their personal experience with Vedic teachings, they could see things outsiders could not, just as ballplayers can see aspects of a game that spectators cannot. (The reverse is also true, of course.) Although relatively small in number, the practitioners helped to change the way Asian religions are understood and taught. Because of them and concomitant cultural factors—the influx of Indian immigrants, increased commerce with India, the gurus and gnostic intermediaries, the easy access to information—Hinduism is now far less likely to be characterized as polytheistic or to have its practices dismissed as idol worship in America's classrooms. In general, the practitioner-*pandits* enhanced the public's understanding of, and respect for, Asian religions.[1] They also helped to legitimize the role of direct spiritual experience in religious life. Their influence played out in a million small ways in classrooms, conferences, and publications. Here is an example that is well known within the academy.

Robert K. C. Forman taught at New York's Hunter College until he retired in 2003, leaving behind a number of frequently cited articles and books.[2] Forman entered graduate school at Columbia University in 1975, having spent the first half of the decade immersed in the TM movement. Early on, when reading an assigned text on mysticism by a distinguished scholar, he found that he disagreed with the author. "At some level, he was challenging my own life," said Forman. "He was arguing that people like me, who were having mystical experiences, were essentially giving themselves self-fulfilling prophecies." According to the prevailing theory, mystical experiences were not what the mystics made them out to be; rather, the seekers' own expectations, created by their religious training, convinced them they were experiencing what the sacred texts and gurus said they should. In general, this perspective was an offshoot of the postmodern or constructivist idea that not only do our experiences determine our beliefs but our beliefs determine our experiences. Such is the immense power of language, concepts, and tradition. The argument was, in part, a refutation of the perennial philosophers' assertion that mystical experiences have certain features in common regardless of the culture in which they arise.

Forman agreed with some aspects of the critique, namely the lack of philosophical rigor in perennialism. He thought the term "perennial psychology" was more accurate, because perennialism describes a common pattern of human development, not a philosophy as such. Nevertheless, based on years of prolonged meditation, he felt in his bones that some aspects of mystical experience are *not* constructed by expectations or beliefs. Certainly they are explained and interpreted according to cultural and linguistic factors, but they are not determined by them. Rather, the yogi's *samadhi* and the Buddhist's *shunyata* are precisely what the traditions say they are: awareness of consciousness itself, without thoughts, feelings, or

other mental constructs.[3] The Upanishadic dictum *Ayam Atma Brahma*—
"This Self is Brahman"—is, in this view, not a belief or a postulate but a
description of a direct perception, something more like "It's raining" than
"The gods have answered our prayers for rain."

This perspective came easily to practitioners because such events—or
reasonable facsimiles of them—had arisen during meditation. Constructiv-
ists would say that they'd been conditioned by gurus and books to believe
exactly that, but the mainstreaming of yogic practices offered counterevi-
dence: people who took them up to reduce stress, knowing nothing about
Eastern philosophy, reported similar experiences. Forman's challenge
was to construct a convincing argument using the rules, methods, and
language of rigorous scholarship. Eventually he worked it out, publishing
some thirty attention-getting articles.

His chief antagonist was Steven Katz, then at Dartmouth and now at
Boston University, the leading spokesperson for constructivism. What became known as the Katz-Forman debate played out over a series of publications and American Academy of Religion (AAR) conferences. Forman,
discovering he had allies, most of whom were closet mystics themselves,
started the Mysticism Group within AAR, published key books on the
subject, and founded the *Journal of Consciousness Studies*.[4] The end result
was that a second perspective—basically, a practitioner's view—on the nature of spiritual experiences gained equal footing with the theory that
they were by-products of social structures. It meant that students might
learn that *samadhi* or *turiya* or nirvana can be seen as actualities, not just
as doctrinal beliefs.

Forman's contribution has been duplicated in ways large and small by
practitioner-*pandits* in various areas of religious scholarship. "I bring in the
sense that there is such a thing as spiritual development, and that maybe
it's worthwhile," says William Barnard, a former Siddha Yoga devotee.
Barnard has his students at Southern Methodist University sample the
practices of religions other than their own to "expand their ideas of worship beyond the confines of their local church." Countering the concern
that they are biased, practitioner-*pandits* argue that their bias, if any, is to
show respect for all spiritual traditions, including nonbelief. Jeffery Long,

the Hindu scholar we met in chapter 1, puts it this way: "Contrary to the view that religious commitment is incompatible with academic rigor, my religious worldview commits me to expressing the most accurate possible representation of the religions and philosophies I teach."

Individually, the practitioners who entered academia during and after the guru wave of the 1970s may have affected only a small number of students and academic specialists, but the sum total of their influence has been significant. Over time, as they earned tenure and entered middle age, they attained the stature to address areas of inquiry that hadn't been considered before. Some were able to obtain the resources for new institutions that will further the study of Vedic traditions. For instance, the Dharma Association of North America (DANAM) was created "to impart knowledge from particular fields of scholarship in Dharma traditions to practitioners in North America." It has convened annually during the AAR conference since 2003. Other examples include Christopher Chapple's Yoga Philosophy Program at Loyola Marymount University; Vasudha Narayanan's Center for the Study of Hindu Traditions at the University of Florida; Nathan Katz's Center for Spirituality at Florida International; and Rita Sherma's School of Philosophy and Religious Studies at Taksha University.[5]

For all the changes instigated by the modern practitioner-*pandits,* however, it has not all been smooth sailing. Countervailing winds have kicked up storms in the hallowed halls of academia.

Inside v. Outside

The sometimes-virulent clash between segments of the Hindu and academic communities centers in part on scholars whose theoretical framework is either Freudian or Marxian. Such perspectives distort religion, critics contend, by either oversexualizing or overpoliticizing the subject. Hindus have been especially offended by these interpretations, and some of them—most prominently Rajiv Malhotra, an Indian-born entrepreneur who created the Infinity Foundation largely to combat what he sees as academic Hinduphobia—have aggressively defended their tradition.[6]

The casus belli of this culture war was the 1995 publication of *Kali's Child: The Mystical and the Erotic in the Life and Teachings of Ramakrishna*, by Jeffrey Kripal, who is now the chair of Rice University's religious studies department.[7] The book won academic awards but was also criticized for what some scholars considered flawed translations. More to the point, Kripal was excoriated by Hindus in both India and America for highlighting what he considers homoerotic overtones in the life of the revered Ramakrishna. Space does not allow for a thorough account of the conflict; suffice it to say that Kripal and defenders of his academic freedom were called anti-Hindu, sex-obsessed, intellectual imperialists, and the author received death threats. Predictably, the intimidation tactics produced a backlash, and even the reasonable Hindu critics were labeled religious fundamentalists and right-wing extremists.[8]

Cooler heads on both sides argued that Kripal's work—like that of any controversial scholar—should be evaluated solely on its merit, with identity politics and personal venom relegated to the sidelines. SMU's William Barnard summarized that position in an e-mail exchange: "To me, the criteria for good scholarship is whether that scholarship is faithful to the facts, and whether the interpretive lens used helps to illuminate areas that might have been previously unseen." The challenge of delivering a respectful, by-the-rules rebuttal was taken up by two monastics from the Ramakrishna order, Indian-born Swami Tyagananda and Pravrajika Vrajaprana, an American. Their exhaustive analysis of *Kali's Child* was published in 2010, fifteen years after the uproar began.[9]

To be sure, Marxist, Freudian, and social scientific perspectives have been applied to all religions; Kripal, for instance, has said, "I've written the exact same things about Catholicism, Islam and Judaism." But there are important differences, say Hindu activists and their supporters inside the academy. One is that Hinduism is associated with one very colorful country. As a result, says theologian Rita Sherma, the religion has been more "heavily anthropologized" than others. Hindus complain that what some call "the caste, cows, and curry syndrome" attributes to India's dominant religion customs that are better seen as vestiges of a long and complex cultural history. To make the point, they ask Americans to imagine that Christianity were to be defined as the religion of racism or imperial conquest. Another analogy is used to illustrate why Hindus get upset when their rituals and symbols are interpreted in ways to which they do not subscribe, as when Emory University's Paul Courtright analyzed the trunk of the elephant-headed god Ganesh as a limp phallus: imagine that the sacrament of Holy Communion were to be described as cannibalism. The objectionable scholarship, says Suhag Shukla, managing director of the Hindu American Foundation, produces "an analysis of Hinduism that is so far removed from how a Hindu perceives her tradition that it is no longer recognizable as the familiar, comforting, enlightening environment of one's own experiential, lived world."[10]

Activists say that the situation is exacerbated by the dearth of native Hindus in religious studies departments. (Distinguished scholars such as Arvind Sharma of McGill University and Vasudha Narayanan of the University of Florida are exceptions.) Whereas the academy has ample numbers of Christians, Jews, and Muslims to counter distortions of those traditions, Hinduism, they argue, lacks protection there; hence misbegotten interpretations tend to be perpetuated unless outsiders come to the rescue. To which the rejoinders include: (1) anyone who comments on academic matters needs to play by academic rules, and (2) the material that Hindus object to constitutes only a small portion of the scholarship in the field, whereas most of it presents the Vedic tradition in ways that Hindus find acceptable. Hindu activists reply that the objectionable scholars happen to be highly influential tone-setters.

The Kripal controversy raged for more than a decade before subsiding, although to some extent it persists today. Other scholars have also come under fire, chief among them Kripal's former mentor, Wendy Doniger, the Mircea Eliade Distinguished Service Professor of the History of Religions at the University of Chicago Divinity School. Doniger, who once had eggs thrown at her at a conference, was in the news early in 2010 when Hindu organizations protested her latest book, *The Hindus: An Alternative History*, on the grounds that it was defamatory and, in places, factually incorrect. Their efforts to petition the publisher, Penguin, to pull it from the shelves fell on deaf ears, as the book was one of five finalists for the National Book Critics Circle Prize in nonfiction (it did not win).

Meanwhile, the larger insider-outsider debate continues, with proponents of each side making cogent arguments. In all probability it will never be settled, which would be fine with everyone who recognizes that no religion can be exhaustively explained by either perspective alone. The general direction seems clear, however. Thanks to the advent of two vital forces—more students and scholars of Indian descent and more practitioner-*pandits*—the academic study of India's spiritual heritage will surely grow deeper and more accurate. This is bound to further advance the assimilation process described in this book.

But university scholars are not the only players in the world of Vedic panditry. In the great tradition of Huxley, Watts, and other lay scholars, some practitioner-*pandits* operate outside of academia, where the demands are less restrictive and they can reach a more diverse audience. Had I not called them *acharyas*, David Frawley, Georg Feuerstein, and Andrew Harvey would count among them. Others include Stephen Knapp (aka Sri Nandanandana Dasa) and Timothy Conway.[11] But by far the most influential of the independent *pandits* is the prolific Ken Wilber.

The Theorist of Everything

It is hard to be in Wilber's company without being dazzled by the breadth of his knowledge and the ease with which he retrieves information from the vast database of his brain. People familiar with his prodigious output imagine him as some kind of extraterrestrial with a swollen cortex. But while his shaved scalp does give him a slightly alien look, it's his neck and shoulders that are huge (he pumps iron), and he's actually a warm, friendly human being. Anyone with the audacity to try to explain pretty

much everything, with charts and diagrams to boot, is bound to have critics, and where they're concerned Wilber's self-designation as "intellectual
samurai" is apt.

Raised in Lincoln, Nebraska, Wilber was a pre-med student at Duke
when the Sixties erupted. Like other baby boomers, he burned with questions and could not find answers in science. A chance encounter with the
elegant *Tao Te Ching* turned him toward the East, where he discovered
"technologies of interior transformation." He transferred to the University of Nebraska, studying chemistry and biology while, in his spare time,
scarfing down Vedantic and Buddhist classics, moderns like Sri Aurobindo and Krishnamurti, and the best of psychology and Western philosophy. He also sampled the meditative practices that had suddenly become
available, eventually favoring Buddhist disciplines, although he makes a
point of saying that he is not a Buddhist or any other "ist." Those formative
years, it would seem, were perfect training for an autodidact with a pen-
chant for synthesis and for diagramming consciousness the way chemists
diagram complex compounds.

At one point in the early 1970s, Wilber left academia, immersed himself in books, and set out to write a treatise that would synthesize the best
of East and West, and of science and spirituality. His key insight was that
every legitimate system of investigation contains some valuable truth in its
own domain. "They were just aiming at different levels," he told me, "so I
didn't have to exclude anything." The result was *The Spectrum of Consciousness*. Published in 1977, it made an immediate splash among leading-edge
psychologists and consciousness researchers.

At the time transpersonal psychology—the first psychological subdiscipline to take spirituality seriously—was about eight years old. Progress
had been made in examining "nonordinary states of consciousness," but
no one had set forth a comprehensive theory. Enter the wunderkind, who
wasn't even a trained psychologist. Wilber described the development of
consciousness as a hierarchical progression that begins in the prepersonal,
or prerational, stage of infancy and moves in predictable steps through the
maturation of a healthy ego structure. That's where traditional psychology
petered out. Wilber saw that consciousness can evolve further, into the

transpersonal or postrational levels described in the mystical texts of the East. Like a builder adding stories to a home, he stacked the higher stages atop those already delineated.

Spectrum was referred to so extensively that the uncredentialed author became the transpersonal movement's best-known theorist. Wilber built on that success, attempting to map human development from bottom to top and to apply his model to ever-widening domains of life. He summarized the perspective this way in *The Atman Project* (1980): "Development is evolution; evolution is transcendence; . . . and transcendence has as its final goal Atman, or ultimate Unity Consciousness in only God. All drives are a subset of that Drive, all wants a subset of that Want, all pushes a subset of that Pull."

So it continued, through a multitude of books and the establishment of his Integral Institute.[12] While his subject matter expanded with his audience, the goal of creating a master template of human development remained a constant. And while the range of his sources has been virtually limitless, what he called "the stuff that came out of India" also remained a constant.

Wilber's many fans compare his enterprise to physics's attempt to create a grand unified theory that explains all phenomena of matter and energy. His detractors accuse him of making the untidy process of human growth seem more schematic than it really is, and of making too much of experimental findings that should be regarded as preliminary. Like all academic arguments, the arcane quibbles will eventually be sorted out. So will fears that a religion of Wilberism, with Wilberians speaking Wilberese, will emerge. Meanwhile his models show up increasingly in textbooks, psychological assessments, business consultations, and other contexts, and his books have turned up on the reading lists of people like Bill Clinton and Al Gore.[13]

Perhaps most important in the present context, Wilber is the go-to intellectual for a great many people in the Spiritual But Not Religious cohort, as well as for adherents of Eastern paths. Several of his contributions have been especially valuable. His four-quadrant model, which is used increasingly in professional contexts, has helped seekers understand the connections between spiritual development and the physical, social, and other aspects of life.[14] His thesis that various "lines" of development—cognitive, emotional, spiritual—move along separate tracks has helped to clarify the relationship between classic Self-realization and life in the world, and to explain conundrums like why enlightened gurus can misbehave. His exposure of the "pre/trans fallacy"[15] helped keep certain New Age blunders, like conflating the innocence of children with the blissful wisdom of realized sages, from doing too much damage. And in recent years, his exposition on the "three faces of God" (one of which is "the Great Thou") helped to legitimize devotional practices in circles where the personal aspect of the divine is typically ignored. Those are only some in a long list of examples.

For most of his career, Wilber was a reclusive egghead, emerging from long meditations in his Boulder, Colorado, home to churn out tome after tome. At one point he descended from his intellectual Olympus and founded the Integral Institute (I-I). A combination think tank and teaching institution, its mission is "to awaken humanity to full self-awareness." "Short definition, tall order," Wilber acknowledges. At its core is "integral spirituality" (the title of one of Wilber's books), one that is "comprehensive, balanced, inclusive, essential for completeness." In essence, it's a Vedantic/Perennialist vision mixed with psychology and science. So far I-I's diverse array of spiritual teachers, scholars, scientists, and artists has attracted a large and surprisingly young constituency to its programs.[16]

The stock in trade of *pandits* is the life of the mind. They analyze ideas and concepts, identify patterns, and quantify whatever can be counted; they reason, infer, and apply logic; they reach deducible conclusions. All of it is necessary to understand religion and spirituality but insufficient to their practice. For that, seekers drawn to the Vedic promise of higher consciousness need guides, mentors, and exemplars. For some, teachers like the ones we called *acharyas* are sufficient. For others, only a guru will do.

14

GURU AMERICANA

A mericans think of gurus as bearded, barefoot, dark-skinned men in robes. That a guru may be female is relatively new to us. That one may have light skin, wear ordinary Western clothing, and speak in an American or European accent—that's *very* new. If the image seems hard to accept, consider it a case of what religious scholar Jeffrey Kripal calls "reversed orientalism," in which "the Indian qua Indian" is assumed to be more spiritual than Westerners. The skepticism is compounded by American cult leaders who have perpetrated calamities. In the early 1970s, for instance, a charismatic New Yorker named Frederick Lenz denounced his guru, Sri Chinmoy, and proclaimed his own ascendancy. He set up shop in California, taking on the name Atmananda and later changing it to Zen Master Rama. By the late 1980s, he had acquired several hundred followers, a sizable fortune, a drug habit, and an assembly line of disciple-lovers. In 1998 his body was fished out of Long Island Sound, saturated with tranquilizers. A young model, covered with bruises, said she and Lenz had a suicide pact.

Despite such incidents, a number of American gurus have had respectable careers. Remember Joya Santana, Ram Dass's antagonist in the mid-1970s? As Ma Jaya Sati Bhagavati, she settled into a more typical guru role, presiding over her Kashi Ashram in Florida with a mix of wise old

India and wiseass Brooklyn. (She grew up as Joyce Green in Coney Island.) She and her global following have earned distinction with various charitable projects, particularly those serving AIDS patients.[1] Other low-profile gurus have been content to meet the spiritual needs of their devotees in their own, quirky American way. Lee Lozowick, a Jersey boy who now looks like a Hasidic Willie Nelson, has been guiding a small band of followers since the 1970s, following a quest triggered by a spiritual experience he calls a "shift of context." He runs a simple ashram in Prescott, Arizona, leads a rock band, and would probably be totally unknown if one of his devotees, psychologist Mariana Caplan, hadn't written about him in *Do You Need a Guru?* and other works.[2] Judging from his website, he might prefer anonymity. It consists entirely of this message, "If you're looking for enlightenment, look somewhere else."[3]

The roster of American gurus is longer than most people realize. Their styles vary widely, as many have reconfigured the guru role to suit their personalities, methods, and the spirit of the times. The gurus described in this chapter have had an impact on the larger spiritual culture, not just on their own constituencies.[4]

The Antique Dealer

For New Yorkers browsing the Chinese landscapes, Hindu deities, and statues of Buddhas in the Greenwich Village shop, it might have been disorienting to see, behind the proprietor's desk, a pink-faced man with a bald, Buddha-like head, a Buddha belly, and a benign Buddha-like smile, especially if he uttered some Buddha-like enigma in a thick Brooklyn accent. His name was Albert Rudolph, and he was way ahead of the East-West curve. Rudi, as he was called, sold ancient Asian art and gave away ancient Asian wisdom.

India entered his life in 1957, when he served as the personal attendant to the Shankaracharya of Puri, an exalted religious figure whose visit was sponsored by Paramahansa Yogananda's disciples. The following year Rudi went to India and met Bhagawan Nityananda, who would become known as Swami Muktananda's guru. That encounter, Rudi wrote, "was of such depth that it changed the course of my life." When the *avadhuta* passed away, Rudi, following custom, transferred his loyalty to the guru's successor. Muktananda initiated him as Swami Rudrananda in 1966. Four years later Rudi financed and organized the guru's first American tour. But things soured between the two, and Rudi continued to teach on his own. The antiques shop supported the teaching (he never charged for it) and got him to India at least once a year. By the late 1960s, he was holding classes on most weeknights. Later he turned an old upstate hotel into an ashram for weekend retreats.

"Rudi didn't encourage students to treat him as guru in the usual way," a retired sociology professor named John Mann told me. "But he didn't take the attitude that he was one of the guys either, because it just wasn't true." Rudi did not go in for scriptures, apparently, and while he some-times delivered talks, the main language of his *satsangs* was silence, and his primary method was the transmission of *shakti*. In his memoir, Mann quotes Rudi on what happens when he works with a student: "I give a higher energy directly to you . . . you have only to absorb the energy that comes from me like water from a faucet."[5] As with Muktananda's *shaktipat*, the transmission could be one-on-one (sans peacock feathers), but also in groups through an eyes-open meditation practice. The process may sound passive, but being Rudi's disciple was apparently no casual matter. Disci-pline was required.

By 1972, with Indian spirituality booming in New York, Rudi was at-tracting a lot of new students. The next February, at age forty-four, he died in the crash of a small plane.[6] His legacy is assured because he is the rare American guru to establish his own Hindu-like lineage. He trained about twenty students as teachers, and several carry on in his name. Stuart Per-rin, for instance, survived the plane crash and afterward taught in Texas and other locations. Another Rudi student, screenwriter Bruce Joel Rubin, leads Kundalini Yoga *satsangs* in New York and Los Angeles. That spiritual subjects are important to Rubin is evident in the life-beyond-the-body themes of his best-known scripts, *Jacob's Ladder* and *Ghost,* which earned him an Academy Award in 1990.[7]

When Rudi died, a close student named Michael Shoemaker consolidated thirteen ashrams into one, in Cambridge, and later moved the operation to Portland, Oregon. Today, as Swami Chetanananda, he leads the Rudrananda Ashram and Nityananda Institute. About eighty followers live under one big roof on four and a half acres of downtown Portland, and two hundred more live nearby. On the grounds are gardens, meditation halls, life-size statues of Rudrananda and Nityananda, and a shrine with the remains of the man who was born Albert Rudolph.[8] In addition, Rudi *satsangs* are held regularly in several cities. But the student of Rudi who left the biggest mark on America's spiritual terrain was the multinamed guru in the on-deck circle.

The Dawn Horse

It is not unusual for disciples to believe that their guru is an avatar with a unique, world-transforming destiny. It *is* unusual for such a one to hail from Long Island and have the surname Jones. Born in 1939 to Lutheran parents, Franklin Jones died in 2008 as Avatar Adi Da Samraj. In between he adopted about a dozen names, beginning with Bubba Free John and running through Da Love Ananda and others, each one purportedly linked to a quantum leap in consciousness.

According to his official biography, Jones was a spiritual rarity, one who is born fully enlightened. He relinquished that status, it is said, in order to experience the rigors of worldly existence, the better to teach others. After majoring in philosophy at Columbia and earning a master's in English literature from Stanford, he diligently pursued what he called his reawakening. For four years he studied with Rudi, then spent time in India with Muktananda, who apparently recognized the American as a "Realizer." In 1970, in the Vedanta Society temple in Hollywood, Adi Da "became re-established in the continuous state of illumination that was his unique condition at birth."[9]

Two years later, around the time that his autobiography, *The Knee of Listening*, was released, he began teaching in a Los Angeles storefront. Eventually he established a community north of San Francisco and an ashram in Fiji, which became his primary home. At its core the path he taught was a traditional guru bhakti, in which progress hinges on the disciple's ability to resonate with the tuning fork of the guru's grace. It is a demanding path, and Adi Da made no bones about it. About ten thousand disciples came and went from his "cooperative culture" over the years, never more than two thousand at a time. Thousands more have been arm's-length followers.[10]

In his thirty-seven years of guruship, Adi Da made only a handful of public appearances. Seekers found him through word of mouth and his flood of written work. Hailed as masterpieces by the likes of Alan Watts, his volumes include plays and a trilogy of novels in addition to spiritual treatises. The books stood out early on because accounts of higher consciousness by Americans were rare, and because few memoirists had Adi Da's blend of philosophical sophistication and creative flair. (He also painted well enough to have his work exhibited at the prestigious Venice Biennale.) Combine a literary gift with charisma and a claim to avatar status, and you have a recipe for attracting devotees. One of them, Bill Gottlieb, was an editor at *Prevention* magazine when he came upon an Adi Da book in the mid-1970s.[11] "I read it in a sweat of delight and surprise," he told me. "It was beautifully written, and a brilliant critique of contemporary spirituality." That Adi Da was a young American, not an older Indian, also appealed to him: "He wasn't culture bound, tradition bound, or history bound." Gottlieb became a formal disciple in 1990 and has lived in the Adi Da community ever since.

Adi Da was steeped in the Vedic canon and professed the utmost respect for tradition, counting both the Ramakrishna-Vivekananda and the Nityananda-Muktananda-Rudi lines as "my present-Lifetime lineage gurus." At the same time, he was an unrepentant iconoclast and a daring provocateur. In the mid-1970s he became the poster boy for "crazy wisdom," taking the sexual and spiritual revolutions to the limits of experimentation. Partner switching, orgies, and all manner of sexual expression were personally choreographed by the guru, who sometimes doubled as lead dancer with partners of his choosing. Sometimes he initiated alcohol-soaked revelry, a radical departure from the disciplined lifestyle he normally advocated. The period was justified by devotees as a master teacher's brilliant burst of boundary-busting and ego-shattering. The logic goes like this: to free up energy for higher spiritual pursuits, we need to be released from our psychosexual hang-ups; Indian traditions are ambivalent about such matters, and in any case they don't translate well to modern life; therefore it falls to an awakened Westerner to shatter the constraints of social convention. To disciples, the possibility that Adi Da was motivated by personal gratification is out of the question. To outsiders, the theory is a giant rationalization for licentiousness and abuse of power. It must be said that to this day, some devotees who were subjected to what most would consider cruelty and humiliation express gratitude for the experience. Others, of course, remain bitter. In the late 1970s, a $5 million lawsuit was filed by former disciples, attracting considerable media coverage. As scandals go, this one made the clandestine affairs of other gurus seem quaintly Victorian. According to the *San Francisco Chronicle,* the suit alleged "imprisonment, sexual abuse, assault, brainwashing, involuntary servitude, and clergy malpractice." (It was settled out of court in 1986.)

By all accounts, Adi Da's world never again came close to the wildness of that period, but some degree of crazy wisdom and psychosexual processing remained part of his methodology. Musician John Wubbenhorst, a disciple since 1997, told me that Adi Da was "not afraid to go into the pit of snakes and reflect people's emotional and sexual hang-ups with complete frankness and depth. He strips away all the ego stuff, and if you're not mature or self-responsible enough to handle it, it can be really difficult." He compared it to mastering his instrument, the Indian bamboo flute. The payoff in both cases is ecstasy, he said. Therein lies the ambiguity: one person's crazy is another's wisdom.

Whatever history decides about him, Adi Da was a catalyst for important inquiries into the meeting of East and West. His behavior prompted several scholars, in particular his own early student, Georg Feuerstein, to examine the phenomenon of crazy wisdom, elucidating why it can be efficacious in some circumstances and disastrous in others.[12] Adi Da also became a case study for a related investigation: how can a presumably enlightened master behave in such a way as to cause pain to others? Unlike other scandalized gurus, Adi Da was not an Indian monk at sea in the land of temptation, so his behavior could not be explained as an artifact of culture shock. Perhaps the leading figure in the inquiry was Ken Wilber, whom critics assailed for his exuberant praise of Adi Da before the revelations surfaced. When asked about it in 2007, Wilber said, "I think it goes to show that you can make significant gains in awareness, including enlightenment, but that enlightenment, per se, does not fix everything in the psyche or the body." That conclusion is now widely accepted.

In addition to Feuerstein, two other former Adi Da disciples have made an impact on the spiritual scene. Saniel Bonder was with Adi Da for twenty years until leaving the fold in 1992 and creating a teaching of his own. Called Waking Down, it is aimed mainly at longtime practitioners who want to get their feet back on the ground. The other is David Deida, whose popular books and workshops explore sexuality and male-female issues in a spiritual context.[13]

Adi Da died suddenly in November 2008. In addition to furious ex-students and adoring disciples, he left behind three daughters with three different mothers, a museum's worth of paintings, about sixty books, and an organizational structure that he designed to keep his legacy alive.[14]

The Radical Evolutionist

Andrew Cohen wears the label of guru proudly, even as he attempts to redefine the role as a twenty-first-century American. Redefining things has been a Cohen trademark ever since 1992, when he launched a magazine with a question mark in its title, *What Is Enlightenment?*

Cohen, whose two identities, guru and publisher, give him double significance, calls himself an "idealist with revolutionary inclinations." He grew up in a secular, upper-middle-class Manhattan home. In 1970, at sixteen, he had a spontaneous experience of what has been called cosmic consciousness. "The doors of perception opened," he told me. "I saw, felt, and knew the whole universe was a cosmic being that was self-aware and intelligent, and whose nature was a kind of absolute, impersonal love. I was overwhelmed by rapture and awe." After the experience faded, Cohen struggled with the typical confusions of a thinking teenager. Six years later, at twenty-two, the memory of the numinous experience started to haunt him. Whatever it was, he wanted it back. When his martial arts teacher turned him on to books about Eastern spirituality, he was "off to the races."

Cohen read voraciously and checked out the spiritual teachers who came through New York. His first mentor was Swami Hariharananda Giri, from the Kriya Yoga lineage that gave us Paramahansa Yogananda. When India beckoned, what was supposed to be a brief trip turned into a two-and-a-half-year odyssey. One morning, after an all-night rooftop meditation, he had another breakthrough. "I knew for the first time that enlightenment wasn't just a theory, but something I could attain, and all I had to do was apply myself." Subsequently, in Lucknow with his guru, H.W.L. Poonja, he experienced a major shift of consciousness: "I realized I've always been free and I've never been *not* free." Eventually, he says, the periodic surges of realization became permanent.

Seekers gathered to hear his story, and Cohen found himself in the role of spiritual teacher. In time, he saw people having breakthroughs in awareness, but, he says, they remained "complacent about their own narcissism." His way of challenging them to break free of their egos was highly confrontational. This led to a rift with his own guru, and with other disciples who disapproved of Cohen's tactics. He held to his conviction that personal behavior is an important aspect of spiritual development. What's more, he says, some of Poonja's behavior bothered him. "My guru really helped to liberate me through his grace," he once said. "But at the same time, there was a disturbing discrepancy between the things that he said and the way that he lived." Cohen gathered followers of his own and created a spiritual community. Visitors to that community, now located on 220 acres in western Massachusetts, a short drive from Kripalu, might think they're in a country inn, not an ashram. There are no saris or *kurtas,* no Hindu deities, no photos of saints, no Sanskrit names for people, rooms, or buildings, and no tributes to the guru's guru or his lineage. No one stands up with breathless excitement when Cohen enters the room. There is no bowing, or touching of feet, or other conspicuous displays of devotion. He is a jazz drummer and a tell-it-like-I-see-it New Yorker, and his typical attire is a shirt and a sleeveless vest. They call him Andrew, not Swamiji or Guru Dev, and his Indian-born wife of many years is a member of the community, not Mother or Amma. "Andrew is my guru. I put my spiritual life in his hands," says Carter Phipps, the executive editor of *EnlightenNext,* as Cohen's magazine is now called. "At the same time, we're partners in a venture." Phipps, who has been a Cohen disciple for more than twenty years, says his guru "comes across as a regular human being, not someone on a throne, but he doesn't go to the other extreme of 'I'm just a regular guy like you.'" The community's residents seem grounded and authentic, with little of the "Look how spiritual we are" pretensions one often sees in ashrams (although some "we're the cutting edge of evolution" occasionally comes through).

As with Adi Da, grateful followers say Cohen has transformed their lives for the better, while a noisy band of ex-students have poured their venom into the blogosphere, accusing Cohen of being authoritarian, abusive, and sometimes cruel. Calling himself "uncompromising," he attributes the "unabated resentment and narcissistic rage" of the disgruntled to their inability to do the ego-transcending work he demanded of them. "Everybody wants to get enlightened but nobody wants to change," he says. Everyone was free to leave, he adds, and in fact many students have departed amicably and remain on good terms with Cohen.[15] (One not-so-amicable deserter is Cohen's own mother, Luna Tarlo, who denounced him in a book titled *The Mother of God.*) In an e-mail exchange, Carter Phipps wrote that "most if not all of the methods that ex-students complain about were used in the past; they're not really used now."[16]

As with many gurus, Cohen's teaching skills will no doubt be debated for some time. His reputation as a publisher is less ambiguous. What started out as a colorless, twenty-page mouthpiece has evolved into an artfully designed, ad-filled, hundred-plus-page glossy, with solid reporting and a diversity of leading-edge voices in spirituality, science, and scholarship. *EnlightenNext* enjoys nearly universal respect among spiritually inquisitive readers whose concerns are not addressed in other publications. "We wanted to be objective and to present different points of view," Cohen told me. "But we also have a position. It's about evolutionary spirituality and leading-edge thinking."

"Evolutionary enlightenment" is now the brand for both Cohen's teaching and the quarterly magazine. "We're convinced that spiritual enlightenment is not a personal matter," states the publication's website, "but an evolutionary potential that really does have the power to change our world from the inside out and create a new foundation for our collective culture."

In addition to the community in Massachusetts, Cohen's organization has public centers elsewhere in the United States and Europe, as well as an ashram in Rishikesh. Like *The New York Review of Books* in literature, or *The Nation* and *National Review* in politics, *EnlightenNext*'s influence extends well beyond its limited subscriber base. No other periodical has done more to advance the understanding of core Vedantic ideas in the West, and to subject those ideas to trenchant analysis.[17]

A Multiplicity of Oneness

Robert Adams, born in the Bronx to a Jewish mother and a Catholic father, reportedly had spiritual experiences as a child that led him to books about Eastern philosophy. During World War II, at age sixteen, he split for California to meet Yogananda, who advised the passionate youngster to go meet Ramana Maharshi (see chapter 7). Adams lived around Arunachala from 1946 until Ramana's passing four years later. For the next thirty-five years, he apparently divided his time between sages in India and his wife and two daughters in the States. In the 1980s, he began teaching a Ramana-inspired Advaita Vedanta in Los Angeles, supporting his family as a handyman. The writings and recorded dialogues he left behind remain available through the Web.[18]

Adams was probably the first American to teach some variation of Ramana's *atma vichara*, which has been translated as "self-inquiry."[19] But he was only the beginning. In recent years, teachers who were born way too late to have met the sage have used his image, words, and methods either to bestow legitimacy on their work or to embellish it. All of them expound Ramana's radical nondualism, which is captured in this typical statement: "The Self alone exists, and the Self alone is real. Verily, the Self alone is the world, the 'I' and God." And this corollary: "If one can only realize at heart what one's true nature is, one then will find that it is infinite wisdom, truth, and bliss, without beginning and without end." For Ramana, "Who am I?" was the first and last question, and so it is with those who claim a connection to him.

To cite two quick examples: the Society of Abidance in Truth (SAT) in Santa Cruz, California, which is "consecrated to the teachings of Advaita Vedanta, especially as revealed by Sri Ramana Maharshi," is led by a fifty-something American who calls himself Nome (as in "no me"). And the Association of Happiness for All Mankind (AHAM) has an ashram in the North Carolina mountains that was created by a Texan who calls himself Arunachala Ramana. Born Dee Wayne Ray in 1929, he claims that Ramana Maharshi, who named no successor and left behind no official lineage, came to him in a vision and authorized him to teach his self-inquiry. In the winter he holds forth in Tiruvannamalai, a ten-minute taxi ride from the official Ramana ashram.[20]

But the self-inquiry Advaita that is associated with Ramana Maharshi really began to make its mark in the 1980s, when a procession of Americans returned from India ready to conduct *satsangs*. Connected only loosely, they constitute what has come to be called the neo-Advaita movement. They eschew the traditional guru role, in that they have no formal disciples or communities, and request no commitments or vows from their students. But they are said to be "awakened" (their preferred term for *moksha*, enlightenment, Self-realization, etc.) and are therefore seen as exemplars. As a result, the neo-Advaita leaders often have a gurulike mystique, sometimes with an assumption of subtle transmission, as in traditional *darshan*, and they work directly with students to prod them into the same awakening they've achieved. Taken together, they constitute an important addition to the spiritual landscape.

The key figure in the neo-Advaita phenomenon is H.W.L. Poonja, known affectionately as Papaji. Born in 1913 in what is now Pakistan, he had a life-shaping spiritual experience at the age of eight, resulting in what he called "an intense and passionate love for the form of Krishna." Ramana Maharshi turned his focus from outer-directed worship to inner-directed self-inquiry, culminating, Poonja said, in realization of the non-dual Self—the archetypal "I am That." A married householder, Poonja's modest meeting room in the northern city of Lucknow was flooded with Westerners from the late 1980s until his passing in 1997. In the opening scene of a documentary about him, he is asked to sum up his teaching. His reply: "No teaching, no teacher, no student." Then why are we here? "To find out who you are."[21]

It is said that in his skillful presence many devotees "woke up." No doubt most of those awakenings were transitory, and some were delusional. But for some, the realization that all is One has apparently endured. From their ranks came the *satsang* leaders who have made Advaitan nondualism a central feature of modern spirituality. Of course, the core of Advaita has been with us ever since the first Hindu texts were unpacked in Boston harbor, but the neo-Advaitans have tweaked the vocabulary and made awakening to our true nature their one and only teaching.

Ironically, the best-known Poonja graduate is Andrew Cohen, who, as we saw, disassociated from his former guru. Of those who lay claim to a Poonja lineage, by far the most popular is the former Merle Antoinette (Toni) Roberson (b. 1942), now known as Gangaji. According to her website, the Texas-born, Mississippi-bred Gangaji "pursued many paths to change her life" until Papaji "opened the floodgates of self-recognition" in 1990. She has since guided thousands in the perennial "Who am I?" inquiry, and some of her students—like Amber Terrell, author of *Surprised by Grace,* and John Sherman, an ex-con who met Gangaji through her prison outreach program—have taught on their own.[22] Other direct Poonja disciples on the circuit include Catherine Ingram, whose Dharma Dialogues are popular, and Arjuna Ardagh, the author of *The Translucent Revolution.*

Two other streams of neo-Advaitans are also active on the *satsang* trail: (1) teachers with no allegiance to a specific guru, but who have purportedly awakened through grace and/or independent effort, and (2) teachers whose primary reference point is one of the more intriguing spiritual figures of recent history, the Bombay cigarette merchant Nisargadatta Maharaj.

It is said that when he was asked about his life, Nisargadatta would answer, "I was never born." He was saying that his true identity—the true identity of *all*—transcends the birth and death of our temporary bodies. Nevertheless, the individual known as Nisargadatta arrived on the scene in 1897 as Maruti Sivrampant Kambli on a small South Indian farm. By the 1930s he was a husband, a father, and the owner of Bombay shops that sold household goods and *bidis* (cigarettes hand rolled in leaves). He was also a disciple of Sri Siddharamesvar Maharaj, a householder guru, and at a certain point attained realization, along with a new name. According to Timothy Conway, who spent time with the sage in 1981, Nisargadatta means "one dwelling in the natural state."

As seekers came to his loft above his shop to pepper him with questions, his reputation as a kind of Socrates of the Self grew. His dialogues were recorded, transcribed, and published in 1973 as *I Am That: Conversations with Sri Nisargadatta Maharaj*. Thousands have been captivated by the massive volume, in which the master, in a raw, cut-to-the-chase style, shows one inquirer after another that whatever he thinks he is, he is not. He is only That—birthless, formless Oneness—and always has been.[23] Between the book's publication and the smoking sage's death from throat cancer in 1981, numerous Westerners sought him out. Some of those in attendance, such as Conway and psychologist Stephen Wolinsky, became teachers themselves.[24]

The neo-Advaitans have their own styles, methods, and angles, but they share the stated purpose of snapping people out of their deluded identification with the ego.[25] In some cases the focus on Oneness is so laserlike as to constitute a kind of Advaita fundamentalism. This has led to what might be called dueling nondualists.[26] In a nutshell, the debate boils down to what "One without a second" (the literal meaning of *advaita*) really means. The basic nondual position is uncontested: everything, including us, is nothing but the Absolute. Always was, always will be, like ocean waves are always ocean despite their apparent separateness. But, critics argue, neo-Advaitans take that principle to absurd extremes, essentially negating the reality of the world we live in, where objects and persons are separate and ever-changing. To them, the attempt to squeeze the square pegs of relativity into the round hole of absolute unity has had unfortunate consequences.[27]

Variations of the following advice have come to permeate neo-Advaitan *satsangs:* "You're already enlightened, so stop with the striving and the seeking, and just snap out of it!" Hearing such statements, seekers often eschew practices that might actually facilitate their realization. The American Buddhist Lama Surya Das calls it "premature immaculation." The no-practice stance also ignores the fact that the great nondualists often advocated traditional disciplines. As David Frawley points out, "A careful examination of [Ramana Maharshi's] teachings reveals that he . . . encouraged whatever might aid a person in their sadhana."[28] Timothy Conway makes the same point about Nisargadatta, who told seekers to meditate and performed daily devotional rituals himself. Ironically, most neo-Advaita teachers engaged in practices for decades before they allegedly woke up, only to preach that practices aren't necessary—which might be compared to a baseball player achieving such mastery that he no longer takes batting practice, and then advising Little Leaguers to do the same. Mystics have always said that the onset of realization is a form of grace. But they also said that it takes some work to become open and ready for grace.

Another concern is that nondual fundamentalism can descend into the world-denying attitude that Swami Vivekananda called "heartless escapism masquerading as illumination." Since all is One and the Self is beyond all dualities—good and evil, right and wrong—one should not make judgments or bother trying to change the world. This, critics contend, can lead to slapdash ethics and indifference to social concerns. As Surya Das told me, you can say "It's all One," but if you care whether your family lives or dies, you drive on the right side of the road.

Kurt Johnson, a retired scientist and spiritual activist, says that in recent years neo-Advaitans have shifted away from renunciation to explore

the application of nondualism to politics, ecology, and interpersonal relations. If true, the trend would bring neo-Advaita into line with the overall
history of Vedanta-Yoga in America.[29] Whatever its future, the movement
has made Vedantic nondualism better known to Americans. Ramana Maharshi's visage is now framed in thousands of homes, a reminder of the
possibility of higher attainment and perhaps a cue to ask "Who am I?"

The American-bred *pandits, acharyas,* and gurus absorbed the teachings of Vedanta-Yoga, filtered it through their unique personalities, backgrounds, and passions, and added their voices to the gathering chorus.
They helped to demystify the ancient teachings, adapted them to the needs
of their constituencies, and moved them further into the mainstream of
society. Other intermediaries have done the same, albeit less overtly and
in different contexts. In the next three chapters, we'll explore the contributions of Vedic transmitters in the arts, sciences, and religion. First, the
creative masterminds who entertained us as they enlightened us.

15

ART-OMATIC TRANSMISSIONS

F ew people outside music circles have heard of Richard Bock, but he is one of the unsung heroes of our story. A music producer and the head of L.A.-based World Pacific Records, Bock met Ravi Shankar before the sitarist was famous and went on to produce many of his albums. Bock's connections also led to historic collaborations between Shankar and leading jazz artists like alto saxophonist Bud Shank and flutist Paul Horn (who later recorded the seminal album *Inside the Taj Mahal.*)[1] In 1961 Bock introduced Shankar to John Coltrane, which led to a friendship that moved the great saxophonist in a new direction and showcased Indian spirituality to a new population. It was also through Bock that David Crosby, then a member of the Byrds, first heard Shankar's music. Crosby shared the discovery with George Harrison, and the rest is musical and spiritual history.

Bock is an example of how individuals become links in the chain of Vedic transmission, influencing others who also become transmitters. Some of the most influential, and certainly the most sublime, were artists.

Sattvic Sounds

Long before Richard Bock, and far removed in time and sensibility from Woodstock, the cognoscenti were exposed to Vedic themes through Indian music and dance. In the early twentieth century, Ruth St. Denis, a pioneer of modern dance and a student of Swami Paramananda, one of Vivekananda's direct disciples, performed original pieces such as "The Yogi," which featured choreographed Yoga asanas and vocalized passages from the Bhagavad Gita. One of St. Denis's most famous pieces was "Radha," a portrayal of a maiden's all-consuming love for Krishna, a traditional allegory about devotion to the divine. Later in the century Uday Shankar's touring dance company (with baby brother Ravi providing *sattvic* sound on sitar) drew sizable crowds in American recital halls.[2] Evelyn Blau, a longtime student and supporter of Krishnamurti, told me that she stepped onto her spiritual path when, as a young dancer in the 1940s, she was swept away by the troupe's performance in New York. The custom of conveying Vedic teachings through Indian dance forms continues to this day.

In the early 1950s the great violinist Yehudi Menuhin met Ravi Shankar in India and quickly introduced him to the West. Shankar's first tour, in 1956 when he was thirty-six, drew small audiences, but they included tastemakers like Bock.[3] In 1959 at the prestigious Bath Festival in Great Britain, Menuhin and the sitarist performed together. The response, while restrained compared to the hippie roar to come, was so enthusiastic that the duo recorded the historic *West Meets East* album, which won a Grammy Award in 1967. (Sequels were released in 1968 and 1976.)

Menuhin's respect for Indian music went beyond aesthetics, just as his passion for Yoga transcended its physical benefits. Readers of his memoir, *Unfinished Journey,* learned that Yoga helped him prepare to play music but was "primarily a yardstick to inner peace." Similarly, the higher purpose of Indian music, he wrote, is "to make one sensitive to the infinite within one, to unite one's breath with the breath of space, one's vibrations with the vibrations of the cosmos."

Many of Shankar's listeners could sense that higher purpose. Being at his concerts was euphoric, not just because you were discovering a musical form that was as spontaneous as bebop and as formal as a sonata but because you felt that it was, for the artists performing it, holy. You could see it in their eyes, and in their repose, and in the way they approached the stage as if it were a sanctum sanctorum. The music itself evoked the cosmic order, with a changeless sound stabilizing a raging, unpredictable dynamism. At the very least, you walked away knowing that a culture that was thought of as backward was capable of producing sublime and sophisticated art. If that were true of its music, why wouldn't it also be true of the spiritual tradition that gave rise to it?

"In India, music is considered as a subtle divine thread that can link the individual soul to divinity," says Gita Desai, an Indian-American filmmaker whose documentary *Raga Unveiled: India's Voice* is an exhaustive exploration of the subject.[4] It is therefore not surprising that the nation's classical music has been an entry point to a new spirituality for many people. Chip Hartranft, for example, was a precocious twelve-year-old drummer in a New Jersey garage band that covered Beatles songs. In 1967 a bandmate's father took the group to a Ravi Shankar concert. Hartranft soon realized that India was the source of the Beatles' mind-expanding musical phase. A few years later, when his band turned to jazz, he discovered the Coltrane-India connection. All of which led him to Yoga and meditation and ultimately to the founding of a successful Yoga center outside Boston.[5]

All That Jazz

In 1957, John Coltrane had a transcendent experience that led him away from drugs and onto an impassioned spiritual quest. According to Peter Lavezzoli, author of the comprehensive history, *The Dawn of Indian Music in the West,* when Coltrane discovered Shankar he "plunged headlong into an investigation of Indian music."[6] In his memoir, *Raga Mala,* Shankar wrote that Coltrane was eager to learn how Indian musicians "create such peace, tranquility and spirituality in our music." Musicologists can hear the Indian influence in Coltrane's subsequent work. Ordinary fans knew something was up from the titles of compositions such as "Meditation," "Om," and "India." The bond between the two legends grew so strong that the saxophonist named his second son Ravi.

Coltrane's interest in India was not just musical. An avid reader, he apparently devoured Yogananda's autobiography, the life of Sri Ramakrishna, the Bhagavad Gita, and other classics. ("Om" features a chanted verse from the Gita.) His goal, he once said, was "to point out to people the divine in a musical language that transcends words." That quest, the fruits of which are preserved for the ages in the breathtaking "A Love Supreme," was cut short by his death from liver cancer in 1967, at age forty. As mentioned earlier, his widow, Alice McLeod Coltrane, went on to become Swamini Turiyasangitananda. The name, she once told an interviewer, means "the bliss of God's divine music."

In the mid-1960s, as Ravi Shankar's fame grew, he influenced two other innovative musicians and through them two additional sets of music lovers. Classical composer Philip Glass met Shankar when both men were hired by Conrad Rooks to work on the score of *Chappaqua*. Glass, who studied and recorded with Shankar (the album *Passages* in 1990), said that "Indian music pushed me towards a whole new way of thinking about music." The result is reflected in Glass's compositions, with their repetitive passages and their emphasis on rhythmic structure. He transmitted Vedic ideas explicitly in two major works: the opera *Satyagraha,* which is based on Mahatma Gandhi's years in South Africa and whose libretto consists of verses from the Bhagavad Gita; and *The Passion of Ramakrishna,* a concert piece for orchestra and voices based on the last months of the legendary saint's life.

Jazz fusion artist John McLaughlin first heard Indian music on the radio as a boy in postwar England. In the 1960s, having earned serious cred by playing with Miles Davis, his blistering guitar licks reached jazz-rock crossover audiences, first with his plugged-in band Mahavishnu Orchestra, and later with an acoustic group, Shakti. The sincerity of his spiritual discipline was respected as much as his virtuosity, says Lavezzoli, which no doubt led many fans to explore the philosophy he embraced.

All Things Must Pass, By George

George Harrison's well-publicized association with Ravi Shankar launched the maestro to superstardom and changed the Quiet Beatle's life as well as the face of music. After Harrison introduced the sitar in 1965 on "Norwegian Wood," other pop stars of the era used the instrument—the Byrds, the Grateful Dead, the Incredible String Band, Stevie Wonder, and others— and decades later the likes of Red Hot Chili Peppers and Janet Jackson did so too. But for Harrison it was about more than the sound. No artist took India's spiritual message more seriously or promoted it with as much fervor. It is front and center on his sessions with the Hare Krishna musicians and on Shankar's *Chants of India* album, which Harrison produced. It is also palpable in lyrics such as "Try to realize it's all within yourself." The line is from "Within You Without You," whose fusion of Eastern and Western motifs opened side two of the shape-shifting *Sgt. Pepper* album.

Some of the songs on Harrison's solo album *All Things Must Pass* were the Vedantic equivalent of gospel music. On "My Sweet Lord," the first number-one single by a former Beatle, Harrison voices the yearning of a God seeker: "I really want to know you," he cries, "I really want to be with you." As he intones variations on "my sweet Lord," the chorus sings "Hallelujah," then Hare Krishna, then a traditional verse invoking Brahma, Vishnu, and Shiva (called Maheswara). Harrison said he wanted to show that Christian and Hindu sounds of praise "are quite the same thing." Because all things must indeed pass, some songs on that album warned about attachment. "Beware of Darkness" counsels us to beware of "falling swingers" and "thoughts that linger." He also posed spiritual solutions. "Awaiting on You All" says you don't need a horoscope or microscope or a church or temple; just chant the names of the Lord, and you'll be free. He advises us to learn "The Art of Dying," a classic metaphor for transcending bodily identity, and he argues for reincarnation: "There'll come a time when most of us return here."

Thousands heard such Harrison lyrics at the historic Concert for Bangladesh in August 1971, which packed Madison Square Garden for two performances, and millions more heard them on the Grammy-winning album and on the documentary of the events. (They also heard a stunning set by Ravi Shankar, Ali Akbar Khan, and other Indian virtuosos.) But eventually Harrison's overt spiritual messages began to turn off his fans. At one point in the 1970s, writes Joshua Greene in *Here Comes the Sun*, Harrison "grappled with the depressing realization that most people simply didn't care to hear about Krishna or maya or getting liberated from birth and death."[7]

In his remaining years, Harrison recorded and performed infrequently, and when he did, he subdued his missionary zeal. But his commitment to his spiritual path never diminished. He continued to meditate, chant, and study, always retaining some degree of involvement with Krishna devotees, the TM movement, and Yogananda's lineage. Nor did he hold back when interviewed. When John Lennon was murdered, millions heard George reference the Bhagavad Gita on reincarnation. In a 1987 profile in *People*, Harrison proclaimed, "The purpose of our life is to get to God-realization," and "there's a science that goes with that."[8]

All of this has made Harrison a spiritual mentor to a great many seekers. "The fact that George's lyrics reflected the same sensibility I was getting into at age thirteen or fourteen made me feel a bond with him that's hard to describe," religious scholar Jeffery Long said. "I know all his lyrics by heart, and I see him as a role model, in terms of expressing his Hindu beliefs and experiences through his Western culture." Long's book, *A Vision for Hinduism: Beyond Hindu Nationalism*, is dedicated to his musical hero.

Harrison died in November 2001. The title song on his posthumously released album, *Brainwashed*, was a spiritual valedictory. He runs through the many ways that *maya* deceives us, then offers a Vedic answer, calling God "the wisdom that we seek" and evoking the classical attributes of the divine: existence *(sat)*, knowledge *(chit)*, and bliss *(ananda)*.[9] He quotes a passage from a yogic text on the nature of the soul and, joined by his son

Dhani (named for two notes on the Indian musical scale), he closes with an invocation to Shiva and his consort Parvati, the supreme embodiment of the Divine Mother. Harrison's ashes were scattered in the Ganges in accord with Hindu tradition.[10]

Shabda Power

The *shabda*[11] transmission continues through masters of Indian music such as sitarists Nishat Khan and Anoushka Shankar, Ravi's daughter, whose album *Rise* earned a Grammy nomination in the Contemporary World Music category. In addition to playing classical ragas, both artists collaborate with Western musicians. (A song on Shankar's album *Breathing Under Water* features her half-sister, Norah Jones.) The fertile fusion of Indian motifs and jazz continues to be explored by musicians of Indian ancestry—like pianist (and physicist) Vijay Iyer and saxophonist Rudresh Mahanthappa—and Americans such as John Wubbenhorst, who studied jazz at the Berklee College of Music and the *bansuri* (bamboo flute) with an Indian master. Then there's Charles Lloyd, who has been at it since Coltrane's day. A longtime meditator and a regular at the Vedanta Society in Santa Barbara, Lloyd has mixed straight-on jazz with meditative moods for over forty years, dipping occasionally into Indian themes. In his 2004 release *Sangam*,[12] his ensemble includes the tabla master Zakir Hussain, who played with John McLaughlin in Shakti. In his interviews, which are as quirky as they are rare, Lloyd is unambiguous about his path. "We make a direct connection with the Man, and render unto God what's God's, and render unto Caesar what's Caesar's," he told one writer. "But Caesar can't come in there, because you hear the sound, and Brahman is in the sound."

The *shabda* tradition of transformative sound is being tapped by more and more artists for explicitly sacred purposes—not just by the *kirtan wallahs*[13] mentioned in chapter 12 but by Yoga and meditation teachers. Russill Paul, who spent years in India as a Hindu-Christian monk, says his study of Indian spiritual and musical forms "laid the foundation for my ministry, The Yoga of Sound." His albums, including *Shabda Yoga,* a collection of Vedic chants, come with booklets explaining how to "deepen your experience of the sound through methods of breathing and focused awareness."[14]

As ever, pop stars inspired by Indian teachings expose their fans to samples of the Veda. In 2005 a group called Cynic, for instance, recorded a song called "Veils of Maya." On the superstar end of the spectrum, Madonna's 1998 album *Ray of Light* contains a cut titled "Shanti/Ashtangi," with Sanskrit *shlokas* (verses) taken from the Yoga Taravali. Reportedly, she took pronunciation lessons from a Sanskrit scholar. And the award for Vedic kitsch goes to the irrepressible Cher. On her farewell tour, she included an extravagant rendering of the Gayatri Mantra from the Rig Veda. She sang it while seated atop an ersatz elephant, surrounded by dancers decked out in what someone called India-meets-Vegas, to the same intoxicating arrangement used by Deva Premal on her popular album *The Essence.* Deva and her partner-collaborator Miten (the couple met at the Indian ashram of Rajneesh-Osho in the 1980s) told me that Cher, like thousands of others, had used their recording as background music for her Yoga routine. Now a multitude of Cher fans have heard the most revered mantra in all of Hinduism, albeit in rather glitzy fashion.

A new generation of musicians continues to blend East and West in novel ways. To cite one very cool example, Nick Giacomini, who teaches Yoga in Point Reyes, California, doubles as a rapper named MC Yogi. On his album *Elephant Power,* he cleverly raps about yogic ideals, pays homage to Gandhi, and tells the tales of Ganesh, Hanuman, and other Hindu deities. Sample lyrics from his paean to Shiva, who is called the King of the Yogis: "To the old school mystic, who's non dualistic / Shiva guides my mind so that I can shift it / away from a place that's materialistic / into a space that's more holistic."[15]

Ever since the days of Yehudi Menuhin, the media have been happy to disclose the yogic proclivities of musical celebrities, even if their music contains no spiritual references. No one would know from her songs, for instance, that folk goddess Judy Collins is a longtime practitioner of Yogananda's Kriya Yoga. She revealed it in her memoir, and she's talked about it in interviews. "As a habit," she told one reporter, "I try to give myself the silence." That silence, the Vedas say, is the source of all sound, whether primeval mantras or Collins's transcendent version of "Amazing Grace."

Vedantic Verse

If the Romantic poets—William Blake, Percy Bysshe Shelley, William Wordsworth, Samuel Taylor Coleridge—did not read Vedic texts, they were at least familiar with the idealist philosophers who did. One way or another, a Vedanta-like voice found its way into some of their verse. Blake's "Auguries of Innocence" for instance: "To see a world in a grain of sand / And a Heaven in a wild flower / Hold infinity in the palm of your hand / And Eternity in an hour." Shelley may as well have been describing Brahman when he wrote, in "Adonais," "The One remains, the many change and pass." So too Wordsworth, who sang of "A motion and a spirit, that impels / All thinking things, all objects of all thought, / And rolls through all things." And Coleridge, who was definitely acquainted with Vedanta, wrote of seeing in unspoiled nature "the translucence of the Eternal through and in the temporal."

Later in time, between Whitman and the Beats, came two poets in whom the influence of India is most explicit: William Butler Yeats and T. S. Eliot. Yeats, the most beloved of Irish bards, wrote that "the mystical life is the centre of all that I do and all that I think and all that I write." He discovered Vedanta when he was about thirty and found that it "confirmed my vague speculations and seemed at once logical and boundless." Harry Oldmeadow, in *Journeys East,* notes that Yeats's poems often express "distinctively Indian ideas about *karma,* transmigration, the four stages of life and the interdependence of the inner and outer worlds."[16] The poet was directly influenced by friendships with three Indian men: Mohini Chatterjee, a Theosophist; Rabindranath Tagore, his fellow Nobel laureate in literature; and Shri Purohit Swami, a monk whom Yeats met in his sixties.

He wrote introductions to Purohit's autobiography, *An Indian Monk: His Life and Adventures,* and to his translations of the *Mandukya Upanishad* and the *Yoga Sutras.* He also shared writing credit with the swami on *The Ten Principal Upanishads,* one of the bestselling translations of the classic texts.

The St. Louis–born T. S. Eliot spent two years at Harvard studying Vedantic texts with America's finest Indologists. Eliot, who learned Sanskrit and Pali (the language of the Buddha), once remarked that the subtleties of Indian sages "make most of the great European philosophers look like schoolboys," acknowledging that his own poetry "shows the influence of Indian thought and sensibility." In "Burnt Norton," the first of his celebrated *Four Quartets,* the Nobel laureate evokes the Vedantic transcendence of time and space and points the reader toward infinity at "the still point of the turning world." In "The Dry Salvages," the third quartet, Eliot draws upon the Bhagavad Gita, which he first read in his early twenties, pondering Krishna's message to Arjuna and invoking central themes, such as "do not think of the fruit of action."

Eliot's masterpiece, *The Waste Land,* begins with the famous line "April is the cruellest month" and proceeds to paint a bleak picture of modern life on the brink of collapse. But he closes on a hopeful note with what have been called the Three Cardinal Virtues from the *Brihadaranyaka Upanishad: datta* (charity, or generosity), *dayadhvam* (compassion), and *damyata* (restraint, or self-control). The last line is "Shantih shantih shantih," the traditional ending for Hindu invocations. In his published notes, Eliot equates *shantih* with "the Peace which passeth understanding."

It is easy to dismiss the influence of poetry nowadays, but before the explosion of audio and visual technologies, verse was a prime source of knowledge and inspiration, and Yeats and Eliot were among the most widely read poets of the twentieth century. It has been through the art of fiction, however, that the literary transmission of Vedanta has been the most profound.

Puranic Prose

As early as 1897, when Mark Twain wrote of his travels in India ("the most extraordinary country that the sun visits on his rounds"), lovers of literature have learned about the exotic land through storytellers. Many got their first taste from the yarns of Rudyard Kipling, E. M. Forster, and other bards of the British Raj. There was, to be sure, a strong undercurrent of imperial arrogance in Kipling's work; nonetheless a tale like *Kim* could stir a sympathetic interest in the colonized nation. Forster's *A Passage to India,* published in 1924, depicted the social and spiritual tension between Brits and the native population, offering intriguing glimpses of mystical India in the bargain. Paul Scott introduced a later generation of readers to India, beginning in 1966 with *The Jewel in the Crown,* the first installment of his epic Raj Quartet and the title of the hugely popular 1984 miniseries based on all four books.

The main novelists who pointed readers toward India's spirituality, as opposed to its cultural wonders, were (in addition to Huxley and Isher-wood) Hermann Hesse, Somerset Maugham, and J. D. Salinger. Hesse's *Steppenwolf, Siddhartha,* and *Journey to the East,* written by the German Nobel Prize winner between the world wars, were virtually required reading in the Sixties counterculture, as was his magnum opus, *The Glass Bead Game* (aka *Magister Ludi*), an enigmatic masterpiece that includes three short stories "written" by the novel's protagonist, one about a shaman, another about a Christian mystic, and a third about a yogi that could stand as a modern Upanishad. In one way or another, Hesse's most popular works were about transcendence, reflecting his lifelong fascination with India, where his parents had been missionaries.

For romantics in the World War II era, Maugham's *The Razor's Edge* was an inspiration, and its American protagonist, Larry Darrell, was a role model. The novel's title derives from a passage in the *Katha Upanishad* that Maugham used as an epigraph: "The sharp edge of a razor is difficult to pass over; thus the wise say the path to Salvation is hard."[17] It follows Darrell, a well-educated, well-bred dropout, whose search for an alternative to the rat race takes him to an ashram and the lotus feet of a guru named Shri Ganesha.[18] What he discovers adds up to a synopsis of Vedanta. A sampling of his dialogue:

> Shri Ganesha [said] that the satisfactions of the world are transitory and that only the Infinite gives enduring happiness.

> The Self, which they call the Atman and we call the soul, is distinct from the body and its senses, distinct from the mind and its intelligence.

> Advaita doesn't ask you to take anything on trust; it asks only that you should have a passionate craving to know Reality; it states that you can experience God as surely as you can experience joy or pain.

In the end Larry heads to New York, where the libraries are well stocked and driving a taxi can support a life of "calmness, forbearance, compassion, selflessness and continence." In the 1960s and 1970s, if your cab driver was young and somewhat scraggly, he might have read *The Razor's Edge* and was saving up his tips for passage to India.

But no literary figure can match the impact of J. D. Salinger on modern spirituality. A determined seeker of spiritual truth, the author studied Zen after the war and segued to Vedanta in the early 1950s, after the publication of *The Catcher in the Rye,* that masterful depiction of a young soul hungry for meaning. He was a regular at New York's Ramakrishna-Vivekananda Center, where Joseph Campbell also hung out. Apparently Salinger was torn between the monk and householder paths, having learned that worldly concerns were distractions on the path to enlightenment. In his 1953 short story "Teddy," the ten-year-old title character says the only reason he was incarnated again was because, in his previous life, "I met a lady, and I sort of stopped meditating." The author's daughter, Margaret Salinger, says her father was relieved to find out that marriage can be a legitimate pathway to spiritual attainment. He made that discovery when reading about Yogananda's guru, Lahiri Mahasaya, who was a family man. Salinger and his wife-to-be were initiated into Kriya Yoga, and he gave his kids pictures of Lahiri Mahasaya to carry in their pockets.[19]

"Teddy," the last in the collection *Nine Stories* (1953), ends with Teddy calmly, even cheerfully, walking Christ-like to an accidental death that he's foreseen—Salinger's portrayal of a highly evolved soul who knows that discarding a body is no more tragic than shedding a garment. The book's opening story, the enigmatic "A Perfect Day for Bananafish," also features a voluntary death: Seymour, the saintly main character, blows his brains out, presumably because modern life's corruption of innocence is too much to bear. If decades of obsession by Salinger freaks is any measure, the mystifying deaths are captivating storytelling devices. As teachings, however, most Vedantins would consider it naïve to think that enlightenment translates to suicide or indifference to childhood death. Be that as it may, since the early 1950s, "Teddy" has introduced readers to reincarnation, nonattachment, and other concepts that Salinger imbibed on his personal quest.

His understanding of Vedanta grew more sophisticated with each subsequent work, beginning with *Franny and Zooey*. The sibling tales about two siblings were first published in *The New Yorker* (1955 and 1957 respectively), and then together in a 1961 book. They introduce Salinger's immortal Glass family and foreshadow the journey upon which thousands of baby boomers would soon embark: a smart, sensitive college student sinks into an existential crisis, tries to unlock the secrets of an esoteric text, and climbs out of her dark night of the soul with the help of Vedantic ideals articulated by a representative of a guru lineage. In this case, the "ashram" is the Manhattan apartment Franny grew up in, and the spiritual guide is her older brother Zooey, who imparts wisdom transmitted by the next oldest sibling, Buddy, who in turn is the chief "disciple" of their late brother Seymour, the family *sadguru*. In the end, Franny "lay quiet, smiling at the ceiling," and we know her spiritual quest can now begin in earnest. Along the way readers learn about karma, Atman, and chakras, and about yogic challenges such as acting without attachment to outcomes and seeing everything, even the remedial chicken soup of a fussbudget mother, as consecrated.

Franny and Zooey was followed in 1963 by two novellas, also published originally in *The New Yorker* (1955 and 1959), *Raise High the Roof Beam, Carpenters* and *Seymour: An Introduction.* The stories round out Salinger's portrait of swami Seymour and his sibling *chelas,* all karma yogis trying their damnedest to live authentic spiritual lives while performing their dharmic duties with dignity. They may be precocious kids, ridiculously sensitive adolescents, and eccentric adults, but they speak in modern vernacular and struggle with the same neurotic concerns as anyone who's ever wondered what it's all about or why the world is populated by phonies and sleepwalkers. Salinger's answers are invariably lifted from Vedanta or a sister wisdom tradition.

He completed his Glass chronicles with a prequel. Written in the form of a letter from camp by the seven-year-old Seymour, "Hapworth 16, 1924" ran in *The New Yorker* in 1965. The last work the author made public before hunkering down to his long, famous seclusion, it contains repeated references to past lives ("appearances"), instructions for a yogic breathing technique, allusions to Tantric sexual practices, and an homage to Swami Vivekananda, whom Seymour calls "one of the most exciting, original, and best-equipped giants of this century."

In 1963 *New York Times* reviewer Orville Prescott said of the Glass family saga to date: "Rarely if ever in literary history has a handful of stories aroused so much discussion, controversy, praise, denunciation, mystification and interpretation."[20] While the number of readers today is no doubt less than it was half a century ago, Salinger's books—not just the perennial *Catcher in the Rye*—are still remarkably popular (there's even a rock band named Raise High the Roof Beam), and they still turn on readers to Vedantic ideas. A few years ago I wrote an essay about *Franny and Zooey*'s impact on me as a young seeker. After it was published, I received a thank-you e-mail from a woman whose eighteen-year-old daughter had become a spiritual seeker but had sunk into a Franny-like dark night of the soul. My essay led her to *Franny and Zooey,* which showed her daughter that she was neither crazy nor alone.[21]

Cinema *Bharata*

Hollywood films have often reinforced negative images of Indian culture and religion. Comedic actors, from Peter Sellers's bumbling thespian in *The Party* (1968) to Mike Myers's horny Guru Pitka in *The Love Guru* (2008), have trafficked in stereotypes. Even the Beatles succumbed: *Help!* involves a cult, led by Swami Clang, that sacrifices human beings to the goddess Kali. If that sounds familiar, it may be because Steven Spielberg portrayed a bloodthirsty Kali cult two decades later in *Indiana Jones and the Temple of Doom.* Of course, whatever bad karma the Beatles acquired for Swami Clang was offset when they turned on a generation to India's wisdom. Karmic balance was probably also achieved by Sellers, who was a public advocate of Yoga, and by Myers, who is a friend and student of Deepak Chopra. Unfortunately, the countless parodies of gurus and Hindu cults have no doubt kept many from taking India's traditions seriously.

On the plus side, Western audiences have been enchanted by cinematic India ever since 1917, when a young Mary Pickford starred in a silent film version of Frances Hodgson Burnett's novel *A Little Princess.* The story is about a girl who is taken from India to London, where her burning desire to find her missing father is aided by the wise Indian servant next door, named Ram Das. It was remade twice, in 1939 with Shirley Temple and Cesar Romero, a debonair Cuban-American who played Ram Das, and again in 1995, with New York replacing London. It is, of course, impossible to know how many viewers acquired an interest in the spiritual tradition that presumably made Ram Das so sagacious, but it is interesting to note that Hodgson Burnett was an early New Thought proponent. Another of her books, *The Secret Garden,* also touches on Indian philosophical principles, and was twice adapted for film (1949 and 1993).

In 1951 Jean Renoir's *The River* offered a breathtaking vision of life along the Ganges. Shot in colors as saturated as any put to canvas by the director's father, the great Impressionist Pierre-Auguste Renoir, the film was a revelation to many film buffs, and its success enabled Renoir's assistant, Satyajit Ray, to make his first film. Starting in 1955, when the first installment was released, Ray's celebrated Apu Trilogy was seen by thousands of foreign film aficionados, for whom the director was cinema *Bharata*'s answer to Akira Kurosawa and Federico Fellini.[22] With their understated Ravi Shankar scores and indelible black and white images, the trio of masterpieces drew a great many viewers irresistibly to India. Bill Drayton, for instance, was an adolescent in New York when he saw the trilogy in the 1950s. He went to India the first chance he could, but first he established the Asian Society at his prep school, Andover. Eventually, inspired by Gandhi's legacy and "the tolerance and openness of India," he created Ashoka, a nonprofit that sponsors innovative social entrepreneurs around the world.[23] Others for whom Ray's films were pivotal trekked to ashrams and became the students of visiting gurus.

The longtime collaboration of producer Ismail Merchant, director James Ivory, and screenwriter Ruth Prawer Jhabvala brought India to life with *The Householder* (1963); *Shakespeare Wallah* (1965); *The Guru* (1969), which depicted a George Harrison–like Brit who goes to India to study sitar; and the captivating *Heat and Dust* (1983), based on Jhabvala's Booker Prize–winning novel. In addition, some of the novels mentioned earlier were turned into films seen by millions. The 1946 version of *The Razor's Edge,* with Tyrone Power, earned an Academy Award nomination for best picture; the 1984 remake, with Bill Murray trying his hand at drama, earned a bouquet of downturned thumbs. Conrad Rooks's stylized version of Hesse's *Siddhartha* was panned by critics in 1972 but was lapped up by the counterculture. In 1984 David Lean's acclaimed *A Passage to India,* based on the Forster novel, pulled in big box-office numbers and eleven Academy Award nominations.

Perhaps the pinnacle of cinematic transmission was Richard Attenborough's epic *Gandhi,* which won eight Academy Awards, including best picture, in 1982. *Gandhi* brought Indian spirituality to life for millions, including schoolchildren who were paraded to theaters for history lessons. Anyone who thought the Mahatma was just a nonviolent version of George Washington learned what Martin Luther King had: that everything he did was grounded in his spiritual tradition. Filmgoers who were inspired to learn more about Gandhi would have read statements of his, such as: "The soul of religion is one. It is encased in many forms. The final goal of all religions is the realization of this essential oneness of Spirit."

In recent years, with India's new-found respect on the world stage, films about India and Indians have become more common. The apotheosis, of course, was the triumph of *Slumdog Millionaire* in 2008.[24] But even minor efforts like *Outsourced* and *Darjeeling Limited* provide more nuanced versions of Indian life than the films of an earlier era, in which Indians were portrayed mostly as decent but inferior functionaries or as noble primitives in need of rescue by Westerners.[25] Perhaps the most important development has been the emergence of talented Indian filmmakers such as Mira Nair. Since *Salaam Bombay!* in 1988, and continuing with *Mississippi Masala* (1991), *Kama Sutra: A Tale of Love* (1996), *Monsoon Wedding* (2001), and *The Namesake* (2006), the Harvard grad has revealed aspects of Indian culture previously unseen by most Westerners. Though she lives in New York now, the name of Nair's company, Mirabai Films, tells you where her heart is: Mirabai was a sixteenth-century female devotional poet who is beloved in India.

With gifted filmmakers like Nair, and with celebrated novelists like Anita Desai (and her daughter, Kiran Desai), Amit Chaudhuri, and Aravind Adiga providing source material, we are likely to see ever more authentic depictions of India and its people in the coming years.[26] Some of those films will inspire spiritual seekers to explore the Vedic legacy. And there will always be the late Satyajit Ray, whose films can still mesmerize. In 2009 a retrospective of his work played to sold-out houses at Lincoln Center.

Senses and Sensibilities

Music, poetry, fiction, and feature films have been the primary artistic vehicles of Vedic transmission, but not the only ones. Nonfiction artists have made their mark with documentary films and literary memoirs. On the serious side, recent documentaries such as Paula Fouce's *Naked in Ashes*

(2005), Maurizio Bennazo's *Short Cut to Nirvana: Khumb Mela* (2004), and Gita Desai's *Yoga Unveiled* (2004) have explored the history and variety of Indian spiritual expression. But no documentary has ever matched, for either splendor or impact, Louis Malle's majestic *Phantom India*. The seven-part, nearly seven-hour masterpiece was released in 1969, a year after the Beatles brought images of India to mainstream attention, and it may have inspired more treks to the subcontinent than any film in history.

Several memoirs have achieved commercial success while teaching readers about Indian spirituality. The apotheosis of the genre was Shirley MacLaine's 1983 bestseller, *Out on a Limb*. For all its New Age clichés and occult woo-woo, the book introduced a legion of readers to Vedantic ideas and sent many of them scurrying for the deeper stuff. Stan Madsen, one of three aerospace engineers who quit their jobs in 1970 to open L.A.'s legendary Bodhi Tree bookstore, told me that traffic multiplied about fivefold when the shop was mentioned in MacLaine's book and depicted in the TV miniseries based on it. In recent years, the most spectacular memoir has been Elizabeth Gilbert's *Eat, Pray, Love* (2006). One-third of the runaway bestseller takes place in an unnamed Indian ashram although it doesn't take a Sherlock Holmes to deduce that it's the Siddha Yoga ashram in Ganeshpuri and her guru is Gurumayi. (By now, tens of millions have visited the movie version of that ashram, with Julia Roberts as Gilbert.)

Network TV has occasionally tuned into Eastern mysticism, from the much-loved *Kung Fu* (sixty-three episodes from 1972 to 1975) to the karmic reverberations in *My Name Is Earl*. Comedians also get into the act, often with spoofs that humorist and public speaker Steve Bhaerman calls "shallow, mean-spirited and inaccurate." As his alter ego, the turbaned Swami Beyondananda, Bhaerman has been spinning sagacious spiritual satire for about two decades at conferences and in writing (as in his book *Driving Your Own Karma*). His humor respects Vedic tradition and transmits useful advice, largely through aphoristic puns, like "there's no place like om" and "curb your dogma."[27]

The influence of India's visual arts has been minor compared to that of the Chinese and Japanese. Art historian Debashish Banerji says that is because Indian painting has mainly been representational and somewhat gaudy—the opposite of Western trends toward abstraction and minimalism. In the twentieth century private collectors and major museums displayed Hindu statuary, but few aficionados delved into its spiritual underpinnings. The leap from art to spiritual inquiry was more common in the Sixties, when colorful Krishna posters were tacked to the walls of many a hippie pad. For the most part, however, the Hindu visual esthetic did not catch on.

That is, until the twenty-first century, when India's spiritual heritage was introduced to a new generation of Westerners through a quintessentially American art form: comic books. Around the time hippies started meditating, Indian graphic artists started producing adventure comics about Vedic gods and goddesses. The form was digitalized and adapted to video games and animated film. One company depicting epic tales as superhero fantasies is Bangalore-based Liquid Comics, which was cofounded by American-born Gotham Chopra (Deepak's son). The genre, which is huge in India, sells well to American youngsters, and in 2009 the Los Angeles County Museum of Art mounted an exhibit titled "Heroes and Villains: The Battle for Good in India's Comics." To get to it, visitors passed through the museum's Asian galleries, where they saw Durga, Shiva, Rama, and the rest depicted in traditional sculpture.

Some Western artists have drawn from Indian motifs to portray spiritual ideas. In the late 1930s a group of Americans who were influenced by Theosophy and Eastern philosophy formed the Transcendental Painting Group, whose stated purpose was "to carry painting beyond the appearance of the physical world, through new concepts of space, color, light and design, to imaginative realms that are . . . spiritual." In its brief existence, the group reached art lovers through exhibits, lectures, and publications. (Wassily Kandinsky and Piet Mondrian were also Theosophists.) Also strongly influenced by the East was the Russian painter Nicholas Roerich. A spiritual teacher in his own right, Roerich and his wife founded the Himalayan Research Institute in India and later moved to New York, where their Agni Yoga Society attracted a following. Roerich's paintings, with their Buddhist and Hindu imagery and Himalayan landscapes, are housed in their own Manhattan museum.[28] Modern artists influenced by Eastern themes range from the Tantric "spiritualized anatomy" in Alex Grey's Chapel of Sacred Mirrors, to numerous abstract works depicting meditative states of awareness, to Madeline De Joly's *Veda Project,* which consists of forty related pieces depicting the artist's impressions of Vedic texts.[29]

For centuries now, the arts have made India attractive to Western sensibilities. For some, the appeal was strictly aesthetic or anthropological: India the exotic, the colorful, the mysterious. Regardless of the initial charm, many were led to the nation's spiritual essence. Some got hooked, and some of the hooked became disseminators of Vedanta-Yoga. A remarkable number of people interviewed for this book were turned eastward through the arts. Three of them are leading scholars: Ramdas Lamb, whose ninth-grade mind was blown by a Ravi Shankar album and who went to India as soon as his marine hitch was over; Christopher Chapple, who read *The Secret Garden* at age ten, prompting curiosity about his college-age sister's copy of the Upanishads; and Jeffery Long, who had an adolescent double whammy with George Harrison followed by the movie *Gandhi.*

"Only through art," wrote the French novelist Marcel Proust, "can we get outside of ourselves and know another's view of the universe which is not the same as ours and see landscapes which would otherwise have remained unknown to us like the landscapes of the moon." For a great many people, the arts have been a portal to the spiritual landscape of India, and through that to the landscape within themselves.

16

THE SOUL OF SCIENCE,
THE SCIENCE OF SOUL

Ever since the seventeenth century, when the Enlightenment (aka the Age of Reason) first dawned, science had spread like kudzu, taking over one domain of inquiry after another and establishing itself as the preeminent mode of acquiring reliable knowledge. As one astonishing discovery and life-altering invention followed another, the juggernaut rolled on, and its confidence swelled, until it seemed there was no mystery that the scientific method would not eventually solve. Then science turned its lens on itself. In the mid-1920s Werner Heisenberg's uncertainty principle showed that, on the quantum mechanical level, what is observed cannot be entirely separated from the observer. Kurt Gödel's incompleteness theorems in 1931 proved that no formal mathematical system—the tools on which science depends—can be both complete and consistent. These and related discoveries did nothing to diminish the scientific method's preeminence, but it was a blow to *scientism* as an ideology that views science as the only valid path to knowledge—a postulate that, ironically, cannot be proved by scientific means.

In the ensuing decades, as the implications of uncertainty and incompleteness slowly sank in, and knowledge of the new quantum mechanical reality spread, scientists and scholars were increasingly exposed to Eastern philosophy because of the social forces chronicled in earlier chapters.

Some of them were surprised to find that the mystical traditions were not as antithetical to science as the familiar faith-based religions seemed to be, since they did not postulate a Jehovah-like overseer or a creation story that was incompatible with evolution and scientific dating. Romain Rolland's assertion that "religious faith in the case of the Hindus has never been allowed to run counter to scientific laws" appeared to be true.

Come the Sixties, and the Eastern winds that had whipped through the enclaves of metaphysical seekers, bohemians, and artists started to waft into the spaces where brainiacs in lab coats and rumpled corduroys pondered conundrums. Since then the sciences—physics, psychology, and medicine in particular—have been influenced by systems of knowledge with Vedic roots. In turn, representatives of those disciplines have adapted Vedantic ideas and yogic practices in ways that furthered their dissemination.

The Dance of Shiva

In a plaza outside the European Organization for Nuclear Research (CERN) in Geneva, Switzerland, stands a human-size statue of the deity Shiva. A more fitting image of the meeting of Eastern spirituality and Western science is hard to imagine. Inside the CERN fortress, subatomic particles are made to accelerate and collide, as physicists ponder the origins of the universe. Outside, under the sun and stars, stands Vedic cosmology in symbolic form. Depicted as Nataraja, the Lord of Dance, Shiva stands with his right foot planted on a slayed demon, symbolizing the destruction of ignorance. His raised left leg, his four arms, and his torqued body are frozen in perfect balance, as if captured midwhirl in a photo. Taken as a whole, it depicts cosmic creation and destruction, in which infinite dynamism coexists with eternal, changeless Being. "It is the clearest image of the activity of God which any art or religion can boast of," said the philosopher and art historian Ananda K. Coomaraswamy. That quote is etched on the statue's pedestal, along with one from physicist Fritjof Capra, author of the seminal bestseller *The Tao of Physics:* "In our time, physicists have used the most advanced technology to portray the patterns of the cosmic dance. The metaphor of the cosmic dance thus unifies ancient mythology, religious art and modern physics."[1]

As some physicists delved deeper and deeper into the substructure of the atom, unveiling a whirligig of abstract energies, others turned their sights to the sky and discovered an expanding universe of seemingly infinite space and time.[2] Some imaginative physicists recognized that this two-pronged expansion of awareness parallels that of yogis in meditation: inward to the deepest layers of mind and outward to infinite consciousness. They also saw that each style of inquiry is an attempt to discern the unseen order beneath appearances, and that each one points to an ultimate unity: physics in the still-to-be-formulated unified field theory; mystics in the Upanishadic maxim "All this is That." The more adventurous found intriguing parallels between Eastern metaphysics and quantum mechanics, each of which demonstrates in its own way that reality is not exactly what we perceive through our ordinary senses.

The Early Days of East-Meets-West

The confluence of modern Indian philosophy and modern science began in the 1890s when Swami Vivekananda spent time with luminaries Sir William Thompson (aka Lord Kelvin), Hermann von Helmholtz, and Nikola Tesla, the legendary inventor. The swami and Tesla apparently saw eye to eye on a vision of nature that seems axiomatic now but would have seemed as fanciful as unicorns at the time. "Mr. Tesla thinks he can demonstrate mathematically that force and matter are reducible to potential energy," Vivekananda said in a letter to a friend, adding, "I am working a good deal now upon the cosmology and eschatology of Vedanta. I clearly see their perfect unison with modern science." Tesla did not succeed in constructing his proof, and Vivekananda died three years before Einstein's $E = mc^2$ united matter and energy forever. But both men were remarkably prescient, and their meeting must have impressed Tesla, judging from his subsequent use of Sanskrit terms such as *akasha* and *prana*.[3]

Einstein's friend and colleague Erwin Schrödinger was a student of Vedanta, perhaps inspired by the harmony between that philosophy and the work that earned him a Nobel Prize. "Vedanta teaches that consciousness is singular," wrote the Austrian theorist. "All happenings are played out in one universal consciousness and there is no multiplicity of selves." Elsewhere he said: "This life of yours which you are living is not merely a piece of this entire existence, but in a certain sense the whole . . . what the Brahmins express in that sacred, mystic formula which is yet really so simple and so clear; tat tvam asi, this is you." Schrödinger, who died in 1961, expressed the hope that a "blood transfusion from the East" might cure what he called the West's "spiritual anemia."

Schrödinger's biographer, Walter Moore, wrote that the quantum revolution, which overturned the model of the universe as a great machine, was "entirely consistent with the Vedantic concept of All in One." Heisenberg, who spent time in India, wrote: "One cannot always distinguish between statements made by eastern metaphysics based on mystical insight, and the pronouncements of modern physics based on observations, experiments and mathematical calculations."

Perhaps the most famous use of Vedanta by a physicist came in 1945 when an atomic bomb first exploded in the New Mexico desert. J. Robert Oppenheimer, who directed the Manhattan Project that had produced the bomb, said that when he saw the mushroom cloud, a verse from the Bhagavad Gita came to mind: "Now I am become death, the destroyer of worlds." Oppenheimer, who had studied Sanskrit at Berkeley and called the Gita "the most beautiful philosophical song existing in any known tongue," also read from the text at a memorial service for President Franklin D. Roosevelt and named it, for a Christian magazine, among the books that shaped his philosophy of life.

The Unified Field of Brahman

In the late 1960s and early 1970s, younger physicists, products of their time, found inspiration in Eastern thought, and gurus, eager for scientific legitimacy, were happy to oblige. None pursued those connections more aggressively than the former physics student Maharishi Mahesh Yogi. He volleyed ideas with the likes of Brian Josephson, who had just won a Nobel Prize at the ripe age of thirty-three, and at one point got a Hampshire College professor named Lawrence Domash to quit his job, cut off his ponytail, and join his movement. Domash infused terms like *quantum vacuum state, phase transition,* and *superfluidity* into the TM vocabulary. The lingo may have flown over the heads of the public—and of most TM teachers—but the language of Einstein opened more doors than the language of religion.

The courtship of physics and Eastern philosophy climaxed in 1975, when Fritjof Capra announced their engagement in *The Tao of Physics.* The Vienna-born Capra said in a 2009 interview that he had been influenced equally by Heisenberg's struggle to comprehend quantum physics and by the Beatles' embrace of India. His bestseller explained how the new physics rendered obsolete the mechanistic worldview that had prevailed since the days of Newton and Descartes, as well as the dualism that separates mind from body and the human observer from that which is being observed.

"The mechanistic world view of classical physics is useful for the description of the kind of physical phenomena we encounter in our everyday life," wrote Capra. "It is inadequate, however, for the description of physical phenomena in the submicroscopic realm." There what we call particles are actually "dynamic patterns which do not exist as isolated entities, but as integral parts of an inseparable network of interactions." Somehow the interactions "give rise to the stable structures that build up the material world," but those objects—this book, your chair—actually "oscillate in rhythmic movements." The conclusion, writes Capra, is that the universe is "engaged in endless motion and activity, in a continual cosmic dance of energy." He illustrated that dance with what most Westerners would have seen as a quaint religious icon: the Shiva Nataraja.

In 1980 more people than will ever read Capra's books saw the same ancient image when Carl Sagan took TV viewers on a journey through the known universe. In the tenth episode of the phenomenally popular *Cosmos,* and in Sagan's bestselling companion book, the ebullient astronomer visits a South Indian temple and explains that Hinduism is the only religion whose proposed time-scale for the universe matches the billions of years documented by science. *Cosmos* attracted more viewers than any PBS program in history, making Vedic cosmology respectable to millions who may have dismissed it as prehistoric drivel.

Capra went even further. He asserted that quantum theory was compatible with Eastern metaphysics, illustrating his contention with copious examples from Hinduism, Buddhism, and Taoism. He also proposed that the introspective methods of mystics and the objective methods of scientists are equally valid means of gaining knowledge. Each, he said, penetrates the surface of things—the mind in one case; matter in the other—to arrive at insights that turn out to be remarkably similar.

The book was attacked by both scientists and spiritual purists, who thought Capra had taken East-West analogies way too far. But it had an enormous impact, unleashing a flood of books (notably, Gary Zukav's *The Dancing Wu Li Masters*, and, later, Deepak Chopra's *Ageless Body, Timeless Mind*), articles, conferences, and seminars that built upon Capra's theme. In New Age circles, it became fashionable to line up quotes from physicists and Eastern sages side by side. Soon the term "new paradigm" came into vogue, based on philosopher Thomas Kuhn's famous analysis of scientific revolutions, in which the governing theoretical framework (the paradigm) gives way to another, more efficacious one.[4] The concept was applied to the worldview of the culture as a whole.

In the late 1970s, another physicist stepped up to the plate, bearing credentials that made Capra look like an undergrad by comparison. David Bohm had done his graduate work at Berkeley under Oppenheimer and taught at Princeton when Einstein was on campus. He was also influenced by his two-decade-long dialogue with J. Krishnamurti (see chapter 3). Bohm theorized that the domain we think of as reality, with its separate objects and events, is actually enfolded within (and unfolds from) a realm of unbroken wholeness in which everything—all of matter and all of consciousness—is simultaneously connected to everything else.[5] "The sphere of ordinary material life and the sphere of mystical experience," said Bohm, "have a certain shared order [that] will allow a fruitful relationship between them."

Bohm's theory evoked a compelling image: the hologram, in which each piece of the whole is mirrored in every other piece. Another Vedic visual now came into use: Indra's Net, a vast network of jewels, each of which reflects the image of all the others. Throughout the 1980s, as Reagan reigned in Washington, conversations about the "holographic universe" and the "holographic paradigm" ranged over a variety of disciplines. Many of the participants had been influenced by Eastern philosophy, and now their ideas were heard by the public.[6]

Capra and others created such excitement among spiritual practitioners, consciousness researchers, and New Age dabblers that a paradigm shift to a holistic, organic, unified worldview was deemed the next—and in some eyes inevitable—step in human evolution. To the chagrin of many scientists, the language of physics was mixed with psychobabble and Eastern mysticism by laypeople who wouldn't know a supercollider from the Super Shuttle. Nevertheless, the enthusiasm furthered the penetration of Vedanta-Yoga (and Buddhism and Taoism) into the cultural zeitgeist.

Other physicists have since stepped forward to carry the Vedic torch, perhaps most visibly John Hagelin and Amit Goswami, both of whom were seen in 2004's *What the Bleep Do We Know!?*, a film that carried the paradigm shift mania into the new century with intriguing but questionable connections between science and spirit. Goswami, himself an East-West bridge, is a professor emeritus of physics at the University of Oregon's Institute for Theoretical Physics. His website describes him as "a revolutionary in a growing body of renegade scientists who in recent years have ventured into the domain of the spiritual." Coining the term "quantum activist," Goswami has taken on with a sense of urgency the task that Capra and others began thirty-plus years ago. "We have literally managed to train a whole generation of students on the idea that everything is material," he writes, "but this Newtonian world view that has shaped our understanding for centuries is now giving way to the revelations of quantum physics which goes beyond materialism; to show that consciousness, not matter, is the ground of all being."[7]

Hagelin, a Harvard Ph.D., turned down offers from top-notch universities to start the physics department at Maharishi University of Management in the Iowa boonies so he could, as he put it, "explore the connections between pure consciousness as the foundation of the mind and the unified field as the foundation of matter." Because of his close association with the TM movement, he is seen by many colleagues as a former wunderkind who went over to the dark side of religion. But he is convinced that when physics finally unifies all the laws of nature in one neat formulation, it will stumble upon what the Vedic seers asserted thousands of years ago, that consciousness and cosmos are one.

That unification is the holy grail for those who see the connection of Eastern philosophy and Western science as more than metaphorical. To them, the unified field that theoretical physicists are groping toward is, literally, the eternal, unmanifest Brahman of the Vedas. Time will tell, but one thing is already clear: iconoclastic physicists from Schrödinger to Capra and beyond have made Vedanta credible to people who would otherwise have taken it about as seriously as astrology.

Healthy, Stealthy, and Wise

To commemorate the fortieth anniversary of that *annus mirabilis*, 1968, *Newsweek* devoted an entire issue to the enduring impact of "the year that made us who we are." Science editor Sharon Begley's piece was titled "What the Beatles Gave Science." Referring to the group's sojourn in India, she noted that "the high-profile visit still echoes 40 years later—in, of all places, science, for the trip popularized the notion that the spiritual East has something to teach the rational West." It turned out that some of what the East had to offer could be studied with empirical methods. As noted in chapter 8, the seminal research on TM was conducted by UCLA graduate student Robert Keith Wallace, who then teamed with Harvard cardiologist Herbert Benson for studies that were published in specialized journals and in *Scientific American*.[8] As Begley noted, the ripple effect was of historic proportions, as experiments on meditation multiplied geometrically. By now thousands have been published, changing everything from health-care protocols to our knowledge about the brain.

Wallace's Ph.D. dissertation was titled "The Physiological Effects of Transcendental Meditation: A Proposed Fourth Major State of Consciousness." Note that subtitle. Taken together, Wallace claimed, the physiological changes he measured added up to a state distinctly different from sleeping, dreaming, and ordinary waking: "transcendental consciousness," or what the yogic tradition calls *turiya* (literally, "fourth") and Vedanta calls *savikalpa samadhi* (pure consciousness alone, with no mental content). When the same data was written up in *Science* magazine, the subtitle did not make the cut. Right from the start, it seems, the scientific world was interested in the potential medical benefits of meditation—the lowered blood pressure, the indices of deep relaxation, the reduced drug abuse—not in anything "spiritual."

Wallace has served the TM movement in a variety of capacities ever since. Because of that affiliation, his subsequent research, like that of other TM scientists, has been greeted with an extra measure of skepticism.[9] Benson had no such difficulty. Having stayed connected to Harvard, where his Mind/Body Medical Institute was located for many years, he is lauded as a pioneer of integrative medicine. His rise to fame began when he reasoned that TM was not the only way to produce the effects he and Wallace had measured. He labeled that constellation of physical changes "the relaxation response" and published a huge best seller with that title, offering readers what TM teachers could not: written instructions for meditation.

Essentially Benson did what pharmaceutical companies do when they discover the health benefits of a naturally occurring substance: isolate the active ingredient (the property that causes the effect they wish to duplicate) and manufacture a means of delivering it (as when the pain-reducing substance in willow bark was turned into aspirin). In addition to its presumed medical benefits, the approach has the advantage of generating a product that can be patented. Benson did not invent a pill, but he identified the ingredients he thought gave TM its potency and tossed out what he considered superfluous. Gone was the *puja* ceremony that TM teachers performed; gone were the individualized instructions and the follow-up sessions; gone was the framework of consciousness and spiritual development; and gone were the Sanskrit mantras (students could use *one* or any old word instead).

To the trained eye, it was obvious that Benson had eliminated some of the components that make meditation a technique for transcendence, not just relaxation. But to those interested solely in medical benefits, it seemed a perfectly reasonable thing to do. Also reasonable—and also deemed a high crime by serious meditators—was the assumption that all mental techniques that produced a modicum of relaxation were pretty much the same and worthy of the name *meditation*. Cosmic consciousness? That's metaphysics. Blood pressure? Now you're talking—fill out this grant application. Forty years on, more people probably see meditation as a preventive health measure—a way to relax and reduce stress—than as a spiritual practice. This reductionism is a major concern among advocates of Vedic spirituality.

Common Denominators

Benson basically redefined meditation according to the parameters that could be measured at the time. He then reconfigured and rebranded it and, incidentally, sold over four million books. The basic premise of *The Relaxation Response* was quickly repeated in virtually every mainstream article on stress and eventually found its way into medical textbooks. "All I've done," said Benson at the time, "is put a biological explanation on techniques that people have been utilizing for thousands of years." But it was only a partial explanation, say his critics, and when you reduce a complex phenomenon to a small set of components, you denude it of its larger significance. To detractors, Benson was selling Tang and calling it fresh-squeezed orange juice. His technique may have helped millions of people relax and possibly spared many from serious illness, but what about the original purpose of meditation? What happened to higher states of consciousness? Where did you hide enlightenment?

The reductionist dilemma runs through the entire history of Eastern spirituality in the West. In recent years, to cite the most prominent example, we've seen Hatha Yoga reduced to a form of fitness training, with one component, asanas, separated out from a multifaceted system. Now, newly minted forms of stretching and breathing are being marketed as Yoga whether or not they have any connection to the tradition. Philosophically, the concept "Truth is one, the wise call it by many names," has been reduced absurdly to "All religions are the same." These developments raise serious questions, such as: What is lost and what is gained when a Vedic import is redefined (dumbed down, some would say) for Western consumption? What constitutes a reasonable adaptation, and when does adaptation become a form of cultural imperialism?

Rajiv Malhotra, founder of the Infinity Foundation, uses the term *U-Turn Syndrome* to describe the phenomenon by which Westerners appropriate ideas and practices from India, reshape them to suit their purposes, and claim the product as their own, failing to give credit to the source. "It is like the referee holding the stopwatch at the Olympic hundred-meter dash receiving the gold medal because he timed the winning runner," says Malhotra. Even worse, he contends, some adapters *malign* the source. "What we need, we assimilate," he says. "What we don't need, we denigrate."

Theologian Rita Sherma, the executive director of Taksha University's School of Philosophy and Religious Studies, has a different analogy. "I call it the Salmon Instinct," she told me. "Salmon can be in the ocean and play about, but when it comes time to spawn, it is time to go back home." In other words, those adapting Vedic concepts and practices are returning, salmonlike, to the comfort zone of their origins—the language of their own discipline and culture. "I see it as a part of the fluidity of the tradition," says Sherma.

The adaptation process itself adapts. For years, those who were knowledgeable about meditative practices were annoyed by the blithe and unscientific assumption that all forms of meditation are pretty much the same. As the science, and the scientists, grew more sophisticated, that assumption gave way to studies comparing the various practices. The results confirm that while there are commonalities among the techniques, their effects on mind and body are no more identical than that of different drugs or foods.[10] In the long run, knowing which practices produce which

results under which circumstances is likely to produce protocols for recommending appropriate disciplines to specific people.

There is another way of looking at the modification of spiritual practices for therapeutic purposes: imitators are not pirates but importers
whose products are no more sinister than Bombay's film industry adapting an American art form to India's cultural norms. In fact, this argument
runs, taking liberties may allow more people to benefit from the practices.
"Sure, it would be more authentic, and more fair, to have swamis initiate
our patients into traditional Hindu meditation," one physician told me.
"But replacing the orange robe with a white lab coat opens it up to a
lot more people." So does calling meditation a stress-reduction technique,
not a *sadhana* for achieving *moksha*. We will never know how many heart
attacks were prevented, or how many millions of pills were not taken, because of that decision.

The tension between those dedicated to the integrity of India's holy traditions and those who wish to freely adapt what they find useful in them
will no doubt persist. Meanwhile, the barrage of data on meditation has
indisputably had an enormous impact, from psychotherapists' offices to
the most prestigious hospitals, where, *Newsweek*'s Begley reported, "They
have instituted meditation programs for patients suffering chronic pain
and other ailments." Say what you will about the American health-care
system, it has been a prime disseminator of yogic technologies—and not
just meditation.

Stretching Toward Wellness

As a stressed-out medical student, Amrita McLanahan (then Sandra) read
an article by Swami Satchidananda that changed the course of her life (see
chapter 10). It said that our natural state is one of ease, and that losing
that state causes *dis*-ease; the task of medicine, therefore, is to treat what
disturbs the ease. McLanahan spent as much time with Satchidananda as
she could while completing her training. As an M.D., she made a dozen
trips to India with him, learning about the use of Yoga in healing. She

has lived at Yogaville, the Integral Yoga community in Virginia, since its inception, helping to train teachers, giving classes on anatomy and physiology, and writing articles and books, while also maintaining a private practice in Richmond.

In the early 1970s a Baylor University medical student read one of McLanahan's articles and invited her to speak at the school. The student was Dean Ornish, whose groundbreaking research at his Preventive Medicine Research Institute in Sausalito, California, is recognized worldwide. Swami Satchidananda saved his life, he told me. As a Rice University freshman, he was so depressed that he made plans to kill himself. But a funny thing happened on the way to extinction: he got mononucleosis and was forced to recuperate in his parents' home. Knowing that their older daughter had benefited from Satchidananda's Yoga, the Ornishes thought it might do the same for their troubled son. So they arranged for the swami to speak in their living room on his visit to Dallas. "I began studying with him, and we developed a very close personal relationship," says Ornish. "The guiding principles in all my work I learned from him."

He and McLanahan packaged the main ingredients of the Integral Yoga lifestyle into a program for heart patients and gathered data. "We used expensive, high-tech, state-of-the-art measures to prove how these low-tech, low-cost interventions can work," he said. They showed that the progression of heart disease can be reversed. Other studies followed. The results were published in medical journals, and insurance companies perked up when they saw that lifestyle changes could preclude expensive surgery. McLanahan and Ornish worked together for about twenty years, she as director of stress management training, he as lead researcher and public spokesman. During that time, as anyone who watches talk shows or reads national magazines knows, Ornish turned out a string of bestsellers, such as *Dr. Dean Ornish's Program for Reversing Heart Disease*. While most of the attention has been on his advocacy of a low-fat diet, from the beginning his program has included traditional yogic practices: asanas ("stretching"), pranayama ("breathing exercises"), and meditation ("stress management"). It is a measure of successful assimilation that the practices are now called by their proper names. In 2008 Medicare agreed to cover the Ornish program.

Dr. McLanahan also introduced Yoga to another medical superstar: Mehmet Oz, director of the Cardiovascular Institute and the Complementary Medicine Program at New York-Presbyterian Hospital. Ever since McLanahan gave him a private lesson in his father-in-law's backyard, Dr. Oz has practiced and promoted the ancient system. It is no small thing that someone who appeared on fifty-five episodes of *Oprah*, wrote bestsellers *(YOU: The Owner's Manual)*, was named by *Time* magazine one of 2008's hundred most influential people, and now stars on his own syndicated TV show openly endorses Yoga.

It is hard to imagine a more credible pair of advocates than Oz and Ornish.[11] And while healing the body is obviously of great importance to both men, they see Yoga primarily as a means of spiritual transformation. "The real benefit of the spiritual practice is that it can help you quiet down your mind and body enough to experience what is there already," Ornish told me. "Not only peace and well being, but, if you take it deep enough, the realization that we are part of something that connects us." Dr. Oz put it this way in the documentary *Living Yoga:* "Although the asanas of yoga are important . . . I don't think that you can truly achieve health—surely the health that will make you happy and glow in life—without dealing with the spiritual issues."[12]

Therapeutic Yoga, Old and New

In March 2009, as part of the Obama administration's preliminary work on health care reform, Drs. Oz and Ornish testified at a hearing titled "Integrative Care: A Pathway to a Healthier Nation."[13] Also on the panel was another medical celebrity, Dr. Andrew Weil, director of the Arizona Center for Integrative Medicine. He too has been influenced by the Vedanta-Yoga tradition, with a particular interest in pranayama. "If I had to limit my advice on healthier living to just one tip, it would be simply to learn how to breathe correctly," he has said. Thanks to the efforts of Weil, Oz, Ornish, and other health professionals, Yoga and meditation have become central components of complementary and alternative medicine (CAM), some form of which, surveys show, is used by 35 to 40 percent of Americans.[14] Among the categories listed in the CAM surveys, "deep breathing" is the second most popular methodology, meditation is third, and Yoga is sixth. ("Natural products" is first.)

"The appearance and practice of yoga as a therapeutic intervention began in India early in the 20th century," says neurophysiologist Sat Bir Khalsa. By the 1960s, "yogic hospitals" were established. In the West, Yoga therapy is a relatively new concept, but it has spawned an impressive amount of research in a short period of time. If you consult a medical database, you will find over a thousand references to studies on Yoga, not counting those on meditation. Khalsa, a Canadian-born Sikh trained in Yogi Bhajan's Kundalini Yoga, points out that the range of Yoga research is remarkably broad: some studies focus on a single practice, while others examine combinations of techniques or entire lifestyles; some measure the effect on biochemical variables, while others look at changes in performance, mood, or medical conditions from asthma to diabetes to heart disease.[15] Every week, it seems, the results of another health-related study is announced.

Recent years have also seen the professionalization of Yoga therapy. In 1989 two veteran Yoga teachers, L.A.'s Larry Payne and Richard Miller, a Bay Area psychologist, founded the International Association of Yoga Therapists (IAYT). It grew slowly, and then, between 2004 and 2009, its membership tripled to over 2,300. With a journal, research and training programs, and annual conferences that draw about a thousand Yoga teachers, it is attempting to make Yoga therapy an ordinary clinical option. Payne, the author of *Yoga Rx,* also heads up a certificate program called Yoga Therapy Rx at Loyola Marymount University. And Miller, through his Integrative Restoration Institute, conducts research on the effects of yogic techniques on conditions as serious as post-traumatic stress disorder among Iraq War veterans.[16]

Reductionism has already become an issue in the new discipline. By prescribing individual asanas for specific ailments are Yoga therapists turning the holistic system—which many see as a lifestyle, not a medical intervention—into just a variation of physical therapy? Or are they addressing a medical need and at the same time introducing Yoga to people who might otherwise not be exposed to it? Sat Bir Khalsa favors the second interpretation. "Anything that becomes extremely popular in society undergoes diversification," he says, adding that "without the experience of limited Yoga," many individuals would never have availed themselves of "deeper involvement."[17] A mountain of anecdotal evidence suggests that many people who try Yoga for a specific complaint such as back pain get a taste of something more profound and begin to explore the possibilities.

One thing is certain: it's a lot easier to obtain funding for an experiment on the prevention or treatment of illness than on the nuances of spiritual development. For that reason, health-related studies have dominated the research. Still, from the beginning, other variables have also been investigated: mental skills, personality development, behavior and performance, neurobiology, and more. Each area of inquiry has added to the body of knowledge about—and furthered the respectability of—practices derived from India's spiritual heritage.

Becoming Conscious of Consciousness

"For thirty years meditation research has told us that it works beautifully as an antidote to stress," Daniel Goleman, the psychologist and author of several bestsellers, told *Time* in 2003. "But what's exciting about the new research is how meditation can train the mind and reshape the brain." Looking at meditators' brains is actually old hat; even Wallace's initial TM study recorded EEG patterns. But today's imaging technology makes the early equipment seem like opera glasses compared to the Hubbell Space Telescope. Researchers such as Andrew Newberg at the University of Pennsylvania and Richard J. Davidson at the University of Wisconsin have been looking at brain activity during a variety of meditative practices.[18] Conferences on the subject have attracted a mountain of press coverage, largely aided by the presence of today's most compelling spiritual celebrity, the Dalai Lama.[19] The findings have given rise to unfortunate "nothing but" talk, as in "transcendence is nothing but neurons firing" and

"God is nothing but electrochemical events in the brain." But it has also contributed to what Ken Wilber calls the Human Consciousness Project.[20]

By this he does not mean a formal discipline, although a growing number of universities have consciousness studies programs, but rather a loose interdisciplinary endeavor that draws from neurobiology, psychology, and even physics. What is striking, and potentially revolutionary, is that a small but growing number of scientists think of consciousness not as a consequence of electrochemical activity in the brain, as has long been assumed, but as a reality unto itself. In this view, consistent with Vedic suppositions, consciousness is the substratum of existence and assumes the form of thoughts, feelings, and perceptions through the operation of the brain. In other words, the brain is not the creator of consciousness, but a kind of processor, just as a television set processes electromagnetic signals and converts them to images on a screen.

This is, to be sure, a minority position. That's why it is voiced mainly at small conferences and places like the Esalen Center for Theory and Research.[21] But it can also be heard at more mainstream institutions, like the University of Arizona, where anesthesiologist Stuart Hameroff started the Center for Consciousness Studies in 1998. The center has run biannual conferences (titled Toward a Science of Consciousness) in Tucson ever since. Hameroff and Oxford physicist Roger Penrose have advanced one of the more intriguing new theories of consciousness, known as Orch OR (for orchestrated objective reduction). In a comprehensive interview in *EnlightenNext* magazine, Hameroff summed up the idea: "Most people think that consciousness emerged over eons as a byproduct of random mutations and the inherent complexity of natural selection, but I look at it the other way around. I think a fundamental field of protoconscious experience has been embedded all along—since the big bang . . . and that biology evolved and adapted in order to access it and to maximize the qualities and potentials implicit within it."[22]

The nonphysical view of consciousness has gained traction in recent years, thanks in large part to scientists inspired by Eastern philosophy and informed by their own meditative practices. "When science sees consciousness to be a fundamental quality of reality, and religion takes

God to be the light of consciousness shining within us all, the two worldviews start to converge," writes Peter Russell in *From Science to God*. Russell, one of the leading popularizers of consciousness theories, is not alone in concluding that "this meeting of science and spirit is crucial, not just for a more complete understanding of ourselves and the cosmos, but also for the future of our species."[23] If that transpires, history might declare it to be the most profound result of the East-to-West transmission of ideas.

From Couch to Cushion

On January 6, 1966, at San Francisco's Grace Cathedral, Abraham Maslow gave a lecture titled "Toward a Psychology of Religious Awareness." His message, writes Maslow biographer Edward Hoffman, was that "psychology and religion are building an important bridge joining two previously separated shores of human nature." The following year, on September 14, Maslow appeared at the First Unitarian Church in the same city. In a speech called "The Farther Reaches of Human Nature," he announced the establishment of a new branch of the discipline he straddled both as a revolutionary and as an establishment figure. What came to be called transpersonal psychology launched its own journal about a year and a half later; Maslow's talk was reproduced as a lead article.

The two speeches were pivot points in the tense relationship between psychology and spirituality. Maslow was the perfect mediator. He was president of the American Psychological Association in 1967 and 1968, while at the same time he was challenging some of the discipline's tightly held assumptions. A self-proclaimed atheist, he nonetheless saw value in religion and did more than almost anyone else to legitimize the study of transcendence. After earning a doctorate at the University of Wisconsin, he returned to his hometown of New York City to do research at Columbia. In the late 1930s, the city was aflame with progressive ideas, kindled in part by recent émigrés who had escaped Hitler's grasp. The group included important psychologists such as Alfred Adler, Erich Fromm, Karen

Horney, and Max Wertheimer, the cofounder of Gestalt psychology, who introduced Maslow to Eastern philosophy.

At the time the discipline was dominated by two schools of thought: psychoanalysis and behaviorism. The primary focus of the former was psychopathology, and its attitude toward religion was contemptuous. Freud called it "a system of wishful illusions together with a disavowal of reality." He compared the state of blissful union described by mystics to "infantile helplessness" and "regression to primary narcissism." As for behaviorism, it considered the entirety of inner life—consciousness, emotions, beliefs—to be outside the reach of empirical science and therefore of no interest. Aspiring to scientific purity, its method was to apply stimuli to subjects—more often lab rats than human beings—under controlled circumstances and to measure their behavioral responses.

A small group of psychologists saw that, in Maslow's words, "a large portion of the theoretical structure of current psychology is based upon the study of men at their worst." They thought it would be fruitful to look at the happier, more fulfilled members of the species, just as, Maslow said, if you want to know how fast human beings can run, you study Olympic sprinters, not ordinary plodders. He and colleagues such as Carl Rogers, Virginia Satir, Gordon Allport, and Rollo May called for a "third force" to study psychological wellness. It came to be called humanistic psychology, and by 1961 it had its own professional association and journal.

Some of Maslow's insights, such as the hierarchy of needs, the distinction between *deficiency needs* and *being needs,* and *self-actualization* became as much a part of the Sixties vocabulary as *far out.* He proposed that we are driven to self-actualize—that is, to realize the totality of our potential—just as an acorn is impelled to become an oak. When our basic survival needs (for food, shelter, and the like) are met, other innate needs (for love, belonging, and meaning) rise up to motivate our actions. Among the qualities he found in self-actualizing individuals was the occurrence in their lives of "peak experiences," yet another Maslowism that entered the lexicon. These euphoric moments were characterized by wonder, awe and beauty, the absence of fear, a sense of connection to the cosmos, and the transcendence of time and space. Often, Maslow noted, peak experiences gave rise to a greater sense of meaning, purpose, and overall happiness.

The resonance between his budding ideas and Eastern philosophy was not hard to discern. Maslow read, among others, Krishnamurti, Alan Watts, and Carl Jung, the Swiss psychiatrist whose famous break with Freud was motivated in part by differences in how the two viewed spirituality. Jung took the matter seriously, and because of the renown he ultimately achieved, he may have done more than any other early psychologist to make Asian religions respectable, even though he concluded— erroneously, as history bears out—that yogic disciplines were a bad fit for Westerners.[24] According to Hoffman, in 1955 Maslow "began to ponder yogic descriptions of the ecstatic state known as samadhi" and eventually "amassed perhaps more up-to-date material on the subject of mysticism than any major American psychologist" since William James, half a century earlier.

Maslow's interest in mystical experience was unorthodox to say the least, but he soon found like-minded colleagues in the Bay Area. In an often-described event, one dark night in 1962 Maslow and his wife, Bertha, were driving on the winding coastal highway of Big Sur when they saw what looked like a motel. Whether by happy coincidence, Jungian synchronicity, or divine intervention, the tired couple glided down the long driveway and inquired about a room. It was not a motel but the newly established Esalen Institute, and the person at the desk freaked out when he saw Maslow's signature. It seems that Michael Murphy, Esalen's founder, had just given his entire staff copies of Maslow's *Toward a Psychology of Being* because he was inspired by the book's central premise, that "we need something 'bigger than we are' to be awed by and to commit ourselves to in a new, naturalistic, empirical, non-churchly sense." Thus was born Maslow's close relationship with Esalen, and his fruitful association with men and women who were rethinking what it means to be an evolving human being.

The Fourth Force

Before long, progressive voices called for a "fourth force" that would account for "non-ordinary" states of awareness and the spiritual dimension of human experience. To humanistic psychology's self-actualization they added self-transcendence. Virtually all the founding transpersonalists—Robert Frager, Anthony Sutich, Stanislav Grof, and others—had significant exposure to Eastern traditions. Those teachings not only described peak experiences in painstaking detail; they also outlined reliable methods for inducing them safely.

The fourth force took steps to establish itself as a bona fide subdiscipline, creating a professional organization (the Association for Transpersonal Psychology or ATP), a peer-reviewed journal, national and international conferences, and books for both scholars and lay readers.[25] In time academic institutions with accredited programs cropped up.[26] Leading transpersonalists crossed into the mainstream with popular books: in addition to the likes of Ram Dass, Ken Wilber, and Daniel Goleman, they include Roger Walsh, Frances Vaughan, Charles Tart, and Jack Kornfield.

The primary task was to study the higher regions of consciousness and personal development. Theorists charted developmental stages beyond the well-adjusted ego that conventional psychology considers the apex of growth but which the Eastern traditions see as a state of delusion—what Charles Tart calls our "consensus trance." Researchers like Charles Alexander, who had one foot in Harvard and the other in TM's research juggernaut, extended the "endstages" of human growth identified by Jean Piaget, Lawrence Kohlberg, Jane Loevinger, and other developmentalists. By adding hard data gleaned from meditators, Alexander helped fuel the work of other theorists such as Susanne Cook-Greuter.[27]

On the clinical side, therapists added traditional spiritual practices to their bag of tricks, and the *Journal of Transpersonal Psychology* published their findings. In addition to reducing stress and anxiety, the practices made clients more receptive to therapy. They were also of value to therapists, by enhancing qualities such as intuition, detachment, compassion, and empathy.[28]

Instead of sick people in need of treatment, the transpersonalists saw clients as evolving souls with unlimited potential for growth. The hidden regions of the psyche contained untapped treasures, not just buried secrets and dark instincts. "I view psychological healing within the larger context of spiritual unfolding," says Brant Cortright, a therapist who teaches at CIIS. "It is a movement from alienation or isolation to authenticity and greater connection . . . from darkness to light." It is not a coincidence that Cortright's language is reminiscent of the famous passage in the Upanishads: "Lead me from the unreal to the real. Lead me from darkness to light. Lead me from mortality to immortality."

Prior to the humanistic and transpersonal movements, the psychiatric establishment had been so antireligion that ordinary religious conflicts, such as doubts about received dogma, were dismissed as being outside the purview of therapy. Anyone driven by an intense spiritual longing was usually considered delusional, and sudden transformations of consciousness were often treated as pathological. Misdiagnoses and improper treatment, sometimes including medication and institutionalization, were not uncommon.[29] Transpersonalists, led by Stanislav and Christina Grof, responded by creating the Spiritual Emergence Network to help therapists distinguish between psychotic episodes and spiritual crises that are better seen as chapters in an ongoing growth narrative. The idea that some upheavals can be attributed to the activation of kundalini energy led to the investigation of that phenomenon by, among others, psychiatrist Lee Sannella, whose *The Kundalini Experience: Psychosis or Transcendence?* became a standard reference. His Kundalini Clinic, established in 1975, became a center for research and treatment. (Since 1983 it has been run by Stuart Sovatsky, copresident of the ATP.)

In all these ways and others, the transpersonal movement adapted Eastern concepts and practices to modern psychology. At the same time, it supplied a needed dose of psychological sophistication to the lives of starry-eyed yogis, who naïvely thought that spiritual practice would wash away all their "stuff" in a flood of bliss. Seekers learned the hard way that dysfunctional behavior patterns can be stubborn. Concepts such as "spiritual bypass," which was introduced by Buddhist therapist John Welwood, and Frances Vaughan's notion of "spiritual intelligence" added a measure of discernment to the mix, and practitioners came to see that psychotherapy, in the right hands, can come in handy on the path to enlightenment.[30]

The Self-Help Mavens

By the late 1970s and early 1980s, the transpersonal ethos had carried over to the self-help/New Age world. It was the rare book or workshop that did not contain some form of meditation instruction, as well as key ideas about the mind, healing, and human potential derived at least in part from Eastern philosophy. Check out the work of Gerald Jampolsky *(Love Is Letting Go of Fear)* and Ken Keyes Jr. *(Handbook to Higher Consciousness),* to name just two popular authors of the time. By now, pop psych's absorption of Hindu and Buddhist psychology—like pop music's appropriation of rhythm and blues—is so ubiquitous we hardly notice it.

Inevitably, principles of ego transcendence are twisted into techniques of ego inflation. But to a surprising degree authentic teachings come through. Take, for instance, two of the more popular self-help personalities. Joan Borysenko, who worked with Herbert Benson at Harvard, draws from all spiritual traditions as well as science. In *The Way of the Mystic,* to cite an explicit example, you'll find, in addition to endorsements of Yoga and meditation, concepts like karma and the chakra system, with links to science, as in: "Yoga research correlates the heart chakra with the cardiac plexus and the thymus gland." You'll also find Eastern referents in Wayne Dyer, who hit the self-help market running in 1976 with *Your Erroneous Zones.* In *Getting in the Gap,* he writes, "We can make conscious contact with God, transcend the limitations of a dichotomous world, and regain the power that is only available to us when we're connected to the Source." The gap he refers to is the space between thoughts, which he calls "the powerful silence we can access through meditation." Buddhists would call it *shunyata* (usually translated as "emptiness"); yogis would call it *turiya* or *samadhi.* Even Anthony Robbins, the powerhouse behind *Unlimited Power* and *Awaken the Giant Within,* has added Indian spirituality to his repertoire, advocating for the Oneness Movement, which was started by a Chennai-based couple known as Sri Bhagavan and Sri Amma.[31]

Most of the self-help borrowing is more covert, and sometimes it is camouflaged beyond recognition. John Gray, the author of *Men Are from Mars, Women Are from Venus,* spent most of his twenties in monkish celibacy as one of Maharishi Mahesh Yogi's assistants. To make up for lost time, he then learned all he could about sex, relationships, and other aspects of worldly life. Eventually, he blended cutting-edge psychology and the spiritual insights of his renunciate years to create his own seminars. Vedantic concepts were never mentioned explicitly, and you will search in vain for any mention of them in the pages of his books, which have sold upward of fifty million copies worldwide. But they're there. When Gray advises people to examine their own contributions to troublesome situations, rather than see themselves as victims, he is in effect applying the karmic law of cause and effect. He gives the Vedantic concept of *maya* a therapeutic application, he told me, when he teaches that "things are not what they appear to be, and there is always a higher perspective that points to unity rather than separation." In fact, he says, the core of his work is a variation on yogic self-sufficiency and nonattachment: find your own fulfillment within, then build a relationship on that foundation.[32]

Read between the lines of most pop psych and self-help books, and you'll find similar adaptations of Vedanta-Yoga: neutral (some would say neutered) language, despiritualized yogic practices, and references to science to bestow legitimacy. At this point, self-help mavens may not even know that some of their principles and practices originated in India—any more than a chef cooking up a new pasta dish realizes that the main ingredient was invented in China.

Psyche and Soul

As a movement, transpersonal psychology never coalesced into a unified school like behaviorism. It is classified by the American Psychological Association as an "interest group" within the division of its progenitor, humanistic psychology. Many transpersonalists, following Ken Wilber's lead (and Sri Aurobindo's before him), now use the term *integral psychology,* which CIIS faculty member Bahman Shirazi defines as "a framework that not only addresses the behavioral, affective and cognitive domains of the human experience within a singular system but is concerned with the relationship among the above-mentioned domains in the context of human spiritual development."

But the impact of the transpersonalists can't be measured in membership numbers. Nor is it diminished by the fact that their perspective is shared by only a small percentage of psychologists. In the course of time their ideas have filtered into the mainstream to a surprising degree, just as medical treatments once considered quackery are now paid for by HMOs. Spiritual and religious issues are now regarded as legitimate areas of concern, not dismissed as irrelevant. The shift is reflected in a plethora of books, websites, journal articles, professional conferences, and specialized organizations.[33] In 2007, for instance, the American Academy of Psychoanalysis and Dynamic Psychiatry devoted its annual meeting to "Psychodynamic Psychotherapy and Spirituality." Among the sessions was a panel titled "Dialogues with Eastern Spirituality," and one of the presenters was a former Ramakrishna order nun. Another presenter, psychiatrist Anthony Stern of the Albert Einstein College of Medicine, told me, "It's been a long road from Freud's *The Future of an Illusion* to this conference." Stern, who studied with both Rudi and Krishnamurti, attributes the "sea change" to consumer demand (patients took their spiritual lives seriously even if their analysts didn't) and to Eastern practices, which provided both hard data and a way to frame spirituality as something more than a religious belief system.[34]

Perhaps the most significant sign of spirit-psyche integration is the fourth edition of the *Diagnostic and Statistical Manual of Mental Disorders (DSM-IV),* the official handbook of clinicians, mental health organizations, and insurers. For the first time, the category "Religious and Spiritual Problems" was included among conditions that are addressed in therapy but are not considered disorders. (Marital problems and bereavement are other examples.) The new addition was a victory for a group of transpersonal psychologists spearheaded by David Lukoff, the copresident of ATP. Among their goals, Lukoff told me, were reducing the harm done by misdiagnosis and mistreatment, creating a context for clinical research on spirituality, and training therapists to deal with issues related to religion and spiritual experience. In a 1994 *Psychology Today* article titled "Desperately Seeking Spirituality," psychologist Eugene Taylor, who teaches at Harvard, cited the *DSM-IV* listing as evidence that "our conception of spirituality is undergoing enormous change."[35]

Of course, any significant change in a large and diverse profession is the result of many contributing factors, but in this instance the exposure of key players to Eastern teachings was clearly one of them. In 2006 Roger Walsh and Shauna L. Shapiro, writing in *American Psychologist* (the journal of the American Psychological Association), gave a status report on the relationship between "meditative disciplines" and Western psychology.[36] The article described three historical stages: first, "a prolonged period of mutual ignorance" and misunderstanding; second, a "paradigm clash," in which each side saw the other through its own distorted lens; and third, the current period of "open-mindedness and mutual exploration." While encouraged by the progress, the authors caution against a "colonization of the mind" in which psychology views Eastern practices solely through its own framework and "overlooks much of the richness and uniqueness of the meditative disciplines." They predict subsequent stages of mutual enrichment. As Walsh's wife and transpersonal colleague Frances Vaughan expressed it, "You can't really separate the psychological and the spiritual. They interact and affect each other all the time."

The open-trade policy between ego-building Western psychology and ego-transcending Eastern psychology has only begun; if it proceeds in mutual respect, the enterprise is likely to yield increasingly rigorous and valuable rewards. To cite one example of an area rich in possibilities, Stuart Sovatsky told me in an e-mail that "Transpersonal psychology has been (unwittingly) applying Indic teachings to American householders that were specifically meant for monastics." The skewed emphasis on renunciation, often resulting in misguided attempts to squelch nonharmful desires, has been mentioned by other observers as well, suggesting that

India's rich legacy of householder teachings might soon yield fresh inter-pretations and applications. It also suggests that Vedic teachings rooted in an older, simpler cultural context might benefit from an update with modern psychological insights.

As we've seen, virtually every Vedanta-Yoga institution that set down roots in the West has cultivated a relationship with men and women of science, as if trying to prove Einstein's famous maxim, "Science without religion is lame, and religion without science is blind." Even that most out-wardly religious guru, A. C. Bhaktivedanta, established a nonprofit, sepa-rate from his Hare Krishna organization, whose goal is "to have spiritual reality accepted and incorporated into scientific research and advance-ments, and to have scientific principles and methods integrated into the practice of spirituality."[37] Recent years have seen a number of science-meets-spirituality conferences in which Eastern traditions are front and center. In October 2009, for instance, about six hundred people convened north of San Francisco for the Science and Nonduality Conference, the first of what is expected to be an annual event. Its symbol was Einstein's $E = mc^2$, only in place of the E was the symbol for the sacred syllable om.[38]

Mircea Eliade famously said that one side effect of science and technol-ogy was to "desacralize" the world. In recent decades, however, science has been resacralizing itself, with considerable help from the Vedic legacy. Vivekananda would no doubt be pleased by these developments. Over a century ago, he told a European audience, "In the light of Vedanta you will understand that all sciences are but manifestations of religion, and so is everything that exists in this world." As it happens, religions had similar lessons to learn.

17

INTO THE MYSTIC

One day during the nine years he lived as an ascetic in the jungles of India, Ramdas Lamb was asked by his guru's guru what religion he grew up in. Lamb said that he was raised Catholic. "Did you pray to Jesus?" the teacher asked. Lamb said he had done so as a boy, adding flippantly that he'd stopped when he left the church as a teenager. The sadhu smacked him in the head. Then he gave Lamb new marching orders: Pray to Jesus every morning. His explanation, as Lamb recalls it, was, "On the road to wisdom, a wide vision of God is needed. Moving from one narrow view to another narrow view will not accomplish anything."

Another baby boomer who spent time in an ashram in the 1970s was asked about his ancestral faith. He said his parents were nonpracticing Jews. He knew virtually nothing about the religion, and he didn't much care to. The guru sent him to Cochin, in South India, to visit the dwindling community of Jewish descendants of Mideast traders who settled there hundreds of years ago. In the ancient synagogue, the American visitor had an unexpectedly moving experience. He is now an orthodox rabbi.

Lamb, now a professor of religion at the University of Hawaii, says of the sadhu's slap, "That's Sanatana Dharma—doing whatever it takes to get you there." He was referring to the Vedic imperative for individuals to follow their own paths to the divine. That perspective has sparked changes in American Judaism and Christianity, proving that Dorothy Parker was wrong: You *can* teach an old dogma new tricks.

A great many Americans have come to see their birth religions in a new light after being exposed to Eastern spirituality. Harvard's Diana Eck, for example, wrote in *A New Religious America:* "Through the years I have found my own faith not threatened, but broadened and deepened by the study of Hindu, Buddhist, Muslim, and Sikh traditions of faith. And I have found that only as a Christian pluralist could I be faithful to the mystery and the presence of the one I call God."[1] Lessons gleaned from Vedic teachings have enabled many to reconcile deeply held grievances toward their religious heritage, or to find value in theologies and rituals they had rejected. As a result of that reconciliation, many were able to reestablish—or establish for the first time—some degree of active involvement with their ancestral faith, bringing a new understanding of what religion is, what it can offer, and how it can be practiced in a rational, pluralistic society.

Perhaps the biggest shakeup caused by the Eastern winds has been the awakening—or, more accurately, the reawakening—of Western mysticism. When the baby boomers started meditating and chanting and dashing off to ashrams and zendos, clerics who were not busy denouncing the phenomenon asked themselves whether there might be something in their own traditions that would give seekers what they were looking for. Laypersons asked the same question, and many searched for answers on their own. As a result, the long sequestered vaults of contemplative Christianity and Jewish mysticism began to be unlocked.[2]

That Old-Time Religion

Where religion is concerned, until the post-1960s era, the long history of Western contact with India was a mostly one-sided affair. As mentioned earlier, missionaries poured into the subcontinent to win souls for Christ and scholars helped them out with skewed depictions of native beliefs and practices. But on occasion the triumphalism was interrupted by a voice of respect, or at least mixed feelings.

Among the most profoundly ambivalent were a handful of missionaries who were theologically committed to the doctrine of salvation in Christ, but who also found profundity in Vedanta. They saw that Hindus were quite content with their own religion and more than willing to accept Jesus as an exceptional sage, perhaps even an avatar on a par with Krishna and Rama, but not the savior of all mankind, thank you very much. They came to wonder why they were trying to convert the natives instead of learning from them. One such open mind belonged to a French priest named Jules Monchanin. In 1950 Father Monchanin created a hermitage for Christians in South India called Shantivanam, whose stated goal was to "grasp the authentic Hindu search for God in order to Christianize it, starting with ourselves first of all, from within." According to Harry Oldmeadow, Monchanin struggled with "the missionary dilemma" until his death in 1957, unable to reconcile his vow to bring salvation to India with the realization that India "was in no need of salvation."[3]

Shantivanam's cofounder, the Benedictine monk Dom Henri Le Saux, apparently found a way to resolve that ambivalence. Two years after arriving in India, in the same year the monastery opened, Le Saux met Ramana Maharshi. The encounter led to two extended retreats in the caves of Arunachala. Afterward he met a guru named Sri Gnanananda Giri and took initiation as a sannyasi with the name Swami Abhishiktananda. "Advaita is already present at the root of Christian experience," said Le Saux. "It is simply the mystery that God and the world are not two." He left Shantivanam and lived as a wandering monk for some time before settling in the Himalayas. Along the way he wrote extensively of his "double belongingness," describing himself, says Oldmeadow, as "at once so deeply Christian and so deeply Hindu, at a depth where Christian and Hindu in their social and mental structures are blown to pieces, and are yet found again ineffably at the heart of each other." His books, written mainly between the mid-1960s and his death in 1973, were widely read in Europe and America.

Beginning in 1968, Shantivanam was run by an eloquent, charming, energetic British monk named Bede Griffiths. Griffiths had gone to India in 1955 "to seek the other half of my soul," and it did not take long before he took on the task of "Hinduizing Christianity," as one scholar put it.

Shantivanam prospered as a pilgrimage destination, and Griffiths came to be seen as a living link between the mystical East and Christianity's mystical past. Although he attempted to maintain the integrity of both traditions, as opposed to blending them indiscriminately, he was attacked by Christians and Hindus alike. Mostly, however, the outspoken monk was beloved by ashram visitors, readers of his articles and books, and the crowds who attended his lectures. In a recorded speech he gave at San Francisco's Cultural Integration Fellowship in 1983, which he opened and closed with Vedic chants, Griffiths expressed the hope that the future would see a confluence of Asian mysticism, science, and Christianity. When he died, a decade later, that confluence was much further along, thanks in part to his efforts.[4]

Father Bede, as he was called, turned thousands of Christians toward the Christ within and taught them that each religion is "a face of the one Truth, which manifests itself under different signs and symbols." Among those who acknowledge a spiritual debt to him are the scholar and activist Andrew Harvey; the innovative biologist Rupert Sheldrake, who says that Father Bede helped him to integrate science and religion; Russill Paul, whose time at Shantivanam shaped his work with sacred sounds (see chapter 15) and his book, *Jesus in the Lotus;*[5] and the late Brother Wayne Teasdale, who lived in Chicago as a Christian sannyasi.

"Bede awakened in me a sense of the eternal value of India's spiritual traditions in the inner search and a powerful desire to discover the 'other half' of my own soul," Teasdale said. He took sannyasi vows at Shantivanam and made Father Bede the subject of his Ph.D. dissertation. (It was turned into the book *Towards a Christian Vedanta.*) Teasdale, who taught at Catholic educational institutions, predicted in his most popular book, *The Mystic Heart: Discovering a Universal Spirituality in the World's Religions* (1999), that what he called "interspirituality" would be the religion of the future. "The necessary shifts in consciousness require a new approach to spirituality that transcends past religious cultures of fragmentation and isolation," he wrote.[6] A tireless proponent of religious cross-fertilization, he played a key role in reviving the World's Parliament of Religions in 1993 and was creating an interspiritual monastic order when he was stricken with cancer and died in 2004.

But no Christian did more to popularize Eastern religions than Thomas Merton. Born in France in 1915 and raised Anglican, Merton moved to New York to attend Columbia University and plunged headlong into literature, politics, jazz, wine, and women. While in graduate school, he had an experience that would be repeated by thousands of others: an Indian monk led him back to Christianity, in this case by getting Merton to read St. Augustine and Thomas à Kempis. He converted to Catholicism, became a priest, and was drawn inexorably to the monastic way. In 1941 he entered the Abbey of Gethsemani, a Trappist monastery in Kentucky. From his humble quarters emerged a torrent of poems, essays, books, and letters to spiritual leaders of the East and West. Beginning in 1948, with his bestselling memoir, *The Seven Storey Mountain,* Merton became a public figure. His admiration for Eastern mysticism came as a revelation to Catholics, many of whom took it as permission to explore those pathways themselves.

While he was drawn primarily to Zen Buddhism, Merton also wrote about the Bhagavad Gita, Mahatma Gandhi, and other aspects of the Vedic tradition. In his last work, *The Asian Journal of Thomas Merton,* published after his accidental death in Thailand in 1968, he describes his travels in India, where he visited sacred sites and met with sannyasis. The journal contains a passage that describes precisely what many seekers had already experienced and what thousands more were about to: "I believe that by openness to Buddhism, to Hinduism, and to these great Asian traditions, we stand a wonderful chance of learning more about the potentiality of our own traditions."[7]

The Center of Prayer

Merton, Griffiths, Teasdale, et al. were mystics in the tradition of Meister Eckhart, John of the Cross, Teresa of Àvila, and other luminaries in the Christian past. All controversial in their time, they were seen by moderns—to the extent they were known at all—as exceptional beings, graced by God. Thanks in large part to perspectives drawn from the East, many Christians came to see them as spiritual exemplars, the way Hindus and Buddhists see their great adepts.[8] It soon became known that the meditative practices developed in Christian monasteries had grown rusty with age, having been placed off limits to laypersons and even to most monks and nuns. That began to change in the 1970s, and the best-known result is the practice called Centering Prayer.

Father Thomas Keating, then abbot of St. Joseph's Monastery in Spencer, Massachusetts, was one of the rare priests who understood the instinct that was driving youngsters to Asian disciplines. "Many of them," he wrote, "were disaffected from the religion of their youth because of the legalistic and overmoralistic teaching that many had received in their local parishes and Catholic schools." Keating invited Eastern teachers to dialogue with his fellow Trappists. Some of the monks sampled Buddhist meditation forms (Vipassana from Americans at the nearby Insight Meditation Center; Zen from Joshu Sasaki Roshi) while others learned TM, mainly from a Maharishi-trained teacher named Paul Marechal, who had been a Trappist novice. (He later returned to the Christian monastic life.)

Keating thought it was time to revive the contemplative practices of his own tradition. They "had gotten lost in the historical shuffle," he said in a phone conversation from St. Benedict's Monastery in Snowmass, Colorado, where he has lived since 1981. Based on what he'd learned from the East, he concluded that a methodology with "clear directives" was needed "to access the mystery that is closer than we are to ourselves." He posed this question to his fellow monks: "Could we put the Christian tradition into a form that would be accessible to people in the active ministry today and to young people who have been instructed in an Eastern technique and might be inspired to return to their Christian roots if they knew there was something similar in the Christian tradition?"

Fathers William Menninger and Basil Pennington took up the challenge. Menninger discovered that the fourteenth-century classic, *The Cloud of Unknowing*, penned by an anonymous mystic, contained instructions remarkably similar to mantra meditation.[9] The key passage, in chapter 7, reads, "Take thee but a little word of one syllable: for so it is better than of two . . . With this word, thou shall smite down all manner of thought under the cloud of forgetting." In 1974 Menninger developed a meditation method based on *The Cloud*, which was taught to priests on retreat and turned into an audio series. Father Pennington adapted the practice for lay retreatants. It was dubbed Centering Prayer, a name derived from Merton's description of deep prayer as "centered entirely on the presence of God and His will and love."[10]

What Keating describes as a watershed moment came two years after he moved to Colorado, when he conducted a retreat at the Lama Foundation in New Mexico. His presentation described how various traditions, including contemplative Christianity, line up with Ken Wilber's model of developmental stages. Among the parallels was this: "The idea of Atman, and of Buddha nature, is not too different from the divine indwelling of Christian spirituality." Based on the success of that and subsequent retreats, he decided to develop Centering Prayer into "a form that would be accessible to lay persons . . . not just a chosen few."

As it happened, Gus Reininger, one of the TM teachers who had spent time at St. Joseph's a decade earlier, went on retreat at Snowmass around that time. Reininger, who had become an investment banker in New York, was exploring the links between Vedanta and his own Catholic roots. "Father Keating asked me how the TM movement structured their courses," he recalled. Together they adapted the language and procedures for their intended audience. "Pure consciousness" became "resting in God," and instead of an assigned mantra, the student would use a self-chosen "sacred word." They rolled it out in a hugely successful workshop in New

York. With the support of the New York archdiocese and lay Catholics, they soon had ongoing groups around the city, and Reininger (who later became an award-winning screenwriter and producer) conducted retreats. In 1984 he, Ed Bednar, and Father Keating created a nonprofit called Contemplative Outreach to train teachers and take the method to the wider Christian community. As of 2008, the organization had ninety-six chapters in fifteen countries, with seventy-four in the United States. More than sixty thousand people had learned Centering Prayer through work-shops, and many more had picked it up through books, pamphlets, and other sources. (Slightly more than half are Roman Catholic.)

Father Keating and Centering Prayer have been criticized by some as a rip-off of mantra meditation, like a religious version of the "relaxation response." Those familiar with the procedures followed by TM teachers see their traces as plainly as fingerprints. But the criticism is muted by the presence of similar practices in the Christian mystical past, like the one in *The Cloud of Unknowing,* and by proponents' need to position the method as 100 percent Christian. Father Keating, who acknowledges his debt to the East, has also come under fire from the other side: conserva-tive Christians say he's been contaminated by paganism and is out of line with biblical precepts. Those critics evidently missed Sunday school the day Matthew 6:6 was discussed. In that passage, from the Sermon on the Mount, Jesus decries the showy public prayers of hypocrites. "When you pray," he says, "go into a room by yourself, shut the door, and pray to your Father who is there in the secret place."[11]

New Testaments

Centering Prayer is the most prominent example of Christians reclaiming their contemplative heritage by way of the East, but it is far from the only one. In 2001 *Los Angeles Times* religion writer Teresa Watanabe wrote an article titled "Looking Inward, Looking Back," asserting that "Christians across the spectrum" were turning to ancient practices out of "a hunger for a deeper faith and a direct experience of God." Her reporting confirmed the catalytic role of Asia: "The Eastern masters brought methods of cultivating inner spiritual experiences—not just outwardly religious affirmations such as church attendance." Despite warnings from the Vatican and apocalyptic rants from fundamentalists, the trend has grown. One can see the evidence in bookstores, websites, religious periodicals, and the topics of discussion at Christian retreats. Google "Christian meditation," and you'll find 464,000 entries ("Christian Yoga" has 338,000). To cite one example, James Finley, a psychotherapist who was a novice at Gethsemani when Thomas Merton was there, draws from Eastern nondualism in books such as *Merton's Palace of Nowhere* and *Christian Meditation: Experiencing the Presence of God.* He also leads popular retreats with titles such as "Buddha's Four Noble Truths for Christians."[12]

Evidence can also be seen in the use of Vedantic and Buddhist concepts to reinterpret the Gospels. Martha Dewing, who grew up Episcopalian and is now an Interfaith Minister, told me that her studies of Advaita Vedanta at the School of Practical Philosophy in New York changed the way she saw her inherited faith. "It opened me up and broadened my perspective," she said. "I see a bigger Jesus. I see what he meant rather than what they *say* he said." For decades Christians have found new meaning through works such as Swami Prabhavananda's *The Sermon on the Mount According to Vedanta* and, more recently, Yogananda's *The Second Coming of Christ,* Russill Paul's aforementioned book, *Jesus in the Lotus: The Mystical Doorway Between Christianity and Yogic Spirituality,* and Deepak Chopra's *The Third Jesus: The Christ We Cannot Ignore.* The scientist and philosopher Beatrice Bruteau opens *What We Can Learn from the East* with this statement: "The first thing we can learn about religion from the East is that it is a matter of direct experience." The book, which is based on talks Bruteau gave to retreat leaders, applies Vedanta to a Christian context. She suggests, for instance, that "Take my yoke upon you" can be interpreted as Jesus's invitation to "take up my yoga," and in her extended meditation on the story of the Samaritan woman at the well, the "husbands" in the woman's past are metaphors for stages of spiritual development linked to the system of ascending chakras. Dr. Bruteau herself exemplifies the meeting of East and West: a devoted Catholic with advanced degrees in

mathematics, philosophy, and religion, she is a longtime member of the
Vedanta Society (and former editor of *American Vedantist*); she draws on
both Teilhard de Chardin and Sri Aurobindo in her musings on spiritual
evolution.

Eastern-inspired interpretations of the Gospel, while no doubt blasphe-
mous to many Christians, have come as a revelation to those who prefer
to see Jesus as a great holy man rather than as the son of God. For many,
that position is strengthened by *The Gospel According to Thomas,* one of the
long-buried Gnostic Gospels discovered in Egypt in 1945 and published
in book form in 1959. The slim volume reads like an Upanishad, with a
gurulike Jesus pointing followers inward toward unity consciousness:[13]

> If those who lead you say to you: "See, the Kingdom is in heaven,"
> then the birds of heaven will precede you. If they say to you: "It is in
> the sea," then the fish will precede you. But the Kingdom is within
> you and it is without you. If you will know yourselves, then you will be
> known and you will know that you are the sons of the Living Father.

> When you make the two one, and when you make the inner as the
> outer and the outer as the inner and the above as below, and when
> you make the male and the female into a single one . . . then shall you
> enter the Kingdom.

> If you bring forth that within yourselves, that which you have will
> save you.

Some Christians have come to see Jesus as their *ishta devata,* the form
of God chosen by an individual as his or her object of devotion. As a young
woman at a Yoga center put it, "I'm a *bhakta* for Jesus." (Some, drawn
to the divine feminine, consider Mother Mary their *ishta devata*.) Rachel
Fell McDermott, the chair of the Asian and Middle Eastern cultures department at Barnard College, grew up outside Philadelphia in a home
that doubled as the city's Vedanta Society; her parents were devotees who
also attended an Episcopalian church. She told me that the Kali worship

in the Ramakrishna Order not only pointed the way to her academic specialty—the goddess-centered Hinduism of Bengal—but also changed her approach to Christianity. She adopted a bhakti attitude toward Jesus, using pictures of Christ for worship, the way a Hindu might use a depiction of her favored deity.

In the course of my research, I also met a number of clerics and theologians whose faith was enriched by Vedic teachings. Francis X. Clooney, a Jesuit priest with a Ph.D. from the University of Chicago and a professorship at Harvard Divinity School, has written academic books with titles such as *Theology After Vedanta* and *Divine Mother, Blessed Mother: Hindu Goddesses and the Virgin Mary*. By studying Hinduism, he told me, he came to better know Catholicism. "It kind of broadens the horizons and changes the context," he said. "It didn't change my practices in the sense of adding or subtracting, but it has affected how I pray as a Christian, how I think of images of God, how I imagine how God works in the world." Such personal religious shifts occur every day. Just recently, the well-known political journalist Andrew Sullivan came out as a TM-practicing Catholic.[14]

Eastern teachings have also led a great many Jews to see Jesus in a different light. Speaking personally, as the child of atheists of Jewish descent, I grew up equating Christianity with oppressive popes, superstitious beliefs, and a hatred of fun and sex. After reading Yogananda in my twenties, I thought I must be missing something if he was so fond of Christ, so I picked up a New Testament. I came away thinking that Jesus was a *siddha* and a *jivamukti* of the highest order and has been tragically misrepresented. Krishna Das, the *kirtan* star who says he was "born Jewish on my parents' side," told me he had a similar turnaround in the presence of Neem Karoli Baba. When a Westerner asked the guru to teach him to meditate, the response was, "Go meditate like Christ." As everyone present wondered what he meant, Neem Karoli closed his eyes for a few minutes, then said, "He lost himself in love."

Oy Veda!

Remember Mickey Finn, the con man–turned–Sri Aurobindo devotee described in chapter 7? When I finished my interview with his widow, I told her that I enjoyed hearing about such a classic Boston Irish character. "Oh no, dear," she said, "his real name was Finkelstein."

If you hang around *satsangs, sanghas,* and Yoga studios even a little while, you will probably notice that a remarkable number of the people you meet are of Jewish descent, considering that Jews constitute a mere 2 percent of the American population. Among Buddhists, the observation gave rise to a new species, the JewBu, perhaps best exemplified by Sylvia Boorstein, the author of *That's Funny, You Don't Look Buddhist.* It also led a group of soul-searching Jews, about half of them rabbis, to hold a historic meeting with the Dalai Lama in India. Chronicled by Rodger Kamenetz in the best seller *The Jew in the Lotus,* the purpose of the trip was to learn why so many Jews were drawn to the East.

The equivalent of the JewBu in Vedanta-Yoga circles is called a Hin-Jew, and you could fill a large synagogue with wise guys who believe they coined the term themselves. I was stunned by how often during my research Swami So-and-So turned out, on questioning, to have once been a nice Jewish boy or girl, more often than not from New York. By now Jews who found their way to—or back to—Judaism via India are as easy to find as a poppyseed bagel.

Several interconnected factors, each complex in its own right, have contributed to the phenomenon, experts say: the severed connection to mystical Judaism; the virtual extinction of Europe's rabbis in the Nazi era; Jews' post-Holocaust rejection of God as traditionally defined; the traditional Jewish emphasis on spirited inquiry and higher education. Like their Christian counterparts, some Jewish seekers became exclusively devoted to an Eastern path; others returned to their ancestral heritage with new eyes and ears; still others combined the two. In response, teachers reconfigured yogic practices for a Jewish context, and made ancient mystical practices more accessible.

The Jewish equivalents of Thomas Merton were rabbis like Shlomo Carlebach, "the Singing Rabbi," who said of other traditions, "We're all on the same path; we're just wearing different shoes," and Zalman Schachter-Shalomi, one of the founders of Jewish Renewal, who has collaborated frequently with Buddhist and Hindu leaders during his long, distinguished career.[15] They and others revived interest in Jewish mysticism among a generation of younger Jews, some of whom became cross-pollinators themselves. One of them is Rabbi Michael Lerner, author of several books, including *Spirit Matters,* and founder of *Tikkun* magazine, in whose pages one frequently finds writers from Eastern traditions. Another is Rabbi Rami Shapiro, who calls himself, only half joking, an Advaita rabbi.

Shapiro's exposure to the East began in high school, when a history teacher spoke about his trip to India. In his college years, a professor of Hinduism taught Shapiro to meditate. On his way to becoming a Zen monk he decided to check out the tradition of his birth. Now the rabbi draws from Vedanta and Buddhism in his effort to modernize the esoteric practices of his own tradition. He does this through ongoing workshops, a column in *Spirituality and Health* magazine, a series of books, and his religious studies classes at Middle Tennessee State University. On his desk is a photo of Ramana Maharshi, whose personal example and self-inquiry methods have inspired him.[16] In recent years, Shapiro has emphasized the bhakti element in Judaism, specifically the celebration of the divine feminine (the title of his 2009 book). In this he was guided in part by similarities between the Hindu concept of *shakti* and the Hebrew *shekinah.* "Everything I teach is actually from Jewish texts," he said, "and all my study and practice within Buddhism and Hinduism helps me interpret it, shape it, and teach it." That includes his own version of *kirtan,* using Hebrew phrases.[17]

"I go to an orthodox synagogue," says Nathan Katz, professor of religious studies at Florida International University. "But I got there by way of India." As he recounts in his memoir, *Spiritual Journey Home: Eastern Mysticism to the Western Wall,* when Katz was an undergraduate at Temple University in Philadelphia, he saw every guru who came to town and took a course in Hinduism from Swami Nikhilananda of New York's

Ramakrishna-Vivekananda Center. After graduating, he spent three years in India, taking initiation in several lineages. "I fully embraced the dharma world," he says. "At the time, Judaism was the farthest thing from my mind." A series of incidents brought his heritage closer. While earning his Ph.D. in Indology at Temple, he learned about Kabbalah from Zalman Schachter-Shalomi. Later, when Katz was teaching at a small college, he was asked, because of his ethnic background, to teach a class in modern Jewish thought. The forced study of his own tradition was illuminating. The next time Katz was in India he researched the famous Jewish settlement in Cochin. "Without my conscious knowledge, Judaism had crept into my bones," he says.

Now Katz can be found most mornings in a Miami Beach synagogue before assuming his triple duties at FIU as a professor, founder-editor of the *Journal of Indo-Judaic Studies,* and director of the Program in the Study of Spirituality. "I don't believe I would have found my way into an Orthodox Jewish life had it not been via a Buddhist/Hindu route," he once wrote. That same route also led him to teach Jewish meditation in synagogues. "I learned to meditate in ashrams and Buddhist monasteries," he told me. "Once you learn to meditate properly from qualified teachers, you can adapt it to other practices reliably." [18]

Google "Jewish meditation," and you'll be led to scores of books, articles, classes, and retreat centers.[19] Some of the meditation practices were unearthed from Jewish mystical sources; others were adapted from Eastern methods, most commonly by substituting Hebrew for Sanskrit mantras. The widespread interest in Kabbalah alone is extraordinary; once so esoteric that only select Jewish males over forty were eligible to study it, the system is now available to virtually anyone.[20] Some prominent Kabbalah teachers found their way to it via India. In his introduction to *God Is a Verb: Kabbalah and the Practice of Jewish Mysticism,* Rabbi David A. Cooper writes that, as a young businessman in the 1960s, "I read every book I could find on Buddhism and Hinduism, searching for the secret of existence and the purpose of life." After discovering Jewish mysticism at forty-one, he went on to write books, lead retreats, and create the Heart of Stillness Hermitage in Colorado.[21]

Do a search for "Jewish Yoga," and you'll find another mother lode. For instance, Torah Yoga was created by Diane Bloomfield, who defines her creation as "classic yoga instruction in the light of traditional and mystical Jewish wisdom." You'll also find "Gentle Jewish Yoga," whose founder, Avivah Winocur Erlick, assures students that it's strictly kosher. Search further, and you'll find Susan Deikman, aka Yofiyah, who uses Indian instruments and musical forms in her Kaballistic Kirtan, which she describes as "the intense devotional chanting of Hebrew texts, and the Names of God."[22]

Like Christians reinterpreting the Gospels, Eastern-influenced Jews have taken a fresh look at Hebrew scripture. The Book of Psalms has attracted a good deal of attention: New York rabbi Asher Block analyzed several psalms in the light of Vivekananda's four types of Yoga; Norman Fischer's *Opening to You* features "Zen-Inspired translations"; and the prolific Stephen Mitchell's *A Book of Psalms* gives off a distinctly Eastern scent. Mitchell, a translator of sacred works (among them the Bhagavad Gita and the *Tao Te Ching*), also penned a commentary on the Book of Job. In an e-mail exchange, I asked if his interpretation of Job was influenced by chapter 11 in the Gita. "Yes," he replied, "from top to bottom, from inside to out." Mitchell, who grew up in a synagogue-attending Brooklyn family, told Krista Tippett of public radio's *Speaking of Faith* that when he first read Hindu texts, "my whole sense of God blew to smithereens. There was something much vaster than what I had thought I was praying to." In his novel *Meetings with the Archangel,* Mitchell's narrator writes: "I began to study the Upanishads . . . From their first lines, they made my heart stand up and clap its hands," and "The Gita was stunning in its depth, its tolerance, and its beauty."

Finally, there is New York rabbi Joseph Gelberman, an interfaith pioneer and a friend of Swamis Satchidananda and Vishnudevananda, who taught him Yoga back in the 1960s and 1970s. Gelberman evidently learned well. In 2007, when he was about to turn ninety-five, he was teaching Florida's bagels-and-lox brigade a combination of Yoga and Jewish mysticism he called Kabbalah in Motion.

Inter to Multi to Trans

In *Mystics and Zen Masters,* published in 1967, a year before his death, Thomas Merton wrote that "genuine ecumenism requires the communication and sharing, not only of information about doctrines which are totally and irrevocably divergent, but also of religious intuitions and truths which may turn out to have something in common." At the time, attempts at interfaith dialogue consisted of what he called "polite diplomatic interests in other religions and their beliefs." Most gatherings opened like the setup to a joke: *A priest, a minister, and a rabbi walk up to the dais . . .* Each would speak about some aspect of his (they were invariably male) tradition. The others would listen politely and, just as politely, speak about how the rituals or doctrines of their faith were different. They would all call for tolerance and understanding and, in some laudable instances, follow up with some mutual effort for a charitable cause or a social justice campaign. The audience would learn something about other faiths, and perhaps their own, and everyone would feel very good about themselves for having reached across the religious divide with an open hand instead of a fist. What they did not do was what Merton called for: to seek "the inner and ultimate spiritual 'ground' which underlies all articulated differences."

Merton's message was rooted in the perennialist observation that all paths that lead practitioners to deep, authentic spiritual experience ultimately converge in the Ground of Being—the One with many names. Religious leaders and their congregants became increasingly exposed to that perspective, as more gurus and *roshis* arrived from Asia, as Americans listened to them and read more widely about Eastern traditions, and as Swami Satchidananda, Sri Chinmoy, the monks and nuns from the Vedanta Society, Buddhist teachers, and others crashed the interfaith party. As a result, religious interaction has changed over the past few decades.

That evolution progressed along a scale of increasing inclusion, intimacy, and respect. In terms of participation, the motion has been from an inter-Christian ecumenism, to a Judeo-Christian interfaith, to an Abrahamic interfaith (that is, with the occasional Muslim thrown in), to an all-inclusive global pluralism. It took some time for interfaith programs to start including the Asian traditions, however. The experience of New Yorker Dena Merriam, a Yogananda devotee since the 1970s, illustrates the point. In 2000, while working at a major public relations firm, she was asked to help organize the UN's Millennium World Peace Summit of Religious and Spiritual Leaders. She was disturbed to find that "the Abrahamic traditions were so dominant in interfaith, it was as if Hindus and Buddhists didn't exist." She invited Eastern representatives, prompting a rebuke from the Vatican. Since then interfaith activism has become Merriam's life's work. "Every few months I take another interfaith delegation somewhere in the world, and I always try to include Hindus and Buddhists," she says, adding that in some places "it's still revolutionary."[23] That may be so, but it's a whole lot *less* revolutionary than it was a couple of decades ago, thanks to the efforts of people like Merriam and the sheer exposure of ordinary people to the Eastern traditions. Nowadays, religiously diverse gatherings in major U.S. cities are colorful affairs, with silky whites, oranges, and yellows blending happily with the dark-suited Abrahamic clergy.

The quality of interaction has also evolved. Think of it as a motion from inter to multi to trans. By interfaith, or interreligious, I mean the sort of get-together described above, where official representatives of the major faiths lecture to what amounts to a combined congregation. Such gatherings emphasize the communication of beliefs and the cultivation of tolerance (although too often that has meant "I'll tolerate the presence of your religion and keep quiet about the superiority of my own"). These are, to be sure, worthy endeavors that have accomplished a great deal of good. But they lack depth. Multifaith suggests not only the inclusion of multiple religions but also a wider range of activities—not just lectures by clerics and scholars but interaction among the laity, with a sampling of rituals and other participatory events. Finally, what might be called *trans*faith assemblies have begun to emerge. Here the hard boundaries of tradition are transcended in several ways without denying or obliterating differences. The circle's circumference expands further to include variations *within* the Asian religions as well as aboriginal traditions, fringe groups such as pagans and wiccans, and sometimes even the unaffiliated spiritual but not religious types. Lay participation is greater and, significantly, spiritual practices are shared and engaged in, not just demonstrated. At its best, the atmosphere transcends tolerance and reaches genuine respect, and the experience switches from horizontal foraging to a vertical dive into the depths of being, where differences of belief, ritual, and history dissolve.

Toward the end of his life, Swami Abhishiktananda (né Henri Le Saux) wrote that "dialogue about doctrines will be more fruitful when it is rooted in a real spiritual experience at depth . . . and when each one understands that diversity does not mean disunity, once the Center of all has been reached." That the attempt is made at all, and that the one amidst the many is reached even rarely, is a testament to America's transcendent openness and to the presence of Eastern thought on the religious frontier. By now there are very few interfaith participants who have not at least heard the Vedic dictum *Ekam sat vipraha bahudha vadanti* ("Truth is one, the wise call it by many names") if not tasted it in the silence of being.

18

THE ONCE AND
FUTURE RELIGION

In five to thirty minutes from my home in Los Angeles, I can be at any of the following: the Self-Realization Fellowship's Lake Shrine; the Sivananda Yoga-Vedanta Center; the Hare Krishna temple; Ananda L.A.; the Siddha Yoga Meditation Center; the Sri Aurobindo Center; the Universal Shaiva Fellowship (the Kashmir Shaivism of Lakshman Joo); the Transcendental Meditation center; Radha Govinda Dham;[1] classes at Loyola Marymount's Yoga Philosophy Program; regular *satsangs* or study groups with devotees of Sathya Sai Baba, Mata Amritanandamayi, Ramana Maharishi, Neem Karoli Baba, Swami Rudrananda (Rudi), Adi Da Samraj, Ma Jaya Sati Bhagavati, Eckhart Tolle, or Krishnamurti; at least five weekly *kirtan* evenings; and more Yoga studios than there are Starbucks. If I'm willing to drive another ten or twenty minutes, I can be at the Vedanta Society's temple and monastery; SRF's Mother Center or its Hollywood temple; the Sai Anantam Ashram; the Art of Living Foundation (Sri Sri Ravi Shankar); the Malibu Hindu Temple; the Brahma Kumaris World Spiritual University; some neo-Advaita *satsangs;* several Ayurvedic clinics; and still more Yoga studios.

That menu would keep the most fervent devotee of Vedic spirituality busier than a theater buff in London, and it doesn't include special events with visiting gurus, Yoga masters, workshop leaders, and *kirtan* singers. Yes, the spiritual buffet on the west side of Los Angeles is as abundant

as the sunshine; but it's remarkable how easy it is to find similar offerings, albeit fewer, in other locales, and how many ashrams and yogic retreat centers there are—not just in the hills of California and Colorado,
or outside Boston, or in upstate New York in what used to be called the
Borscht Belt, but in places like Tennessee and North Carolina and Arizona. Stressed-out urbanites of any religious persuasion, or none, can easily find refuge and take meditation or Hatha Yoga classes—and in some
places, add on spa services and gourmet vegetarian meals. Plus, anyone
who wants a taste of ordinary Indian-style worship can pop into one of
the many Hindu temples that have added an ornate touch to the spires
and minarets on the religious skyline. The sheer availability assures that
the Vedization of America will continue to advance. Here are some of the
more salient trends.

A Different Breed of Gurus

Gurus still come to America, but they have fewer doors to break down,
and they no longer attract overheated media coverage and trigger extremes
of rapture and hostility. The recent crop differ from their predecessors in
other ways too. More of them are women, for one thing, including the
most popular one of all.

It is of no small significance that Mata Amritanandamayi gives far
more hugs than lectures. Affectionately known as Amma (mother), she
has become known worldwide as the "Hugging Saint" for her unique,
tradition-defying trademark: marathon *darshan* sessions in which she sits
for hours on end, hugging all comers, sometimes thousands of them. It is
a remarkable sight to observe, as she presses the supplicants' heads to her
shoulder like a diminutive auntie, rocks them gently, whispers blessings in
their ears, and hands them Hershey's Kisses as a parting offering. The assembly line goes on for as long as someone is on it, and the guru displays
no sign of fatigue or annoyance, and no need to stand up, eat, or attend
to bodily functions.

The girl who became Amma was born in an impoverished fishing village in the South Indian state of Kerala in 1953. As a girl she was ill-treated by family members who were dismayed by the ecstatic, God-intoxicated states she slipped into and out of. She was considered crazy, but as she matured, seekers started coming around, gathering at first in a cowshed. Now her ashram, Amritapuri, a twenty-building complex, is built on that very spot. Four thousand people live there, and about ten thousand a year come for retreats of varying lengths. While the hugs have attracted the most attention (she dispenses an estimated one million a year), Amma is an all-purpose guru, teaching a primarily bhakti path, but with plenty of meditation, discourses, chanting, and *seva* as part of her *sadhana* package. As a presumed incarnation of the Divine Mother, she is her disciples' focus of devotion, but she states on her official website, "It matters not whether one believes in Krishna or Christ, Mother Kali or Mother Mary; a formless God or even a flame, a mountain or an ideal."

Amma's early trips to America, beginning in 1987, are recalled wistfully as a time when devotees could hang out with her as she came and went in virtual anonymity. In 2009, on her annual tour, she stopped in eleven North American cities, drawing four to ten thousand people a day. With ashrams, centers, and *satsang* groups all over the world (the U.S. ashram is in San Ramon, California), as well as high-profile charitable operations, she is a global presence of the first order.[2]

The only frequent visitor from India with a profile that approaches Amma's is Sri Sri Ravi Shankar. Born in 1956 in the south, he is said to have recited the Bhagavad Gita at age four. He was evidently a precocious student of both Western science and the Vedas, studying the latter as a youth with the same guru who tutored Gandhi. Beginning in his late teens, he spent several years working for Maharishi Mahesh Yogi's India operation, arranging conferences, performing recitations, and teaching. In 1982, during a ten-day silent retreat, an original breathing practice came to his mind unbidden, the way melodies sometimes sneak up on composers. Folding what he called Sudarshan Kriya into a package of teachings, he set off on his own.

During an interview in 2007, Shankar told me he'd had no plan and no ambition. "I started teaching small groups here and there, and they told friends, and everything naturally unfolded," he said—a familiar story in the annals of successful gurus. Now his Art of Living Foundation is said to be one of the largest volunteer-based NGOs in the world, active in 140 countries and huge in India, where Shankar is a major public figure.[3] Like Amma, he spearheads an impressive program of service endeavors.

Sri Sri, as he is commonly called, travels constantly from his spacious Bangalore ashram. In the United States, his trained teachers conduct introductory and advanced courses pretty much everywhere. Regular *satsangs,* with breathing, meditation, and chanting are held regularly for graduates of those courses, of which there are more than two hundred thousand. Most Art of Living activities in the United States take place in rented facilities and devotees' homes, but the organization has twenty-two permanent centers, the grandest of which is a huge, domed, former Christian Science church in Los Angeles that was purchased in 2010.[4]

There are plenty of other gurus on the scene, some with sizable followings.[5] Sri Karunamayi, who is said to have been a spiritual prodigy as a child, has been coming to America annually since 1995. On her 2009 visit to L.A., about three hundred attended her public talk and about two hundred devotees showed up for a fire ceremony *(homa)* in a private home. Another female guru, Mother Meera, was made famous by devotee-turned-denouncer Andrew Harvey (see chapter 12). Born Kamala Reddy in 1960, she gives *darshan* in silence, touching each person on the head and staring into their eyes. At the session I attended in a hushed UCLA auditorium, over four hundred people waited their turn. Her website says, "She doesn't lecture, nor does she have a movement." She does, however, produce books, *sadhana* guidelines, and other teaching tools at her main ashram in Germany.[6]

Also coming and going are some lesser-known male gurus. Yogiraj Siddhanath, a householder guru in the tradition of Hamsa Yoga, has been coming to the United States since the late 1980s. Dressed in white, with thick, wavy, snow-white hair and matching beard, he looks part Himalayan, part Hebrew prophet. He speaks perfect, well-educated English and uses science, current events, and names like Trump and Jobs to illustrate his points. On the T-shirts for sale at one of his programs was this slogan:

"Humanity our uniting religion. Breath our uniting prayer. Consciousness our uniting God."[7] Another guru in late middle-age is Sadhguru Jaggi Vasudev, founder of the Isha Foundation, with headquarters in India and centers worldwide. That includes the twelve-hundred-acre Isha Institute of Inner Sciences in central Tennessee, where a 39,000-square-foot meditation dome was erected in 2008. Dubbed "the Rational Guru" by Indian journalists, he teaches what he calls Sahaja Sthithi Yoga, or Effortless Living, a package of techniques "to help people experience and express their divinity."[8]

Two youthful gurus, both born in 1978, began to make a mark in post-millennium American only to succumb to old-fashioned sex scandals. According to his official biography, Paramahamsa Nithyananda became enlightened at age twenty-two and felt "the intense need to share this precious gift with humanity." His organization, Dhyanapeetam (Life Bliss Foundation in the West), attracted a huge following in India and established several centers and temples in the United States. Then, in April, 2010, a video captured him in compromising circumstances with two Indian actresses. Swami Vishwananda, originally from the island of Mauritius, which has a large Indian population, had built a sizable following in America when, in 2008, his world was rocked by the revelation that the handsome and purportedly celibate swami was having sexual relations with other men. Clearly, seekers of Vedic wisdom will always need discernment upgrades.

Like most of the gurus who came to the West, the current ones uniformly assert that they are not promulgating Hinduism as such but a universal spirituality for people of all faiths. Also like earlier gurus, they attract a mostly white, well-educated, middle-class population, but reflecting changes in the population as a whole, their followings are visibly more diverse and include a growing number of Indian Americans. Some— Amma and Sri Sri Ravi Shankar in particular—have attracted baby boomers who once followed the 1970s gurus. They are attracted in part by the personal touch of a living master, but also by the current gurus' emphasis on humanitarian service and their devotional orientations. But the new gurus have also attracted eager seekers who weren't even born when the earlier wave of gurus prevailed. The lines for Amma's *darshan* are multi-generational, and the tables selling Vedic tchotchkes are manned primarily by chipper twenty-somethings in loose white cottons who are eager to tell customers about the charitable work their purchases finance.

Longtime observers of Vedanta-Yoga have been intrigued by what one called the feminization of the subculture. Evidence includes the rise of female gurus, the predominance of women in the empire of Yoga, the ascendancy of devotional practices like *kirtan* (and, within that phenomenon, the rise of the divine feminine as an object of devotion), the growth of service work as a spiritual practice, and the democratization of teaching organizations. Even the male gurus seem softer, less authoritarian, less didactic, than their predecessors. Sri Sri Ravi Shankar's public appearances, for instance, almost always feature chanting, a marked contrast with the straight-up lecture style of his mentor, Maharishi Mahesh Yogi. By way of explanation, a cosmic hypothesis has made the rounds: dynamic, masculine energy was needed to till the soil and plant the seeds of Vedanta-Yoga in the West; it is now being balanced by the nurturing energy of the feminine. Who knows? Whatever the reasons, the new equation—more singing, more sweetness; fewer lectures, less control—seems to appeal to today's seekers.

Yogis and Yoginis

The lead story in any account of India's twenty-first-century exports has to be the soaring popularity of Hatha Yoga. The system is so in vogue that, counting outfits, mats, and other accessories, it adds up to a $6-billion-a-year industry. A 2008 survey by *Yoga Journal* (whose paid circulation exceeds 350,000) found that 6.9 percent of U.S. adults—almost sixteen million people—are practitioners.[9] Ever on target, *The Onion* captured the trend satirically with the headline: "One in Five Women Training to be Yoga Instructors."

The millions who schlep their sticky mats to classes also carry a range of motivations. But it is generally agreed that the majority of students, especially in the early phases of their yogic involvement, are in it for reasons of fitness, appearance, or health. Those who consider asanas and pranayama the physical components of their spiritual repertoire are comparatively few in number. This concerns many in the Yoga community. Judith Lasater, who founded *Yoga Journal* in 1975 by charging $500 to a credit card, told an interviewer, "I mourn the fact that many people in the United States know about asana just as a way of working out." Decoupling the stretching and bending from the rest of the eight-limbed package, implying that asanas are just a calmer version of aerobics, has obscured the system's function as a catalyst for spiritual transformation. This trend could accelerate, as state governments attempt to license Yoga teacher training programs and promoters campaign to make Yoga an Olympic event—a prospect that many find as chilling as giving out medals to those who pray the loudest.

The emphasis on fitness and health has undeniably made Yoga accessible to the masses. But most leading yoga professionals are determined to prevent the breadth of outreach from killing the golden goose of depth.[10] For years, they have been striking a delicate balance between supplying the asanas that most students come to learn and conveying the philosophical-spiritual foundation of the physical practices—both conceptually, with language, and experientially, with meditative techniques. Steve Ross, the founder of L.A.'s Maha Yoga and author of *Happy Yoga,* says he follows the dictum of the legendary saint Shirdi Sai Baba:[11] "I give them what they want so they want what I have to give." He sneaks in deeper messages "through the back door" and offers retreats and workshops for those who hear the call.

You can see this attempt at balance throughout the Yoga world. Sara Ivanhoe, a popular teacher in L.A., sends out a regular e-newsletter that contains both health and fitness information, such as links to her column in *Health* magazine (e.g., "The Belly-Busting Pose"), and spiritually oriented features such as a selected mantra and "Amma's Corner," with sayings from the aforementioned guru. In fact, anyone who samples a range of Yoga classes will find that only a few are exclusively physical—although some studios are proudly so, like the one in Venice, California, with the sign outside saying "No Sanskrit. No chanting. No granola." Most classes at least nod toward Yoga's larger purpose, even if it's blandly phrased as finding inner peace or a deeper connection to the natural world. Those who train new teachers—such as John Friend, who founded Anusara Yoga, and Lisa Walford, who designs the teacher training curriculum for Yoga Works—are taking steps to ensure that their trainees are grounded in the bigger picture and don't become glorified fitness instructors.

Most Yoga leaders are confident that the rewards of commercialization outweigh the risks. They recognize, as noted earlier, that many students who start out wanting only to look good and feel better find a doorway into something deeper. At the very least, they might experience a measure of inner silence or hear some point of philosophy that prompts them to stop in the boutique on the way out and purchase one of the books along- side the leotards and T-shirts. That asana-dominated Hatha Yoga can be a key purveyor of Vedantic ideas and practices is supported by data: in a 2009 survey of over four thousand American adults by the Pew Research Center's Forum on Religion and Public Life, 23 percent said that Yoga is "a spiritual practice, not just exercise." In fact, some of America's lead- ing proponents—Lilias Folan, Sharon Gannon, and Larry Payne among them—initially got interested in the system to heal their back pain.

One thing is certain: no one will have difficulty finding a suitable Yoga class. There is already a specialized form for just about every- one: Yoga for elders, Yoga for prisoners, Yoga for the injured and ill, Chris- tian Yoga, Jewish Yoga, Yoga for recovery, hip-hop Yoga, laughter Yoga, Yoga for spas, Yoga for airline passengers, even Yoga wine-tasting tours. And Yoga in schools. For a growing number of college students, Yoga can be a credit-bearing elective; in high school it might be a phys ed option; in the lower grades it is "quiet time" or a stretch break. Tara Guber, a former schoolteacher and prominent Hollywood citizen, started Yoga Ed. in 2002; the nonprofit has certified hundreds of Yoga teachers to lead ses- sions for K–12 students. It also provides schoolteachers with simple tools for their classrooms.[12]

Another development gives hope to *Yogacharyas* who wish to preserve

Yoga's spiritual roots. While some studios brand themselves as a different kind of gym, others are more like learning centers or even churches, offering philosophical discussions, seminars, meditation classes, *kirtan* evenings, and ritual celebrations on special occasions. Loosely knit spiritual communities have developed around them. In West Los Angeles, for instance, Lauri Ashworth opened a studio called the Hub in large part to provide "conscious community" for yogis and yoginis who are not affiliated with any institution. Another new studio, Santa Monica's Bhakti Yoga Shala, was started by a couple named Govindas and Radha (he's American, she's Australian) to blend the physicality of asana with the bhakti of *kirtan*. Yoga-studio bulletin boards and mailing lists have also become marketing channels for tribal gatherings.

Embodied and Engaged

There has long been a tendency in Vedanta to favor the transcendental Absolute over the relative domain of transience and decay. When gurus in the strife-torn 1960s and 1970s held up renunciation as superior to the path of the householder, aspirants to enlightenment eagerly withdrew from the vulgar, noisy, stressful, painful mundane world, either taking monastic vows or, more commonly, living quiet lives prioritized around spiritual practice and the avoidance of *Sturm und Drang*. But many are called and few are chosen. Vows were rescinded, families were started, ambitions surfaced, and worldly duties became unavoidable. In time, the joys and sorrows of the world came to be seen not as illusions or traps but as part of the spiritual curriculum.

Today's scene—symbolized perhaps by the shift in advertising images from the seated meditator with eyes closed to the lithe yogini stretched in dynamic repose—is marked by spiritualized bodies, spiritualized relationships, and spiritualized service. Younger practitioners are, by and large, more socially engaged and vigorously embodied than the boomers were when they first turned eastward. By embodied I mean more physically grounded, more real, more here-and-now; less cerebral, less ethereal, less repressed, and less obsessed with the long-term goal of spiritual liberation. This is perhaps why the religious scholar Jeffrey Kripal and others contend that the dominant strain of contemporary spirituality is Tantric. The tendency to associate Tantra with great sex is like reducing Yoga to weight loss—a worthy goal, to be sure, but a trivialization of sophisticated teachings centered on converting what is usually regarded as profane (sexuality included) into vehicles for spiritual advancement. (Because, in India, the membranes separating sects and teaching traditions are porous, most of the Vedantic gurus and Yoga masters who came here were strongly influenced by Tantra, even if they didn't use the term or refer specifically to Tantric texts.)

Today's embodiment is seen not only in the lithe, flexible figures in Yoga classes but also in ecstatic *kirtan* singing and devotional rituals. The earlier practitioners engaged in such activities too, but for the most part in closed circles of devotees. Today's venues are open to the public and draw participants with a range of spiritual outlooks and affiliations. Traditional *pujas* take place not only in ashrams and Hindu temples but also in Yoga studios, small shrines, and makeshift settings. Kali Mandir in Laguna Beach, California, for instance, was founded in 1993 by Usha Harding, who grew up Catholic in Germany and discovered the Ramakrishna lineage in the 1960s, when she was an actress in Hollywood. The temple is "dedicated to the worship of Goddess Kali in the mother/child relationship," Kali being "the ultimate power of creation, preservation and destruction." About half of those who attend the daily and monthly *pujas,* and the annual two-day festival, are of Indian descent. The rest are a mélange of ethnicities, including the resident priest, Swami Bhajanananda Saraswati, a young man of Mexican origins who was raised in southern California.[13]

Kirtan has become so hot that there is talk of it becoming a Grammy category. A concert by Deva Premal and Miten I attended in late 2009 drew about six hundred people, ranging from teenagers to pre-boomer grandparents. There are all-*kirtan*-all-the-time websites such as Sacred Sound Radio ("Yoga for your ears"), a creation of singer-songwriter Larisa Stow. And the summer of 2009 saw two yogic Woodstocks in California: The Wanderlust Music and Yoga Festival in the Sierras and Bhaktifest,

"3 Days of *Kirtan*—Yoga—Meditation—Bodywork—Celebration & Fire Ceremonies," which drew about two thousand to the high desert above Palm Springs.

One of the most successful *kirtan* artists, Wah! (she received the name as a teenager from a Yoga master), told me that her initial audience was mainly baby boomers who, as she put it, "heard the Hare Krishna mantra on a Beatles record." Today's crowds are younger and bigger. Some show up because it is a smoke-free, alcohol-free concert that leaves you feeling good. But, she says, just showing up can trigger a heart-and-mind expansion that opens new spiritual vistas. When asked if anything is lost when traditional chants are mixed with Western melodies and rhythms, Wah!, who was musically trained at Oberlin College, said, "The mantras are incorruptible," comparing them to medicine that can be sweetened with different flavors of syrup.

The embodiment trend is seen by some observers as a logical development: paths that are heavy on meditation and study can leave practitioners craving something that stirs their emotions, not to mention loosens their aching joints. Hence you'll find longtime meditators mixing with trendsetting yogis, keeping limber and ramping up the devotional element of their *sadhana*. It should also be emphasized that the ascent of bhakti does not contradict the rational, pragmatic image that Vedanta-Yoga has enjoyed. Americans see activities such as *kirtan* and *puja* as proven ways to expand consciousness and connect to the sacred, and their efficacy is confirmed by personal experience. Scientific studies on the effects of chanting can't be far off.

Another expression of the new embodiment is what Andrew Harvey calls sacred activism. Boomer spirituality was marked to a large extent by retreat from the sociopolitical battlegrounds of the era. Protest-driven activism was disparaged in many circles as lacking the vital ingredient of personal development. After a few decades of waiting for inner peace to flow from individual hearts to the collective bloodstream like oxygen molecules, many now-middle-aged citizens realized that cosmic consciousness without skillful action will not solve real-world problems. Sally Kempton, who transitioned in the mid-1970s from politically engaged journalist to monastic spiritual leader Swami Durgananda (to the consternation of her activist friends), told me she didn't get interested in politics again until the Clinton administration. For others, it took 9/11 and Iraq. Since then, Harvey and other veterans have argued for combining the spiritual and the political.[14]

The younger generation is not taking thirty years to get there. Whereas the supercharged intensity of the 1960s and 1970s made Eastern spirituality seem antithetical to social activism, today, with the fate of the natural environment a burning issue, Vedanta-Yoga seems a natural fit, with its emphasis on connectivity and the sanctity of all living things. The Green Yoga Association, for instance, says it is "dedicated to fostering ecological consciousness, reverence and action in the Yoga community." Green Yoga conferences have been held every eighteen months since 2005.

Other devotees are offering the fruits of their inner work to service. Yoga teacher Seane Corn created Off the Mat Into the World, whose name says it all. The organization defines service as "feeling empowered to make a difference in the world from a place of balance, connection, and fierce love!" Yoga Aid conducts the Yoga Aid United States Challenge "to raise awareness for the benefits of Yoga and to raise money for various charity projects." And Krishna Kaur, a longtime teacher of Yogi Bhajan's Kundalini Yoga, founded two organizations: the International Association of Black Yoga Teachers "to utilize the art and science of yoga to better serve the African Diaspora and other communities around the world," and Y.O.G.A. for Youth, which "provides urban youth with tools for self-discovery" and works with incarcerated youngsters.[15]

Those are just a few examples of Vedanta-Yoga devotees who are working to embody the lesson that former Siddha Yoga official Robert Rabbin expressed this way: "The seminal spiritual question of 'Who am I?' is incomplete without 'How shall I live?'"

As the Karmic Wheel Turns

"We are witnessing nothing less than the reinvention of spirituality," wrote the pollster Daniel Yankelovich in 1997. "It is an extraordinary event that will endure far beyond our lifetimes." By all indications, Yankelovich was correct, and the history documented in this book has been a major reason why. That new spirituality will no doubt continue to evolve, fueled in good measure by Vedantic ideas and yogic practices. Only those who believe their religion is the one true way to God would not think this is a good development. It would seem that a society split by polarities such as faith versus reason and science versus religion can't help but welcome a non-dogmatic spirituality that is friendly to both science and religion and has shown that it can add value to each. Scientific research will no doubt grow, because the demonstrable benefits of meditation and Hatha Yoga cannot be denied. For the same reason, clinicians will continue to adapt and apply Vedic modalities for therapeutic purposes. Research on the brain and the nature of consciousness will no doubt continue to find theoretical inspiration in Eastern texts and experimental application in meditative disciplines. Artists will continue to incorporate Vedantic themes and Indian motifs in their work. Scholars will compile a more complete and accurate portrait of Eastern religious traditions. (It is estimated that less than 20 percent of Vedic literature has been translated.) Self-help authors will not stop improvising on the Vedic repertoire, even if they disguise their sources. Memoirs by writers whose lives were affected by Vedanta-Yoga will continue to draw readers. And celebrities will never stop touting the discoveries that enrich their lives.

Spiritual seekers will continue to find their way to the established institutions: the Vedanta Society, SRF, Siddha Yoga, the Himalayan Institute, and the rest. People will still learn TM, whether drawn to it for spiritual, psychological, or health benefits. The older Yoga lineages, such as IYI and Sivananda Yoga-Vedanta will always attract serious seekers, while the hipper studios, with their emphasis on fitness, will draw others, and both groups will take retreats at yogic spas and places like Kripalu. Students will learn about Mahatma Gandhi in school, and pilgrims will pay homage at the Martin Luther King Center in Atlanta, where they will see a statue of the Indian apostle of *ahimsa* and learn about his spiritual roots.[16]

Mostly, the Vedization process will continue to expand because we are increasingly becoming a nation of pragmatic mystics. More and more Americans draw from spiritual teachings that make sense to them, regardless of their source, and they utilize whatever methods work. As long as the Hindu-Buddhist-Tantric-Vedantic-Yogic menu continues to serve up transformation and transcendence, people will fill their plates. Similarly, the Vedantic worldview will continue to be adopted as long as those principles hold up to reason and help people make sense of the cosmos we inhabit.

Everything points to a further expansion of spiritual choice, which should make fans of free-market consumerism proud indeed. In the American spirit of autonomy and religious freedom, and the Vedantic spirit of personalized *sadhana,* religion is becoming both increasingly nonsectarian and increasingly individuated. Already 24 percent of American adults worship outside their own faith, according to a 2009 study by the Pew Research Center's Forum on Religion and Public Life. This does not portend a do-your-own-thing spiritual anarchy, as traditionalists fear. Nor will organized religion disappear. It simply means that individuals are taking responsibility for their own relationship with the divine. The trend parallels the evolution of health care away from the physician-as-God model to one that sees patients as educated consumers who make autonomous decisions in consultation with experts. There will surely be backlash from the forces of exclusivism and triumphalism, but they are on the wrong side of history.

Demographic Diversity

The generation that will largely determine the future may be even more amenable to Eastern spirituality than the baby boomers were. The so-called Millennials, born between 1982 and 2003, are twice as numerous as the record-setting boomers and have come of age in a far more pluralistic world. About 40 percent of them are Asian, African American, Latino, or racially mixed; 20 percent have immigrant parents. Famously wary of ethnic, racial, and religious divisiveness, studies show they mistrust authority, value authenticity, and distinguish readily between religion and spirituality. They are also exploratory, and as the most plugged-in generation ever, their curiosity is easily satisfied. With a few clicks of a mouse, one can locate anything from a study group to an ashram, or browse through texts that can't even be found in university libraries.

According to Princeton sociologist Robert Wuthnow, the "typical pattern of religious behavior" of the hundred million souls in that cohort is "tinkering," which he characterized as "the quest to update one's beliefs about spirituality."[17] In a major study released in 2009, the Search Institute's Center for Spiritual Development surveyed 12-to-25-year-olds in seventeen countries. It found that 23 percent called themselves spiritual but not religious, and another 34 percent were spiritual *and* religious. Nearly a third said they don't trust organized religion. This complements data from the 2009 American Religious Identification Survey: 16 percent of Americans said they had no religious affiliation, but only 4 percent called themselves atheists or agnostics. The others, presumably, have spiritual inclinations but do not identify exclusively with any one tradition. And a 2008 Pew survey found that "people not affiliated with any particular religion stand out for their relative youth" (31 percent under thirty, 71 percent under fifty).

A significant portion of that generation grew up around meditation and Yoga, and some are now furthering the integration of Vedic teachings themselves, in up-to-the-minute formats. Deepak Chopra's own children, Mallika and Gotham, have each authored books and together founded Chopra Media, which has so far launched Intentblog and Liquid Comics; and Max Simon, son of David Simon, the longtime medical director at the Chopra Center, is a brand consultant who, in his spare time, teaches meditation, hosts Conscious Indulgence events, and organizes "public displays of meditation."

Another demographic trend, the Hindu diaspora, will also bolster the Vedization process. Already Americans of Indian descent are more than two million strong, and many have achieved positions of prominence that allow them to further the understanding of their religious heritage. Varun Soni, the dean of religious life at the University of Southern California, is the first Hindu to hold that position at an American university. (It is called university chaplain at some schools.) Rajan Zed, president of the Universal Society of Hinduism, was the first Hindu to offer the opening prayer in the U.S. Senate (in 2007) and writes for the *Washington Post*'s "On Faith" blog. Anju Bhargava, a banker and a female Hindu priest, is on President Obama's faith-based advisory council. Chandrika Tandon, founder of her own financial advisory firm, is on the boards of both business schools and Indian-American nonprofits; when not restructuring banks, she records devotional music for her label, Soul Chants. Navin Doshi, a retired engineer and entrepreneur (and author of *Transcendence: Saving Us from Ourselves*), endowed a chair in Indian History at UCLA and a chair in Indic Studies at Loyola Marymount.

Like other ethnic and religious groups before them, Hindu Americans have also formed associations to maintain the integrity of their tradition.[18] Already textbooks with misleading descriptions of Hinduism have been corrected under pressure from such organizations.

Each successive generation of diaspora Hindus is better assimilated, more confident, and more outspoken in defending their heritage from misconceptions and stereotypes. Plus, India's emergence as an economic power and strategic partner guarantees that individuals will be shuttling between the two countries at an ever-accelerating clip, furthering respect for its religious legacy. While Hindu Americans still have their work cut out for them, things are a lot better than they were a few years ago, when delegates of the Hindu American Foundation meeting with congressional representatives on Capitol Hill were asked, "Are you Shia or Sunni?"

Vedic teaching institutions not mentioned elsewhere in this book have grown in size and reach in recent years. They include the Kauai Aadheenam, a Hindu temple-monastery in Hawaii that was started by an American swami, Sivaya Subramuniyaswami, and that publishes *Hinduism Today* magazine; Arsha Vidya Gurukulam in the Pennsylvania Poconos, founded in 1986 by Swami Dayananda Saraswati; and the Chinmaya Mission, a worldwide organization founded by Swami Chinmayananda in 1953. Forays into higher education are also under way: Hindu University of America offers degree programs and noncredit classes online.[19]

It should be noted that these efforts are not being conducted solely by Indian Americans. They have allies from other ethnic groups, including the gnostic intermediaries described in this book and non-Indian Americans who are, for all intents and purposes Hindu. One American even runs a temple. Sri Dharma Pravartaka Acharya, originally Frank Morales of Brooklyn, is a traditionally ordained Hindu priest. Aside from his duties at the Hindu Temple of Nebraska, in Omaha, he is a major voice for his adopted religion, founding the International Sanatana Dharma Society and the Center for Dharma Studies.[20]

The diversity that has made America unique among nations is accelerating as recent immigrants reproduce and new ones arrive from foreign shores.[21] As Diana Eck, director of the Pluralism Project at Harvard, observed, "Our classrooms have become the laboratories of a new multicultural and multireligious America." More and more children of Asian descent—Buddhists, Sikhs, Jains, and Taoists, as well as Hindus—will be attending classes with Christians, Jews, Muslims, atheists, and agnostics. (Already India has more visiting students in the United States than any other nation, more than one hundred thousand in 2009.) Like kids thrown together in multiethnic schools in the past, Hindu Americans and their classmates will learn at least a little about one another's religious heritage. That is, unless they become Laodicean. That was the winning word in the 2009 National Spelling Bee. It means "lukewarm or indifferent, especially in religion." The contestant who spelled it correctly was a thirteen-year-old girl of Indian descent named Kavya Shivashankar.[22]

Unnamed and Invisible

While the Vedic influence is almost certain to grow, we won't always recognize it. Stealthy adaptation, as we've seen, can render the source invisible—Rajiv Malhotra's U-Turn Syndrome or Rita Sherma's Salmon

Instinct, take your pick. American Veda in the twenty-first century will probably take on a multitude of forms, some proudly wearing Indian colors, others bleached in secular shades that hide the roots. In the American melting pot, Vedantic, Tantric, and yogic ingredients will continue to mix with a hundred other flavors to create dishes never before tasted. Already new approaches to spirituality—"evolutionary spirituality," "integral spirituality," "interspirituality," "transtraditional spirituality," "spiritual but not religious"—all heavily influenced by Vedanta-Yoga, are being formulated in religiously and culturally neutral language.

Nondual is one generic spiritual term that is used increasingly. Connoting oneness, unity, and nonseparation—of the individual and universal, the immanent and the transcendent, spirit and matter—the word comes directly from Advaita Vedanta. (As mentioned earlier, *advaita* means "not two.") Today's nondual teachers draw upon a variety of influences, from traditional Advaitan lineages, to Mahayana and Zen Buddhism, to Western mysticism, and even to quantum physics—but they speak generically. The most prominent nondualist is Eckhart Tolle, the global phenom whose work is so suffused with Vedantic principles as to infuriate Hindus who would like him to pay proper homage. One of the rising stars is Adyashanti, a young, unpretentious Bay Area teacher who was trained in Zen but teaches a hybrid. "If you filter my words through any tradition or '-ism,' you will miss altogether what I am saying," he states on his website.[23]

We will no doubt see more of this lingua spiritus in the future. We will also see Vedantic precepts expressed in the languages of physics, neurobiology, psychology, and medicine. And the equivalent terminology will be extracted from the esoteric canons of Judaism, Christianity, and Islam, with no indication that the expeditions that led to those rediscoveries were inspired by Buddhism and Hinduism. One hopes that, for the sake of fairness, India gets the credit it deserves; its dazzling heritage has been trashed enough. Even more important, respecting the source can help prevent something vital from getting lost in translation.

Heyam Dukham Anagatam

The above subhead is taken from Patanjali's *Yoga Sutras*. It means "avert the danger that has not yet come"—a maxim worth remembering as we continue to assimilate Vedic ideas and practices. And we surely will. Why would we not want to employ methods that enhance mental capacities and foster compassion, empathy, kindness, and other desirable qualities? Why, given the escalating cost of health care, would we not make use of yogic techniques that alleviate and prevent illness cheaply? And given the perilous state of the planet, why would we not encourage a worldview that rejects materialism and directs the pursuit of happiness inward? But while adaptation is inevitable and desirable, one hopes the process will be carried out with care. If we do not treat authentic Vedic teachings with respect, we will deprive the future of their true value. The task—a delicate and sacred one—is to carefully shape the ancient ideas to fit modern society without distorting them or diminishing their value.

Vedanta's ecumenical spirituality has never been more necessary. In an ever-shrinking world, authentic pluralism—by which I mean genuine respect for religious differences within a framework of underlying unity—is obviously a needed counterweight to the deadly forces of tribalism, ethnocentrism, and fundamentalism. The French philosopher Blaise Pascal argued that since the existence of God can be neither proven nor disproven, belief is the better wager for the soul. One can take a similar position on "Truth is one, the wise call it by many names." While much evidence supports the premise, it might not be scientifically provable—but it is a far better wager for humanity than "Mine is the one true religion."[24]

That worldview is likely to ascend. Studies show that human beings tend to move upward along a continuum of spiritual expansiveness. The best-known model for this was mapped by James Fowler, a developmental psychologist who taught at Harvard, Emory, and Boston College. The first of Fowler's six stages of faith, the Intuitive-Projective stage, is described as the "fantasy-filled, imitative phase" typical of ages three to seven, when self-awareness is first attained. In stage two, Mythic-Literal,

God is anthropomorphic and stories and symbols are taken literally. With Synthetic-Conventional faith, stage three, the believer is governed by unexamined ideology and precepts received from authority figures. In stage four, Individuative-Reflective faith, the individual assumes "responsibility for his or her own commitments, lifestyle, beliefs and attitudes." It is a stage of critical reflection, when stories and symbols are "de-mythologized" and self-actualizing drives begin to emerge. Stage five, Conjunctive faith, is integrative. "Alive to paradox and the truth in apparent contradictions," writes Fowler, "this stage strives to unify opposites in mind and experience. It generates and maintains vulnerability to the strange truths of those who are other . . . freed from the confines of tribe, class, religious community or nation." Finally, in stage six, Universalizing faith, individuals acquire a "taste and feel for transcendent moral and religious actuality . . . devotion to universalizing compassion . . . enlarged visions of universal community."

In his 1981 book *Stages of Faith,* Fowler said that stage sixers are rare.[25] They still are, no doubt, but evidence suggests that they have become *less* rare, thanks in large part to the technologies of consciousness we've imported from India. A 2009 Pew survey found that "nearly half of the public (49%) says they have had a religious or mystical experience, defined as a 'moment of sudden religious insight or awakening.'" That number is "much higher than in surveys conducted in 1976 and 1994 and more than twice as high as a 1962 Gallup survey (22%)." (The report adds that "these kinds of experiences are particularly common among the 'religious unaffiliated.'")[26]

But hey, the world would settle for having more folks at stages four and five; those stuck at two and three have wreaked enough havoc. Research suggests that each stage of development enlarges the individual's center of identity. That is, one's sense of "I" and "we" opens out from the narrow identification with family, tribe, race, political affiliation, religion, and so on, to encompass a broader swath of humanity. With that comes a corresponding expansion of the moral compass. This is not a fanciful imagining of "we are the world" harmony but a living experience of unity with other humans, with nature, and ultimately with the cosmos. The Eastern traditions propose that such an expansion of mind and heart can be cultivated, and so far the research suggests that they are right. "We don't know all that much yet about how to foster human development in an effective way," says psychiatrist and author Roger Walsh, "but what we do know so far is that meditative practices move people through developmental stages, and they do foster the development of certain qualities, like love, compassion, generosity, kindness, and service orientation that we associate with higher consciousness."

The result of such internal shifts can only be an uptick in interreligious and interethnic harmony. But that desirable outcome can only be realized, it must be emphasized, if the experiential components of the Vedic heritage—the practices, not just the philosophical ideas and theological precepts—are maintained in their integrity. Otherwise it would be like a developing nation importing the philosophy of science and not the technologies that emerged from it. We don't just need tidbits of a cosmic philosophy, we need the nuances and the details in all their deep complexity. More important, we need cosmically conscious minds and cosmically compassionate hearts. Vedanta itself says that its own eternal truths are virtually useless unless grounded in the direct experience of ultimate reality. We need to pay attention to that message and not settle for bullet points from an inspiring worldview, even if it is a "new paradigm."[27]

In 1969 the distinguished historian Arnold Toynbee wrote:

> It is already becoming clear that a chapter which had a Western beginning will have to have an Indian ending if it is not to end in the self-destruction of the human race. At this supremely dangerous moment in human history, the only way of salvation for mankind is the Indian way . . . Here we have the attitude and the spirit that can make it possible for the human race to grow together into a single family—and, in the Atomic Age, this is the only alternative to destroying ourselves.[28]

That remark makes for a fitting conclusion to this book, coupled with a traditional Sanskrit prayer: *Loka samastha sukhino bhavantu* (May all beings everywhere be in peace).

NOTES

Introduction

1. Sri Dharma Pravartaka Acharya (aka Frank Morales), the only American to run a Hindu temple, says Sanatana Dharma "represents the prereligious, primordial essence of all true spirituality, philosophy, and yearning to know the higher Reality, as well as the very foundation of any and all attempts to establish a civilization based upon eternal ideals."

1: *NAMASTE,* AMERICA!

1. Lola Williamson, *Transcendent in America: Hindu-Inspired Meditation Movements as New Religion* (New York: NYU Press, 2010).
2. Durant, *Our Oriental Heritage,* vol. 1 of *The Story of Civilization* (New York: Simon and Schuster, 1935).
3. Some Indian sources date the Vedic period as thousands of years earlier. The American Heritage Dictionary defines *rishi* as "a divinely inspired poet or sage in India, sometimes regarded as a saint." With the prefix *maha* (great), it becomes Maharshi or Maharishi, an honorific given to gurus held to be great seers.
4. The Vedas consist of four foundational collections of verses called *samhitas*—Rig (sometimes spelled *Rg*) *Veda, Sama Veda, Yajur Veda,* and *Atharva Veda*—as well as subsets, or limbs, known collectively as *Vedanga.*
5. The Sanskrit *upanisad* means "sitting near to," as when a student sits near a teacher. The collection of writings known as the Upanishads are said to have been composed between 800 and 500 B.C.E. The *Brahma Sutras* are a collection

of pithy verses attributed to the sage Badarayana and commented upon by Shankara, Ramanuja, and other luminaries. The Bhagavad Gita is actually a section of
the massive epic *Mahabharata*. Its origin is said to be between 200 and 400 C.E.
Together the three texts are considered the *prasthanatrava*, the threefold source of
Vedanta.

6. *Yoga* is used in two ways: as a state of unitive awareness, and as a discipline for
achieving it. Hence it can be said that one performs Yoga to achieve *yoga*. Most
scholars trace what we think of as Yoga to the Samkhya philosophy, but that word
is barely known in the West, and the nuanced differences between Samkhya and
Vedanta are well beyond the scope of this book.

7. Tantra is a rich, diverse, and complex system of texts and practices whose principle aim is to sacralize the mundane. Found in both Buddhism and Hinduism,
Tantra should not be confused with the limited (some would say vulgarized) use
of the term as purely sexual.

8. The saying is sometimes translated as "Truth is One, the wise call it variously." In
other variations, "God" or "Reality" replaces Truth and "sages" stands in for "the
wise."

9. From the *Mandukya Upanishad*, 1.2, and the *Chandogya Upanishad*, 6.8.7, respectively.

10. Most Vedantists delineate four Yogas: Karma Yoga, the path of selfless action;
Bhakti Yoga, the path of devotion; Jnana Yoga, the path of knowledge; and Raja
Yoga, which emphasizes meditation and other psychospiritual disciplines.

11. Scholars describe three different schools of Vedanta: Advaita (pure nondualism,
literally "not two"), *dvaita* (a form of dualism), and Visistadvaita (qualified nondualism). Theologically, these are important distinctions, but in practice they are
virtually meaningless. To keep things simple, I am ignoring them, except in certain instances.

12. Stephen Prothero, *God Is Not One: The Eight Rival Religions That Run the World—
and Why Their Differences Matter* (New York: HarperOne, 2010).

13. The prolific lay scholar of religion, Evelyn Underhill, defined mysticism as "the
science of union with the Absolute," and the mystic as "the person who attains to
this union, not the person who talks about it." (From her 1911 classic, *Mysticism:
A Study in Nature and Development of Spiritual Consciousness,"* p. 86.)

14. I use uppercase *Sixties* when referring to the era as a cultural phenomenon, and
1960s to indicate the time period.

15. Integral philosopher Ken Wilber's distinction between translation and transformation stimulated this line of thinking; I broke that division into additional
pieces.

16. This is not to suggest that organized religions have always fulfilled the first three
functions well. (For that reason, a friend suggested that I add a sixth function:

Transgression.) Nor do I mean to suggest that no transformation or transcendence occurs within Western religions, just that they have not made those elements a priority and have provided few systematic procedures for attaining them. That has begun to change, largely as a reaction to the popularity of Eastern teachings (see chapter 17).

17. Other considerations, such as love for a particular teacher and the opportunity to join a spiritual community, were farther down the list.

18. "In the Guru District," *The New Yorker,* March 10, 2008, p. 118.

19. Mailer added that reincarnation, karma's sister concept, was the only afterlife model that made sense to him, and 50 Cent added, by way of definition, "Shit always comes back to you in one way or another."

20. According to the 2009 American Religious Identification Survey, conducted by the Program on Public Values at Trinity College in Hartford, Connecticut, 15 percent of the 54,461 surveyed said they had no religion. The comparable number in 1990 was 8.2 percent. The fastest-growing religious category was "none." Which does not necessarily mean they are not religious or spiritual. Only 1.6 percent called themselves atheists or agnostics. The study also found that "New Religious Movements" grew faster in the past decade than in the late 1990s. Another study, a national poll by *Spirituality & Health* magazine in 2001, found that 59 percent describe themselves as both spiritual and religious, while 20 percent "see themselves as solely spiritual, and among this group, 47 percent view religion negatively" and 23 percent "view spirituality as the broader concept that embraces religion."

21. Compare that number to an earlier one, a 1985 Princeton study, in which only 20 percent said they are "focused more on spiritual consciousness than on conventional ritual or practice." A 2008 study by the Pew Forum on Religion and Public Life said that almost 40 percent of Americans "report meditating at least once a week." And the data suggest not only that more aspirants than ever are seeking spiritual experience, but more are *finding* it. In 1962, 22 percent of U.S. adults reported having "a religious or mystical experience"; in 1994 the number was 33 percent; in 2009, *Newsweek* reported that a Pew survey found that 49 percent have had "a religious or mystical experience, defined as 'a moment of sudden religious insight or awakening.'" Significantly, 30 percent of that group said they were unaffiliated with any religion.

22. In a 1997 Yankelovich/Roper poll, 86 percent said they "respect people of other beliefs." In 2005, Beliefnet asked visitors to its site, "Can good people outside your faith tradition attain salvation as you understand it?" The majority (57 percent) responded, "Yes, fully, if they are sincere in their efforts to know or worship a deity." In its January 28, 2008, issue, *Newsweek* reported that 48 percent of Americans agreed that "all religions of the world are equally true and good."

23. When asked in a 2005 Newsweek-Beliefnet poll where they feel most strongly connected to the sacred, nearly twice as many (40 percent) chose "praying alone" as "house of worship" (21 percent); "in nature" also scored 21 percent.

24. Robert Wuthnow, *After Heaven: Spirituality in America Since the 1950s* (Berkeley and Los Angeles: University of California Press, 2000). Also, a 2008 Pew study found that only 39 percent of Christians believe that the Bible is the literal word of God.

25. The same cohort has also been called "the unchurched," and "the unaffiliated." In the mid-twentieth century the scholar of religion Frederic Spiegelberg referred to the phenomenon as "the religion of no religion."

26. Robert C. Fuller, *Spiritual, but Not Religious: Understanding Unchurched America* (New York: Oxford University Press, 2001).

27. The number varies, depending on the source. Some examples: In 1999 a USA Today/CNN/Gallup poll of 1,037 adults found that 30 percent were spiritual but not interested in attending church; 54 percent said they were religious, but of that group 45 percent were "more likely to follow their own instincts than denominational teachings." A 2002 USA Today/Gallup Poll found that 33 percent consider themselves "spiritual but not religious" (a 3 percent increase from their 1999 survey). In 2005, *Newsweek* had the number at 24 percent. In 2007, the Barna Group reported that "there has been a 92% increase in the number of unchurched Americans in the last thirteen years."

28. Paul H. Ray, *The Cultural Creatives: How 50 Million People Are Changing the World* (New York: Harmony Books, 2000).

29. Wade Clark Roof, *A Generation of Seekers: The Spiritual Journey of the Baby Boom Generation* (New York: HarperCollins, 1993).

30. Ibid., p. 76. Robert K. C. Forman defines panentheism as "the doctrine that all things are in the ultimate, that is, all things are made up of a single 'stuff' or substance. But that 'stuff' is not limited to the beings in it. It includes but extends beyond them as well." Pantheism, by contrast, holds that "the deity *is* the universe and its phenomena," that is, not both immanent *and* transcendent. See Robert K. C. Forman, *Grassroots Spirituality* (U.K.: Imprint Academic, 2004), p. 52.

31. Wade Clark Roof, *Spiritual Marketplace: Baby Boomers and the Remaking of American Religion* (Princeton, N.J.: Princeton University Press, 1999), pp. 204–5.

32. These data may seem to conflict with the growth of Evangelical megachurches and Pentecostalism. But a major part of the appeal of those movements is that they are powerfully experiential and emphasize a personal relationship with divinity. This is consistent with Yale literary and culture critic Harold Bloom's description of American religion as "a Gnostic quest for the unmediated experience of God." See Harold Bloom, *The American Religion* (New York: Touchstone Books, 1992).

33. In a follow-up to Wade Clark Roof's landmark study of baby boomers, he and

Jackson W. Carroll found that Generation-Xers "attach more importance to exploring different religious teachings, and to learning from them, than do even the boomers, who were often labeled as spiritual dabblers when growing up." Jackson W. Carroll and Wade Clark Roof, *Bridging Divided Worlds: Generational Cultures in Congregations* (San Francisco: Jossey-Bass, 2002).

2: THE VOICE OF AN OLD INTELLIGENCE

1. *The Bhagvat Geeta, or Dialogues of Kreeshna and Arjoon* (1785).
2. Megasthenes is said to be the first European to see the river Ganges and to meet the legendary ruler Chandragupta Maurya, whose reign began after the departure of Alexander.
3. Harry Oldmeadow, *Journeys East: 20th Century Western Encounters with Eastern Religious Traditions* (Bloomington, Ind.: World Wisdom, 2004).
4. Schopenhauer reportedly said of the Upanishads, "In the whole world there is no study so beneficial and so elevating."
5. Quoted in Thomas A. Tweed and Stephen Prothero, *Asian Religions in America* (New York: Oxford University Press, 1999), p. 48.
6. Robert C. Gordon, *Emerson and the Light of India: An Intellectual History* (New Delhi: National Book Trust, 2007).
7. In a poem he composed in his senior year at Harvard, "Indian Superstition," Emerson lamented the "desolation" of "dishonoured India" and predicted that the ancient culture would rise again, its "shackles riven" and its "giant genius" reawakened.
8. Three of my principal sources, Alan Hodder, Richard Geldard, and Robert Gordon, had backgrounds in Vedic teachings, as both scholars and practitioners. The value of such a background in this regard was captured by Schopenhauer in *The World as Will and Representation:* "If the reader has also received the benefit of the Vedas, . . . and received it with an open heart, he will be prepared in the very best way for hearing what I have to tell him. It will not sound to him strange, as to many others."
9. Alan D. Hodder, *Emerson's Rhetoric of Revelation* (University Park: Pennsylvania State University Press, 1989). See also his *Thoreau's Ecstatic Witness* (New Haven, Conn.: Yale University Press, 2001).
10. Chapter 2, verse 19, of the Gita reads: "He who considers this individual self as a slayer, or he who thinks that this individual self is slain, neither of these knows the Truth, for Self slays not, neither is It slain."
11. In *The Essential Transcendentalists* (New York: Tarcher/Penguin, 2005), p. 24, Geldard says that the poem marked Emerson "as both courageous to his supporters and foolhardy to his detractors."
12. Diana Eck, *A New Religious America: How a "Christian Country" Has Become the World's Most Religiously Diverse Nation* (New York: HarperCollins, 2001).

13. Other Fireside Poets included Henry Wadsworth Longfellow, Ralph Greenleaf Whittier, William Cullen Bryant, and James Russell Lowell.

14. Thoreau may also have been the first American to draw parallels between Buddha and Jesus. "I know that some will have hard thoughts of me, when they hear their Christ named beside my Buddha, yet I am sure that I am willing they should love their Christ more than my Buddha, for the love is the main thing, and I like him too," he wrote in *A Week on the Concord and Merrimack Rivers,* p. 85.

15. In his eulogy of Thoreau, Emerson said: "He was bred to no profession; he never married; he lived alone; he never went to church; he never voted; he refused to pay a tax to the State; he ate no flesh; he drank no wine; he never knew the use of tobacco; and though a naturalist, he used neither trap nor gun. He chose, wisely no doubt for himself, to be a bachelor of thought and Nature. He had no talent for wealth, and knew how to be poor without the least hint of squalor or inelegance."

16. Diane Ackerman, "'Leaves of Grass' Still Growing, Still Inspiring," read on *All Things Considered,* National Public Radio, October 8, 2007.

17. Bloom was quoted by Christopher Lydon on his blog at http://blogs.law.harvard.edu/lydondev.

3: NEW THOUGHT IN OLD WINESKINS

1. Eddy asserted that the healing methods she espoused sprang from her unique revelation, but New Thoughters who saw her work as directly derived from Quimby regarded that as self-aggrandizement. She kept her distance from the New Thought community, but the Christian Science connection to the movement is well accepted.

2. Mary Baker Eddy, *Science and Health with Key to the Scriptures* (Boston: Beacon Press, 1875).

3. Wendell Thomas, *Hinduism Invades America* (Boston: Beacon Press, 1930), reprinted in 2003 by Kessinger Publishing.

4. Helena Petrovna Blavatsky, *The Key to Theosophy* (London: The Theosophical Publishing Society, 1893), p. 28.

5. Harry Oldmeadow, *Journeys East: 20th Century Western Encounters with Eastern Religious Traditions* (Bloomington, Ind.: World Wisdom, 2004), pp. 131–32.

6. For the Theosophical Society in America, see www.theosociety.org. For Krotona, see http://www.theosophical.org/local_groups/krotona/index.php. For Quest, see http://www.questbooks.net and http://questmag.com.

7. Mitch Horowitz, *Occult America* (New York: Bantam, 2009). Gandhi, who met Blavatsky and Besant, told a biographer that Theosophy was "Hinduism at its best."

8. The documentary *The Challenge of Change* is available on DVD at www.kfa.org.

See Evelyn Blau, *Krishnamurti: 100 Years* (New York: Stewart, Tabori & Chang, 1995).

9. Oak Grove is also the name of an Ojai private school rooted in Krishnamurti's educational ideas. See www.oakgroveschool.com.

10. Titled "Credo," the poem contains the passage "The God in his mind, creates an ocean more real than the ocean."

11. For the dialogues, see J. Krishnamurti and David Bohm, *The Ending of Time* (New York: Harper & Row, 1985), and the DVD, *The Nature of the Mind: J. Krishnamurti, David Bohm, Rupert Sheldrake, and John Hidley* (KPA, 1982).

12. See David Bohm, Peter M. Senge, and Lee Nichol, *On Dialogue,* rev. ed. (London: Routledge, 2004).

13. Contact the Krishnamurti Foundation of America, www.kfa.org, for information on their library, archives, conferences, and retreats.

14. See Neal Vahle, *The Unity Movement: Its Evolution and Spiritual Teaching* (West Conshohocken, Penn.: Templeton Press, 2002). Vahle also published biographies of Myrtle Fillmore, Charles Fillmore, and Ernest Holmes.

15. The names included Society of Silent Unity, Unity Society of Practical Christianity, Unity Church of Christianity, and Unity School of Christianity.

16. DeLuca is also the author of a compilation of Swami Vivekananda's speeches, *Pathways to Joy* (Makawao, Hawaii: Inner Ocean, 2006). His website is www.davedeluca.com.

17. Interview by Krista Tippett, "The Spirituality of Addiction and Recovery," on *Speaking of Faith,* American Public Media, May 15, 2008; www.speakingoffaith.org. Susan Cheever, *My Name Is Bill* (New York: Simon & Schuster, 2004).

18. The current edition of *The Science of Mind,* published by Tarcher/Penguin, has sold over 125,000 copies since 1998.

19. Another metaphysician who started teaching in L.A. at this time and became quite popular in the 1940s and 1950s was P. Manley Hall, the author of *The Secret Teachings of All Ages.* According to Mitch Horowitz, author of *Occult America,* Eastern teachings were a secondary source in Hall's broad knowledge base but nevertheless important. (He made trips to India.) He no doubt exposed a significant number of people to Indian philosophical concepts.

20. *The Essential Ernest Holmes,* ed. Jesse Jennings (New York: Tarcher/Putnam, 2002), pp. 149–50.

21. The circulation of *Unity* magazine is about 25,000, and over 1.5 million readers in 180 countries receive inspirations and affirmations in the church's other publication, the *Daily Word.* (It is now available every day on the Internet.) *Science of Mind* magazine reaches about 100,000 readers a month.

22. Michael Bernard Beckwith, *Spiritual Liberation: Fulfilling Your Soul's Potential* (New York: Simon & Schuster, 2008).

4: THE HANDSOME MONK IN
THE ORANGE ROBE

1. Some accounts say he slept in a box in the corner of the station.
2. Another progressive reform group was active at the time as well: the Arya Samaj. Created by Swami Dayananda Saraswati, it is considered the more Vedically orthodox.
3. Following Ram Mohan Roy's death in 1833, the movement was led by Devendranath Tagore, whose son, Rabindranath, would win the Nobel Prize for literature, and then by Keshab Chandra Sen.
4. The Ramakrishna movement has always downplayed Kali worship in the West, knowing that the strange and often frightful depictions of the goddess would reinforce the image of Hinduism as idol worship. When discussed at all, it is explained as a preference, Kali being Ramakrishna's *ishta devata,* or "favored form of God." This is consistent with Vedanta in general, and with Ramakrishna's own teachings.
5. Another of Ramakrishna's metaphors: "As one can ascend to the top of a house by means of a ladder or a bamboo or a staircase or a rope, so diverse are the ways and means to approach God, and every religion in the world shows one of these ways."
6. Some translators have rendered it "more intensely."
7. Marie Louise Burke, *Swami Vivekananda in the West: New Discoveries* (Mayavati, India: Ananda Ashram, 1983), pp. 51–52. This is the most complete account of Vivekananda's years in America.
8. Ibid., p. 20.
9. Ibid., p. 60.
10. All accounts of the parliament and Vivekananda's pre- and post-parliament activities are taken from Burke and the following sources: Carl T. Jackson, *Vedanta for the West: The Ramakrishna Movement in the United States* (Bloomington: Indiana University Press, 1994); Swami Tathagatananda, *Journey of the Upanishads to the West* (New York: Vedanta Soceity of New York, 2002); Rev. John Henry Barrows, *The World's Parliament of Religions* (Chicago: The Parliament Publishing Company, 1893); and unpublished documents from the Vedanta Society archives and individual collections.
11. Jon Monday, a filmmaker and longtime Vedanta Society devotee, did a painstaking study of the newspaper coverage and found that portions of the official story are exaggerations. But as he put it, "The truth is impressive enough." See Jon Monday, "For the Historic Record," *American Vedantist* 3, no. 3 (Fall 1997).
12. Jackson, p. 34. See also Jackson's *The Oriental Religions and American Thought: Nineteenth-Century Explorations* (Westport, Conn.: Greenwood Press, 1981).
13. Ibid., p. 27.

14. Personal correspondence.

15. Elizabeth De Michelis, *A History of Modern Yoga* (London: Continuum, 2004), p. 50.

16. The New York Vedanta Center has been on West 71st Street since 1921; a separate institution, the Ramakrishna-Vivekenanda Center, has been on East 94th Street since 1933.

17. Marie Louise's last name is unknown. She is not to be confused with Marie Louise Burke (later Sister Gargi), who was born in 1911 and chronicled the movement's history.

18. *Pravrajika* is the title given to all nuns in the Ramakrishna Order. The received names of all female monastics in the order end in *prana*.

19. *Ananda,* Sanskrit for "bliss," is the suffix in the names of all Ramakrishna monks.

20. Christopher Isherwood, *My Guru and His Disciple* (New York: Farrar, Straus & Giroux, 1980).

21. In addition to numerous articles, Pravrajika Vrajaprana is the author of *Vedanta: A Simple Introduction* (Hollywood, Calif.: Vedanta Press, 1999) and the editor of *Living Wisdom* (Vedanta Press, 1994), an update of *Vedanta for the Western World* (1945).

22. Jackson, p. 108.

5: THE PUBLIC INTELLECTUALS

1. *The Song of God* (Hollywood, Calif.: Vedanta Press, 1944), *Crest-Jewel* (Vedanta Press, 1947), *How to Know God* (Vedanta Press, 1953).

2. Sorokin emigrated to the United States in 1923 and founded the sociology department at Harvard.

3. Dana Sawyer, *Aldous Huxley: A Biography* (New York: Crossroad, 2002), p. 95.

4. Aldous Huxley, *The Perennial Philosophy* (New York: Harper & Row, 1944), p. 14.

5. Henry Miller, *The Air-Conditioned Nightmare* (New York: New Directions, 1945), p. 18.

6. Swami Prabhavananda, *The Sermon on the Mount According to Vedanta* (Hollywood, Calif.: Vedanta Press, 1963). With Frederick Manchester, he also translated sections of the Upanishads as *The Upanishads: Breath of the Eternal* (Hollywood, Calif.: Vedanta Press, 1957).

7. Gerald Heard, "What Vedanta Means to Me," *Vedanta and the West,* January–February 1951, pp. 26–27.

8. Hal Bridges, *American Mysticism: From William James to Zen* (New York: Oxford University Press, 1970).

9. Huxley, p. iv.

10. See Huston Smith's foreword to the new edition of Gerald Heard's *Pain, Sex and*

Time (Rhinebeck, N.Y.: Monkfish, 2004), p. vii. The book was originally published by Harper & Row in 1939.

11. Ram Dass, *Be Here Now* (San Cristobal, N.Mex.: Lama Foundation, 1971), p. 116.

12. Stephen and Robin Larsen, *A Fire in the Mind: The Life of Joseph Campbell* (New York: Doubleday, 1991), p. 282.

13. Arnold's book was the first English-language version of the life of Buddha. When it was published, in 1870, it was an immediate sensation in New York and New England, selling over half a million copies and igniting the country's first enchantment with Buddhism.

14. Stephen and Robin Larsen, p. 64.

15. Ibid., p. 105.

16. Ibid., p. 66.

17. Ibid., p. 283.

18. His real name was Mahendranath Gupta.

19. Glass's composition premiered September 16, 2006, at the Orange County Performing Arts Center in Costa Mesa, California.

20. The book is *The Hero's Journey: Joseph Campbell on His Life and Work* (1990; reprint New York: New World Library, 2003); the film is *The Hero's Journey: The World of Joseph Campbell* (1987). See http://www.philcousineau.net.

21. Joseph Campbell, *The Hero with a Thousand Faces* (New York: Meridian, 1956), p. viii.

22. Joseph Campbell, *Myths to Live By* (New York: Viking Penguin, 1972), p. 94.

23. Gerald Heard, *Pain, Sex and Time* (New York: Harper, 1939); it has been reissued in paperback by Monkfish Publishing.

24. The title was changed in 1989, when the book was updated. A shorter version, with pictures, was published as *The Illustrated World's Religions* (Harper SanFrancisco, 1995).

25. To commemorate the book's fiftieth anniversary in 2008, HarperCollins began awarding an annual prize to the author "whose unpublished work best reflects the spirit of Huston Smith's life's work." See http://www.harpercollins.com/features/Smith/index.aspx.

26. Huston Smith, *Forgotten Truth* (New York: Harper & Row, 1976), and *Why Religion Matters* (New York: HarperCollins, 2001).

6: THE YOGI OF THE AUTOBIOGRAPHY

1. Because of unreliable record-keeping, SRF could not tell me exactly how many copies have been printed since the book was published in 1946. They do know that between 1998 and 2008, about 350,000 were sold.

2. Shri Yogendra was unable to return after 1924 because of changes in immigration laws; his institute in Bombay became an important center for the study of Yoga.

3. Stephen Prothero, "Mother India's Scandalous Swamis," in *Religions of the United States in Practice,* ed. Colleen McDannell (Princeton, N.J.: Princeton University Press, 2001). See also Thomas A. Tweed and Stephen Prothero, *Asian Religions in America: A Documentary History* (New York: Oxford University Press, 1999).

4. See Robert Love's article about the lurid press coverage of Yoga before it became trendy: "Fear of Yoga," *Columbia Journalism Review,* November–December 2006.

5. Yogananda, *Autobiography of a Yogi* (Los Angeles: Self-Realization Fellowship, 1946), p. 357.

6. Yogananda expanded the speech for publication by his Self-Realization Fellowship in 1924.

7. That definition of Kriya Yoga is essentially the same as the one on page 231 of *Autobiography of a Yogi.* There Yogananda explains the root: *kri,* "to do or to act" (*karma* has the same root), thus "union *(yoga)* with the Infinite through a certain action or rite." In fact, the term *kriya* is used by teachers for their favored psychophysical practices. As a brand, Kriya Yoga generally refers to the lineage that Yogananda represented, which he claimed his guru's guru revived in the modern era.

8. It was originally called Yogoda Sat-Sanga Society of America; the organization's name in India is still Yogoda Satsanga Society of India.

9. Evidently an earnest seeker, Wilson later studied with Swami Nikhilananda at the Ramakrishna-Vivekananda Center of New York (she helped him and Campbell edit the *Gospel of Sri Ramakrishna*) and also studied the teachings of Sri Aurobindo (see chapter 7).

10. Doris Duke, the tobacco heiress, is also said to have been a follower and a major benefactor.

11. The Lake Shrine is the only place outside India where Mahatma Gandhi's ashes are buried. See http://www.lakeshrine.org.

12. According to one source, he also said, "I prefer a soul to a crowd, but I love crowds of souls."

13. Information about the lessons and everything else about SRF can be found at http://www.yogananda-srf.org.

14. That page is also reproduced on the back cover of some editions and appears as well in other SRF publications.

15. Paramahansa Yogananda, *The Second Coming of Christ: The Resurrection of the Christ Within You* (Los Angeles: Self-Realization Fellowship, 2004).

16. For information, see www.lifecamp.com.

17. An internal upheaval led to the departure of many monks and nuns in 2000–2001. For a summary of those events, see Lola Williamson, *Transcendent in America* (New York: NYU Press, 2010), p. 76.

18. For the Kriya Yoga International Organizations, see www.kriya.org.

19. The Self-Revelation Church of Absolute Monism is at www.self-revelationchurch
    .org. For the Gandhi Memorial Center, see www.gandhimemorialcenter.org.

20. For information about Davis's Center for Spiritual Awareness, see www.csa
    -davis.org.

21. Two of the San Francisco locations where he spoke, the American Academy of
    Asian Studies and the Cultural Integration Fellowship, are discussed in chap-
    ter 7.

22. In addition to Ananda Village, the organization (Ananda Sangha Worldwide) has
    sister communities in Seattle, Portland, Sacramento, Palo Alto, and Los Angeles;
    Ananda Italy is in Assisi, and India's community is outside Delhi.

7: BLOWIN' IN THE WIND

1. Gandhi was depicted on *Time*'s cover on the editions of May 31, 1930; January 5,
   1931 (Man of the Year); and June 30, 1947.

2. *Life* magazine, May 30, 1949, text by Winthrop Sargeant, photographs by Eliot
   Elisofon.

3. Winthrop Sargeant, *The Bhagavad-Gita: An Interlinear Translation* (Albany: SUNY
   Press, 1984). A revised edition was released in 1994 by SUNY Press, with a foreword by Christopher Chapple.

4. The official Ramanasramam website is www.sriramanamaharshi.org. Another
   excellent source is David Godman, a tireless advocate of Ramana's teachings:
   http://davidgodman.org.

5. See www.larsonpublications.com.

6. See Thomas A. Forsthoefel, "Weaving the Inward Thread to Awakening: The
   Perennial Appeal of Ramana Maharshi," in *Gurus in America,* ed. Thomas A.
   Forsthoefel and Cynthia Ann Humes (Albany: SUNY Press, 2005), pp. 47–51.
   Clooney's book was published in 1998 by Orbis.

7. Sri Aurobindo's other works include *Essays on the Gita, The Secret of the Veda,* and
   The Synthesis of Yoga. All of his books are distributed in the United States by Lo-
   tus Light Publications. Also recommended is *The Essential Aurobindo,* ed. Robert
   McDermott (West Stockbridge, Mass.: Lindisfarne Press, 2001). The most recent
   Sri Aurobindo biography is Peter Heehs, *The Lives of Sri Aurobindo* (New York:
   Columbia University Press, 2008).

8. For the Sri Aurobindo Ashram, see http://www.sriaurobindoashram.org. For Auroville, see www.auroville.org.

9. Archives of the California Institute of Integral Studies.

10. Alan Watts, *The Book: On the Taboo Against Knowing Who You Are* (New York:
    Random House, 1966), p. ix.

11. The official Watts website is www.alanwatts.com.

12. In another irony, the caretaker hired to do the job was Hunter S. Thompson, the future grand master of gonzo journalism.

13. For information, www.anandaashram.org. Brahmananda Sarasvati's books include *A Textbook of Yoga Psychology,* based on Patañjali's *Yoga Sutras.*

14. Murphy was associate editor of the *Journal of Transpersonal Psychology* at its inception (Sutich was the editor) and contributed his first published article ("Education for Transcendence") to the initial issue. Murphy has written a number of well-regarded books, and his novel, *Golf in the Kingdom* (New York: Penguin, 1997), has sold over a million copies. Its main character, Shivas Irons, has a society named for him.

15. Jeffrey John Kripal, *Esalen: America and the Religion of No Religion* (Chicago: University of Chicago Press, 2007). An earlier history, more journalistic than scholarly, is Walter Truett Anderson, *The Upstart Spring: Esalen and the American Awakening* (Reading, Mass.: Addison-Wesley, 1983).

16. *Integral Yoga,* a documentary film about Haridas Chaudhuri's efforts to bring Sri Aurobindo to the West, is available on DVD. Also see Haridas Chaudhuri, *Integral Yoga* (Wheaton, Ill.: Quest, 1965). For information about the CIF, see http://www.culturalintegrationfellowship.org. For the CIIS, see www.ciis.edu. Two nonprofit organizations dedicated to Sri Aurobindo's vision, the Foundation for World Education and Auroville International USA, cosponsor an annual conference called AUM (All USA Meeting). For information, see www.collaboration.org/aum.

17. Brant Cortright, *Integral Psychology: Yoga, Growth, and Opening the Heart* (Albany: SUNY Press, 2007). See also Cortright, *Psychotherapy and Spirit: Theory and Practice in Transpersonal Psychotherapy* (Albany: SUNY Press, 1997).

18. For the history of the psychedelic era, see Jay Stevens, *Storming Heaven: LSD and the American Dream* (New York: Grove Press, 1987); and Don Lattin, *The Harvard Psychedelic Club: How Timothy Leary, Ram Dass, Huston Smith and Andrew Weil Killed the Fifties and Ushered in a New Age for America* (New York: HarperCollins, 2010).

19. For Stephen Gaskin, who still presides over his Tennessee community, see www.stephengaskin.com.

20. For the Blue Mountain Center, see www.easwaran.org.

21. To see the cover and read the story, see www.time.com/time/covers/0,16641,19660408,00.html.

22. Robert Love, "Fear of Yoga," reports that in the mid-1960s, the *New York Times* estimated that there were at least 20,000 Yoga practitioners in the United States and perhaps as many as 100,000.

23. Maslow's book sold 200,000 copies in hardcover, an enormous number for what was basically an academic tome.

24. The Be-In had been organized to protest a 1966 California law making LSD illegal.

25. For an account of Ginsberg's Indian sojourn, see Deborah Baker, *A Blue Hand: The Beats in India* (New York: Penguin, 2008).

26. In 1968 Ginsberg took out his harmonium and performed a Krishna chant on William F. Buckley's *Firing Line* program. Recognition of "the unity of being, and of that great consciousness that we are all identical with," Ginsberg told the conservative Buckley, was the grounding awareness of the motto "make love, not war." The episode can be viewed on YouTube.

8: *MAHA* MASS MEDIA

1. *Maharishi* is an honorific meaning "great sage." It was bestowed upon the man whose given name was Mahesh, along with *Yogi,* by followers in India. When he became famous in the West, it was used as if it were his name, and I've stuck with that custom even though *the* Maharishi, like the Dalai Lama, would be more proper.

2. Videos of the interviews can be seen on YouTube.

3. The quotes from the David Frost interviews are taken from Keith Badman, *The Beatles Off the Record* (U.K.: Omnibus Press, 2001), pp. 320–23.

4. Kurt Vonnegut Jr., "Yes, We Have No Nirvanas," *Esquire,* June 1968.

5. Jerry Jarvis, former leader of the TM movement in the United States, has Maharishi's expired passport with the 1918 birthdate.

6. The four *varnas,* or primary castes, are *brahmin,* priests; *kshatriya,* warriors; *vaishya,* merchants; and *shudra,* workers and artisans. For an analysis of the significance of caste in Maharishi's history, see Cynthia Ann Humes, "Maharishi Mahesh Yogi: Beyond the TM Technique," in *Gurus in America,* ed. Thomas A. Forsthoefel and Cynthia Ann Humes (Albany: SUNY Press, 2005).

7. The remark is quoted in Paul Mason, *The Maharishi: The Biography of the Man Who Gave Transcendental Meditation to the World* (Lanham, Md.: Element Books, 1994). It cites a publication by Maharishi called *Thirty Years Around the World.* Mason's website, srigurudev.net, contains additional information.

8. Most scholars place Shankara in the ninth century C.E., although some Hindus believe he lived hundreds if not thousands of years earlier. He established four major *maths* (monasteries) to preserve his teachings, at north, south, east, and west points in India.

9. *Bal* means "from childhood" and *brahmachari* means "celibate," hence "a lifelong celibate."

10. The excerpts are taken from *Beacon Light of the Himalayas,* published in India in 1955 or 1956. It can be read at www.paulmason.info.

11. As a nonbrahmin, Maharishi departed from orthodoxy by teaching at all. By initiating nonbrahmins and women into mantra meditation, he was departing even further.

12. On those early years, see Helena Olson, *A Hermit in the House* (1967) and Nancy Cooke de Herrera, *Beyond Gurus: A Woman of Many Worlds* (Blue Dolphin, 1992).

13. Both books are still in print and readily available on the Web. His commentaries on the remaining twelve chapters of the Gita have not been published.

14. Ray Manzarek met Robby Krieger and John Densmore at a TM course in L.A., then introduced them to Jim Morrison, who never learned TM because he refused to stay off drugs for the requisite fifteen days.

15. As Lola Williamson notes in *Transcendent in America: Hindu-Inspired Meditation Movements as New Religion* (New York: NYU Press, 2010), Maharishi's application of meditation to worldly life places him more in the Tantra camp than in traditional Advaita Vedanta. Maharishi himself said that Advaita's emphasis on renunciation was a tragic misinterpretation.

16. The Ginsberg-Maharishi encounter was reported in "The Yogi Dusts Off His Cosmic Truths," *New York Post,* January 22, 1968.

17. It appeared in the February 9, 1968, issue of *Life.*

18. The headline on *Look*'s cover for February 6, 1968, read "And Now—Meditation Hits the Campus. How Hindu Monk Maharishi turns the students on—without drugs."

19. *Mad* magazine's cover (September 1968) depicted a bearded Alfred E. Neuman, with a red *tilak* on his forehead, held aloft by Maharishi, Mia, and the Beatles. Around him swirled Sanskrit-looking letters: "Swami, how I love ya, how I love ya, my dear old swami . . ."

20. The use of course fees, rather than basket-passing or voluntary donations, was consistent with the TM movement's decision to register as an educational nonprofit, not a religious one.

21. Harry Oldmeadow, *Journeys East: 20th Century Encounters with Eastern Religious Traditions* (Bloomington, Ind.: World Wisdom, 2004), p. 269.

22. These and other data were taken from the records of the Students International Meditation Society, which were provided by Jerry Jarvis.

23. Full disclosure: I was one of those trained teachers and worked for the TM organization in several capacities until 1975.

24. At the beginning of 1970, there were 253 TM teachers in America; at the end of 1975, there were 6,468; at the end of the decade, there were more than 10,000.

25. The mantras were traditional *bija* (seed) mantras. I will keep my word by not revealing how they were selected, although anyone can look it up on the Internet.

26. R. K. Wallace, "Physiological Effects of Transcendental Meditation," *Science* 167 (1970), pp. 1751–54.

27. R. K. Wallace, H. Benson, and A. F. Wilson, "A Wakeful Hypometabolic Physiologic State," *American Journal of Physiology* 221 (1971), pp. 795–99, and R. K.

Wallace and H. Benson, "The Physiology of Meditation," *Scientific American* 226 (1972), pp. 84–90.

28. Carl T. Jackson, *Vedanta for the West: The Ramakrishna Movement in the United States* (Bloomington: Indiana University Press, 1994), p. 136.

29. A separate organization, called Transcendental Meditation Centers (TMC), was created to bring the technique to African Americans. It reached a significant number of professionals and celebrities (including Stevie Wonder), and some of the teachers would later bring meditation to urban schools and conduct studies on TM's effect on African Americans with hypertension.

30. Harold Bloomfield, Michael Peter Cain, and Dennis T. Jaffe, *TM: Discovering Inner Energy and Overcoming Stress* (New York: Delacorte, 1975).

31. Denise Denniston and Peter McWilliams, *The TM Book* (New York: Price/Stern/Sloan, 1975); Herbert Benson, *The Relaxation Response* (New York: Morrow, 1975). Jack Forem, *Transcendental Meditation: Maharishi Mahesh Yogi and the Science of Creative Intelligence* (New York: Dutton, 1973), was rushed into paperback as well, as were two books by British physician Anthony Campbell, *Seven States of Consciousness* and *TM and the Nature of Enlightenment* (New York: Harper & Row, 1974 and 1975, respectively).

32. Adam Smith, *Powers of Mind* (New York: Random House, 1975).

33. According to TM sources, the number of initiates worldwide now exceeds six million.

34. Hixon's show was on the air from 1971 to 1984.

35. Not to be confused with the European Enlightenment, also known as the Age of Reason.

36. The customary spelling is *siddhi*. The TM movement eliminated one of the *d*'s, presumably for trademark purposes.

37. TM reps cite this passage from the *Siva Samhita* as an example that the claim has traditional support: "When the Yogi, though remaining in Padmasan [lotus position], can rise in the air and leave the ground, then know that he has gained Vayu siddhi, which destroys the darkness of the world."

38. The tipping point for peace and invincibility, say TM scientists, is the square root of one percent of a population. It was rarely met. In 2008 the movement achieved critical mass by importing Indian monks whose sole task is to perform yogic flying and Vedic rituals *(yagyas)* to pacify the world.

39. Two practitioners came directly from the TM movement: John Douilliard in Boulder, Colorado (www.lifespa.com) and Vaidya Kant Mishra in Los Angeles (www.vaidyamishra.com). For Dr. Vasant Lad's Ayurvedic Institute, see www.ayurveda.com/. For the California College of Ayurveda, see www.ayurvedacollege.com. For the National Ayurvedic Medical Association, see www.ayurveda-nama.org.

40. David Friend, "The Return of Mister Bliss," *Life*, November 1990, pp. 83–92.

41. Stern's eulogy can be heard at www.rencapp.com/Howard_Stern_on_Maharishi _02_06_2008.mp3.

42. Joel Stein, "Just Say Om," *Time*, August 4, 2003.

43. For a complete overview of TM research and responses to its critics, see psychologist David Orme-Johnson's website www.truthabouttm.org.

44. They include Jungian psychologist Connie Zweig (*Romancing the Shadow*, 1999, and *The Holy Longing*, 2003) and Dean Sluyter (*Cinema Nirvana*, 2005, and *The Zen Commandments*, 2001).

45. For information on the Lynch initiative and TM school programs, see www .davidlynchfoundation.org and www.stressfreeschools.org. Lynch also published a quirky book called *Catching the Big Fish: Meditation, Consciousness and Creativity* (New York: Tarcher/Putnam, 2006).

9: THE BABY BOOMERS' BABAS

1. *Life*, February 9, 1968.

2. Christopher Chapple, "Raja Yoga and the Guru," in *Gurus in America*, ed. Thomas Forsthoefel and Cynthia Ann Humes (Albany: SUNY Press, 2005).

3. Gaudiya Vaishnavism sees Krishna as the source of all that is and as having many manifestations, including that of Vishnu. "Krishna is Bhagavan, the Supreme Personality of Godhead," writes Vaishnavite scholar Steven J. Rosen. "He is not merely a portion or manifestation of God, as are so many other divinities in India" (*The Hidden Glory of India* [Los Angeles: Bhaktivedanta Book Trust, 2002], p. 46). It is, at the same time, profoundly monotheistic and not incompatible with the monism of Advaita Vedanta, which emphasizes the impersonal aspect of the divine.

4. "Hare Krishna, Hare Krishna, Krishna Krishna, Hare Hare. Hare Rama, Hare Rama, Rama Rama, Hare Hare."

5. They were to intone the *mahamantra* 108 times, once per bead on the string *(mala)* they wore, and repeat the process sixteen times each day. The routine could take over two hours.

6. Published by the Bhaktivedanta Book Trust, it has reportedly sold over five million copies.

7. Radha is the name of Krishna's beloved consort; as the feminine side of God, she is worshipped equally. The album is now called *Chant and Be Happy*.

8. Joshua M. Greene, *Here Comes the Sun: The Spiritual and Musical Journey of George Harrison* (New York: Wiley, 2006).

9. The Hare Krishna mantra can be heard on Harrison's "My Sweet Lord" (1971). His "Living in the Material World" (1973) contains a line about "the Lord Sri Krishna's grace." In 1984 the group Hüsker Dü recorded a song called

"Hare Krisna." The *mahamantra* is the chorus. Boy George's 1991 song is "Bow Down Mister." Kula Shaker's is the 1996 "Govinda." For a complete list of pop culture references, see http://en.wikipedia.org/wiki/Hare_Krishna_in_popular _culture.

10. Those scholars include: E. H. Jarow, assistant professor of religion and Asian studies at Vassar; Graham Schweig, a Harvard Ph.D. who teaches at Christopher Newport University and has written several books and stacks of journal articles; Edwin Bryant, who teaches at Rutgers and leads workshops on aspects of Hindu philosophy; and two who operate outside of academia: Steven Rosen, the founding editor of the *Journal of Vaishnava Studies* and author of some twenty books, and Stephen Knapp, a prolific writer on, and advocate of, Vedic philosophy.

11. From "Awaiting on You All," on Harrison's 1970 album *All Things Must Pass.*

12. For the early years of Hare Krishna in America, see Hayagriva Dasa, *The Hare Krishna Explosion* (San Rafael, Calif.: Palace Press, 1985).

13. *Shakti* (also spelled *sakti*) is associated with the feminine aspect of divinity, often depicted as a consort of the masculine god Shiva. It is so inseparable from *kundalini* that the two terms are often used interchangeably and sometimes referred to as *kundalini-shakti.*

14. Sir John Woodroffe wrote an early kundalini classic, *The Serpent Power* (1919). In 1967 a Kashmiri office worker named Gopi Krishna attracted attention with *Kundalini: The Evolutionary Energy in Man,* an account of his own remarkable experiences. He spent the next seventeen years lecturing and writing on the subject. In the late 1960s the Sikh guru Yogi Bhajan started teaching his brand of Kundalini Yoga through his 3HO organization (for "healthy, happy, holy").

15. The claim that Nityananda formally anointed Muktananda as his successor has been disputed; others also teach in Nityananda's name.

16. Lola Williamson defines *siddha* as "one who has attained perfection and who can lead others to this same perfection." See her essay on Muktananda, "The Perfectability of Perfection," in *Gurus in America,* ed. Forsthoefel and Humes.

17. Douglas Renfrew Brooks et al., eds., *Meditation Revolution: A History and Theology of the Siddha Yoga Lineage* (South Fallsburg, N.Y.: Agama Press, 1997), p. 436.

18. According to the historical overview by Swami Durgananda (née Sally Kempton) in *Meditation Revolution,* by 1982 fifty-one men and fourteen women had taken vows.

19. In the 1980s, after Muktananda's passing, two adjacent hotels were purchased, expanding the property, renamed Shree Muktananda Ashram by his successor, to over one hundred acres.

20. William Rodarmor, "The Secret Life of Swami Muktananda," *CoEvolution Quarterly* (Winter 1983).

21. Swami Nityananda started his own organization, Shanti Mandir (Temple of

Peace). One of its ashrams is in the Catskills, not far from his estranged sister's. See http://www.shantimandir.com.

22. Lis Harris, "O Guru, Guru, Guru," *New Yorker,* November 14, 1994.

23. The PRASAD Project (www.prasad.org) operates health, education, and sustainable-development programs; the Muktabodha Indological Research Institute works to preserve India's scriptural heritage (www.muktabodha.org).

24. Salacious rumors have circulated regarding Gurumayi's lack of public appearances: she's physically ill; she's living with a lover; she had a botched face-lift; and so on. All have been refuted by SYDA.

25. James Strohecker, who ran Muktananda's library in Ganeshpuri, created Healthy. net, the largest alternative health site on the Web. Robert Rabbin, who learned about organizations working in SYDA for ten years, is now an executive coach (www.robertrabbin.com). Diana Denton is a professor of communication at Ontario's University of Waterloo and a leader in the spirituality and education movement. Gorakh Hayashi brings yogic practices into courses such as "Mystical Consciousness, East and West" at Columbia College Chicago. Douglas Renfrew Brooks and Paul Muller-Ortega, both at the University of Rochester, have done scholarly work on Tantrism and Kashmir Shaivism. William Barnard of Southern Methodist University has written, among other things, biographies of William James and the French philosopher Henri Bergson.

26. Muktananda's last public appearance was at the 1982 International Transpersonal Conference in Mumbai, which featured a number of well-known scholars. The proceedings, edited by Stanislav Grof, were published as *Ancient Wisdom and Modern Science* (Albany: SUNY Press, 1984).

27. Kempton's website is www.sallykempton.com.

28. Other devotees who have become spiritual teachers include Swami Shankarananda (originally Russell Kruckman), who runs the Shiva School of Meditation in Australia; Charles Cannon, once a swami and now Master Charles, who created the Synchronicity Foundation in Virginia; and Kumuda (Sharon Janis), a devotional singer, author of *Spirituality for Dummies,* and the creator of the well-stocked website www.nightlotus.com.

29. See www.dreugenecallender.com.

30. The official SYDA website is www.siddhayoga.org.

31. Kusumita Pederson, "The Teachings of Sri Chinmoy: Values and Spiritual Practices for Human Transformation," in *Bengal Studies 1994: Essays on Economics, Society and Culture,* ed. Sachi G. Dostidar (Old Westbury, N.Y.: SUNY Press, 1996).

32. The organization's official website, www.srichinmoy.org, contains videos of Sri Chinmoy.

33. The Divine Light Mission is not to be confused with the Divine Life Society in Rishikesh, India.

34. *Prem* means "love" in Sanskrit. It connotes a pure, or spiritual kind of love, as contrasted with *kama*, which signifies sensual and sexual love (as in *Kama Sutra*).

35. The four techniques included a conventional meditation form plus three esoteric practices that were said to awaken the subtle senses to divine light, divine music, and divine nectar.

36. Davis's former antiwar comrades excoriated him for abandoning the cause for what they saw as a delusional religious quest. He went on to lead self-improvement seminars and create a venture capital company.

37. According to official sources his message is "available in 197 countries in over 70 languages. He has spoken personally in 54 countries to audiences that number 12.6 million." For information see www.wopg.org.

38. Published in 1974, the breakaway bestseller was dedicated to Guru Maharaj Ji.

39. *Bhagwan* is a derivative of *Bhagavan,* an honorific that refers to a form of God. *Shree* (often spelled *shri* or *sri*) is a term of respect akin to *sir* and *madame.*

40. *Zorba the Greek* was adapted from the Nikos Kazantzakis novel and directed by Michael Cacoyannis.

41. Georg Feuerstein, *The Yoga Tradition* (Prescott, Ariz.: Hohm Press, 1998), p. 19.

42. The company represents all of Osho's works. See www.oshointernational.com.

43. From Urban's chapter, "Osho, From Sex Guru to Guru of the Rich," in *Gurus in America,* ed. Forsthoefel and Humes.

44. Mount Madonna: www.mountmadonna.org.

45. Based in Portland, Oregon, Ashley-Farrand has produced a number of books (e.g., *Healing Mantras,* 1999) and audio CDs, and teaches workshops around the country. See www.sanskritmantra.com/.

46. Christopher Key Chapple, "Raja Yoga and the Guru: Gurani Anjali of Yoga Anand Ashram, Amityville, New York," in *Gurus in America,* ed. Forsthoefel and Humes. His website is myweb.lmu.edu/cchapple. The LMU Yoga Philosophy Program is at www.lmu.edu/Page3891.aspx.

47. For the Desert Ashram in Arizona and the Sacred Mountain Ashram in Colorado, see www.light-of-consciousness.org/TC_Ashrams.htm.

48. On Hariharananda, see www.hariharanandakriyayoga.org/index.html. On Vidyadhishananda, see www.swamahiman.org/monastery.html.

49. "Joy-Permeated Mother" is a translation of the name she was known by; her birth name was Nirmala Sundari. Timothy Conway's valuable *Women of Power and Grace* features a chapter about her. She died in 1982. The website http://www.anandamayi.org contains complete information about her.

50. Google "Sai Baba tricks" for YouTube videos.

51. The official Sai Baba website is www.sathyasai.org. For Sai Maa, see www.humanityinunity.org. For Shanti Anantam Ashram, see www.saiquest.com.

10: THE YOGA BEARERS

1. The key verse in the *Yoga Sutras* (chapter 1, sutra 2) reads: "Yoga is the cessation of the movement of thought." Other translations are "the stilling of . . . ," "the control of . . . ," and "the suppression of . . . ," and there are variations on "movement" as well (e.g., "fluctuations"). The choice of terms is not trivial, as it leads to the employment of different types of practices to attain the results Patanjali describes.

2. Eliade's major works include *The Sacred and the Profane: The Nature of Religion* (1957), *Myth and Reality* (1963), *The History of Religious Ideas* (three volumes, 1978, 1982, 1985), and *Encyclopedia of Religion* (1987).

3. For the Sivananda network of centers and ashrams, see www.sivananda.org. For the Divine Life Society in Rishikesh, see www.dlshq.org. Also see Sarah Strauss, *Positioning Yoga: Balancing Acts Across Cultures* (Berg, 2005).

4. For Satchidananda's account of the event, and other information about him, see the documentary *Living Yoga,* coproduced by Joshua M. Greene and Shiva Kumar, www.LivingYogaMovie.org.

5. Satchidananda's Integral Yoga should not be confused with Sri Aurobindo's use of the same term.

6. Other performers drawn to Satchidananda in those days included Laura Nyro and members of the Young Rascals.

7. New Seminary was the forerunner to other institutions that ordain interfaith ministers, such as One Spirit in New York and the Spiritual Paths Foundation in Santa Barbara.

8. The lotus is a common symbol in both Hinduism and Buddhism, because it grows in mud (symbolic of worldly life) and floats on the surface of the water without getting wet. For details about LOTUS, go to www.lotus.org/index.htm.

9. The Yogaville website is www.yogaville.org. IYI centers have their own sites. New York's is www.iyiny.org; San Francisco's is www.integralyogasf.org.

10. Originally the Sivananda Ashram, it was later renamed the Yashodra Ashram.

11. They have similar, but different names: Sivananda Ashram Yoga Retreat in Nassau; Sivananda Ashram Yoga Farm in Grass Valley, California; and Sivananda Yoga Ranch Colony in Woodbourne, New York.

12. The official Sivananda Yoga Vendanta website is www.sivananda.org.

13. See Elmer Green and Alyce Green, *Beyond Biofeedback* (New York: Delacorte, 1977). Accounts of Swami Rama's time at Menninger can also be found in Tony Schwartz, *What Really Matters: Searching for Wisdom in America* (New York: Bantam, 1995), and in Pandit Rajmani Tigunait, *At the Eleventh Hour: The Biography of Swami Rama* (Honesdale, Penn.: Himalayan Institute Press, 2001).

14. *Diet and Nutrition* was published by the Himalayan Institute Press. Ballentine's most recent book is *Radical Healing: Integrating the World's Great Therapeutic*

Traditions to Create a New Transformative Medicine (New York: Three Rivers Press, 1999). He served for some time as president of the Himalayan Institute.

15. For complete information, see www.himalayaninstitute.org.

16. They include Swami Ajaya, a clinical psychologist and author of several books; Swami Jaidev Bharati (aka Justin O'Brien), a philosophy professor and author of a memoir of his time with Swami Rama (*Walking with a Himalayan Master,* 2006); and Swami Veda Bharati, whose Association of Himalayan Yoga Meditation Societies is based in Minneapolis.

17. See http://www.RaganiWorld.com.

18. Stephen Cope, *Yoga and the Quest for True Self* (New York: Bantam, 2000).

19. For the Kripalu Center for Yoga and Health, see www.kripalu.org.

20. See www.amrityoga.com.

21. Yogi Bhajan also wrote several books. He died in 2004 at age seventy-five. See www.3HO.org, www.sikhdharma.org, and for the natural foods lines, www.yogiproducts.com.

22. See Elizabeth De Michelis, *A History of Modern Yoga* (London: Continuum, 2004).

23. He was mostly in England, visiting New York only briefly in 1956.

24. The official website for Iyengar Yoga is www.bksiyengar.com. For Patthabhi Jois's Ashtanga Yoga Institute, see www.kpjayi.org.

11: SEX, LIES, AND IDIOSYNCRASIES

1. The allegations about Sri Chinmoy, Swami Satchidananda, and Swami Rama can be found online.

2. Vijali Hamilton, *World Wheel: One Woman's Quest for Peace* (Castle Valley, Utah: World Wheel Press, 2007). The allegations constitute only a small portion of the book and are not presented with bitterness.

3. Katharine Webster, "The Case against Swami Rama of the Himalayas," *Yoga Journal,* November–December 1990. For the story of a man who claims to be the offspring of one of Swami Rama's affairs, see http://www.sonofaswami.com.

4. SYDA leaders did not respond to my request for an official statement.

5. Psychologist Stephen Cope, now scholar in residence at Kripalu, describes the saga in *Yoga and the Quest for the True Self* (New York: Bantam, 2006). See also Connie Zweig, *The Holy Longing* (New York: Tarcher/Putnam, 2003).

6. The other two are the Buddha, which can mean either the historical person or the state of enlightenment; and the Dharma, the teachings.

7. Some of the abuses were perpetrated by American and European disciples in positions of authority. This, of course, does not exonerate the gurus at the top, any more than the pope is off the hook for priestly misconduct.

8. Amrit Desai, interview by Andrew Cohen, *What is Enlightenment?*, Spring–Summer 2000. The magazine is now called *EnlightenNext*.

9. For more on the guru scandals of the era, see Joel Kramer and Diana Alstad, *The Guru Papers* (Berkeley: Frog, Ltd., 1993).

12: MADE IN THE U.S.A.

1. Robert Love, *The Great Oom: The Improbable Birth of Yoga in America* (New York: Viking, 2010).

2. Theos Bernard's other books are *Penthouse of the Gods: A Pilgrimage into the Heart of Tibet and the Sacred City of Lhasa* (New York: Scribner's, 1939); *Heaven Lies Within Us: The Attainment of Health and Happiness Through Yoga* (Scribner's, 1939); and *The Philosophical Foundations of India* (London: Rider, 1945), which appeared in America as *Hindu Philosophy* (New York: Philosophical Library, 1947).

3. For Patanjali Kundalini Yoga Care, see www.kundalinicare.com. See also Joan Harrigan, *Kundalini Yoga: The Science of Spiritual Transformation* (Knoxville, Tenn.: Patanjali, 2005).

4. For advanced yoga practices, see www.aypsite.com. In 2009 the site attracted 100,000 visitors.

5. Merrell-Wolff's best-known book is *The Philosophy of Consciousness Without an Object* (Julian Press, 1973). For information about him, see www.merrell-wolff.org.

6. For the Mirabai Devi Foundation, see www.mirabaidevi.org. She is now based in Hawaii.

7. Each of the three is scholarly enough to be considered a *pandit*. But I classified them *acharyas* because they address issues of spiritual development and, to one degree or another, teach spiritual practices.

8. David Frawley's American Institute of Vedic Studies offers a broad range of training programs, resources, and publications: www.vedanet.com.

9. Feuerstein's other books include *The Shambhala Encyclopedia of Yoga* and *Yoga for Dummies,* coauthored with Yoga therapy pioneer Larry Payne. His website is www.traditionalyogastudies.com.

10. Harvey declared Mother Meera's divinity in a book titled *Hidden Journey* (New York: Penguin, 1991) and denounced her in *The Sun at Midnight* (New York: Tarcher/Putnam, 2002).

11. *The Hope: A Guide to Sacred Activism* (Carlsbad, Calif.: Hay House, 2009). For information about Harvey and his Institute for Sacred Activism, see www.andrewharvey.net.

12. I have focused on the most influential American disseminators of Vedanta-Yoga. As it happens, almost all are independents. But there are many American lineage-holders in Vedic organizations, some of whom are mentioned elsewhere in the book.

13. Ram Dass, *Be Here Now* (San Cristobal, N.M.: Lama Foundation, 1971). (The pages in the opening section are not numbered.) It is now distributed by the Crown Publishing Group.

14. Alpert, Leary, and Ralph Metzner reinterpreted *The Tibetan Book of the Dead* in *The Psychedelic Experience* (New York: Citadel Press, 1964).

15. Neem Karoli Baba's male devotees received names ending with Das, which means "servant." Ram Dass means "servant of God." The extra *s* came courtesy of the silent yogi Hari Das Baba, who misspelled the name on a chalkboard.

16. Ram Dass's talks at the Menninger Foundation and Spring Grove Hospital in Maryland were edited into book form and published as *The Only Dance There Is* (New York: Anchor/Doubleday, 1974).

17. Ram Dass, "Egg on My Beard," *Yoga Journal,* November–December 1976.

18. Ram Dass and Stephen Levine, *Grist for the Mill* (Santa Cruz, Calif.: Unity Press, 1976).

19. Ram Dass wrote about the stroke and its aftermath in *Still Here: Embracing Aging, Changing and Dying* (New York: Riverhead, 2000). For information about the film *Fierce Grace*, see http://www.lemlepictures.com.

20. The most comprehensive website for Ram Dass is http://www.ramdass .org. There you will find a page for the Love, Serve, Remember Foundation, which was established in 2009 to disseminate the teachings of Neem Karoli Baba and Ram Dass's work. In addition, http://www.ramdasstapes.org/rdtl.htm hosts a library of Ram Dass recordings. His newest book, *Be Love Now,* is scheduled for publication in October 2010.

21. The Buddhist connection developed, in part, because one of the meditation teachers Neem Karoli sent followers to was the Vipassana master S. N. Goenka.

22. The book was Jack Forem's *Transcendental Meditation* (New York: Dutton, 1973), the earliest book on the subject by an American author.

23. H. M. Sharma, B. D. Triguna, and Deepak Chopra, "Maharishi Ayur-Veda: Modern Insights into Ancient Medicine," *Journal of the American Medical Association* May 22–29, 1991. The critical pieces appeared in *JAMA*'s August 14 and October 2 issues.

24. For the Chopra Center, see www.chopra.com. For Chopra's personal site, see http://deepakchopra.com.

13: NOT JUST ACADEMIC

1. American Buddhist scholars did the same in their areas of expertise, forming a kind of intellectual pincer movement for Eastern religion.

2. Full disclosure: Robert Forman and I have been friends and sometime colleagues for more than thirty years. I verified the information in this section with several scholars in his field.

3. Forman called it a pure consciousness event (PCE), avoiding the word *experience* because every experience involves a subject and an object, whereas in a PCE the subject-object distinction disappears.

4. Forman's key books on the subject are *The Problem of Pure Consciousness* (New York: Oxford University Press, 1990) and *The Innate Capacity: Mysticism, Psychology and Philosophy* (New York: Oxford, 1998). For the *Journal of Consciousness Studies,* see http://www.imprint.co.uk/jcs.html.

5. For information on those institutions, respectively: www.lmu.edu/academics/extension/crs/certificates/yoga_phil.htm; www.clas.ufl.edu/chitra/index.html; spirituality.fiu.edu; and www.taksha.org/page/sprs.

6. Most of the controversy centers on interpretations of Vedic literature and the symbols of Hindu worship, not on the Vedanta-Yoga familiar to most Americans. But the way Hinduism is taught influences the public's understanding of the Vedic tradition as a whole.

7. Jeffrey J. Kripal, *Kali's Child: The Mystical and the Erotic in the Life and Teachings of Ramakrishna* (Chicago: University of Chicago Press, 1995).

8. Most academics I spoke to contend that Kripal and other criticized scholars are neither anti-Hindu nor anti-India but admirers of both, who are doing what scholars do: analyzing their subjects through their own peculiar lenses and letting the chips fall where they may. Similarly, it is understood that most Hindus who object to the work of those scholars are neither fundamentalists nor fanatics, just citizens attempting to protect the heritage they hold dear. For the anti-Kripal perspective, see www.infinityfoundation.com/ECITkalichildframeset.htm. For Kripal's, see www.ruf.rice.edu/~kalischi/.

9. Swami Tyagananda and Pravrajika Vrajaprana, *Interpreting Ramakrishna: Kâlî's Child Revisited* (India: Motilal Banarsidas, 2010).

10. For an exhaustive account of Hindu objections to academic analyses of the religion, see Krishnan Ramaraswamy, Antonio de Nicolas, and Aditi Bannerjee, eds., *Invading the Sacred: An Analysis of Hinduism Studies in America* (New Delhi: Rupa & Co., 2007).

11. For Knapp, see www.stephen-knapp.com; for Conway, www.enlightened-spirituality.org.

12. Wilber has published twenty-five books; at his rate there may be more by the time this book is released. His collected works have also been published, a rare occurrence for a living philosopher barely sixty years old.

13. JFK University's School of Holistic Studies is particularly Wilber friendly. The Bay Area school has a program in integral psychotherapy, an integral psychology master's degree, and an online M.A. program in integral theories, all based on Wilber's model. It also hosted integral conferences in 2008 and 2010.

14. The quadrants are formed by two columns (interior and exterior) and two rows (individual and collective). Hence an integral understanding of *anything* requires

looking at four dimensions: the interior of the individual (inner consciousness, the primary focus of Vedantic spirituality); the exterior of the individual (bodily functions, outer behavior, etc.); the interior of the collective (interpersonal relations, shared values, language, etc.); and the exterior of the collective (social institutions, politics, group dynamics, etc.). The phenomena in each quadrant necessarily affect those in all three others.

15. The basic idea is to avoid lumping together prerational and postrational phenomena, as when transcendent states of awareness are equated to the "oneness" of infants or the magical animism of prerational cultures.

16. For information on Wilber, see http://www.kenwilber.com/. For the Integral Institute, see: http://www.integralinstitute.org.

14: GURU AMERICANA

1. For information about Ma Jaya and her Kashi Ashram, see www.kashi.org.

2. Mariana Caplan, *Eyes Wide Open* (Sounds True Press, 2009); and *Do You Need a Guru?* (Thorsons, 2002).

3. Since http://www.leelozowick.com contains only this satirical announcement, if you want to know more about him, Google will lead you to articles and interviews. He has written more than twenty books and cut several CDs, all available through HOHM Press.

4. Some American gurus have larger constituencies outside the country than they do here. One of them is the former Mary Holland, now known as ShantiMayi. A lineage holder in the ancient Sacha lineage, of which her guru Swami Hansraj is the current head, she spends most of her time in Rishikesh, working with followers from Europe and the United States.

5. John Mann, *Rudi: 14 Years with My Teacher* (Portland, Ore.: Rudra Press, 1973).

6. The other three passengers walked away with minor injuries.

7. For Stuart Perrin, see www.stuartperrin.com. For Bruce Joel Rubin, see http://www.brucerubin-class.com.

8. For Swami Chetanananda's ashram and the Nityananda Institute, see www.nityanandainstitute.org. Chetanananda's Rudra Press has published two compilations of Rudi's talks: *Rudi: In His Own Words* and *Rudi: Entering Infinity*.

9. From the official Adi Da website, www.adidam.org.

10. Those numbers are an estimate provided by one of his close disciples.

11. He later became editor in chief of Rodale Books.

12. Georg Feuerstein, *Holy Madness: The Shock Tactics and Radical Teachings of Crazy-Wise Adepts, Holy Fools, and Rascal Gurus* (Paragon House, 1991). It was revised in 2001 with a new subtitle, *Spirituality, Crazy-Wise Teachers, and Enlightenment*.

13. Bonder's organization is called Waking Down in Mutuality. See: www.wakingdown.org. Deida's official website is www.deida.info.

14. Of Adi Da's books, the most historically significant are his autobiography, *The Knee of Listening,* and the massive *The Dawn Horse Testament.* The official Adi Da website is www.adidam.org. See also Jeffrey Kripal, "Riding the Dawn Horse," in *Gurus in America,* ed. Thomas Forsthoefel and Cynthia Ann Humes (Albany: SUNY Press, 2005).

15. At least one former student is making a mark of his own. After thirteen years in Cohen's community, eight as senior editor of the magazine, Craig Hamilton created a Web-based "academy for evolutionaries" called Integral Enlightenment. He calls it an attempt to create "an authentic, transformative spiritual path for today's world" in the context of collective evolution. See www.integralenlightenment.com.

16. Phipps also wrote in a personal correspondence: "We have been embarking on a multi-year transformation of the organization on many levels. We've established a much stronger management team, a functional and effective board of directors, integrated a whole range of initiatives to establish good governance standards, employee relations, and strategic thinking. We are also working with high-level outside consultants and forming an advisory council, all while fully maintaining the context of a student teacher/guru relationship and a spiritual movement."

17. As of spring 2010, *EnlightenNext* had twenty-five thousand subscribers with an estimated readership of seventy-five thousand. For the magazine, with archives of back issues, see www.enlightennext.org. Cohen's books include *My Master Is My Self* (1989), *Enlightenment Is a Secret* (1991), and *Living Enlightenment: A Call for Evolution Beyond Ego* (2002).

18. The website www.robertadamsinfinityinstitute.org claims to be the official Adams site. There are also several pages of information about Adams, and transcripts of his talks, at www.itisnotreal.com/. One of his students, Pamela Wilson, has a following of her own: www.pamelasatsang.com.

19. *Self-inquiry* is a somewhat unfortunate term, because it makes the process sound analytical. But when practiced as intended, it moves beyond analysis to realms of feeling, and beyond feeling to the primal sense of I-ness, and beyond I-ness to the Source of all, where consciousness knows itself as Atman—which is nothing but Brahman.

20. Society of Abidance in Truth: www.satramana.org. For AHAM: www.aham.com.

21. The documentary, *Call Off the Search,* is available on DVD from www.avadhuta .com. That and http://www.satsangbhavan.net are good sources of information on Poonja. Also see David Godman's three-volume biography, *Nothing Ever Happened* (Boulder, Colo.: Advadhuta Foundation, 1998).

22. In 2008 I was told that Gangaji does about thirty public meetings and several weekend and longer retreats a year. Her official website is http://www.gangaji.org.

23. *I Am That: Conversations with Sri Nisargadatta Maharaj* (Durham, N.C.: Acorn Press, 1973). See also *Seeds of Consciousness: The Wisdom of Sri Nisargadatta Maharaj* (Mumbai, India: Chetana Press, 2003).

24. For information about Nisargadatta and his teachings: www.maharajnisargadatta .com. Timothy Conway's site, www.enlightened-spirituality.org, contains exhaustive material on nondualism, including an essay on Nisargadatta. Footage of Nisargadatta, and commentary by Stephen Wolinsky, can be found on CDs and DVDs from Neti Neti Films: www.netinetifilms.com.

25. Other nondualists on the circuit include: Neelam, Pamela Wilson, Wayne Liquorman, Stuart Schwartz, Loch Kelly, Adyashanti, Frances Lucille, Tony Parsons, and, in their own way, the highly popular Byron Katie and Eckhart Tolle. All are easily located on the Web. Search "Advaita," and you'll find everything you want and more.

26. For detailed critiques, see David Frawley at www.vedanet.com/index.php?option= com_content&task=view&id=38&Itemid=2; *What Is Enlightenment?* magazine, Fall–Winter 1998 and September–December 2006; and Timothy Conway at www .enlightened-spirituality.org/neo-advaita.html.

27. Philosophically, it is argued, neo-Advaitans misconstrue the meaning of *nondual*, turning it, ironically, into a form of dualism by setting the one against the many, whereas true nondualism enfolds the many into the one without denying the obvious existence of separate forms. Classically, Vedanta uses the terms *absolute* and *relative* to indicate the two aspects of existence: the uncreated, eternal, infinite transcendent; and the manifest, ever-changing realm of opposites and individuated forms. Advaita asserts that the relative and absolute are one. This does not mean that the relative doesn't exist, but that its manifold forms are transitory expressions of the absolute, just as individual waves are transitory disturbances of the ocean. The concept of *maya*, usually translated as "illusion," doesn't mean that the phenomenal world is really nonexistent. It's more like a magician's trick that distracts one from seeing the undifferentiated unity behind the multiplicity of appearance.

28. In one exchange with a devotee, Ramana says, "Effortless and choiceless awareness is our real nature. If we can attain it or be in that state, it is all right. But one cannot reach it without effort, the effort of deliberate meditation . . . That meditation can take any form which appeals to you best." See Robert Butler, T. V. Venkatasubramanian, and David Godman, "Bhagavan and Thayumanavar," at www.davidgodman.org.

29. For a concise but thorough explanation of Advaita philosophy, see Eliot Deutsch, *Advaita Vedanta* (Honolulu: University of Hawaii Press, 1969).

15: ART-OMATIC TRANSMISSIONS

1. The album's remarkable success led many to call Horn "the father of New Age Music," although the title might go to clarinetist Tony Scott, who recorded *Music for Zen Meditation* with Japanese musicians in 1964.

NOTES 377

2. *Sattva* is one of the three fundamental qualities or tendencies, called *gunas,* that comprise manifest existence *(prakriti).* *Sattva* is the most healthful, pure, intelligent, and benign *guna.* The *guna* called *rajas* is dynamic, energetic, and vigorous. The third, *tamas,* produces inertia, decay, entropy, and destruction.

3. Shankar had been invited to the United States the year before. He couldn't make it, so his brother-in-law, sarod virtuoso Ali Akbar Khan, came in his stead. Khan got to star on the first American recording and the first TV broadcast of Indian classical music. He later performed with Shankar before huge audiences and opened a famous music school in the Bay Area, the Ali Akbar College of Music.

4. For information on the film, see http://www.ragaunveiled.com. Desai also produced the comprehensive history *Yoga Unveiled* (www.yogaunveiled.com).

5. Hartranft's studio is called the Arlington Center. His translation of *The Yoga Sutras of Patanjali* is highly regarded.

6. Peter Lavezzoli, *The Dawn of Indian Music in the West: Bhairavi* (London: Continuum, 2006).

7. Joshua M. Greene, *Here Comes the Sun* (Hoboken, N.J.: Wiley & Sons, 2006), p. 219.

8. Cited in Greene, pp. 239–40.

9. *Chit* is usually translated as "consciousness."

10. Martin Scorsese is filming a documentary about Harrison's spiritual life, to be titled *Living in the Material World.*

11. *Shabda* means "sound." It sometimes refers to the systematic use of sound to induce spiritual transformation in the listener.

12. The word *sangam* refers to the confluence of sacred rivers and is also used for the coming together of people for a sacred purpose. Lloyd's official website is www .charleslloyd.com. For Anoushka Shankar, see www.anoushkashankar.com; for John Wubbenhorst, www.facingeast.com.

13. *Wallah* refers to the person in charge of, or employed at, something, hence chai wallahs, ticket wallahs, and so on.

14. Paul is the author of *The Yoga of Sound: Tapping the Hidden Power of Music and Chant* (New York: New World Library, 2004). His website is http://www.russill paul.com.

15. For MC Yogi, see www.mcyogi.com.

16. Harry Oldmeadow, *Journeys East: 20th Century Western Encounters with Eastern Religious Traditions* (Bloomington, Ind.: World Wisdom, 2004), p. 29.

17. "Salvation" gives the passage a peculiarly Christian slant. Other translators use terms like *liberation* or *the Self,* and some use lines like *difficult to traverse* instead of *hard.*

18. Maugham based the guru on Ramana Maharshi.

19. Margaret Salinger, *Dream Catcher* (New York: Pocket Books, 2000).

20. Orville Prescott, "Books of the Times," *New York Times,* January 28, 1963.

21. After Salinger's death in 2010, the Ramakrishna-Vivekananda Center of New York posted on its website (http://www.ramakrishna.org) four letters from Salinger to Swami Nikhilananda, written during the author's years of seclusion (in 1967, 1972, 1973, and 1975).

22. *Bharata* is the official Sanskrit name for the Republic of India.

23. Ashoka is named for the legendary Buddhist ruler whose reign brought a period of enlightened harmony to India.

24. While *Slumdog Millionaire*'s Academy Awards made India proud, many Indians objected that the film perpetuated negative images of the country.

25. For the noble primitive genre, rent any movie with the Indian actor Sabu, who became an American citizen and earned a Distinguished Flying Cross in World War II. Sabu appeared in twenty-three films made in England and Hollywood, like *Elephant Boy, Jungle Book,* and *Song of India.*

26. Adiga's novel, *The White Tiger,* won the Man Booker Prize in 2008. Anita Desai has been shortlisted for the award three times, and Kiran Desai won it in 2006. Amit Chaudhuri's most recent novel is *The Immortals* (2009).

27. The Beyondananda website is www.wakeuplaughing.com. *Driving Your Own Karma* (Rochester, Vt.: Destiny Books, a division of Inner Traditions International, 1989).

28. For information about Roerich and the Nicholas Roerich Museum in New York, see www.roerich.org.

29. Alex Grey's website is www.alexgrey.com. For information about his Chapel of Sacred Mirrors: www.cosm.org. Madeline De Joly's *Veda Project* can be seen on her website: http://www.madelinedejoly.com/vedaproject. See "Visualizing the Vedas," *Yoga Journal,* May–June 2003.

16: THE SOUL OF SCIENCE, THE SCIENCE OF SOUL

1. The Capra quote is from Fritjof Capra, *The Tao of Physics* (Berkeley: Shambala, 1975), p. 245.

2. Stay tuned: the Vedas say the universe will one day contract, and some physicists theorize the same.

3. In an article titled "Man's Greatest Achievement" (published in the *New York American,* July 6, 1930), Tesla wrote: "What is to be [man's] greatest deed, his crowning achievement? Long ago he recognized that all perceptible matter comes from a primary substance, or a tenuity beyond conception, filling all space, the akasha or luminiferous ether, which is acted upon by the life-giving prana or creative force, calling into existence, in never ending cycles, all things and phenomena." *Akasha* can be understood as the primal substance of the universe. *Prana* has been equated with "life energy" and, in humans, the breath.

4. See Thomas S. Kuhn, *The Structure of Scientific Revolutions* (Chicago: University of Chicago Press, 1962).

5. Bohm called the observable realm the "explicate order" and the invisible the "implicate order."

6. In addition to Bohm, participants included Stanford neurosurgeon Karl Pribram, who conceived of the brain as a hologram; Stanislav Grof, whose "holotropic mind" incorporates holographic principles; biologist Rupert Sheldrake, with his theory of "morphogenic fields" that transcend time and space; and Ken Wilber, the master synthesizer, who explored the implications of the holographic model in several publications. See Ken Wilber, ed., *The Holographic Paradigm and Other Paradoxes* (Boulder, Colo.: Shambhala, 1982).

7. For information on Dr. Goswami and his Center for Quantum Activism, see www.amitgoswami.org. He also produced a documentary film titled *The Quantum Activist*.

8. R. K. Wallace, H. Benson, and A. F. Wilson, "A Wakeful Hypometabolic Physiologic State," *American Journal of Physiology* 221 (1971), pp 795–99; R. K. Wallace and H. Benson, "The Physiology of Meditation," *Scientific American* 226 (1972), pp. 84–90; H. Benson and R. K. Wallace, "Decreased Blood Pressure in Hypertensive Subjects Who Practiced Meditation," *Circulation* (1972); H. Benson and R. K. Wallace, "Decreased Drug Abuse with Transcendental Meditation: A Study of 1,862 Subjects," *Drug Abuse: Proceedings of the International Conference* (1972).

9. Most of the experts I spoke to said that the bulk of the TM studies in peer-reviewed journals—now numbering more than six hundred—rise to professional standards. Some expressed concern about the way TM proponents have interpreted the findings, accusing them of proselytizing. Psychologist David Orme-Johnson, who headed up the TM research program for years and is now a semiretired spokesman, responds that "enthusiasm for your data does not make the data wrong." See www.truthabouttm.com.

10. "Although relaxation techniques and TM both lower blood pressure, for instance, the effect of TM is twice as big," Sharon Begley wrote in *Newsweek*. David Orme-Johnson told me in an e-mail that "randomized clinical trials that controlled for expectation, placebo, and other design features, as well as meta-analyses and reviews of over 790 studies, provide strong evidence that different techniques are not equivalent and they have specific effects."

11. In January 2003 Oz was featured in a special *Time* issue on "How Your Mind Can Heal Your Body." That same week *Newsweek*'s cover story featured Ornish.

12. Dr. McLanahan's books include *Surgery and Its Alternatives.* For information about her, see www.integralyogaprograms.org/flyers/amrita.pdf. Dr. Ornish's latest is *The Spectrum Book.* For information about him and his institute, see http://www .pmri.org. Dr. Oz's best known book is *YOU: The Owner's Manual.* His website is http://www.doctoroz.com.

13. The panel was convened by the U.S. Senate Committee on Health, Education, Labor, and Pensions.

14. According to a 2007 U.S. government survey, Americans spent $33.9 billion out of pocket on complementary and alternative medicine in a twelve-month period.

15. From an interview with Dr. Khalsa.

16. International Association of Yoga Therapists: http://www.iayt.org. Larry Payne's website is www.samata.com. Richard Miller's Center of Timeless Being: www .nondual.org/index.html.

17. Sat Bir S. Khalsa, "A Perennial Debate," *International Journal of Yoga Therapy*, no. 16 (2006), pp. 5–6.

18. Davidson is Vilas Professor of Psychology and Psychiatry and director of the Laboratory for Affective Neuroscience. Newberg is associate professor in the department of radiology and psychiatry, adjunct assistant professor in the department of religious studies, and director of the Center for Spirituality and the Neurosciences. See Andrew Newberg and Mark Robert Waldman, *How God Changes Your Brain* (New York: Ballantine, 2010).

19. Much of the attention nowadays centers on studies of Buddhist meditation forms, especially the mindfulness practices championed by Jon Kabat-Zinn. The Mind and Life Institute has been a driving force: www.mindandlife.org.

20. For a compelling recent contribution to the literature in this field, see Allan Combs, *Consciousness Explained Better* (Paragon House, 2009).

21. For information on the Esalen program, see www.esalenctr.org.

22. In that interview, Hameroff also says, "I think that when you meditate and attain nothingness . . . it isn't quite nothingness. I think it's actually spacetime geometry, and you're accessing the source of enlightened wisdom by tapping into that fundamental field." See Tom Huston with Joel Pitney, "Finding Spirit in the Fabric of Space and Time," *EnlightenNext,* Spring/Summer 2010, pp. 44–57. For the Center for Consciousness Studies see www.consciousness.arizona.edu. For Stuart Hameroff and the Penrose-Hameroff Orch OR model, see www.quantumconsciousness .org.

23. For Russell's website, see www.peterrussell.com.

24. In 1936, Jung wrote: "If I remain so critically averse to yoga, it does not mean that I do not regard this spiritual achievement of the East as one of the greatest things the human mind has ever created. I hope my exposition makes it sufficiently clear that my criticism is directed solely against the application of yoga to the peoples of the West." (*Psychology and Religion: West and East. The Collected Works of C. G. Jung,* Volume 11 [Princeton, N.J.: Princeton University Press, 1958], p. 537.)

25. For the Association for Transpersonal Psychology, see www.atpweb.org. Pertinent journals include: the *Journal of Transpersonal Psychology;* the *International Journal of Transpersonal Studies;* the *Journal of Consciousness Studies;* and *ReVision: A Journal of Consciousness and Transformation.* Among the books aimed at laypersons are

Roger N. Walsh and Frances Vaughan, eds., *Beyond Ego: Transpersonal Dimensions in Psychology* (New York: Tarcher/Penguin, 1980), and their *Paths Beyond Ego* (New York: Tarcher/Penguin, 1993).

26. The California Institute of Integral Studies (CIIS), the Institute for Transpersonal Psychology (ITP), Saybrook Graduate School and Research Center (originally the Humanistic Psychology Institute), JFK University's School of Holistic Studies, and Naropa University. Naropa is in Boulder, Colorado; the other schools are in the Bay Area.

27. See Charles Alexander and E. J. Langer, eds., *Higher Stages of Human Development: Adult Growth Beyond Formal Operations* (New York: Oxford University Press, 1988). For Wilber's analysis of developmental theories, see *The Eye of Spirit: An Integral Vision for a World Gone Slightly Mad* (Shambhala, 1997), especially chaps. 1, 9, and 10. Susanne Cook-Greuter's site is www.cook-greuter.com.

28. See John J. Prendergast et al., eds., *The Sacred Mirror* (Paragon, 2003), and *Listening from the Heart of Silence* (Paragon, 2007). Both books are anthologies on "nondual wisdom and psychotherapy."

29. To cite one prominent example, prior to cofounding Esalen, Richard Price had a psychotic episode accompanied by an ecstatic spiritual opening; he was hospitalized for months and given shock treatment.

30. See John Welwood, "The Psychology of Awakening," *Tricycle: The Buddhist Review,* Spring 2000, p. 43.

31. The Oneness Movement's central feature is the Oneness Blessing, a hands-on transfer of "divine intelligent energy." It enjoyed a brief flowering in the United States in the mid-2000s.

32. For information on John Gray, see www.marsvenus.com.

33. For example, the Bay Area–centered Nondual Wisdom and Psychotherapy, www.wisdompsy.com, and the New York–based Association for Spirituality and Psychotherapy, www.psychospiritualtherapy.org.

34. The trend is also evident in the new field of positive psychology. One of its leaders, Jonathan Haidt, draws on Eastern teachings in *The Happiness Hypothesis: Finding Modern Truth in Ancient Wisdom,* and in a well-circulated speech at the 2008 Technology, Entertainment, Design conference, where he evoked the Hindu dyad of Shiva the destroyer and Vishnu the preserver.

35. In the article that appeared in the November 1, 1994, issue, Taylor writes: "The new category alerts psychiatrists to patients who might be going through a crisis of the spirit that is nonpathological. Such patients, instead of being misdiagnosed, medicated, and hospitalized, need only to be assisted with philosophical problems of meaning and identity."

36. Roger Walsh and Shauna L. Shapiro, "The Meeting of Meditative Disciplines and Western Psychology: A Mutually Enriching Dialogue," *American Psychologist* 61, no. 3 (May 2006), pp. 227–39.

37. The Bhaktivedanta Institute, located in Denver, holds conferences attended by major scientists and religious leaders. See www.binstitute.org.

38. A second conference is scheduled for October 2010. See www.scienceandnonduality.com.

17: INTO THE MYSTIC

1. Diana Eck, *A New Religious America* (New York: HarperCollins, 2001), p. 23.

2. If, at the time, the Muslim community had been larger and more assimilated, the same scenario might have played out in Islam; as it is, its mystical branch, Sufism, has attracted sizable interest from non-Muslims, mainly due to interest in Rumi, the bestselling poet in America.

3. For Oldmeadow's account of Monchanin, Le Saux, and other missionaries in India, see chapter 9 of *Journeys East*.

4. Among Griffiths's books are the autobiographical *The Golden String* (1964), *Return to the Center* (1976), *The Marriage of East and West* (1982), *The Cosmic Revelation: The Hindu Way to God* (1983), *Christ in India* (1984), and *A New Vision of Reality: Western Science, Eastern Mysticism and Christian Faith* (1992). For information see www.bedegriffiths.com/index.htm.

5. Russill Paul, *Jesus in the Lotus: The Mystical Doorway Between Christianity and Yogic Spirituality* (Novato, Calif.: New World Library, 2009).

6. Wayne Teasdale, *The Mystic Heart* (Novato, Calif.: New World Library, 1999), p. 12. Some of Teasdale's colleagues have carried on his vision in a new organization, InterSpiritual Dialogue 'n Action. See www.isdna.org.

7. For the Thomas Merton Center and the International Thomas Merton Society: www.merton.org. For the Merton Institute for Contemplative Living: www.mertoninstitute.org.

8. The writings of Meister Eckhart resemble the nondual Eastern masters. A sampler: "The Spirit is free of all names, it is bare of all forms, wholly empty and free." "The seed of God is in us. Given an intelligent and hard-working farmer, it will thrive and grow up to God, whose seed it is; and accordingly its fruits will be God-nature." "The eye with which I see God is the eye with which God sees me."

9. *The Way of a Pilgrim,* the Russian book that obsesses Franny in Salinger's *Franny and Zooey,* also describes a practice much like mantra meditation.

10. Something similar happened to John Main, a British Benedictine monk, who learned mantra meditation from a swami in Kuala Lumpur in the 1950s. He was given a Christian mantra. Main taught the method to Anglicans and Catholics until his death in 1982. His work continues through the efforts of the World Community for Christian Meditation.

11. The official website for Contemplative Outreach and Centering Prayer: www

.centeringprayer.com. See also Thomas Keating, M. Basil Pennington, and Thomas E. Clarke, *Finding Grace at the Center* (Still River, Mass.: St. Bede Publications, 1978), and Thomas Keating, *Open Mind, Open Heart* (New York: Continuum, 1986).

12. *Christian Meditation* was published by HarperSan Francisco in 2004. *Merton's Palace of Nowhere* was published by Ava Maria Press in 1978 and was adapted as an audio series by Sounds True.

13. Princeton scholar Elaine Pagels, whose *The Gnostic Gospels* (New York: Random House, 1979) made the new discoveries known to the general public, compared the Jesus depicted in them to descriptions of the Buddha.

14. On his blog, The Daily Dish (andrewsullivan.theatlantic.com/the_daily_dish), April 13, 2010, Sullivan wrote: "Over the last year or so, I've been trained in and have been practicing transcendental meditation. I don't consider this in any way a contradiction of my faith in Christ; in fact, I think it has helped me pray more deeply and helped me get closer to the 'being with God' that prayer is really all about."

15. For information see the Alliance for Jewish Renewal: www.aleph.org.

16. When asked to state his religious philosophy on a bumper sticker, Shapiro's response was *"Neti Neti,"* Sanskrit for "Not this, not this" and a classic Advaita dialogic in the Ramana Maharshi vein.

17. Shapiro's website is www.rabbirami.com.

18. Katz's website is www.indojudaic.com. For the Program in the Study of Spirituality at Florida International University: spirituality.fiu.edu/?c=home.

19. A sampling of books: David A. Cooper, *The Handbook of Jewish Meditation Practices: A Guide for Enriching the Sabbath and Other Days of Your Life;* Avram Davis, *The Way of Flame: A Guide to the Forgotten Mystical Tradition of Jewish Meditation;* Aryeh Kaplan, *Jewish Meditation: A Practical Guide.*

20. As of this writing, the Kabbalah Center, the best-known purveyor of the tradition, has twenty physical centers and fifty study groups in the United States, even in outposts like Boise, Idaho. See http://www.kabbalah.com.

21. See www.rabbidavidcooper.com.

22. For Torah Yoga: www.torahyoga.com. Gentle Jewish Yoga: www.gentlejewish yoga.com. Yofiyah and Kabbalah Kirtan: www.kabbalahkirtan.com/index.html.

23. Dena Merriam's own organization is Global Peace Initiative of Women: www .gpiw.org.

18: THE ONCE AND FUTURE RELIGION

1. A branch of Jagadguru Kripalu Parishat (www.jkpla.org).

2. For information on Mata Amritanandamayi, see www.amma.org.

3. In 2009 *Forbes* magazine named him the fifth most influential person in India.

4. For information on Sri Sri Ravi Shankar and the Art of Living, see us.artofliving .org/index.html.

5. The ashrams, gurus, centers, temples, and organizations are more numerous than I could mention. See www.AmericanVeda.com for a more complete listing.

6. For Karunamayi, see www.karunamayi.org. For Mother Meera, see www.mother meeradarshan.org.

7. For information on Yogiraj Siddhanath, see http://hamsa-yoga.org.

8. For information on Sadhguru Jaggi Vasudev and the Isha Foundation, see www.isha foundation.org.

9. *Yoga Journal* was created in 1975, printing three hundred copies of ten mimeo-graphed pages. Its nine issues per year are now read by an estimated 1.2 million.

10. Among the longtime Hatha Yoga leaders I interviewed are the grande dames, Rama Jyoti Vernon and Lilias Folan; Ganga White, founder of White Lotus in Santa Barbara; David Life, cofounder with Sharon Gannon of Jivamukti Yoga in New York; Steve Ross, founder of Maha Yoga in Los Angeles; John Friend, founder of Anusara Yoga; teacher-researcher-psychologist Richard Miller; Larry Payne, founder of Samata Yoga in L.A. and cofounder, with Miller, of the Interna-tional Association of Yoga Therapy; Lisa Walford of Yoga Works; Julie Deife, edi-tor of *Yoga Therapy Today;* and Felicia Tomasco, publisher of *LA Yoga* magazine.

11. Not to be confused with Sathya Sai Baba, who was discussed in chapter 9. Shirdi Sai Baba lived from 1835 to 1918.

12. Both atheists and conservative Christians are trying to keep Yoga out of schools on church-state grounds, claiming it's a disguised form of Hinduism. The debate is complicated by this irony: for practical purposes, Yoga teachers try to flush any sign of religion from their presentations, while Hindu groups proudly claim Yoga as part of their religious tradition.

13. For Kali Mandir, see www.kalimandir.org.

14. In addition to Harvey's sacred activism venture, other spiritual veterans are at-tempting to address sociopolitical issues. Robert Rabbin, a former Siddha Yoga official, started Radical Sages; and a group associated with the Forge Institute (founded by scholar Robert Forman) created the Global Spiritual Citizens initia-tive. See www.globalspiritualcitizenship.org. (Disclosure: I sit on the board of the Forge Institute and worked on its Call to Global Spiritual Citizenship.)

15. See www.offthematintotheworld.com, www.yogaaid.com, and www.blackyoga teachers.com.

16. The statue of Gandhi in the Martin Luther King National Historic Site is the only memorial statue of a non-American citizen to be erected on federal property.

17. Robert Wuthnow, *After the Baby Boomers: How Twenty- and Thirty-Somethings Are Shaping the Future of American Religion* (Princeton, N.J.: Princeton University Press, 2007).

18. Organizations include the Vedic Foundation, the Forum for Hindu Reawakening, the American Institute of Indian Studies, the American Institute of Vedic Studies, the Sringeri Vidya Bharati Foundation, the Vedic Friends Association, and the Hindu American Foundation.

19. Hindu University of America is based in Orlando, Florida: www.hua.org.

20. See www.dharmacentral.com.

21. A Pew study predicted that 82 percent of America's expected population increase in the first half of this century will consist of new immigrants and their descendants.

22. Indian American youngsters won the National Spelling Bee in 2008, 2009, and 2010.

23. Adyashanti's website is www.adyashanti.org.

24. Indophiles like to point out that the religions that evolved from the Veda—primarily Hinduism but also Buddhism, Sikhism, Jainism, and their myriad variations—never started a holy war against another religion, never conducted an Inquisition or a Crusade, never burned heretics or exiled apostates, and never launched a conversion campaign.

25. James Fowler, *Stages of Faith: The Psychology of Human Development and the Quest for Meaning* (New York: Harper & Row, 1981).

26. The report also found that mystical experiences are particularly common among "those who describe their religion as 'nothing in particular' and say that religion is at least somewhat important in their lives."

27. Theologian Rita Sherma cautions against "the eagerness to pluck low-hanging fruit" and leaving the rest of the tree unexamined: "When the fruits of a civilization are viewed as available for the picking, and the tree and roots are forgotten in the process, a loss of depth occurs and the potential for deep transformation of the receiving civilization remains unrealized." From "Lost in Transmission? The Problem and Promise of Eastern Wisdom in the West," presented at the 2010 South Asian Studies Association Conference.

28. The statement appeared in Toynbee's introduction to Swami Ghanananda, *Sri Ramakrishna and His Unique Message*.

INDEX